Reginald F. Broom
1947

Nev Beal – Stuart McGlashan
Peter Yeldon – Paul Orsborn
Nick Holmes – Barry Blankley
2007

To our wives, Anne, Jackie, Joan and Margery
without whose tolerance and support this book would
not have been written.

The authors + 1 and how they came to discover the Whites at an early age.

17 years

David Thear: I saw the whole first season's home programme (1947/48) and, with what seemed to be a majority of small boys in Salisbury, became totally hooked on the club's activities. Autographs were collected after matches and news of the club was eagerly sought. The classic 1-1 draw with Weymouth was the highlight of that season. Despite living away from Salisbury for most of the intervening years I still have that enthusiasm albeit I've given up autograph hunting ! !

16½ years

Richard J. Walker: The date was 5th November 1949 when, whilst away at school, I returned home and decided to visit my local football club who were playing their second season in Western League Division I. On this day they were playing a Southern Command IX in a friendly, winning 2-1. I was impressed by the quality of play, the size of the crowd, 2000 and the picturesque surroundings. I have been attending ever since, sharing in the truimphs and disappointments along the way.

12 years

Peter J. Waterhouse: When I was a young schoolboy way back in 1947, a father of a school-mate, Vernon Major recommended us to watch a new Salisbury Football Club. They were competing in the Western League Div. II, playing at Victoria Park and Stratford Road grounds, so we made the journey across the city to see the team play. From just our first game we were hooked for life. I can recollect the game at Victoria Park against a strong Arsenal side which ended in a 1-1 draw.

17 years

Peter D. Wood: Around about 1951 one of my occasional pastimes was watching football played in West Harnham. Sometime way back then we had a visit by a Salisbury F.C. XI and I saw the Whites run out easy winners. I was well impressed by the Salisbury players skills so much so that my father suggested I should visit Victoria Park. After but a few games watching Dennis Rogers' trickery on the wing and accurate crossing of the ball to the seemingly ever-present Roy Fisher I was hooked, (except for the odd girlfriend) seemingly for ever, Harnham.............who?........a distant memory.

Salisbury City F.C.

The first 60 years

Published by Citywhite Publishing

David Thear

Richard Walker

Peter Waterhouse

Peter D. Wood

Design & development of the book, which includes: insertion of all photos + captions, make-up of F.A. Cup and Trophy sections, headings within text and all typesetting.

The Book Team would like to express their gratitude to **Salisbury Newspapers** especially the **Journal** publisher Bill Browne and the **Journal** Sports Editor Mike Turner. With appreciation we thank the management of the **Journal** who kindly gave permission for the use of press clippings and photographs from the **Journal** archives in the chapters of this book.

We acknowledge the enormous help and expertise given to us by all the staff at **Mathematical Composition Setters (MCS)** especially Keith and Paul Winch, Ian Clarkson, Matt Holmes, Darren Hull and Roger Hunt.

The ` S.C.F.C. the first 60 years' production team gratefully acknowledge the support given by the **Salisbury City F.C. Board of Directors** to make the publication of this book possible.

The production team would like to acknowledge with gratitude the use of press reports and photographs from the **Southern Daily Echo**.

ISBN 978-0-9554170-0-9

Typeset in 11/13 Galliard

Printed and bound by Salisbury Printing, Greencroft Street, Salisbury, Wiltshire.

contents

Contents

preface

Probably Summer Lightning

It all started over a pint at the Salisbury City F.C. Beer Festival five years ago. David Thear, Richard Walker and Peter Waterhouse were celebrating the resurrection of the club after its near demise in the summer of 2002 and in doing so, started reminiscing. All had been supporters since its early days and had witnessed its fortunes and misfortunes since then.

What then became apparent was that all this history, affecting not only the fans but the City of Salisbury itself, would have been lost had the club ceased to exist. This they felt, could not be allowed to happen and decided, there and then, to record the clubs' activities since 1947 to its 60th anniversary in 2007.

At this point, the three were joined by Peter Wood, the organiser of the Beer Festival and a retired printer who volunteered to undertake the design and setting of the print, which he has done with enormous help from his former employers. He has also assisted with the research activities, particularly photographs. No significant official records existed so the authors had to research the local and regional press, matchday programmes and other enthusiasts' memories and memorabilia.

A few weeks later two of the book team met David Bull (football writer, academic and *hagiologist) who gave valuable advice on all aspects of book production from research to marketing and sales. The book team met every four weeks at Peter Waterhouse's house where deadlines and progress were discussed. Copious amounts of orange juice were consumed, resulting in a very high vitamin 'C' intake.

Peter Wood was given a further task, that of tracking down several ex-managers. This he did through telephone directories and his dogged persistence produced a 100% success rate. It soon became apparent that many ex-managers and players of the club still held very deep affection for S.C.F.C., with ex-players occasionally meeting socially.

One of the least enthralling aspects for the team members was the researching at Salisbury library using the micro-film system. Within 15 minutes any member of the team would suffer severe queasiness searching the screen for information on S.C.F.C., but Evelyn Bunce, a research helper had the stamina to work for hours in front of it.

Two local organisations, The Salisbury Journal and MCS Publishing Services, have been absolutely magnificent with their help: no doubt both companies will be thankful when the book is published.

*P.S. for those puzzled by the phrase 'hagiologist' used in relation to David Bull, the word means 'writer about Saints lives' and David has, of course, been involved in several excellent books on Southampton F.C.

Salisbury in goalmouth action at **Stratford Road.**

Another almost full house enjoying the football at **Victoria Park.**

Players thanking supporters at **Ray McEnhill Stadium** after their win in the F.A. Cup 4th Qualifying Round 2003.

foreword

by Mike Channon

Mike Channon
photo David Bull

I am delighted to be asked to write the foreword to this history of Salisbury City F.C. for two main reasons.

The first is because the Whites were the nearest senior football club to Orcheston, the tiny village on Salisbury Plain that I grew up in. The second is because the manager is Nick Holmes, a former colleague at Southampton and a good friend. We played together at the Dell and were both members of the Cup winning team of 1976. Nick was a talented player whose honesty and hard work made him an indispensable member of the team. Those qualities will serve him well in his managerial role and, I am sure, bring success to Salisbury.

Although, on occasions, I saw Salisbury play I, effectively, left the area in 1964 when I joined Southampton. Before this, however, I played some games for Shrewton in the Salisbury and District League, and this really got me started in football when I was 14 or 15. I remember playing with Brian and Bernard Sainsbury, the Youngs and the Withers, also the away matches right through the area, from Wilton and Salisbury to Amesbury and Durrington.

I was also involved with schools football with Amesbury Secondary Modern where Terry Bates was the teacher who helped me shape my career. I played at Victoria Park on a number of occasions including, as a Saints player, against Bristol City.

As I write this, after Christmas 2006, Salisbury have just gone further in the F.A. Cup than ever before, are handily placed in the league and are still in the Trophy. It looks as if the 60th season could well be the best yet and I hope this proves to be the case.

My present job leaves little time for football but I shall continue to view the Whites progress from afar.

Mike Channon played mainly for Southampton in a career which started in 1964. He scored more goals than any other Southampton player and won 46 full England caps. He is now a successful racehorse trainer. Full details of his career are given in the excellent books about the Saints from Hagiology Publishing.

7

Acknowledgements

The producers of this book are indebted to:
The family of the late Cyril Smith and his son-in-law Alan Hunt.

Former Salisbury managers and players, Norman Crocker, Alan Grant, Alan Green, Alan Kingston, Robin North, Roy Onslow, Cyril Rutter, Derek Rattue, Dennis Rogers, Sean Sanders, Alan Tyler and Christopher Waters as well as the family of the present player Wayne Turk for putting their collection of photographs and press clippings at our disposal.

Photographs have also been made available from Tom Kelly, Roy King and the late Roy Fisher.

Thanks also to Hazel Best, Paul Dible, H.C. Hatcher, Jenny McEnhill, Jim Palm, Gorden Plumb and Phillip Read for the use of their private photographs and press clippings.

Special thanks also are to Mrs Jean Harvey for allowing us to use her late husband's collection of Salisbury City F.C. memorabilia.

David Bull for invaluable assistance and advice.

Very special thanks to the excellent Salisbury Journal photographers David Smith and Roger Elliott for their good humour, patience and considerable help in the production of this book.

The Conference, Isthmian, Southern and Western Leagues for the use of their league tables.

Phil Smith who produced all the cartoons plus caricatures (except pages 43, 50).

We would also like to thank Dave Todd, David Beaven, David Macey and Alec Hayter for providing statistical notes and programme information.

Others who also gave considerable help in the production of this book include Evelyn Bunce for hours of research assistance and Jill Riley for her administration work.

We also thank all those who provided information etc. which we were unable to use and, if we have missed anyone we apologise.

I

Birth of the club

David Thear

The Beginning

In 1946 there was one senior football club in Salisbury. It played in the Hampshire League and was called Salisbury City Corinthians. Its home ground was Victoria Park and the players were amateurs. The club had a substantial following and played before World War II as well as during the war when many well-known footballers who were in the Services and stationed locally guested for them. One of its pre-war players, George Marks, who came from Figheldean, subsequently played in goal for Arsenal and England. George returned to the area after the war and played for Bulford.

There was also considerable residual support for Salisbury City F.C. a club which had played professional football before the war but had folded in the late Thirties. This club had played in the Southern and Western Leagues.

Foundations laid for Salisbury F.C.

On the 12th February 1947 local sportsmen interested in football were invited to attend a meeting in the Guildhall to consider the formation of another senior football club in the City. The aim was to have a first class amateur team backed up by outstanding local players. It was not the intention to compete with the Corinthians but to be of equal standing and provide senior football every

Saturday at the Victoria Park. The meeting was the brain-child of Reg Broom, manager of the Corinthians until he resigned in January 1947, Bill Metherall and Messrs. F. Macey and L. Lodge. Mr Alf Sainsbury, headmaster of St Paul's School and a keen local sportsman, took the chair and over 300 people attended.

The formation of the new club, to be called Salisbury F.C., was proposed by George Searle, the manager of Salisbury Swimming Baths and the league referee who timed Doug McGibbon's second-half goal for Southampton in the match against Chelsea at the end of the 1945, at 4.6 seconds from kick-off. Saints won 7-0 and Doug McGibbon scored six. The seconder was Mr W.A. Rogers and the proposal was carried. The meeting then elected the following:

President	Councillor Adlam
Chairman	A. Sainsbury
Vice-Chairman	W.G. Metherall
Secretary	A. Bull
Treasurer	L.G. Horner
Manager	R.F. Broom
General Committee	
Messrs	Waters, Nash, Fleming, Herring, Rattue, Bevis, Elliot, Leaver
Entertainment Committee	
Messrs	Lodge, Lemon, Butcher, B. Davis, B. Smith, H. Thear, W.A. Rogers

The club headquarters were in the rear of Osmond's Cafe in Fisherton Street; the team colours, white shirts, black shorts and black and white socks. Matches were to be played at Victoria Park. All club duties were to be carried out by the officials and committee including manning gates, sale of programmes and the putting up and taking down of goal-posts and nets.

A true step on the first rung of a long ladder

The first team gained entry to Division II of the Western League and the reserves to Division I of the Salisbury and District League.

A substantial number of players who had represented the Corinthians the previous season signed for the new club namely

Eric Fountain, Roy Pickering, Peter Noss, Fred Colmer, Dennis Rogers, Cyril Smith, Roy Fisher, Jack Parker and Peter Childs. In addition Tommy Williams a Welsh amateur international, joined from Cardiff City and Dave Abbott, the Hampshire County centre-half signed to play at wing-half. Three Bemerton players, Stokes, Fry and Sanger also joined.

On the financial side the club was started with £150 made up of £50 collected at the February meeting, £50 from Mr W. Shipsey who owned a local catering firm and £50 from fund-raising by the Committee. Incidentally Shipsey's is still catering for the club's functions to this day. The scene was thus set for the season with the first match away at R.A.F. Locking on 23rd August 1947.

Local social scene

Before we proceed to the history itself it is probably helpful to the modern reader to comment on the social climate existing at the time of the club's founding and to detail some of the changes to the game's structure over the past 60 years.

Firstly 1947 was just two years after the ending of WWII and the country was still subject to food rationing, fuel shortages and an almost total reliance on public transport for travel. Most people

High Street scene in the early 50s. The Royal George Hotel is where the Mall is now.

worked on Saturday mornings, the five-day week being some years away. There was nowhere near as much choice of entertainment as there is now, the cinema being virtually the only regular outlet. Pubs were for drinking in with little food available other than crisps. Few people had cars and if they had, petrol was not easy to come by.

In addition, the shortages of the war years had sharpened people's appetite for entertainment and this need was met most readily by sport particularly for the spectator. What will strike the reader most forcefully is the size of the crowds which attended the new club's matches in the early seasons.

It was not unusual to have several thousand spectators at Victoria Park for Western League matches particularly when the opponents were local rivals. Indeed the club's record attendance was achieved at the end of the first season on the 28th April 1948, when Salisbury drew 1-1 with Weymouth. Farm carts and flat bed lorries were placed around the pitch to cater for the 8902 spectators who attended. Over 7000 fans were present when Salisbury lost to Dulwich Hamlet in the F.A. Amateur Cup in 1949.

These figures are many times the very best gates which attend today's matches. Having said that, there has been a similar decline in all football except the best teams in the Premiership.

Amateurs or Professionals?

There has also been a major change in the financial structure of the game. In 1947 and until 1973 there were amateur and professional players. Amateurs were not paid to play but could receive expenses while professionals received wages. Anecdotal evidence indicates that some amateurs, at all league levels, received some form of remuneration over and above expenses but this when discovered was firmly dealt with. Amateurs could play for professional clubs and there were 'permit' players who were former pros. who were reinstated to play for amateur clubs. These players could not play in the F.A. Amateur Cup which was the principal trophy for which amateur clubs in senior football competed.

The Whites had considerable success in this competition over the years and were, for some time, considered to be the best amateur side in the southwest of England.

The division between amateur and professional ended in 1973 when the Amateur Cup became the F.A. Vase to be contested by the more junior clubs playing senior football. It is worth noting that Wembley was a sell-out for the Amateur Cup Finals when, after World War II, such teams as Bishop Auckland, Wimbledon and Pegasus made their marks in the competition.

Last, but now least, there are a number of quotations from Salisbury F.C. match programmes and other documents throughout the book. Modern day readers will, I am sure, be intrigued by the quaint prose used in the early days. The regular emphasis on 'sportsmanship' is not something seen in contemporary publications.

A view of the Blue Boar Row at about the time the Club was founded. Buses still park as in the picture but not cars.

What is the book about?

First and foremost it is an attempt to chronicle the club's failures and successes since inception in 1947. To keep the record to a reasonable size the emphasis has been on the activities of the first team although mention is made of the other teams which have paraded in Salisbury colours over the years.

In some instances league tables are not totally comprehensive and it has not been possible to ascertain crowd numbers for all fixtures.

Lack of club records has not helped. We have done our best with the information available to us.

MEMORY LANE

The First Home Game

Salisbury v Cheltenham Town Reserves 30 August 1947

At last the day had arrived and 1300 persons came to see Salisbury play their first match in the Western League Division II at Victoria Park.

Cheltenham took the field with an 11 goal reputation of a weeks standing and stormed the home goal from the kick-off.

The home supporters were left speechless by their team's very shaky start and within a minute, Cole for the visitors had registered the first goal against Salisbury. Five minutes later, whilst I and most others in the crowd were still wondering what had happened, the Whites had taken control and Cheltenham were rarely in the game. Two brief visits to the visitors goal were soon followed by the equaliser.

Peter Child edged his way into the centre and released a jet propelled drive which the goalkeeper never saw. Roy Fisher headed the second goal before the interval from a right wing cross from Dennis Rogers.

Salisbury attacked continuously in the second-half. The third goal was scored by Jack Parker, who chased a long pass up the centre, tricked the defence and shot past the advancing goalkeeper. Dennis Rogers scored the final goal with a curling free kick which left the Cheltenham goalkeeper helpless.

The team could congratulate themselves on their display that day and I went home with the knowledge that the Whites had nothing to fear in this new league.

Anon

The Salisbury team that day was:
Eric Fountain, Ron Pickering,
Len Scullard, Dave Abbott,
Tommy Williams, Fred Colmer,
Dennis Rogers, Cyril Smith,
Roy Fisher, Jack Parker, Peter Child.

1947 48 The first season

Peter J. Waterhouse

Getting Back Into Shape

Manager
Reg Broom

As previously stated, the country was still emerging from wartime austerity with food and petrol rationing still in force. Nevertheless the health and fitness of the nation, I believe, was as high as it had ever been and this was due, in no small measure, to the better balanced diet during food rationing. Shipments of the more exotic fruits were now coming into the UK and queuing outside shops was becoming less apparent for items such as bananas and oranges.

The buying of the luxury item, ice cream, was becoming easier. Once again one saw the old familiar sight of the Walls Ice cream cycle cart, 'Stop Me and Buy One' doing its rounds of the city centre. However, large queues still formed outside the baker's shops for bread and cakes.

Onward Salisbury F.C.

The first ever match in Western League Division II was played on Saturday 23rd August 1947 when Salisbury's legendary captain,

Tommy Williams, lead the team out at R.A.F. Locking. The result was a 3-0 victory.

The team played very constructive football, the defence being solid and the forwards well supplied by the half-backs. Half-time saw them leading 1-0, Parker scoring from a centre by Child, with Fountain preventing an equaliser by saving a penalty.

Salisbury F.C. inaugural squad 1947
Back row, l/r: R. Pickering, E. Fountain, L. Scullard
Centre: R. Mordue, D. Abbott, T. Williams, D. Timms, F. Colmer
Front: D. Rogers, F. Miller, C. Smith, R. Fisher, L. Bayford, J. Parker, P. Child
Only those in football shirts are named with the exception of Manager Reg.
Broom who is on Mordue's right.

In the second-half with a gentle breeze and a slight slope in Salisbury's favour, R.A.F. Locking's defence could not prevent the addition of two more goals, both headed in by Roy Fisher, from passes by Dennis Rogers. The Salisbury team that day was, E. Fountain, R. Pickering, L. Scullard, D. Abbott, T. Williams, F. Colmer, D. Rogers, C. Smith, R. Fisher, J. Parker and P. Child.

Salisbury's first home game was at Victoria Park on Saturday 30th August 1947 against Cheltenham Town Reserves in front of a crowd of approx. 1300. Salisbury ran out 4-1 winners with goals by Rogers, Fisher, Parker and Child. An anonymous supporter's view of this game is given on page 14.

Action from Salisbury's first home game at Victoria Park in the Western League Div. II on Saturday, 30th August 1947. Roy Fisher beats the Cheltenham goalkeeper for the second of Salisbury's four goals.

Stratford Road ground

In the formative years two grounds were used by Salisbury F.C. for the home matches, namely, the council controlled Victoria Park and Stratford Road grounds. Both of these grounds were situated on the northern side of the city.

The homely Stratford Road football ground was fenced off, with galvanised corrugated iron fencing, from the open public playing fields of Hudson Field. The pitch itself contained a slight slope

Above: Seated right is a young and happy Joan Plumb at the Stratford Road ground. Joan later to become Mrs Joan Wilmer, was a great stalwart and supporter of the club.   *photo from G. Plumb*

running down to the Stratford Road and the ground could only accommodate standing viewing. The players dressing room was situated at the Stratford Road end of the ground. Although the ground lacked any covered seating structure, it was popular with all of Salisbury's supporters.

Evidence of a grandstand, which was destroyed by fire before World War II, is a small mound which ran along the Hudson's Field side of the pitch. The Stratford Road ground is now the home of Salisbury Rugby Club.

Victoria Park

Victoria Park originated as The Jubilee Recreation Ground to mark Queen Victoria's Golden Jubilee. It is situated between Castle Road (A345) and Stratford Road and still boasts many fine trees and flower beds. The sports facilities include a bowling green, tennis courts, two football pitches and children's play area. In 1947 a bandstand was still in place.

The main football pitch measured 116 × 75 yards. With a flat smooth playing surface, it was also used for athletic meetings and civic celebrations.

Tommy Williams' looks on as Roy Fisher signs a match ball.

A small stand ran along the Stratford Road side of the pitch with the players' changing rooms situated in the pavilion on the Castle Road side of the pitch.

Busy season ahead for Salisbury F.C.

Not only were Salisbury winning their matches they were also winning the hearts of the City's sporting citizens. Thousands of spectators began flocking to the Victoria Park and Stratford Road grounds.

Many of the Salisbury football aficionados made the matches a social occasion, dressing in their 'Sunday Best'.

The men, who served in World War II, had been issued with a two-piece suit, one overcoat and one trilby-hat on demobilisation.

The Salisbury man-about-town had the choice of an abundance of men's tailors and outfitters in the City to meet his sartorial needs.

Where have all the 'Tailors' gone?

Not many persons will remember Shaddock and Mitchell, Burtons, Hepworths, Fifty Shilling Tailors, Randalls, Whaleys, Ropers, Elliots, Eldridge & Young, Carters and Fosters who were all men's outfitters in the City.

Thankfully we still have Chas H. Baker & Son in Milford Street, who celebrated their centenary in 2002. Designer labels in 1947!

In the late forties very few people were car owners. The majority of supporters went to home matches by public transport, cycle or on foot. The pace of the crowds appeared to quicken in anticipation before reaching the ground.

Wilts & Dorset double-decker buses stretched along Stratford Road to convey the supporters back to the city centre after the matches.

Salisbury's first venture into the magic of the F.A. Cup

The 1st Qualifying round saw Salisbury away at Winchester, where Cyril Smith scored their first ever F.A. Cup goal in a 1-0 victory. The 2nd Qualifying Round on Saturday 20th September 1947 against Basingstoke created another first, being that it was played at Salisbury's alternative ground, Stratford Road. The game saw Salisbury 1-0 down at half-time, but what a change in the second half; Salisbury scored five goals without reply.

In the 3rd Qualifying Round Salisbury played Newport I.O.W. at home but they could only draw 0-0 and in the replay they went down 2-0.

F.A. Cup Results 4/10/47

| Salisbury | 0 | Newport I.O.W. | 0 | Wells City | 0 | Newton Abbot Spurs | 0 |
| Clevedon Town | 4 | Paulton Rovers | 1 | *replay* Newport I.O.W | 2 | Salisbury | 0. |

One of the highlights of the club's first season was the friendly match against an Arsenal XI at Victoria Park on the 13th December 1947.

The Salisbury F.C. official programme for Saturday, 6th December 1947 read:

Extra Special Attraction

Next Saturday, 13th December, we are to have a real tit-bit, for the ARSENAL are sending a team to oppose us at the park, the kick-off is at 2.30 p.m.

We consider ourselves high favoured and we hope a record gate will give our visitors the welcome they have earned. For whatever the constitution of their eleven we know that each man will be a polished footballer and to encourage our men when opposing first class professionals.

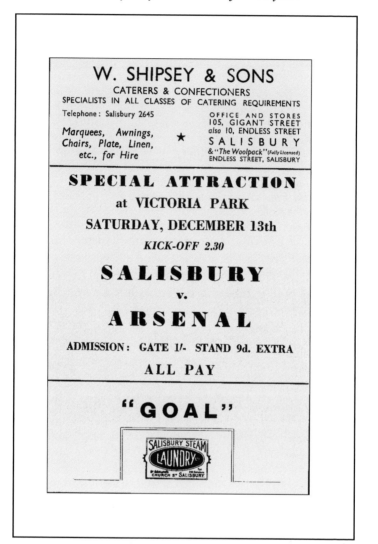

The Arsenal team included seven players from their London Combination side, some of whom went on to play for the first team. The match ended in a 1-1 draw.

The club notes from Boxing Day, 26th December 1947 recorded the match as follows.

> *'We believe that all concerned look back on the Arsenal game as a great success. It was full of action, with our men giving a clever exhibition against a strong team most of whom had played in the London Combination side. '*

Those in charge of the visitors were greatly impressed by the quality of our eleven. 'Let there be no mistake', they said, 'We gave nothing away and were out to win. In the last phase of the game an impartial spectator would have thought that your team was the highly trained one and not ours.

Next year when we hope to come again we shall deem it expedient to send along a still stronger side.'

In this criticism the opposition have voiced the thanks to our team, which we could not convey in a more generous manner. A draw was a very fair result even the manner of the scoring of the goals helping to keep the scales level.

It was a record crowd which greatly encouraged the management for their enterprise. Even so, a considerable number must have been in such a hurry to view the match, that they hadn't time to follow the legitimate road. To those we say, 'come along early on Boxing Day and join the queue formed by those who cherish the name of sportsmen and honourably pay for their entertainment'.

Arsenal F.C. and Salisbury F.C. 1947

B/row, l/r: Broom, R. (Sal. manager), Child, P., Pickering R. (S), Gray, J., Daniels, R., Babes, (A), Fountain, E., 'keeper (S), Male, G. (3rd team manager, A), Scullard, L. (S).
M/row: Miller, F., Parker, J. (S), Holton, C., Platt, 'keeper (A), Abbott, D. (S), not known, (A), Colmer, F. (S), Ollergenshaw, (A).
F/row: Fisher, R. (S), Collett, (A), Williams, T. (S), Bowden, (A), Rogers, A. (S), Taylor, (A) Clelland, Vallance, Holland, and Dolby for Arsenal are in the photograph but not identified.

I can remember prior to the match the Salisbury F.C. publicity team swung into action. Posters advertising the game were placed all around the city and a portable p.a. system toured the city to promote the match.

Returning to league matters, by the 8th of November 1947, Salisbury had played only three league matches because of runs in

The 'good old times'. Warm sunny days, packed grounds, plenty of goal-mouth action – its all here the camera never lies!

the F.A. and Amateur Cup. Cheltenham Town Reserves, the league leaders, had played eleven matches gaining eighteen points.

Start of a famous record

On 15th November 1947, playing at home, Salisbury F.C. defeated Welton Rovers 2-1 to register four wins from four matches. They were now free from the F.A. and Amateur Cup commitments, and the city programme for the Welton Rovers home game read:

' Still, it's an ill wind etc., and Salisbury F.C. are now free to concentrate on the league, which we hope will prove a pointed consolation'.

By the 21st February 1948 they had moved up to third place in the league table.

The top of the table then read:

	P	W	D	L	F	A	Pts
Cheltenham Town Res	25	19	4	2	107	33	40
Weymouth	21	16	3	2	81	27	35
Salisbury	**16**	**16**	**0**	**0**	**81**	**16**	**32**
Frome	20	16	4	0	78	38	32

The Whites still had a backlog of matches and it was not until 28th February 1948 that they reached the half-way point in their fixtures. They then faced the task of having to play all their remaining league games (17) in just two months.

On Saturday 13th March 1948 their league record read:

	P	W	D	L	F	A	Pts
Salisbury	**19**	**19**	**0**	**0**	**92**	**17**	**38**

a quite remarkable effort.

The team lost its first match in the Western League away to the National Smelting Co. 3-1 on 17th March 1948; Peter Child scoring the solitary goal for Salisbury.

The titans of the Western League II

Salisbury and Weymouth clashed for the first time at Weymouth on 24th January 1948. The Weymouth team were a strong professional side, which started after World War II, and like Salisbury had to commence in the Western League Division II.

Not the best of starts

Salisbury found themselves 1-0 down inside the first five minutes, with goalkeeper Eric Fountain and team captain Tommy Williams nursing injuries and, to compound matters Len Scullard the City left-back, returned to the dressing room. The Salisbury 10 men went in at half-time still 1-0 down.

In the second-half Len Scullard came back onto the field at outside-left and, with a goal apiece from Dennis Rogers and Dusty Miller, a precious victory was gained.

Don't get too excited

The club made this special request prior to the home game on 28th April against Weymouth.

A Special Request

The Committee anticipate a great crowd on this occasion and solicit the graceful co-operation of every spectator especially by keeping behind the ropes.

This applies particularly to budding enthusiasts who have failed to take the previous hints, but this time there must be no lapse and **No Questioning**.

If too, our supporters would obtain their tickets before the day of the match, congestion at the gate would be obviated, and disappointment prevented.

A match never to be forgotten

The match at Victoria Park on Wednesday is now part of Salisbury F.C. folklore.

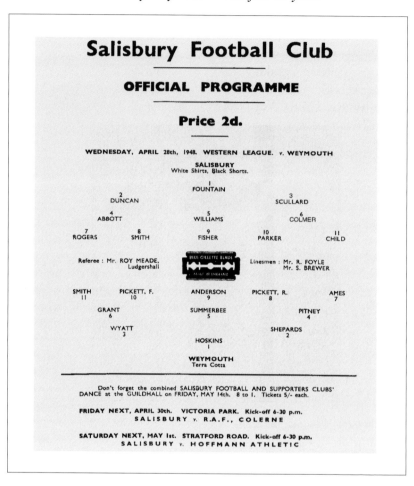

Weymouth won the toss, and from the kick-off went on the attack, but were caught in the Salisbury offside trap. The game was played at a remarkably fast tempo and both goalkeepers were in constant action.

One of the features of the first-half was the tussle between the Weymouth centre-forward Andy Anderson and the Salisbury centre-half Tommy Williams. Neither team scored in the first-half but Weymouth had slightly the better of the exchanges.

Salisbury opened the second-half with great determination and Weymouth were forced onto the defensive.

Salisbury's left back Len Scullard ventured up field to strike a terrific shot which forced the Weymouth goalkeeper into making an excellent save by tipping the ball over the bar. However, in the 55th minute Weymouth developed a neat move from a throw-in which saw the ball breaking to the Weymouth centre-forward Andy Anderson and, in a flash he swept the ball into the back of the Salisbury net, 1-0 to Weymouth.

The captains Williams, Salisbury and Sheppards, Weymouth shake hands before the epic game at Victoria Park to decide the Western Division II Championship. Salisbury had the advantage of only needing to draw.

Salisbury stepped up the tempo and Roy Fisher had a goal disallowed for off-side cutting short local celebrations. With their supporters giving them great support, they consistently tested the Weymouth defence. Even more pressure was applied with the two wing-halves, Abbott and Colmer moving up with the forwards.

Time running out

With full-time approaching rapidly they were awarded a free-kick just inside the Weymouth half. Dennis Rogers stepped up to take it and his celebrated right foot sent an exquisite ball for Jack Parker to head the equaliser.

The supporters were ecstatic and seconds later the referee Mr R. Mead blew the final whistle.

This report and tribute appeared in the Salisbury programme for the following match:

Jack Parker

What a crowd! What a number? Well, since we have never had such a crowd at a football match before it is difficult to estimate, but a shot somewhere near the target is 8–10 thousand, which the fleet of charabancs from Weymouth helped to swell.

Five minutes before the kick-off the ground presented a picture never to be forgotten. A photograph from the air would have produced a permanent and interesting record as well as a pleasing reminder of the enthusiastic support given the club throughout the season 1947–48.

Praise for the behaviour of the crowd cannot be too highly expressed: it was admirable! The arrangements made helped of course, and in the words of Weymouth's Chairman 'The club deserves the highest praise for the way in which the match was staged.' To Mr J. Lampard we are grateful for providing the trolleys which did excellent service, and to Mr Osmond for supplying the forms which gave comfort to many and also did duty as a barrier.

Yes! We all agree the match was a thriller. On it rested a possible chance of Weymouth beating us on the post for the Championship, and as we saw they went all out. So too, did our men who fully deserved to share the spoils, and though perhaps our visitors returned somewhat disappointed, we believe that they would admit the result was justified on the overall run of the play.

The referee, Mr Roy Mead, deserves congratulations on his handling of a difficult game and the neutral linesman ably backed him up.

This evening in giving R.A.F., Colerne a warm welcome, we recognise that the match is of vital importance, for, if we win, the Championship is ours.

Official Attendance 8,220

Gate receipts £290

Thank You!

Editor's note:

Subsequent information revealed that the attendance was 8,902

Victoria Park 1948

Tommy Williams has just received the Western League Division II Champions Cup after playing Southampton in the St. Dunstan's Cup.

People spotting ! !

Dave Abbott and Fred Colmer can be found in the happy crowd and the little girl sitting on the raised platform is Leslie, the daughter of Cyril Smith, with Cyril's wife Joyce close at hand. The lady sporting the very stylish sun glasses is the late Joan Wilmer.

The following tribute to Nobby Trussler was also inserted in the programme:

A TRIBUTE

*HE BREWS THE CUP THAT CHEERS THE TEAM
PREPARES FOR ALL THE BATH THAT STEAMS
A WATCH-DOG O'ER THE DRESSING LOBBY
THANK YOU FOR ALL YOU DO, OUR NOBBY*

Nobby Trussler was a real character. He ran a Boot and Shoe repair business from a small workshop in the back garden of his house in Polden Road, in an area of Salisbury known as Waterloo Gardens. I was brought up in Polden Road and was part of a closely knit group of sports mad schoolboys from that area.

Get your news here!

Nobby was our source of inside information from Salisbury F.C.; he appeared to know everything about the club, new signings, injuries, team news, etc.

I well remember him giving us the responsibility and privilege of delivering by hand, Cyril Smith's newly repaired football boots to his house nearby.

Salisbury's highest score yet

On the Friday evening after the Weymouth game Salisbury hit their highest score of the season, easily beating RAF Colerne 11-1 with goals from Fisher 5, C. Howard 3, Williams 1, Smith 1 and Parker 1.

The next day they entertained Hoffman Athletic at Stratford Road, winning 4-0 in the final league game of the season.

Salisbury F.C. v Southampton F.C.

There was another bumper gate on 8th May 1948 when Southampton were the opposition in the St. Dunstan's Cup.

On a hot spring day the Whites went down 2-0 to a strong Saints side, which was Salisbury's only home defeat of the season. The Southampton goalkeeper Ephgrave looked unbeatable that afternoon.

SATURDAY NEXT —

MAY 8th, 1948   VICTORIA PARK

Kick-off   3-15 p.m.

ST. DUNSTAN'S CUP

SALISBURY

v.

SOUTHAMPTON

DON'T   FORGET !   the Combined

Football and Supporters Club

DANCE

at

THE GUILDHALL, SALISBURY

on

FRIDAY, MAY 14th

Victoria Park May 8th 1948
A young and determined Cyril Smith winning the ball in a tackle that would probably be deemed a foul in the modern day game.

No wonder the club attracted such large crowds in the 17 league games played at home. Salisbury recorded 16 wins and only 1 draw, scoring 95 goals at 5 goals per game and conceding only 10 goals in the 17 at 0.58 a goal per game, an incredible record.

Centre-forward Roy Fisher in another fair tussle is just unable to reach the ball this time.

A proud properly turned-out Salisbury F.C. mascot maybe wishing he'll get a game. (thought to be Terry Cannings.)

Salisbury Football Club Season 1947/48

	P	W	D	L	F	A
Western League	34	29	1	4	145	32
F.A. Cup	4	2	1	1	6	3
F.A. Amateur Cup	5	3	1	1	19	6
Wiltshire Cup	2	1	0	1	7	8
Friendlies	1	0	1	0	1	1
St Dunstan's Cup	1	0	0	1	0	2

'Come on the Whites', 'Up the City'

At this time Salisbury supporters were becoming more vocal. There had always been a solitary voice shouting 'Come on the Lillywhites' and this led to a spontaneous chain reaction of fans accompanying him.

To add extra value a few Salisbury supporters, perhaps nostalgic for the old Salisbury City F.C., voiced 'Up The City'.

What a combination – the Lillywhites and the City. That should confuse the opposition. It would take some years for the club to incorporate the noun 'City' into the club's title, (1992 the club's name was officially changed to Salisbury City) and of course, 'The Famous Whites' evolved from 'The Lilly Whites'.

So, all together, raise our voices with, 'Come on The (you) Whites' or 'Up The City', with the occasional 'Tally Ho' from one long standing supporter.

A very impressive 145 league goals were scored in the first season:

Fisher 33, Childs 21, Rogers, 20, Smith 14, Parker 13, Scullard 6, Abbott 6, Miller 6, Colmer 6, Williams 5, Pearce 5, Cavanagh 4, Howard 3, Bayford 3, and 1 own goal

---

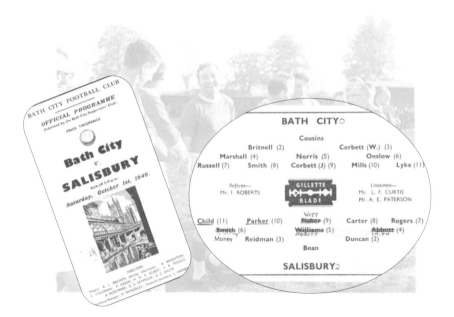

The First Season

Stepping Stones of the 1947/48 Season

23/8/47	Salisbury F.C. inaugurated a new era.
30/8/47	Salisbury F.C.'s first home game was played at Victoria Park against Cheltenham Town Reserves resulted in a 4-1 victory.
Oct 1947	Salisbury F.C. were eliminated in the F.A. Cup 3rd Qualifying Round away to Newport I.O.W. 0-2 after drawing 0-0 at Victoria Park.
Oct 1947	Dennis Rogers rejected the opportunity to join Swindon Town.
8/11/47	Salisbury F.C. suffered a shock defeat away to Pewsey Vale in the F.A. Amateur Cup 4th Qualifying Round.
13/12/47	Salisbury F.C. held Arsenal to a 1-1 draw at Victoria Park.
13/3/48	Salisbury F.C. played 19 consecutive league matches without dropping a point.
24/4/48	Salisbury F.C. secured promotion from Western League Division II with a 5-0 home win against Cinderford.
28/4/48	Salisbury F.C. drew 1-1 against Weymouth in an epic game witnessed by a capacity gate of 8,902 at Victoria Park.
30/4/48	Salisbury F.C. were crowned Western League Division II Champions with an emphatic 11-1 home victory against R.A.F. Colerne. Scorers for Salisbury were: Roy Fisher 5, C. Howard 3, Tommy Williams 1, Cyril Smith 1, Jack Parker 1.
8/5/48	Salisbury F.C. were defeated 2-0 by a strong Saints side in the St Dunstan's Cup Final at Victoria Park.

The two following pages have edits from the 1947—48 Souvenir Programme plus a photograph of those famous players of Salisbury F.C. and their autographs..........lest we forget what this 'famous Salisbury' is all about.

Roy Pickering (right-back): Regular player until he was kept out of the team through injury received during Easter games. Also distinguished himself as a school-boy footballer, playing for Ludlow Road School. At the age of 19 he was playing for Woolston Youth, and later featured in the White Sports side.

Eric Fountain (goal): Born at Greenwich on 11th Nov. 1928, played for Newton School, Hertfordshire at the age of 11 and Woolston Boys when he was 14. At the age of 16 he was in the successful Southampton B' team when they won three cups. Played for the 'Saints' in London Combination games and had one game for the first team.

Len Scullard (left-back): Native of Southampton who commenced his football career with Portswood School team. Member of Pirelli General side when they won Cup and league during 1938-39 season. When in the R.A.F. played for Trowbridge Town in the Western League Div. I and with them when they were defeated by Exeter City in the First Round of F.A. Cup.

Robert Mordue (right-half): Had a wide range of football experience, having played three seasons in the London League, also in the East Kent League, and was included in a Shorncliffe Garrison representative XI. Since the age of 18 played senior football, and during his service played for several army teams.

Dave Abbott (right-half): Born in Calcutta, but came to England when quite young, and played for Itchen School, Southampton. Represented Hampshire three times.

Tommy Williams (centre-half): Born in Cardiff, in his early days played for Adams Down School, later captained the Welsh Schoolboys. Was amateur for Cardiff City when he played as a Welsh Amateur International.

Don Timms: Southampton born, member of Woolston Boys' team.

Fred Colmer (left-half): Southampton born, started his football with Highfield School, played with Southampton Boys XI. Also played for Swaythling Youth team, Botley and the City Corinthians. Had a trial with Tottenham Hotspur.

Dennis Rogers (outside-right): Most popular player in the team, scorer of many excellent goals. Chester born, started his football career with Saltney School. Before joining the Royal Artillery he played for Everton 'A', also played for Peterborough. After demob played a few games for Chester. Appeared for Wiltshire.

Fred Miller (inside-right): Native of Salisbury, started his football with St. Thomas' School team and later was in the St. Edmund's side. Joined Salisbury F.C. on its formation. Capped for Wiltshire.

Cyril Smith (inside-right): A sound inside forward, who could not only go for goals, but did a lot of running and carrying. Was in the Royal Air Force during World War II. Played five games for Arsenal.

Roy Fisher (centre-forward): Native of Southampton, played for Merry Oak School and Woolston Boys' Club. During the 1945—46 season played for Southampton 'B', also had six games for Southampton Reserves.

D. Bayford: Army player who had games with Stoke 'A'.

Jack Parker (inside-left): Born in Southampton and played for Hampshire, also captained Ludlow Road School team. During the 1943—44 season played for Woolston Boys and the following season for Southampton 'B' when they won the Southampton Senior League and Cup plus the Hants Intermediate Cup. Also played 14 games for Southampton Reserves.

Peter Child (outside-left): Southampton born, played his first football for Bitterne School. With Woolston Boys' Club from 1942—45. Played for Southampton 'B' when they won the league and two cups. Also selected for Hampshire Boys.

Salisbury Football Club – for the autograph collector. Signatures of players only. Read from back row left to right.

MEMORY LANE

All in an April Evening

Salisbury v Weymouth 28 April 1948

A fever was gripping Salisbury – `Football Fever'. The forthcoming game, Salisbury versus Weymouth was the talk of the town. The general consensus was that the victorious team would go on to become the Western League Division II Champions.

The headmaster at my old school, St Thomas' gave the school permission to leave early for the evening match (floodlights would follow several decades later).

Arriving at Victoria Park one was greeted by a transformation, the pragmatic Salisbury F.C. management team had transformed Victoria Park into a temporary football stadium. Trailers were placed on the outside of the cinder track, also bench seats were situated at the City end, nearly every conceivable space was fully utilised.

By the time we took up our positions on a trailer at the City end, spectators were streaming in.

A carnival atmosphere prevailed, chanting was breaking out all around the ground followed by a crescendo of rattles and bells. By the time of kick-off a record 8,902 spectators were crammed in, virtually 25% of the population of Salisbury.

When the influential Captain, Tommy Williams led Salisbury F.C. onto the pitch the atmosphere was electric. With both of the teams playing the old 2-3-5 formation the play was open and fast. Weymouth's prolific goal scorer, Andy Anderson, opened the score for Weymouth and with the sands of time running out and dusk falling rapidly it was becoming difficult to watch the flight of the brown ball.

Salisbury's unbeaten home record was in serious jeopardy. Then a free-kick was awarded to Salisbury just inside the Weymouth half.

From the kick, Dennis Rogers' educated right foot projected a precision ball into the Weymouth penalty area, resulting in Jack Parker's stunning,

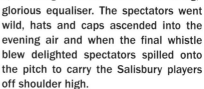

glorious equaliser. The spectators went wild, hats and caps ascended into the evening air and when the final whistle blew delighted spectators spilled onto the pitch to carry the Salisbury players off shoulder high.

Dancing and celebrating in the streets of Salisbury City that night......................
'NOT ARF '

Peter Waterhouse

3

western League

The 1948–49 Season — Richard J.A. Walker

After promotion the previous year, the club eagerly looked forward to their first season in Western League Division I, since the the old Salisbury City had finished bottom of that division in 1928. The reserves were in the Hampshire League Division III.

There were few changes in the playing staff, who were still amateurs and now found themselves playing against mostly professionals, employed extensively by the strongest teams in the league.

Short run in F.A. Cup

The season opened on the 21st August with a home fixture against the previous season's runners-up Glastonbury, which Salisbury won 4-1, Dennis Rogers scoring a hat-trick. Success at Poole was followed by a visit from Purton who proved doughty fighters in the F.A. Cup, before a goal from Jack Parker saw Salisbury safely through.

In those days the team from North Wiltshire were a strong side and formidable opposition for a small village. After a win away against W.C. Mental Hospital, Peasedown Miners Welfare were beaten after extra time in the next

round, when Jack Parker scored a brace in
a 3-2 win. The next round saw a visit
to Trowbridge, which ended the
Whites interest in the
competition for that year
in a 4-1 reverse.

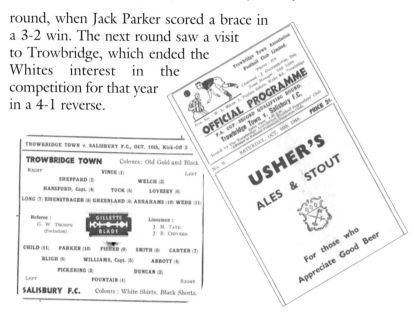

F.A. Cup Results 16/10/48

Trowbridge Town	4	Salisbury	1	East Cowes Vics	1	Poole Town	2
Longfleet St Mary	0	Weymouth	4	Glastonbury	1	Gloucester City	1

Controversy at an Amateur Cup match

The club was still very much involved in the F.A. Amateur Cup.
The reward for beating Shepton Mallet away and Welton Rovers at
home was a trip to Division II opponents Frome Town.

Salisbury suffered a 4-1 defeat at Badger's Hill before it was
found that the opposition had used an ineligible player. This was
in the days when ex-professionals were barred from participating in
the Amateur Cup, even if they were currently playing without
payment.

Our own Cyril Smith and Tommy Williams were absent as they
were ineligible for the competition for the same reason. This
proved costly for the Somerset team as they were ordered to re-play
the match at Salisbury and they were also fined one guinea!
(110 pence now) To rub salt in the wound they lost the match
2-1.

Salisbury F.C., bound for some Channel Island sunshine in 1948.

Whilst all this was going on league fixtures were taking a back seat and when Salisbury entertained Purton once again on the 13th November in the Amateur Cup, (a game they won 3-1 after extra time, although they only equalised in the very last minute) they had in fact still only played four league games, none of which had been lost.

Purton were subsequently to gain some revenge for their previous defeats when a third visit to Victoria Park on New Year's day saw them beat the reserves in the Wiltshire Senior Cup. The club's reward for continuing Amateur Cup exploits, was an away trip to Barnstaple, who played in Division II of the Western League. The Whites played some brilliant football in front of a record crowd of 3000 and an excellent result saw them run out 5-2 winners.

The clubs' Christmas stocking filler

Salisbury F.C. had by now tasted defeat in the league and travelled to Jersey over the Christmas break to defeat the Islanders 4-2 in a friendly match. One player who probably enjoyed it more than most was Roy Fisher, who scored all four goals.

Large crowd at local derby

They where brought down to earth when they returned home, being beaten by their Wiltshire rivals Trowbridge 4-3 at Frome Road. The Trowbridge winner came with the last kick of the match before an attendance of over 4000. By this time all eyes were on a visit to Wimbledon in the first round proper of the Amateur Cup. The team and supporters travelled on a special train which left Salisbury station at 10.50 a.m. at a cost of 10/- (50p) return. Salisbury were acknowledged to have played extremely well against their strong London opponents before losing 2-1 in heavy conditions to a disputed goal.

It was now back to league fixtures, and a poor run of form ensued. It was brightened on the 29th January, when a young Bristol City Colts side were beaten 5-1 at Victoria Park.

Above: Salisbury are seen here playing in their away strip against old Wiltshire rivals Trowbridge Town. Salisbury's Roy Fisher tussles for the ball while Vic Carter looks on.

Below: Players, officials and fans are waiting for the off at the City station on their way to Wimbledon for their F.A. Amateur Cup tie.

Appearing for the visitors was Terry Compton, who was later to play for the Whites during some halcyon years. Len Scullard, who was a very important member of the team and who had been out injured, returned. Somewhat better form then followed in February, although no great consistency was shown and a home defeat by Poole Town on the 30th March left the crowd particularly frustrated.

Bank Holiday games were now strong crowd pullers and on Easter Monday, county rivals Trowbridge Town were beaten at home by a solitary goal from Roy Fisher in front of over 6000 spectators.

Club's 'first Western League Div. I top scorer'

A crowded fixture list was complete with a decisive win at home against Clandown. Roy Fisher finished with another hat-trick to place himself at the top of the Western League scorers with 24 goals. Tony Syrett was overall top club scorer with 72 goals, although 51 of these were in the Hampshire League team. There will be more of the Syrett family in later chapters.

The club finished their first season in the top flight in a respectable sixth position.

Salisbury proud winners of the Pickford Cup against Newport I.O.W. in 1954.

Front l/r: unknown, Dennis Heagren, Cyril Smith
Back l/r: Tommy Williams, Dennis Rogers who scored a hat-trick and Ron (General) Booth.

The 1949–50 Season — Richard J.A. Walker

Owing to the success in the early rounds of the Amateur Cup during the previous season, the team was exempt until the divisional finals of that competition, so fixture congestion was not expected to be so severe as in previous years.

Salisbury continued to operate in the Western League Division I, and the reserves having won Division III of the Hampshire League, were now in Division II.

The Whites started again with a home fixture on 20th August against Bath City Reserves which they won 4-0 and two further wins left them leading the table after three games had been played. Nearly all members of the same team that had been available during the previous two seasons were still with the club. The unbeaten record did not last long however because Glastonbury, the previous year's champions ran out 2-1 winners at Victoria Park.

Excellent crowd — wrong result

Success in the F.A. Cup was expected and achieved by substantial wins against Warminster and Clandown and was a prelude to a visit to Twerton Park to take on Bath City who were already an established Southern League team.

Another special train was organised for fans who were to travel at 1 p.m. at a cost of 5/- (25p) return. The club confounded the sceptics by deservedly toppling their hosts 2-0 in front of 5412 spectators, a new record for Twerton Park. Salisbury scorers were Child and Parker. Reward for this achievement, in the days when the draw was pre-arranged until the 4th qualifying round, saw the Whites travel to Trowbridge. Here they put on a excellent display against a strong Trowbridge Town side, before losing by 1-0 in front of a crowd of 7719, of whom 1500 came from Salisbury.

F.A. Cup Results 29/10/49

Trowbridge Town	1	Salisbury	0	Cowes Sports	1	Weymouth	5
Bideford	4	Dartmouth	2	Gloucester City	3	Lovells Athletic	0

Ding-dong battle between two 'City' teams

Because of all the F.A. Cup activity, league fixtures were at a premium. Furthermore Salisbury were also involved in the Amateur Cup and visited Airlie Road, home of Winchester City, who included a later Whites favourite, Frank Grayer in their attack. The result was 1-1 and the replay produced a game which was talked about for years. Salisbury were overwhelmed at the start and found themselves 3-0 down. They fought back to level 4-4 at the end of normal time before running out winners 6-5 after extra time, when the match finished almost in darkness. I wonder how many alive today will remember being at this game?

A county match at Victoria Park provided some relief to the pressure when Hampshire were the visitors on the 3rd of December.

continued on page 45

Faded drawings and some humorous words may bring back some treasured memories of an unforgettable F.A. Amateur Cup game between two ` Cities'.

More action from Salisbury versus Winchester City in the last qualifying round of the F.A. Amateur Cup. Billed by the press as the battle between the two Cities, it did indeed became a real battle as the score see-sawed back and forth, making sure that no spectators dropped off to sleep.

Top picture: Dennis Rogers in the foreground, Jack Parker left, Roy Fisher right and Peter Child in the background all ball watching.

Bottom picture: Sees a fair tussle between the Winchester defence and Salisbury's attack, Fisher and Parker giving it their all.

Dennis Rogers and Dave Abbott played for Wiltshire, with Dennis Reinman as captain. Our own Len Scullard was performing in the ranks of the opposition.

Besides the F.A. Cup and Amateur Cup Salisbury also competed for the Wiltshire Senior Cup and Russell Cotes Cups. County Cup fixtures took precedence over league matches, causing a league backlog once again. When Salisbury took the field against Trowbridge on Boxing Day at Victoria Park, they had only played eight league fixtures winning and losing four. A convincing win followed against the old enemy, with goals from Norridge, Smith and Rogers without reply.

One step........

League form suffered hereabouts but all thoughts were turning to the big match in the 1st Round Proper of the Amateur Cup, when Wealdstone were the visitors. The London Press suggested this should be a formality for their team who were a powerful unit in Amateur Cup circles. On the day they were soundly beaten 4-1, a result which the national press acknowledged with good grace.

It was a great day for Salisbury soccer. After several weeks of average results the city club had made history by reaching the second round and were now going out to improve their status in this, their third season.

Above: Salisbury's Vic Carter fires in a tremendous volley after outstripping the Wealdstone defence. This time the goalkeeper made an excellent save, but in their next attack Salisbury scored a third goal which was soon followed by a fourth to end any hopes Wealdstone had of playing in the next round of the F.A. Amateur Cup.

Above: Two old and faded press clippings show a lively Roy Fisher as a constant worry to the Wealdstone defence and goalkeeper.

Last to arrive at Victoria Park on that day was the Mayor of Salisbury, councillor S.N. Bigwood, well-known for his sporting interests. He promised the players a banquet at the Guildhall if they were to bring the Amateur Cup back to the city.

Terry Cannings, Salisbury's six-year old mascot, led the team out and captain Jack Parker won the toss. He elected to defend the city end. From the outset the inside-left moved the ball like a master and, though Wealdstone were the first to make an impression, Salisbury were soon in the picture.

Wealdstone were lucky as Salisbury pressed and it was no real surprise when their goal fell for the first time in only the fifteenth minute. Norridge put Fisher away and he outstripped the defence before beating the goalkeeper, Wiltshire as he advanced. They came again and Parker brought the goalkeeper to his knees. As Norridge shaped for a corner kick, Fisher who was idling near the penalty spot, slipped his marker as the ball was in flight. He leapt high, skillfully heading the ball into the Wealdstone net for the second Salisbury goal.

One-way traffic

Up to then, little had been seen of the the visitor's attack, although they did give Salisbury one or two scares. Jack Parker rallied his forces who then went on to score two more goals. The first of these was an own goal when Barker, the Wealdstone captain hurried his back pass to goalkeeper Wiltshire, resulting in the ball sailing over his head into an empty Wealdstone net.

Entry into the next round was made certain 10 minutes later when Fisher finished off the scoring by tricking a defender and hooking the ball over the goalkeeper and into the unguarded net.

Salisbury's team was: Amor, Duncan, Scullard, Reinman, Abbott, Money, Rogers, Carter, Fisher, Parker and Norridge.

Some 'National Press' comments

Daily Telegraph: — *There were only two real surprises in the F.A. Amateur Cup 1st round, one in the north and one in the south. Yorkshire Amateurs were defeated by Sheffield, who claim to be the oldest football club, but have rarely gained much prominence since they won the trophy in 1904. Wealdstone who put up a memorable fight against Port Vale in the F.A. Cup, were well beaten by Salisbury, whose lively centre-forward Fisher, scored three.*

Daily Mail: — *'Reminiscent of Bromley, same colours, same hefty side' say Wealdstone of Salisbury, who beat them fairly and squarely 4-1. Fisher a lively centre-forward, who scored a 'hat-trick', and Norridge, a bespectacled outside-left. were the men to give Wealdstone the chief trouble.*

Daily Herald: — *No excuses for Wealdstone. They were well and truly beaten at Salisbury, where Roy Fisher got a ' hat-trick', by a side described by one of the losers' officials as, 'Just like Bromley — they even had the same colours!'*

Sporting Record: — *Wealdstone found Salisbury much stronger opponents than they had anticipated and were well beaten 4-1. Fisher, a very energetic centre-forward, scored three of the goals, and Wealdstone officials were clearly of the opinion that the next centre-half to oppose him is not in for an easy time. Their Edmonds had an unhappy time against him.*

But not two.......

Whites were fortunate to receive a further home draw in the next round when the visitors were Dulwich Hamlet, another famous Amateur Cup team.

In the event Dulwich Hamlet proved a bridge too far, being a bigger and better side and they deservedly won 2-0 to end interest in the major cup competitions for the year.

Bogey team win again

It was now time to get back to the bread and butter of the league matches and wins over Cheltenham Town Reserves and Portland followed. In April, 12 league games had to be played. League results were satisfactory and Salisbury advanced to the semi-final of the Russell Cotes Cup where the Hants League Team took the fixture and were beaten 5-2 by Reading 'A'.

League games kept the club in mid-table although a home win versus Soundwell was outstanding in that the Whites scored seven without reply. Our bogey side, Poole Town, won 3-2 at Salisbury which was particularly disappointing. Clandown also kept their noses ahead 4-3 in a game where we were 3-0 down at half-time. A pleasant interlude took place after Easter, when a trip to Jersey to play the Jersey F.A. was enjoyed by all and the match finished in a draw.

Quiet end to the season

The season drew to a close with a narrow 2-1 win over Weymouth Reserves at home; the visitors first team were by now playing in the Southern League where Salisbury were to perform nearly 20 years later.

A closing league position of 11th was considered satisfactory, but there was now no doubt that the opposition was getting stronger each year. The main reason for this was that more and more teams were turning professional.

Roy Fisher was top scorer for the first team with 22 league goals, Vic Carter, second, with nine.

The Hampshire League team finished fifth in the Hampshire League Division II, only four points away from winning promotion.

Picture left: Peter Child left and Roy Fisher right, maybe wondering if there will be any left as Reg Broom sups from another Salisbury F.C. trophy.

More silverware for the trophy cabinet!

In the early 50s Mr J. T. Mason, Secretary of the Salisbury Group Hospital Management Committee, presents the Hospital Cup to Roy Fisher following Salisbury's 1-0 win over Avonside, who played in the Salisbury and District League.

Amusing drawings from yesteryear. *Above:* 1949/50 Salisbury beat Cheltenham Res 3-2. *Below:* The extra Qualifying Round F.A. Cup 1950/51 versus Westbury United. (For further information see Statstics section).

The 1950–51 Season — Richard J.A. Walker

The new season started on the 18 August. Tommy Williams had announced his retirement but Doug Witt was to prove a capable deputy in the number five shirt.

Initially, a bad start appeared on the cards when Salisbury started the first game against Portland two players short. Portland took an early lead but Salisbury soon returned to a full complement and, at half-time, led 4-1. The result was eventually a rather flattering 4-3 defeat for the hosts when a couple of late goals were scored against the general play.

At this time a special meeting of the Western League proposed that four teams be promoted and four relegated between the top two divisions. Salisbury were one club who voted against the proposed rule change which was defeated.

Jersey F.A.

The Jersey F.A. sent over a side for an exciting friendly fixture which finished 4-4, but, after only four league fixtures, the F.A. Cup was upon us once more with a visit to Westbury United. A special supporters train was chartered and a young John Atyeo led the home attack at the age of 16. He was later to play for England and saw distinguished service at Bristol City and Portsmouth. This was not to be his day, however and a 6-1 win for Salisbury and further progress against Chippenham United and Clandown, saw Salisbury through to the area final at home to Trowbridge Town.

F.A. magic descends on Wiltshire

The 3rd Qualifying tie versus Trowbridge attracted enormous interest in the two towns swelling the crowd at Victoria Park to around 7000. Some climbed trees to obtain a better view. Two Trowbridge supporters fell and were quite seriously hurt, one being detained in hospital for two days.

Trowbridge dominated proceedings in the second-half but the Whites had a first-half lead and held on to win and qualify to visit Gloucester City away at Longlevens in the final qualifying round. Whilst their Southern

League side proved too strong in the end, Salisbury played exceptionally well but failed to hold a half-time lead given to them by Cyril Smith, eventually losing by the odd goal in three to a penalty. Doug Witt was outstanding again and his play was such that he subsequently returned to Gloucester to sign as a professional for them.

F.A. Cup Results 25/11/50

| Gloucester City | 2 | Salisbury | 1 | Dorchester Town | 1 | Glastonbury | 4 |
| Yeovil Town | 2 | Cheltenham Town | 4 | Llanelli | 5 | Weymouth | 0 |

Back to back league fixtures against old rivals Trowbridge over Christmas produced comfortable wins for the hosts on both occasions.

Pegasus, perhaps the best known amateur side of the day and composed of a number of amateur internationals, made a tour of Wessex and, after beating Winchester City, played in a friendly at Salisbury which the Whites won 3-0, Fisher, Howard and Grayer scoring. Appearing at inside right for the visitors was Peter May, subsequently to captain England at cricket.

Amateur Cup

The campaign started with a 3-0 away win against Bournemouth

Gas Works. A sequel to this is that Josh Jenkins, a well respected inside-forward for Bournemouth Gas Works, was not able to play because of injury. Not being cup-tied and because Salisbury were not able to play Cyril Smith because he was a permit player, Salisbury

Goal-mouth action from the Salisbury versus Walton and Hersham Amateur Cup game at Victoria Park, with Salisbury losing 3-1.

approached him to sign for them so that he could play in future rounds of the competition. The Gas Works team sportingly agreed and he duly made an appearance in the next round against Walton and Hersham.

Salisbury, cheered on by 1100 travelling supporters who had boarded a special train which picked up at Porton and Andover Junction, played well to draw 0-0 before losing the replay 3-1 at Victoria Park. Over 5000 attended including 1000 visitors. It was suggested that Salisbury did not do themselves justice and they were losing 3-0 before Fisher scored a very late consolation.

Amateur Cup Results 13/1/51

Walton & Hersham	0	Salisbury	0			
replay Salisbury	1	Walton & Hersham	3			
Wimbledon	2	Sheppey United	0	Gosport Borough 3	Pegasus	4
Brentwood	1	Westbury United	1	Slough Town 4	Poole Town	1

The Whites returned to Western League action against Portland winning 8-2 (Fisher 4). They certainly had better luck than Wiltshire league Pewsey who also scored eight on the same day only to lose by the odd goal in 17.

Fixture pile-up looming

The Whites record at this stage was won nine, drawn three, lost five, which whilst the best so far in the league, again saw them well behind in their fixtures. The Easter programme saw only one point from three games with two home defeats against Barnstaple and

Bristol Rovers Colts. The last six weeks saw 12 fixtures outstanding.

There were strange goings on in the the 3-1 defeat at Poole. Langley scored a goal for Poole with his hand. The referee allowed it in spite of protests but other Poole players confirmed that their team-mate had handled the ball into the goal. The referee then consulted his linesman and the goal was disallowed. Would it happen now??

Overtime?

The fixtures were such that on the 5th May, Cladge Howard played for the Western League side in the afternoon and at home on the same evening for the Hampshire League side.

End of season comment suggested that in spite of the fixture congestion the club had had a successful season in finishing in eighth place. Amateur football was in a healthy condition locally and many hoped that it would remain that way. Little did people realise that change was inevitably coming.

The 1951–52 Season — Richard J.A. Walker

At the opening of the season, Scullard and Parker, two stalwarts from the first year of the club's existence, had left. Bill Metherall, who was Manager of the reserves, had also departed.

Bad omen

The season started with what was considered a bad omen. The club had not lost an opening fixture since its formation but did so this year with a defeat at Barnstaple. They, too, had turned professional

and had signed a number of ex-league players. Defeat in five league games culminated in a win for Chippenham Town at Victoria Park by 5-2 so a cup-tie versus Calne was a welcome relief.

Freddie Rolls, a young local player, had taken over from Fisher in attack and Tony Syrett, a prolific scorer for the reserves, had moved on to Chippenham Town. Although Calne were beaten 2-0, times were changing. Rolls was sent off in the later stages for disputing a decision, which was almost unheard of in those days. It was also at this time that a young Philip Purdie was taken to court in Salisbury, under a local by-law, for shouting to the annoyance of the public. Apparently, whilst selling newspapers, his sin was to shout: 'Evening Standard' 'latest Test' '3.30 Winner'. He was fined 10 shillings (50p).

Rolls, thankfully, was only reprimanded for his indiscretion and was able to play at Badgers Hill where Frome Town were beaten 3-2. Salisbury then lost to Chippenham Town 2-1 after a replay to end their interest in the major cup competition for the year.

F.A. Cup Results 27/10/51

Salisbury	1	Chippenham Tn	1	Lymington Tn	1	Portland United	1
Barnstaple Tn	2	Bideford	1	Chippenham United	0	Bath City	3
Replays							
Chippenham Tn	2	Salisbury	1	Portland United	1	Lymington Tn	2

Lymington march on

This was the season that Lymington Town first appeared in the fourth qualifying round of the F.A. Cup, taking Barnstaple to a replay in North Devon which the hosts won 3-1. It was many years later that the successors of the same club next appeared at the same stage of the competition as referred to later in this book (season 2003–2004).

Inflation was also on the scene in the price of the programme which had risen from 2d to 3d. (unable to round this up to todays prices as 12d = 5p).

Amateur Cup

Salisbury entered the F.A. Amateur Cup at the last qualifying stage and comprehensively beat Bournemouth Gas Works, Josh Jenkins and all, 6-1 at Victoria Park. Dennis Cutbush played for Salisbury and was one of a number of local service players who played for the Navy and appeared for Salisbury at this time. He was, subsequently, to become a full amateur international after moving to Maidstone United. Local interest was not maintained however, as Salisbury lost 1-2 at Brentwood. Many coaches took supporters door to door for 10s.6d (52½p) in an overall crowd of 1200.

Dennis
Cutbush

By this time Salisbury's league form was causing concern. They were in the bottom two of the table and a real relegation struggle was about to begin. Dennis Rogers, who had spent a year out with a leg injury, had fought his way back into the side but things were not looking good.

Pegasus

Pegasus, the Amateur Cup holders, visited Salisbury again for a friendly match in aid of 'Eventide', a local charity. Although Salisbury beat them again they entertained the crowd by their style of football. The crowd was amused to hear the genteel voices of visiting players calling ' pass it down the middle to Peter' (reference again to Peter May).

Welcome back for Dennis Rogers.

The end of March saw the Whites at the bottom of the table and hosting Stonehouse on a grey day which saw driving rain and snow. A 2-0 defeat resulted and only an optimist could find anything to be cheerful about.

Revival

The return fixture on the 5th April saw the start of a revival which was to take the club clear of relegation. A 1-1 draw at Stonehouse was followed by a good Easter where spirits were revived in the home game against Cheltenham Town Reserves. A goal-keeping crisis saw a new ' keeper appear who was carried off injured after five minutes on Easter Monday. In those days there were no subs allowed but Salisbury played the rest of the match with 10 men and won the fixture 2-0. A further seven matches saw only one defeat and the club finished with 29 points, six clear of the relegation places occupied by Bristol Rovers Colts and Poole Town.

Salisbury were not going to be able to hold on to amateur status in a league now dominated by professionalism.

The 1952–53 Season — Peter J. Waterhouse

The 1952/53 League campaign commenced on 23 August with a home game against Dorchester Town. The match ended in a 1-0 victory for the Whites, a very encouraging start to the new season. Newcomer Hibberd, who played at outside-right, hit a powerful drive to secure maximum points.

Heavy rain causes major disaster

Sadly events had taken place in the West Country the previous week which would send the whole nation into deep shock as the Lynton and Lynmouth Flood disaster unfolded.

The football world responds

Many football clubs in the U.K. rallied in support of the relief fund. At the Dorchester Town game at Victoria Park, where the attendance was 2300, a collection was taken at half-time which realised £25.10s.

The following week the Whites travelled to the west country for the Western League game against Barnstaple, when a cheque was handed over from the supporters.

On Tuesday evening 26th August Bristol Rovers sent a team to play at Barnstaple and, with collections taken and the receipts from the match, a further £404 was raised for the Relief Fund.

The club also made donations to the Mayor of Salisbury and the Wiltshire F.A. relief funds. Tragically a Western League linesman was drowned in this disaster.

At Barnstaple Salisbury went down 4-2 while the Hampshire League Division II side recorded a 3-2 victory at Victoria Park in front of a 1300 gate against Romsey Town.

Disappointment in F.A. Cup

Last season the team made an early exit from the F.A. Cup resulting in them starting from the qualifying rounds this season, with home wins against Welton Rovers (7-1) and Chippenham Town (3-1).

The Whites faced Trowbridge Town in the divisional final where the winners would go on to the 4th Qualifying Round. The game at Victoria park on 25th October drew 4100 spectators who saw the hosts beaten 2-0.

F.A. Cup Results 25/10/52

| Salisbury | 0 | Trowbridge Town | 2 | Dorchester Town | 2 | B'mouth Gas Works | 1 |
| Gloucester City | 0 | Bath City | 2 | Basingstoke Town | 2 | Newport I.O.W. | 4 |

More of the same

In the F.A. Amateur Cup Salisbury were exempted until the 4th Qualifying round on the 8th November with an away tie, against Clevedon.

Four coaches travelled down from Salisbury for the game, but, unfortunately didn't arrive at the ground until just before half-time. The Salisbury supporters must have thought it was a bad omen; the Whites went down 2-1.

Football League beckons

Local player Bill Sainsbury was attracting rave notices for his performances with the club. As luck would have it, in November Bill was called up for his National Service, but later he went on to become a professional with Fulham F.C.

A young Bill Sainsbury is soon off to Craven Cottage but via his National Service.

SALISBURY FOOTBALL CLUB

A SPECIAL GENERAL MEETING OF

CLUB MEMBERS

will be held on

MONDAY 1st DECEMBER, 1952

7 p.m.

in the

Oak Room, The Guildhall, Salisbury

for consideration of the future policy of the Club

Please produce your Membership Card

or quote

Membership Number at the door.

The club had now reached a watershed in that they were facing the reality of turning semi-professional. Many clubs similar to Salisbury had already done this because it was virtually impossible to attract good class amateur players.

He who dares!

Basically the choice was that the club would remain amateur and just play in the Hampshire League, or turn semi-professional with a view to recruiting some good experienced players, which would hopefully, take the club forward in the Western League.

Many people still appreciated the old amateur virtues of fair play and sportsmanship. Indeed the club was well respected for the players exemplary conduct. In the club notes of 8th November 1952, after the away defeat to Wells City, 1-0:

'We returned with the referee's opinion that Salisbury possessed a team of outstanding sportsmanship, we entirely agree'

At the Extraordinary General Meeting, held at the Guildhall on the 1st December 1952, it was decided to turn semi-professional by 61 votes to 42

The following statement appeared in the club programme on 13th December 1952.

'Having crossed the RUBICON, the next step is to endeavour to bring the venture to a successful conclusion.

The pros and cons were keenly debated at our enthusiastic meeting, and the decision reached demands undivided support from all who have the welfare of the club at heart, and we believe we shall get it.'For the present it is necessary to be patient and hopeful.

On the 3rd January 1953, Salisbury signed their first semi-professional, Doug Witt, who was with the Whites before signing for Gloucester.

He played his first game for Salisbury on 10th January and this resulted in a 2-1 victory away at Clandown. However, with defeats at Chippenham Town, Wells, Stonehouse and a Boxing Day home defeat against Trowbridge, they found themselves in a precarious position.

Salisbury come good when it matters

Thankfully, by the end of January the tide was beginning to turn in their favour and a run of good results saw them drawing at Trowbridge and Weymouth. Wins at Clandown 2-1 and Dorchester 3-2 lifted the club's spirits and went some way to vindicating the decision to turn professional.

The bottom six teams on the 17th January 1953 read:

	P	W	D	L	F	A	Pts
Portland Utd	18	4	6	8	27	44	14
Glastonbury	16	6	1	9	28	28	13
Clandown	14	3	5	6	14	25	11
Dorchester Town	14	3	3	8	22	31	9
Salisbury	**15**	**2**	**5**	**8**	**22**	**41**	**9**
Paulton Rovers	14	0	3	11	13	62	3

Roy Turner joined the Whites from Portsmouth with Roy Fisher, Dennis Rogers, Dennis Heagren and John Newbury turning semi-professional for the club.

Upward move continues

Moving into mid-February the Whites remarkable turnaround continued. The Western League side recorded a 4-0 score away to Paulton Rovers, with Honey, Glass, Fisher and Rogers all getting on the score sheet. On the same day, 14th February, the Hants League side went out in the 3rd round of the Russell Cotes Cup losing at Thornycroft Athletic, 6-3.

The following Saturday, 21st February, the Western League side's exceptional run continued with a 3-0 home win against Wells City, with Smith, Glass and Fisher all bagging goals. The following Saturday, at the reserves home fixture, it was a announced that the first team had won 2-1 at Glastonbury and a wag in the crowd remarked:

`If we aren't too careful we shall experience difficulty in avoiding championship honours!'

The Whites secretary manager was now able to smile; in fact his justified pessimism had now turned to justified optimism.

Entertainment for all

Salisbury's superb run came to an end when they went down 2-0 to Chippenham United on the 7th March at Victoria Park. On Saturday 21st March the Whites made their longest journey in the Western League when they completed the trip to Bideford where they came away with a 1-1 draw. At the end of the game the Bideford supporters gave both teams a rapturous ovation when they left the field. On the last Saturday of March, Salisbury ran out worthy winners against Glastonbury 3-0 at home.

They commenced their Easter programme at Victoria Park entertaining league leaders Barnstaple Town. Of the team that played away to Barnstaple last August, only five players made the line-up that day; they were Heagren, Abbott, Smith, Fisher and Cutbush. Salisbury secured a very credible 2-2 draw, with goals from Witt (penalty) and Cutbush.

All' s well that ends well

The two final Western League games produced maximum points. Both were played at Victoria Park. On Monday 27th April Stonehouse were beaten 2-1 and, on the following Saturday Bridgwater were defeated 5-1.

The club closed the season on an optimistic note and the following programme notes appeared on 2nd May 1953.

'Like every other club in the country, we have had our disappointments, softened by unexpected successes, but on the whole we can congratulate both teams and our Secretary Manager, Mr R. Broom on the success attained.

Since changing our status, the turn of the wheel has been remarkable, for the senior side has steadily climbed from danger to safety and respectability.

Supporters are already wondering what season 1953-54 has in store for us, they can be assured that the management has not been idle for players of known ability have been recommended, and we have reason to hope, will be signed in due course.

With increased strength in the forward line, we can anticipate the future with optimism, for our defence justifies the confidence placed in it'.

Unfortunately, the club would be losing the services of Dave Abbott due to work commitments. Dave was an outstanding and popular player for the club. He joined Salisbury F.C. when it was formed and played in the first game at R.A.F. Locking in August 1947. He joined the club as right-half but had played at centre and left-half. He had also represented Wiltshire, Hampshire and the Western League.

It' s a colourful world!

Finally away from the world of football, two notable events took place in 1953, both of which, I expect, most people in the countries concerned welcomed. In America the first colour TVs came on line, while in U.S.S.R., Joseph Stalin died.

The 1953–54 Season —   Peter J. Waterhouse

The Fifties saw the people of Salisbury getting on with their lives in post war Britain. The Working Mens and Social Clubs were flourishing in the City and there was a plethora of Youth Clubs; virtually all the churches had youth clubs.

Sports clubs prospered in that decade with Salisbury Amateur Athletic Club being highly successful attracting huge crowds to Victoria Park for the August Bank Holiday Trophy Meeting.

Many outstanding athletes were members of Salisbury A.C. People of that decade may remember, Peter Clark, Dennis and Brian Lillicrap, Stan Eldon and Shirley Amey.

Note from fellow author David Thear: The author of this piece was no mean athlete himself; he was the club's 'senior club champion' in 1954.

The famous, 'Round the Houses' road race used to take place in September on a Saturday evening, attracting teams from all across the country. It started from the Blue Boar Row and finished in a crowded Guildhall Square.

Season underway

The Whites faced a difficult away game at championship candidates Barnstaple on the opening match of the season, Saturday 22nd August 1953.

At half-time, with the advantage of a strong wind, the Whites led 1-0, but could have had two or even three more goals. With the wind Barnstaple took their opportunities and scored three goals in the first half-hour after the restart.

Cyril Smith scorer of the Salisbury goal.

Salisbury were still well in the game but Cutbush had a goal disallowed and a deliberate hand-ball in the Barnstaple penalty area went unnoticed by the referee. Had Salisbury made the most of their opportunities they would have drawn instead of being on the wrong end of a 3-1 scoreline.

Early efforts by professional Salisbury bear fruit

Salisbury's first home match was on 29th August against Clandown. It was their first full season as a professional team and they started in style by winning 6-0, with goals from Long (2), Cutbush (2), Smith (1) and Hall (1). The Hampshire League side won 3-1 away to Ryde with Tommy Muckles scoring a hat-trick (one a penalty).

On Saturday 5th September over 1200 saw the Hampshire League eleven record their third successive victory over Totton at Victoria Park 5-2. At Poole, on the same day, the Western League side went down 3-2. At half-time Salisbury were losing 3-0, but were the superior team in the second-half and fully deserved at least a draw.

First defeat for Hampshire League team

There were two superb results on Saturday 19th September. The Western League side beat Bideford Town 5-1 at Victoria Park with goals from Glass, Hall, Long, Rogers and Ron Booth. The Hampshire League side had a hard struggle at Portsmouth, beating the Civil Service side 2-1, with goals from Wilf Sanger and Roy Fisher. The following week they suffered their first reverse going down 2-1 at Bournemouth.

Salisbury lose out in 'Wiltshire derby'

The F.A. Cup run commenced with a 1st Qualifying Round match at Victoria Park against Andover Town. They found themselves 1-0 down early on in the game which made them jittery. Thankfully, kicking towards the 'City end', the team regained their balance and with goals from Long and Hall ran out 2-1 victors.

In the 2nd Qualifying Round, away at Chippenham Town on 10th October 1953, 1700 spectators witnessed an exciting tie.

In a glorious game, with end-to-end football, the Whites went down 4-2 after being behind 1-0 at half-time. After the restart they were soon two goals adrift but this only spurred their efforts with Muckles getting one back. Chippenham hit back with the best goal of the game putting them two goals ahead. Undaunted Salisbury swept down the field and the score became 3-2, Muckles again being the scorer after Fidler had struck the bar with a powerful drive.

Chance to go all-square lost

Then a penalty was awarded which gave Salisbury the opportunity to equalise but it was missed. Chippenham then scored again leaving the Whites beaten but far from disgraced.

Many Chippenham supporters classed the game as 'the best match this year'. With the epic battle taking place away the Hampshire League side fought back at Victoria Park to win 4-2 against Romsey Town after being two down.

F.A. Cup Results 10/10/53

Chippenham Tn	4	Salisbury	2	Welton Rovers	0	Trowbridge Town	3
Chippenham Unt	4	Bristol St. George	1	Newport I.O.W.	7	Winchester City	0
Dorchester Tn	1	Portland United	3				

Although the team occupied sixth place in the Western League and the Hampshire League side were top of their division, the club was not resting on its laurels.

On 17th October a 4-0 home victory was recorded against Wells City which prompted the following statement in the club programme the following week:

If the 'Battle of the Cities' was not a great game it nevertheless helped us by a victory of four clear goals to retain our home record.

Wells have the weakest side that have worn their colours for several years and their position in the League Table was justified by the opposition.

But what of our team? Added punch was very apparent in the forward line and if a number of opportunities were not pressed home, especially in the first half, it may have been that the Salisbury players visualised ultimate victory and felt that risks should be avoided.

This may have been the case but a glorious opportunity was missed of proving the ability of our forwards to be a penetrating force.

We are not knitting together as a team like we did in our first two seasons and we all know that combination rather than individual effort is more likely to bring reward.

It doesn't behove us to be too pessimistic; let us realise that a championship side has to be gradually built-up.

Scouts are out watching for talent and if it is found no effort will be spared to secure it.

Our Secretary-manager, Mr R. Broom, is fully aware that additional players are wanted and the committee are right behind him in believing that obtaining youthful players of good promise is preferable to signing players that are just passing out.

This is not because were are afraid to spend, for if the right men can be obtained the money will be forthcoming, but it must be wisely spent.

We are anxious to give our loyal supporters the very best entertainment and eventually the efforts of our energetic Supporters' Club will enable us to provide it.

Ironically Salisbury lost the return fixture at Wells by 2-1 on Saturday 5th December when, again, scoring chances were frittered away. On the same day 1300 spectators saw the Hants League side beat Bournemouth 5-2 in the 1st round of the Russell-Cotes Cup.

Roll on Christmas

Supporters were now looking forward to the Christmas home fixtures with games against the Western League pace-setters Weymouth on the 12th December and Trowbridge Town on Boxing Day.

In a thrilling game witnessed by over 2000 supporters, Salisbury defeated Weymouth 3-0, with goals by Ron Booth (penalty) Cyril Smith and Bill Hall. Everyone hoped for this continuation of form away to Portland on Saturday 19th December, but the journey was unproductive, Salisbury going down 3-1.

The game against Trowbridge Town on Boxing Day was a classic encounter, enjoyed by a gate close on 3000.

Trowbridge scored the only goal before the interval but on the restart the Whites marksmen became busy and good goals were scored by Heagren, Taylor, Fidler and Hall. Although three goals behind, Trowbridge never slackened and were rewarded when a goal was headed in from a free kick. Good Christmas Fare, six goals in an excellent local derby.

Dennis Heagren, Salisbury's first goal scorer in the Boxing Day game.

The first half of the season

For the first time since the club was formed both teams had completed the first half of the league programme by the end of December.

Great Honour for Salisbury F.C. Manager

Mr Reg Broom the Salisbury Secretary Manager's ability was recognised when he was selected to manage the 'Western League Eleven' to oppose a 'F.A. Eleven' at Bristol during the League's Diamond Jubilee Celebrations.

The honour paid to Mr Broom was well deserved and proved that his ability was well recognised beyond Salisbury.

The records for the half-way stages in both the Western and Hampshire League follow with the dates when reached in previous seasons.

Western League

Season	*Reached*	P	W	D	L	F	A	Pts
1947/48	2-2-48	17	17	0	0	88	16	34
1948/49	19-3-49	17	7	2	8	43	32	16
1949/50	4-3-50	17	8	0	9	31	35	16
1950/51	24-2-51	17	9	3	5	41	32	21
1951/52	19-1-52	17	4	4	9	34	45	12
1952/53	24-1-53	16	3	5	8	25	43	11

Hampshire League

Season	*Reached*	P	W	D	L	F	A	Pts
1948/49	19-2-49	13	10	2	1	50	22	22
1949/50	13-12-49	13	6	0	7	30	26	12
1950/51	10-2-51	13	4	0	9	17	39	8
1951/52	19-1-52	13	5	2	6	31	33	12
1952/53	26-12-52	13	8	0	5	30	25	16

It will be seen from the Hampshire League team's record below that they held a better mid-season record than when they gained promotion at the end of their first season.

Western League

Half-way stage	P	W	D	L	F	A	Pts
1953/54	19	9	1	9	43	37	19

Hampshire League

Half-way stage	P	W	D	L	F	A	Pts
1953/54	16	13	2	1	65	19	28

It was not since season 1948/49 that the total number of goals scored by both elevens had passed the hundred mark, with the total for the 1953/54 season (107) being passed by one.

At the half-way mark of the season, the Western League side were in the top-half of the table and the Hampshire team led their league.

A spell of hard winter weather in January caused serious fixture congestion. A well-fought point was picked up away to Dorchester Town. With a biting cross-wind which made the ball difficult to control, the 2-2 draw was a fair result. They then experienced a thorough drubbing away at the hands of Bath City Reserves 5-0 on 13th February.

The Hampshire League side went through to the next round of the Russell-Cotes Cup with a 6-1 victory over Sholing Sports at Victoria Park.

February 20th proved a far from happy day for Salisbury, for it resulted in a scrambling 2-1 home victory against Hampshire League Ryde and a surprising defeat at Stonehouse, 5-2.

In the club notes of February 1954 the following was reported.

Our Supporters' Club has handed us over a cheque.

How much?

£2000 — and we are staggered by the amount.

Staggered? Yes! but full of appreciation for the untiring efforts of the officials and to all who have rallied round them.

Success has been deserved and we find it quite beyond us to adequately express our thanks.

On the 27th of February 1954 their home form continued with a 2-0 win against championship aspirants Street.

On 20th March, Salisbury's Western League side rose to the occasion to give the best exhibition of the season, both individually and collectively away to Trowbridge Town with a 3-2 victory, thereby completing the double for the season.

At Victoria Park over 1800 saw another attractive match with the Whites Hampshire League side defeating nearest promotion rivals, Portsmouth Civil Service 2-1.

The league tables for the Western and Hampshire Leagues then made for very exciting reading if you were a Salisbury supporter. The top six of both these leagues read:

Western League

	P	W	D	L	F	A	Pts
Weymouth	26	14	3	9	74	46	31
Poole Town	23	14	3	6	54	35	31
Trowbridge Town	25	14	3	8	63	46	31
Barnstaple Town	25	13	4	8	58	38	30
Salisbury	**26**	**13**	**3**	**10**	**61**	**53**	**29**
Bridgwater Town	25	12	4	9	60	61	28

Hampshire League Division II

	P	W	D	L	F	A	Pts
Salisbury	**19**	**14**	**3**	**2**	**57**	**34**	**31**
Portsmouth C.S.	22	14	3	5	72	44	31
Cowes Reserves	16	10	4	2	52	35	24
Thorycroft Athletic	20	10	4	6	54	42	24
Bournemouth	18	9	2	7	44	43	20

Saturday 20th March 1954 saw goalkeeper, Jim Goodwin, join Salisbury. The following Saturday Trowbridge Town were beaten 2-0 to win a place in the final of the Wiltshire Professional Shield. The following appeared in the club programme for the next match.

Jim Goodwin

Before departing, the Trowbridge captain voiced his opinion that we were the best side they had met and what was even more pleasing that we were also the cleanest!

He thought too, that we still had a chance to be champions, which view seems too optimistic to be entertained, although if we continued to win away it would not be impossible.

But to come to earth, if we find ourselves in the first six at the end of the season we shall have no cause to be dissatisfied

The good form continued at Victoria Park on 3rd April with a 3-0 victory against Bath City Reserves and this was followed by a 1-1 draw at Glastonbury.

The Easter programme commenced with an attractive home game against Western League leaders Barnstaple Town, which resulted in a 1-0 win and on Easter Monday at Victoria Park Chippenham United were beaten 2-1.

In the final weeks of the 1953/54 season the Hampshire league side were crowned Hampshire Division II Champions.

Some you win some you lose

Mixed fortunes came in the Whites cup finals. They went down 2-1 to Swindon Town in the Wiltshire Professional Shield at Swindon and at the Tidworth Oval on Wednesday 5th May they were 2-0 victors over Andover in the Russell Cotes Cup.

The following Saturday at Newport I.O.W. they defeated Newport 4-1 to proudly lift the Pickford Cup.

Under the capable management of Reg Broom in the club's first

Salisbury gained revenge for their earlier defeat at Barnstaple. Above Cyril Smith cracks the ball past their defence and the scrambling 'keeper Scot, to set up a 1-0 scoreline.

full year of professionalism they finished in a creditable position in the Western League and had the nucleus of a team that could be built-up to do even better.

The 1954–55 Season — Peter J. Waterhouse

The citizens of Salisbury were now embracing the great economic, environmental and social changes that were taking place in Britain in this decade. They also liked a good old knees up and, on special occasions, the Guildhall Square was used for public dancing. This and the Eventide Carnivals attracted massive crowds to the streets.

A popular pastime was ballroom dancing. Virtually every teenager of the early fifties hoped to become a proficient ballroom dancer.

Many of these teenagers learnt their basic dancing skills from two local youth leaders, the late Miss Kate Whatley and John Pike. John Pike's father was the Salisbury City F.C. trainer in the 1930s. The two principal Ballroom Dancing Schools were the Percy School of Ballroom Dancing and the Johnson Ballroom Dancing School in Wilton Road. Jack Johnson was an enthusiastic sportsman.

The local dancing fraternity had a good choice of venues such as the Co-operative Hall, Winchester St. (Ted Hardy Band), Assembly Rooms, New Canal (Benny Singer Dance Orchestra), Cadena, Blue Boar Row (Merry Macs), Palais, Wilton Road (Gran Silby) and Michael Herbert Hall, Wilton (Charlie Hart Band).

New age dawning

While all this was taking place in Salisbury, over in Memphis Tennessee, on Monday 5th July 1954, a 19-year-old by the name of Elvis Presley was making his first recording, That's Alright, at Sun Records. Many Salisbury teenagers would soon be dancing a new style, the Jive, to a new sound, called Rock & Roll. Most people who lived in the fifties would probably say it was one of the best decades of their lives.

The season starts

The start of the 1954–55 season saw Salisbury Football Club having the luxury of two sides of almost equal merit, which would foster the keenest competition for inclusion in the teams.

The Hampshire League side included players of considerable experience and talent; players of the calibre of Roy Fisher, Cyril Smith, Roy Owen, Dennis Heagren, Alan Kingston and Dennis Tuck. In reality the Hampshire League side was the reserve team, although perhaps it was good sports psychology not to use the word reserves.

Probably the full squad was ideal material for the player rotation system which is now employed by most sides in the top leagues in the UK.

After a very encouraging pre-season the Western League side played their first match at Barnstaple on August 21st. They found themselves a goal down in the first minute and then two within a quarter of an hour. The home team played with increasing confidence and although Salisbury had a fair share of midfield play they still crossed over two goals down.

The second-half started brightly with a Ron Long goal disallowed for off-side but, with King off the field injured, the Salisbury 10 men could not stop the nippy Barnstaple forwards scoring two more goals, which gave them a deserved 4-0 victory.

The first home league match was against Street on Saturday 28th

Salisbury's goalkeeper, Alan Kingston punches clear in another attack from the Frome forwards, in September 1954. The Whites were defeated 3-2 in this F.A. Cup game but went on to gain revenge in the following season.

August. Andy Prentice opened the scoring with a well-headed goal from an accurate centre by Timms, but Salisbury soon found themselves 2-1 down. Prentice added a second and the spectators then saw a whole-hearted recovery with further goals from Timms and Kew resulting in a 4-2 win for the Whites.

Salisbury's F.A. Cup aspirations ended on the 25th September when they lost 3-2 to Frome Town at Victoria Park. However, the Hampshire League side registered their third away victory in succession beating Fareham 4-1. The Hampshire League game on the 2nd October saw a good attendance of just under 2000 witness a 1-1 draw against Southampton A.

By early October both the Western and Hampshire League sides were hitting top form in their respective leagues. On Saturday 9th October the Western League side ran out 5-1 victors against Glastonbury with a gate of 2750. The scorers were Prentice 2, Cutbush 1, Fleming 1, Taylor 1.

Eddie Fleming scorer of one of the goals in the 5-1 defeat of Glastonbury on 9th October, 1954.

The league positions after the 23rd October games for the top three teams in the Western and Hampshire Leagues Division I read:

	P	W	D	L	F	A	Pts
Salisbury	9	6	2	1	26	13	14
Bath City	8	6	1	1	26	8	13
Chippenham Town	8	5	3	0	18	9	13
Salisbury	8	6	2	0	23	8	14
Portsmouth A	10	7	0	3	29	21	14
Newport I.O.W.	8	5	2	1	29	15	12

The Hampshire League side suffered their first defeat of the season away to Gosport going down 1-0 on the 4th December.

On the 11th December, Salisbury played H.M.S. Daedalus in a friendly match which prompted the following remarks in the club notes the following week:

> H.M.S. Daedalus brought a strong side and provided us with an interesting match at home. They hadn't a weak link in the team, and we did well to hold them to a goal-less draw. It was however obvious from the attendance only 800, that friendly games are far less attractive than those of the league.

Winter tightens its grip in January 1955

Salisbury F.C. made the journey to Bridgwater in atrocious weather conditions. When the officials and team arrived at the ground they found the pitch was covered with four inches of snow, yet the match was played!

Football was out of the question, Salisbury tried to play it and, lost, Bridgwater didn't and won 4-2. If allowed to drop, the ball stopped dead and required the kick of a mule to move it a few yards. Unfortunately two precious points were lost in the bid for Championship honours.

Salisbury sign new forward

At Salisbury's home game against Weymouth on the 22nd January, a new forward was unveiled, Cliff Pinchbeck. He was a player with considerable experience having played for Everton, Port Vale, Northampton and Bath. Although the attendance dropped to 1500, due to inclement weather, Salisbury ran out 3-1 winners with the new centre-forward scoring a brace. A report stated his second goal was one of the best ever seen at Victoria Park.

After the home defeat against Bath City Reserves 1-0 on February 19th Salisbury slipped to fifth place in the league. However, the Hants League side still led the table by three points.

Above: Andy Prentice scorer of one of the goals in the 2-0 win over Barnstaple on Good Friday. Andy was the top goal scorer for Salisbury in seasons 1954/5 and 1956/7.

The Western League side dropped only one point over the strenuous Easter Programme. On Good Friday, they defeated Barnstaple Town 2-0 at Victoria Park. On Easter Saturday the team travelled to Wells City where the game ended in a 1-1 draw. On Easter Monday, Bristol City brought a strengthened side to Victoria Park and a crowd of just under 3000 saw a thoroughly entertaining game with Salisbury running out 3-0 victors and Fred Rolls getting a well-deserved hat-trick.

With the Easter programme behind them the Western League side had to play seven games in 26 days to complete the season.

All fingers crossed

The Hampshire League side with just three home matches to play, only required two more points for the Championship.

Following their successful Easter programme the Western League side gained further success at the expense of Bristol Rovers (2-1) and, by gaining a first point at Chippenham United, had raised their league position from seventh to fifth.

Saturday 23rd April saw a visit to Bristol City. With the team down to only nine fit men and a goalkeeper hobbling from a foot injury, they came home victorious with Cliff Pinchbeck scoring the one goal that mattered.

The following Monday evening the team followed up with another victory at Glastonbury by 2-1. This was Salisbury's fifth double of the season. As a result of these victories, they could still be a danger to the league leaders Dorchester Town and a lot could depend on the last match of the season against them at Victoria Park.

Hampshire League side win the honours

On Wednesday 27th April, the Hampshire League side defeated

Fareham Town 1-0, thanks to a goal by Cyril Smith, to lift the Hampshire League Division I title in their first season.

The following Saturday, saw the Western League side beaten 2-1 at Portland. The final league match, against league champions Dorchester, was lost 2-0 but Salisbury achieved a creditable fourth place in the table.

The last game of the season on May 9th saw Salisbury lose 2-0 to Swindon Town at Victoria Park in the Final of the Wiltshire Professional Shield.

The Western League Division I team finished higher in the league than had ever been achieved before and the Hampshire League side had the honour of winning the Championship at the first time of asking.

A quote from the 11th September 1954 programme.

'We are pleased to announce that the City Council have now given permission for The Salisbury Football Club to erect standing covered accommodation on each side of the existing stand.

It is hoped to start this work during the coming week and when finished will be able to be used by Supporters FREE.'

The final top positions of their two respective tables now read:

Western League Division I (top 4)

	P	W	D	L	F	A	Pts
Dorchester	34	23	5	6	102	46	51
Chippenham Town	34	21	7	6	83	39	49
Bath City Reserves	34	22	4	8	87	52	48
Salisbury	**34**	**17**	**8**	**9**	**71**	**50**	**42**

Hampshire League Division I (top 3)

	P	W	D	L	F	A	Pts
Salisbury	**26**	**19**	**5**	**2**	**64**	**20**	**43**
Newport I.O.W.	26	16	4	6	73	53	36
Portsmouth A	26	15	4	8	60	38	33

T.Q.M. (Total Quality Management) in action

An insight into how quickly the club management responded to an unintentional omission which took place the previous week is shown when the following apology appeared in the club programme on 4th September 1954.

PROGRAMMES

The Committee wish to apologise for the error in not announcing the numbers of two programmes at half-time on Saturday last, 28th August.

It was not realised that the numbers had not been announced until after the match, when most of the supporters had left the ground.

Arrangements have been made to see that this will not occur again. Each Saturday a Committee man will be in charge of programmes.

The Chairman of the Football Club will select two numbers each week, which he will place in a sealed envelope to be handed to the person in charge of programmes. This envelope will be opened at half-time and the numbers announced.

Persons holding the programmes bearing the announced numbers will be entitled to travel with the team at the next away match.

Name and address must be handed in at the Pavilion after each match, to the committee man in charge of programmes on that day.

Committee man in charge to-day September, 4th: Mr Curtis.

The 1955–56 Season — David Thear

As a result of much hard work and many miles travelled during the close season, the Secretary-manager, Reg Broom had assembled a formidable group of players to challenge for the Western and Hampshire League titles. There were 12 new names listed in the programme for the first trial games and of these, nine were to play significant roles in the season's events.

Stan Abbott

The Western League team was considerably strengthened by the introduction of Jackie Knight from Bath, Stan Abbott, Frome and Bill Clancy, Fareham. In fact Stan Abbott and Ray Timms (as reserve) were immediately selected to play for the Western League XI, against Trowbridge Town who were celebrating their 75th anniversary.

Significantly the W.L. XI was captained by Stan Rickaby (Poole) who, only a few years previously, had represented the full England team while playing for West Bromwich Albion.

The season opened with high hopes, but, disappointingly, the first game against Wells City was cancelled when financial difficulties caused Wells to disband only to re-assemble in time to begin playing Western League matches in September. Nonetheless, by October, the Whites were third in the League after a four match winning sequence and being praised for the quality of their football.

History made by the Whites

It was the F.A. Cup, however, that captured the fans imagination. In the 1st Qualifying Round, Devizes were beaten 2-0 away in front of 1360 spectators. This led to a home tie against Bulford of the Wilts League and, with an attendance of 3700, Salisbury won 3-0. The next opponents were Frome Town and, again, the score was 3-0, with the crowd better again at 3800. The last match before the 1st Round Proper was away against Chippenham United and in this the Whites excelled scoring six times while conceding only two. A special train, price 5/- (25p) was run as well as numerous coaches and private cars.

Bond the Bulford goalkeeper, goes full-length to save this goal-bound shot from Andy Prentice in the Salisbury versus Bulford F.A. Cup tie at Victoria Park.

The scene was thus set for the away tie against Weymouth of the Southern League. It was the first time the Whites had reached this round in their history and a tie against Southend was to await the winners.

Again a special train was run, price 6/9d (34p), and at least one RAF National Serviceman went absent without leave during a NATO military exercise in order to see the game. He was fortunate not to be found out and

At Weymouth, Salisbury's goalkeeper Alan Kingston jumps high to safely gather this goal-bound shot.

lived to see out the rest of his two-year term.

Some 1500 supporters went to Weymouth to see the home side play superlative football for most of the first-half which produced for them three goals within a space of five minutes. The second half was a different story with the Whites attacking throughout. The deficit was reduced to one and even this

Salisbury's Jimmy Gray (red shirt/white shorts) outjumps the Weymouth forward Hobbs to thwart this attack.

would've been eliminated if the Weymouth full-back had not kicked off the line with the goalkeeper beaten. The next week's programme records the event with the words 'Weymouth deserved

Come on you Whites and Salisbury till we die.

the verdict but our magnificent effort left us far from disgraced and our men left the field deserving of the highest praise'.

Ironically the next Western League match was at home versus Weymouth

reserves which was lost by 4-3! This was only the Whites second league defeat of the season and, on 26th November, they were eighth in the league, eight points behind the leaders, Chippenham Town with six games in hand. In those days it was two points for a win and one for a draw. The Hampshire League Division I team

F.A. Cup Results 19/11/55

Weymouth	3	Salisbury	2		Swindon Town	4	Hereford	0
Yeovil Town	1	Aldershot Town	1		Crystal Palace	2	Southampton	2
				replay	Southampton	2	Crystal Palace	0

were third in the table with 15 points from 10 games, two points behind the leaders Gosport.

Famous names grace the pitch

Boxing Day brought Poole Town to Victoria Park and, in front of 4000 spectators, the match was drawn 1-1. The attraction of the Poole match, apart from it being a local derby, was the presence in their side of two recent English internationals. Stan Rickaby has already received a mention as captain of the Western League XI, but even more significant was the presence of Wilf Mannion at

Wilf Mannion

inside-left. Wilf, who had been a regular England player, was known as the 'golden boy' of English football and was generally reckoned to be one of the finest forwards to don an England shirt.

So why was he playing for Poole? In those days footballers were subject to a maximum wage, probably around £20 per week. This was not applicable to 'non-league' clubs who could pay what they liked and, because the nature of their football was part time, provide quite lucrative other extra employment. A number of clubs did this, including Weymouth, who had Dave Massart an ex-Walsall centre-forward, on their books.

Turning to the league again it would seem that Salisbury's Cup exploits had blunted their edge for league games. On the 25th Feb. 1956, they were seventh in the league with 23 points from 18 games, but their chances of the Championship were diminishing despite having games in hand over all the clubs above them.

Trowbridge Town led the table with 39 points from 25 games. In the Hants League the reserves were lying second, eight points behind Cowes with a game in hand but, significantly, Andover were third, two points behind with four games in hand.

Fifth place twice

In the Western League Cup, the Whites reached the final by beating Portland United 6-2 at home. In the final they drew 0-0 away to Chippenham and won the return 3-0 at Victoria Park.

In the league Salisbury finished fifth with 41 points from 32 games while Trowbridge took the Championship with 50 points. Also finishing fifth were the reserves in Hampshire League Div. I.

So what else was happening in and around Salisbury in 1955/6? The new NAAFI club located on the corner of New Street and St John's Street was opened by Princess Alexandra on 29th October (it is now the Courts Building). The old NAAFI Club located where Woolworths is now in the High Street, was closed. It had been host to thousands of service men and women of all nations during and after WWII. The author can still remember the marvellous parties given by the Americans during the war for Salisbury school children where ice-cream and other delights were on the menu.

All happening in the City

Does anyone remember the Downbeat Jazz Club which featured the Dave Barton Quartet? They met at the Bell & Crown (now the Cloisters). Dave played vibes, Julian Forder, tenor sax, Geoff Gilbert, drums and Tony (Nobby) Lawrence, double bass. Staying with music, Rosemary Squires, now living at Milford, guested with the Ted Heath Band, before going on to record and TV fame.

Salisbury teenagers along with teenagers worldwide were shocked by the news from America of the tragic death of the young actor James Dean, killed while driving his Porsche Spyder 550 near Chalane, California, on 30 September 1955.

The teenagers of Salisbury had their own age group music; Rock & Roll was the scene. They even had their own and the Cities' first R&R band, The Mambo Rockets with Mark Merrick, piano, Johnny Nicholls, guitar, Mick Andrews, drums and Peter Wood, double-bass and two sax players. For 6d (2½p) you could jive the night away at the Wilton Road Palais or the Fisherton St Youth Club. The 'in' places were the expresso coffee bars, 2 Bare Feet and the Man Friday. A night at the cinema was 1/6d (8p) and a pint of beer was 10d (5p), but, of course the average weekly wage within Salisbury for adults was only £8.10s. (£8.50p)

On the sporting scene Shirley Amey was one of the top 12 women milers in the UK and some years later (mid-60s) her younger brother Ian (Tich) became a member of the best-selling pop group, Dave Dee, Dozy, Beaky, Mick and Tich. Known locally as Dave Dee and the Bostons, they vied for Salisbury's most popular band with The Coasters and Danny and the Detonators.

Also on the sporting front Paddy Hasty, a popular centre-

Salisbury in Europe 1955 versus Union Sportive de Torquennoise

Alan Kingston goes to gather a corner – Roy King and 'General' Booth guard the line, Eddy Fleming and Cyril Smith look on.

forward for the Whites, was capped for Ireland amateurs against England.

Turning to transport, Tidworth railway station closed. In its heyday in WWII, it was heavily used particularly after Dunkirk and when US troops were stationed in the area. Special trains were run daily to Bournemouth and London for their recreational purposes. General Eisenhower, Prime Minister Churchill and Field Marshal Montgomery used it on their way to planning meetings for D-Day, 1944.

The 1956–57 Season — David Thear

Salisbury F.C. Victoria Park 1956 Reds versus Whites

These matches became a regular feature for many a season, supplying the Salisbury supporters with a foretaste of the coming season's strengths or weaknesses.

The season opened with a trial match between Reds and Whites at Victoria Park. It took place on 11th August and comprised most of last year's players with a sprinkling of new signings.

Both Western and Hampshire League teams hoped to, at least, emulate last season's performances in the league and again reach the 1st Round Proper of the F.A. Cup. In addition, the Western League, Hampshire Senior and Russell Cotes Cups were entered together with the Wilts Professional Shield. A full season's football was, therefore, in prospect for the Whites fans with more than a chance of success.

National Service for all males?

However, the season had its problems when in Autumn 1956

the U.K became involved with France in the invasion of Egypt. The Suez crisis captured the whole country's attention to the detriment of almost everything else. The military action lasted only a few days but the after effects were felt for some time. In football terms, teams who relied heavily on players from the Services had to make emergency arrangements to replace those who were involved in, or 'on standby' for, the action. National Service was at its height and many conscripts were involved, a lot of these being really good players. As an example of this Salisbury played the Royal Army Service Corps, Aldershot in the 3rd round of the Hampshire Senior Cup in February 1957 and nine of their players were on the books of league clubs. Salisbury won 3-1 but it took their strongest side to do so.

Glut of goals for Salisbury

Western League action started on 18th August when Bridgwater were beaten 4-0 at home but reality set in on the following Wednesday when Poole Town won 6-2 at the Park in the Western League Cup. They were a very strong side and went on to win the league by nine points from Trowbridge with Salisbury finishing 3rd with 45 points. Poole lost only six league matches all season and happily, one of these was against the Whites at the Park in April when Stan Abbot's goal clinched victory. Third place in the league was, in fact, their best since joining and their 98 goals scored (62 at home) were second only to Poole. The oddest result of the season was the 7-1 reverse at Portland compared with their 4-0 home win over the same opposition.

In the F.A. Cup Warminster were beaten 6-1 away in the First Qualifying Round. Again a special train was run at a cost of 3s.3d (16p). The result sparked off hopes of another Cup run but this was not to be. Chippenham Town came to the Park in the Second Qualifying Round and triumphed by 2-1, Bill Clancy scoring for the Whites. Significantly Chippenham's inside left was Roy Onslow who was later to sign for Salisbury and score in 1959 what was up to then, the most important goal in their history. The only piece of silverware they won was the Wilts Professional Shield when Swindon Town were beaten 1-0 by a goal from Dave Noyce.

The largest gate of the season was achieved on Saturday 4th May when a friendly was played against Union Sportive Tourquennoise of the North of France League. Salisbury won 4-2 before nearly 3000 spectators. Admission was 1/- (5p) stand 9d (4p) extra and cars 6d (2½p).

left to right: Ron Uren, Dave Noyce, Andy Prentice and Bill Clancy scored a goal apiece in the 4-2 win over the French.

The 1957–58 Season — Richard J.A. Walker

Plans were in hand to run a third team in season 1957/8 and local players were invited to sign up. Training sessions were to be held every Tuesday throughout the summer at Victoria Park under the guidance of Roy Owen.

The club started with their biggest ever payroll of 28 professional players and, with additional financial support, fielded teams in the first divisions of the Western, Hampshire and Bournemouth Leagues.

From 1956–57 season 21 players were retained. There were four immediate arrivals namely Len Gibbons, a left back from Hastings, Peter Rushworth from Bournemouth & Boscombe who was to prove a skillful half-back, Ray McAlone, a defender who was to give sterling service at full-back or centre-half and Charlie McNulty, a goal scoring inside-forward.

An opening day defeat by Bridgwater Town and several early injuries saw Reg Broom add to the squad by signing Ian Allen from Bournemouth and Tom Gale. These two were subsequently joined by Gordon Kaile, a local school master, who had played 65 times in the Football League for such teams as Nottingham Forest, Preston and Exeter City.

Early exit for Salisbury

Salisbury's first match in the F.A. Cup saw an

early 2-0 lead against Westbury wiped out before late goals from Prentice and Noyce saw them safely home. The next round saw Trowbridge Town comfortably defeat their hosts at Victoria Park where Vic Lambden, the old Bristol Rovers striker was a scourge to the home side. The crowd was 2700.

F.A. Cup Results 21/9/57

| Salisbury | 0 | Trowbridge Town | 3 | Melksham Town | 0 | Frome Town | 0 |
| Devizes Town | 1 | Chippenham Town | 5 | Calne | 1 | Warminster Town | 2 |

General disappointment was felt by all at the early season's results after so much was expected and this was shared by all the players. They felt it was now noticeable that, whereas they used to let the ball do the work, more running and carrying seemed to be the order of the day. Changes were made with a number of players from the Western and Hampshire Leagues swapping over. Wins against Yeovil Reserves at home and against Bristol City Colts helped. In the latter match Mike Turner, the visitor's keeper, was magnificent and kept the score to 2-1. He subsequently played for Swindon Town and Torquay in the Football League.

Some Christmas cheer

Salisbury continued their up and down performances and remained in the lower reaches of the league table with the team finding goal scoring a problem.

A number of narrow wins saw them climb the table and a good 3-0 win in a friendly fixture at Southern League Gloucester City in early December indicated better times lay ahead. Indeed, at Christmas the club was only three points off the leaders although the lack of goals contributed to lower crowds at first-team fixtures.

Stan Abbott's return after nearly two months out supplied some pep in attack, although he was hardly his old self. Results improved dramatically. Nottingham Forest came in with a substantial offer for full-back Len Gibbons but Salisbury declined and the player was happy to stay. At this time the weekly wage bill of the team was nearly £200 per week.

A crowd of 917 turned up to see the Bournemouth League side defeat Christchurch 11-0 at Victoria Park which was, in fact, a bigger gate than had seen the first team play Frome Town seven days previously. Perhaps they craved the sight of a goal feast.

Tragedy

The Manchester United plane crash cast a shadow over all soccer and this was compounded by the deaths of two Union Sportive de Tourquennoise players in a car accident in France; they had played in Salisbury at the end of the previous season.

Salisbury reached the summit of the League on the 25th February 1958, the first time since joining Division I of the Western League ten years previously. They had a happy Easter when they defeated Barnstaple at home and then drew the two subsequent holiday fixtures at Glastonbury and Barnstaple where they played with only 10 men after Alan Kingston, the goalkeeper, had gone off injured early in the game. Although a first ever Western League Championship was beckoning no great exhilaration seemed to be felt because of the teams dour performances where results were obtained almost exclusively by an expert defence.

'Champions'

A comprehensive 4-0 win at home against Glastonbury saw the title

Salisbury F.C. – Western League Champions 1957/58
Left/right, back row: Mr. A. Sainsbury (chairman), Reg Broom (sec.-manager), L. Gibbons, J. Herridge (assist. trainer), A. Kingston, P. Rushworth, B. Farrell, B. Clancy, T. Williams (trainer), G. Kaile, Mr. G. Wadsley, (vice-chairman)
Middle-row: D. Oakley, I. Allen, T. Gale, C. McNulty.
F/r: S. Abbott and D. Tuck. Missing from the photograph are J. Gray and A. Prentice.

within their grasp for the first time if they beat Cinderford Town in the next home mid-week match. This was duly accomplished 2-0 and a season that had started unpromisingly saw Salisbury lift the title for the first time ever thanks to a magnificent rearguard. The players rightly joined in toasting Reg Broom who had guided the club to this success and whose team selections and changes had been totally vindicated. One worrying fact was that gates had dropped and, strangely enough, fewer were watching at the end of the season than had done at the start.

Although this was to be Stan Abbott's last season he finished with 15 goals despite missing a large part of the season. This still placed him four goals ahead of his nearest challenger.

The season was completed by a further trip to France to play Union Sportive de Tourquennoise once again and although Salisbury F.C. lost 3-1 it was thoroughly enjoyed by all.

At the end of the season Mr Reg Broom stated he would stand down after presenting his report at the AGM. He had placed his resignation before the committee in 1954 but had withdrawn it after visits from players and supporters.

The 1958–59 Season — Richard J.A. Walker

In the event he continued as manager and signed three new forwards in an attempt to cure the goal famine of the previous year. Tony Alexander came from Yeovil, Derek Purvis arrived from Barnstaple and George Forester from Ashford. Terry Compton was signed from Bristol City where he had made 44 appearances at centre-half. He was to prove an excellent acquisition. Unfortunately, he was to die at the comparatively young age of 60 in 1991. Other new additions included Terry Dooler from Arsenal, who was to play at right-back and Jimmy McGowan, a left-half.

Grid-locked city centre?

The team started with a flourish. White nylon goal nets at Victoria Park were a first for the Western League and they were soon put to good use. Eight goals came in the first two games including an opening day league fixture against Taunton Town which was won 3-1 (attendance 1710). This owed something to the initiative of Ian

Allen and Peter Rushworth. Finding themselves stranded in traffic in their car on the edge of Salisbury, they parked on the grass verge. Walking quickly into the city they got a taxi to the ground to ensure a full complement of players started the game.

More goals were certainly forthcoming but suddenly a great many were at the wrong end as twice the team were beaten 5-2 and once 4-3. In three months they had let in significantly more than a third of the total for the previous season.

Some you win — some you lose

In the F.A. Cup the first game saw Salisbury beat Bridport away 5-2 with goals from Alexander (2), Forester, Allen and Clancy. When the Whites took 500 fans to Poole in the next round of the competition they travelled with some optimism, but in wet and windy conditions, the Southern League side triumphed by 2-1.

F.A. Cup Results 4/10/58

Poole Town	2	Salisbury	1	Chippenham United	1	Trowbridge Town	2
Andover Town	1	Fareham Town	0	Chippenham Town	3	Westbury United	0
Portland United	3	Warminster Town	0				

On resuming league fixtures Salisbury had a comfortable win at Cinderford. Terry Johnson, thought to be the League's youngest ever player at 15 turned out at centre-forward for Cinderford. He had scored a hat-trick in his previous match but found Terry Compton a much tougher opponent and received little change in their battles.

Kingston the hero

Form generally continued to be patchy and a number of changes had to be made where players swapped between the Western and Hampshire League sides. Roy Onslow was promoted to the first team and celebrated with a hat-trick versus Glastonbury (6-0). A November revival with an unchanged team saw goals, victories and a leap up the table. At the beginning of December the new league leaders Dorchester, who had only dropped three points in 13 games, were beaten 3-1 at Victoria Park. Unfortunately the gate was less than 2000. Alan Kingston, in goal for Salisbury was outstanding as usual.

It continued to rain goals as further large wins at Plainmoor against Torquay United and Poole Town Reserves at home saw the Whites progress maintained. Chippenham Town felt the full force of Salisbury's prolific attack when they were beaten 5-2 on Christmas Saturday. This was the club's 11th win on the trot. The champions seemed intent on holding onto their crown, although Dorchester and Bridgwater were both pointless away journeys.

School master joins Frome Town

Jackie Knight, an outstanding performer in previous seasons was transferred to Frome Town in February although his new club already looked assured of relegation. The 14th March saw the Whites level at the top of the table with Yeovil Reserves but having played a game more than their rivals. They had already won 20 matches and averaged nearly three goals a game.

Jackie Knight in a match versus Chippenham United.

Easter fixtures

Easter was once again crucial. There was a catastrophic home defeat against Cinderford who were committed to leaving the league at the end of the season, then, trying hard to recover they won at Barnstaple and Minehead over the same weekend. However a couple of draws against Poole Town Reserves and Portland away, coupled with a home defeat against Bristol City and away at Bideford left Salisbury as runners-up to Yeovil Reserves, whose overall consistency proved too much in the end. Yeovil were also the first club to win the league and the Western League Cup in the same season.

Friendly French

Derek Purvis finished top scorer with 30 league goals, with Roy Onslow scoring 16. Once again a friendly against French opponents, Union Sportive Tourquennoise completed the fixtures with the Whites winning 2-0 at Victoria Park.

The 1959–60 Season — Peter J. Waterhouse

Let the good times roll

Reg Broom had now assembled a truly championship quality league team, which was rated one of the finest in the west of England, for ability and sportsmanship.

The club were associate members of the Football Association in recognition of their previous good runs in the F.A. Amateur Cup and became full members of the Football Association this season, due to the club's outstanding F.A. Cup run.

Signed players for new season:

Goalkeepers:

Alan Kingston	Derrick Rattue	Peter Dyer

Full-backs:

Chris Waters	George Cryle	Kenneth Barfoot
Robert McAlone	Selby Dando	Trevor Griggs

Wing-halves:

Douglas Barrington	James Cross	James McGowan
Keith Prosser	Peter Rushworth	

Centre-halves:

Bob Hardy	John Haywood	Terence Compton

Outside-rights:

Derek Oakley	Gordon Kaile	Ian Allen
John Harding		

Inside-Forwards:

Anthony Alexander	Dave Stratton	Roy Watts

Centre-forwards:

Ian Gogan	Roy Onslow

Outside-lefts:

William Clancy	Brian May

Pictured below are just four of the many Salisbury crowd pleasers.

| Ian Allen | Terence Compton | Alan Kingston | Roy Watts |

Sorry we must let you go

The opening Western League game of the season saw the Whites suffer the ignominy of a 5-0 defeat away to Bridgwater on Saturday 22nd August 1959.

The irony of the defeat was that three of the well-taken goals were by Derek Purvis who was the player Salisbury did not retain at the end of the previous season despite being top scorer with 30 league goals because to quote the club's committee: 'he did not make the grade'.

The club lost no time in proving that the form shown at Bridgwater was much below their ability with a fine 3-2 victory over Chippenham Town in the Wilts Premier Shield played at Victoria Park the following Wednesday.

This was the first opportunity for the Salisbury home supporters to see Roy (Ginger) Watts in action. He showed his class when he coolly placed the first goal wide of the capable Chippenham Town 'keeper. Roy Onslow scored the other two goals.

Roy Watts went on to play many games to become the club's most prolific scorer with 180 goals in his career with Salisbury, this season's tally being 49 in all matches.

History making run begins

Salisbury commenced their F.A. Cup exploits in the first Qualifying Round on Saturday 19th September with a tricky away tie at Portland and ran out 3-2 winners with goals from Watts (2) and Clancy (1). The 2nd Qualifying Round played on Saturday 3rd October, saw the club taking the short trip to nearby Warminster Town where they advanced to the 3rd Qualifying Round with a resounding 5-0 victory over their neighbours.

Once more Salisbury were drawn away in their F.A. Cup campaign this time against a strong Poole Town side. Thanks to a last minute goal by Watts the Whites went through to the Fourth Qualifying Round with a 1-0 victory.

First Round beckons

They then faced Basingstoke at Victoria Park with the prospect, for the winner, of going into the draw with Football League teams. In front of a 3408 gate Basingstoke held Salisbury to a 2-2 draw, but, in the replay at Basingstoke, the Whites won by the odd goal in three.

The scene was now set for the F.A. Cup First Round Proper tie with the reigning Athenian League Champions and F.A. Amateur Cup finalists Barnet.

From a miskick by Rushworth, Kingston punches the ball into the Salisbury net for Basingstoke's first goal.

The Barnet team had six amateur internationals on their books at the time of the match. The following pen pictures of their players appeared in the match programme.

PEN PICTURES OF THE BARNET PLAYERS

Brian Goymer (20) goalkeeper:. A stock exchange clerk, joined Barnet from school, played for three seasons with West Ham Youth side, playing in the F.A. Youth Cup Final against Manchester United's Youth Team. Joined Barnet in 1958.

Coin Barker right-back:: Graduated from Barnet's Youth Team. Played for England and Herts County this season. A Master Builder by trade.

Michael Cooper (26) left-back:: While serving in the Army had a short spell with Romford. Joined Barnet last season. He played for the Army, the London F.A., Hertfordshire and Middlesex Wanderers.

Roy Sleap (20) right-half: A product of Barnet's Youth XI. Played in representative matches for Edmonton and Middlesex while at school. An apprentice draughtsman, on Amateur forms for Arsenal. Gained his regular first team place this season. Played for England and Great Britain this season.

Alf D'Arcy (25) centre-half: An engineer. Regular centre-half for England and Great Britain. For the past two seasons apart for a short spell with Hounslow Town, he has always been with Barnet. Is Captain of the team. Also on Amateur forms for Bristol City.

Robert Cantwell (20) left-half:. Has played for the London F.A., F.A. Youth XI when an Arsenal Junior. Was selected for the Middlesex Wanders East African Tour at the end of last season. A carpenter by trade.

John Welch, (24) outside-right: Played at centre-forward season before last with marked success, but switched to the right-wing when Robert Brown was brought into the side. He has played for the Herts F.A. and selected for the Athenian League XI.

Dennis D'Arcy (26) inside-right: Apart from short spells with Hitchin Town and Hounslow Town, he has played for Barnet since 1951. Played for England against Wales last season. A printer by trade, also played for London F.A., Athenian League, Hert and Middlesex Wanders. One of the club's leading goal scorers.

Robert Brown (19) centre-forward: The youngest player in the team. Working in export and shipping. Joined Barnet last season and was the clubs leading goal scorer. Played for England and Great Britain this season also Herts F.A. and F.A. XI. Signed for Fulham as an Amateur. Scored the two goals for Barnet in the Amateur Cup Final.

The Barnet full-backs seemed rooted to the line as the ball sails into the net from the head of the diving Roy Onslow after a nod on from Bob McAlone. Other Salisbury players in the picture, no. 8 Tony Alexander and Bill Clancy.

Tony Harding (20) inside left: Joined Barnet from East Barnet Old Grammarians last season. An insurance clerk, played for England and Herts F.A. this season.

Reg Finch, outside-left: Owing to a broken ankle was not playing in the Amateur Cup Final last season. Has made a splendid recovery to get in the team. Came from Barnet's Youth side, played for Herts County this season. A van driver by trade.

Jim Duncan (30) (reserve): Played at right-back in the Amateur Cup Final, joined Barnet 1957-58 season. Toolmaker by trade. The oldest player in the side.

Salisbury make local football history

The exciting F.A. Cup 1st Round Proper tie was watched by 4349 spectators at Victoria Park on 14th November 1959.

The Whites went about their task against the Athenian League Champions with confidence and determination. Centre-half and captain Terry Compton blotted the Barnet centre-forward Bobby Brown (England amateur international) out of the game in the first-half. This example inspired the rest of the Salisbury team to equal efforts when the Barnet centre-forward adopted a wandering role in the second-half.

The hosts shooting was erratic at times but it was only sheer resolution on the part of Barnet defenders that kept them at bay. Salisbury only scored once but the goal proved decisive.

In the 21st minute they won their first corner, taken by Ian Allen which right full-back Bob McAlone went up for. He nodded it to Roy Onslow the centre-forward, who skilfully headed the ball past

Brian Goymer the Barnet goalkeeper, for one of the most talked about goals in the club's history.

There was a scare for Salisbury when, just two minutes after the interval, the Barnet inside-left sent in a powerful shot. Goalkeeper Alan Kingston got a hand to it and Selby Dando cleared off the line. Salisbury went close to scoring on several occasions and four times the ball was cleared off the Barnet goal-line.

Barnet were now looking for an equaliser coming back again and again throwing everything into attack in what turned out be a do-or-die effort, but their best was just not good enough. Salisbury survived the attacks to take the match 1-0.

The Mayor of Salisbury, Clr. W.J. Rothwell shook each player by the hand as they reached the dressing room.

F.A. Cup fever swept through the city of Salisbury; shops decorated their windows in the Whites colours. There was just one topic of conversation in the pubs and clubs in the city, the forthcoming F.A. Cup Second Round encounter with the first English League side to visit Victoria Park in a National Competition, Newport County.

The Whites now had the chance of becoming one of the giant-killers of the competition. The term giant-killers was used by the sports commentator Raymond Glendenning, who described the draw made over the radio at The Football Association headquarters in London.

Money is not the be all and end all of everything

Secretary-Manger, Reg Broom could have wished for nothing better with the F.A. Cup draw, as he reiterated, 'Its prestige we're after not money'.

The management made the decision that the tie would not be all-ticket as the ground could well accommodate the anticipated 7000 gate.

The club had few financial worries at that time in their history with a manageable weekly first-team wage bill and an average gate of 2500. In 11 years the Supporters Club, under Secretary Ron Lemon had raised £49,000. Mr Broom described them as one of the finest Supporters Club in the south of England.

Newport to treat Salisbury with respect

The Newport County Manager, Bill Lucas the former Welsh

international, was cautious when asked what he thought of his team's chances against Salisbury in this F.A. Cup tie. He stated, 'we treat all our cup opponents with the greatest respect, it would be foolish of us to treat Salisbury lightly'.

All set for the kick-off

The gates at Victoria Park opened at 11.45 a.m. on 5th December 1959 for the eagerly awaited cup-tie and 6368 spectators flocked in to witness the history making match.

Newport kicked off and within minutes the Salisbury defence was in trouble with McPherson the Newport centre-forward and inside-right McSeveney both shooting wide. Salisbury's 'keeper, Kingston was getting a taste of what was to come.

In the 15th minute the Whites hopes were raised when Clancy ran onto a ball down the middle but he was thwarted just two yards from goal before he had time to shoot. Minutes later the Newport no. 9, McPherson was injured in a clash of heads and he left the field with slight concussion. His head injury needed stitches. He returned to the field just before half-time.

In the 30th minute Salisbury's hopes were raised again, when Alexander sent in a tantalising shot from near the corner which dropped just behind the Newport cross-bar. At half-time the game was locked in a 0-0 draw.

In the second-half the home team immediately went on to the attack and long passes cut through the Newport defence but their full-backs Hollyman and Sherwood dealt well with these raids. In the 56th minute Salisbury were rocked when a well constructed move was concluded when the Newport winger, Morgan slipped

continued on page 95

Ian Allen is in Salisbury's net, along with the ball as Alan Kingston is beaten by Newport's Barry Meyer (hidden behind right post) as he cracks in their winner in the second-half.

A 30-yard shot from Bob McAlone (out of picture) looks bound for the top corner of the net. Roy Onslow (centre) and Ginger Watts await the outcome. Unfortunately for the Whites the ball just went over. Ian Allen is the other Salisbury player in the picture.

The flying Newport 'keeper Weare, punches a header away from the diving Tony Alexander seemingly straight to the ever present Roy Onslow.

Once again the ball clears the Newport bar from another Salisbury attack as Ian Allen tangles with Weare the Newport 'keeper.

Everything seems to happen in slow motion as Roy Watts's (second right) shot beats the Newport defence and the goalkeeper, but just misses.

the ball to inside-left Meyer who hit the ball from 20 yards into the back of the Salisbury net.

To the Whites credit they never gave up. Inside-left Watts hit a quality shot beating the Newport 'keeper only to see the ball spinning tantalising past the far post. The solitary Newport goal booked them a home tie against the mighty Spurs in the 3rd Round of the F.A. Cup.

Their thoughts on the game

Mr Reg Broom the Salisbury secretary-Manager:
> 'I think they just had the edge on us on the run of the game they just about deserved to win, we were in the game that was the point'.

Terry Compton, captain of Salisbury:
> The Whites defeat 'was a bit of bad luck', he added, 'with a bit of luck we could have made it a draw'. It was a grand game and I think we gave them something to think about. We matched them for football'.

Newport's Manager, Bill Lucas said of the Salisbury team:
> 'These fellows played well, I think they surprised us. It was much harder than we expected'.

Alf Sherwood, captain of Newport:
> 'I'm as pleased as I could be. I would like to congratulate Salisbury on the way they played and on the very sporting manner they played, I liked the pitch too. It's in grand condition and better than that of many Third Division clubs'.

F.A. Cup Results 5/12/59

Salisbury	0	Newport C.	1	Southampton	3	Southend	0
Reading	4	King's Lynn	2	Crystal Palace	3	Margate	0
Notts County	0	Bath City	1					

Due to the Whites F.A. Cup run they had only played 17 Western League matches up to the end of January 1960, when they defeated Trowbridge Town Res 9-1 at Frome Road Trowbridge. Roy Onslow was in tremendous form personally netting five. Roy Watts netted two with Ian Allen and Jim Cross one each.

The second half of the season saw the club accelerate up the league table with a succession of good results. From 7th April to the 18th the Western League side had crowded in six matches, three had been won, two lost and one drawn.

Roy Onslow

On 13th April an improved Portland side defeated the Whites at

Man of action, Roy Onslow.

home by the only goal scored. On Easter Monday, Barnstaple shared the points after Salisbury had beaten them away on the Good Friday. During this period the team had gathered seven out of 12 points and could now finish the season as runners up.

Having played 12 matches in the last four weeks of the season, Salisbury did finish as runners-up to Torquay United.

Success followed success

This season saw the introduction of the Alan Young Cup to be played for by the League Champions and runners-up. The match which was played the next season was won by Salisbury who beat Torquay United Reserves on aggregate.

Season 1959/60 also saw the Wilts Premier Shield retained when Swindon were beaten at Victoria Park with goals from John Harding and Roy Watts.

The 1960–61 Season — David Thear

Time To Join Our Neighbours?

The 1960/61 season saw the Whites fans very optimistic. Last season's exploits had whetted the appetite for more League and Cup success and in some peoples minds, this indicated a need to raise the level at which the club performed. There were a sizeable number of fans and parts of the local press who believed this could only be done by advancement to the Southern League with a professional manager at the helm. These views were to become more prevalent over the next few seasons.

The season itself was one of outstanding league success. Of 40 Western League matches played 31 were won and only five lost. The side scored 135 goals with only 42 against. Roy Watts top scored with 49 goals. The Victoria Park faithful saw 84 league goals scored in 20 matches with four or more in 11 matches. Home crowds were mostly over 1000. The reserves were also champions of the Hampshire League so the fans were sated with success.

The Wilts Professional shield and the Alan Young Cup, came to Salisbury as a result of wins over Trowbridge and Torquay respectively.

The only disappointment was the 2-0 loss at home to Weymouth in an F.A. Cup replay. Dilwyn Hill, who had been signed from Exeter, suffered a broken leg in this match.

With this kind of season it was no wonder that the fans were looking for better things. Caution was, however, recommended by Reg Broom who saw increased travelling costs and some full-time professional players an inevitability if the move to the Southern League came to fruition.

Tragic death of Salisbury player

There was one sad note when John Harding, a mainly Hampshire League player, was killed in a car crash in January 1961. There were numerous fund raising events to aid his family, the principal one being on the 3rd of May when a match between Salisbury and a combined Bristol Rovers and City side comprising mostly first team players was played at Victoria Park. In total the fund raised £1046.

The 1961–62 Season — David Thear

This season was, again, one of considerable Western League success. A strong Bristol City Reserves side won the league scoring 136 goals with only 36 against. The Whites came second with Roy Watts scoring 34 goals, approximately a third of the team's total of 105. The defence was sound enough being the second meanest in the Division. So far as the playing strength was concerned the team was substantially the same as for the previous seasons and there is little doubt that this played a major part in their success. There was one new signing of note. Robin North came from Andover for a season and played mainly in the Hampshire League side. More of him anon.

Quick exit from major competition

The F.A. Cup was a disappointment inasmuch as the away tie against Oxford United of the Southern League Premier Division was lost 3-2 in front of over 6000 spectators. The Whites had been exempted until the 4th Qualifying Round. The Wilts Professional Shield was won with a 3-1 victory over Chippenham United and the Hampshire Senior Cup came to Victoria Park

Joe McCartney who scored Salisbury's 2 goals at Oxford.

for the first time following a 3-0 win over Fareham Town. The Hants League side came second in their league with 39 points from 30 games.

Roy Onslow, the hero of the F.A. Cup tie against Barnet in 1959 was released. While the fans appreciated the outcome of the season there was still substantial support for a move upwards.

The 1962–63 Season — David Thear

Football All Over Takes a Winter Break

This was the season when the weather took over. During the Western League match against Andover on Boxing Day 1962 snow fell and stopped the football until 9th February 1963 when Salisbury won away to Minehead. Once more the team was substantially the same as the previous seasons although George Petherbridge from Bristol Rovers, Bernie Pask from Basingstoke and Tony McCall from Reading were useful additions. A major loss

Dilywn Hill beats the Chippenham Town defenders and shoots in the 1st Qualifying Round of the F.A. Cup. Watts and Petherbridge scored for Salisbury.

to the club occurred on 19th January 1963 when Dilwyn Hill died in a tragic accident at his home. He was a class player and regular goal-scorer (60 goals with Salisbury).

The final league position was sixth, the lowest since season 1952/53, and again Roy Watts top scored with 25 league goals.

Interest in the F.A. Cup ended at the first hurdle when Chippenham Town triumphed 3-1 after a 2-2 draw at Victoria Park. There was no Wilts Professional Shield this year.

The undercurrents of discontent with the club's position continued throughout the year and in May 1963 it was reported that Reg Broom was considering retirement. However, no new manager was forthcoming and he agreed to carry on although it was nearly July before he could give his full attention to organising the squad. Inevitably with the restricted choice then available the quality was less than would have been wished. Stalwarts of the side like Cross, Petherbridge, McAlone, Clancy, Allen and McCall were not retained. In August, most red-blooded males star of the silver screen, sex symbol, Marilyn Monroe was found dead.

Seasons 1963/4 & 1964/5 — David Thear

End of an Era Looms

These two seasons are dealt with in one chapter, not because they were worth less than the others, but because they mark the beginning of the end of the 'old' Salisbury Football Club and, with that, Reg Broom's retirement after 46 years of service to the game in the Salisbury area.

We have been lucky enough to obtain a copy of a programme for the final matches arranged by Reg Broom in response to requests from former players. The matches were between Bristol City and Southampton, for whom Mike Channon played at inside-left and the 1947 Salisbury F.C. team against Salisbury Old Players. Not only did the programme detail the teams but we are given an insight into the reasons for Reg's retirement and the disparate views which had been raging for some years over the direction the Club was to take.

Time to move on in more ways than one!

In essence it was the age-old conflict between the conservatives, led by Reg Broom, who wanted to maintain the status quo, i.e. the club to remain in the Western League with maximum investment in the playing strength rather than in new facilities such as floodlights. Opposing this were the modernisers who wished the club to join the Southern League (where old rivals, Weymouth, Poole and Trowbridge Town were already in situ) and to install floodlights to add to the club's advancement.

This issue was keenly felt by all concerned and it is to be regretted that the testimonial match arranged to mark Reg Broom's eventual retirement was very poorly attended. Perhaps people forgot what a debt was owed to him and the other founders and what excitement and pleasure the Whites had given to their fans for nearly 20 years.

Turning to season 1963/4 the limited choice of players and the non-retention of so many of the old team undoubtedly led to a poorer standard of football being played than in season 1962/3 and this was reflected in the season's results as at 1st February 1964 viz:

P 25   W 12   D 4   L 9   F 43   A 43   Pts 28

This lack lustre performance, contrasted with the previous years efforts, increased the pressure from supporters and the press for a change of management. Notwithstanding this, three new players were signed for fees, namely, Joe Stocks from Millwall, Barry Fitch and Phil Gilbert from Brighton, the latter two becoming stalwarts of the club for many years to come.

Their arrival did the trick and the final league position was a creditable sixth. The Hampshire Senior Cup was won with a 3-0 win over Aldershot at the Dell while the Hampshire League side achieved fourth place. The F.A. Cup run was curtailed when Dorchester won 3-1 in a replay at Victoria Park.

Season 1964/5 saw a mass exodus of players to Welton Rovers, who then won the league with a record tally of goals scored. The ex-Salisbury players in the Welton Rovers team included Watts, Henderson, Allen, Prosser and Burt. Endeavours were made to sign players of equal quality but without success. Also injuries hit the team before and at the start of the season.

Magic of an F.A. Cup run arrives

However, modest league form was almost forgotten when the F.A. Cup ties started. Dorchester and Poole were both beaten after replays then Portland (5-1) and Yeovil (2-1) in the final Qualifying rounds.

This brought an away tie at Peterborough in front of over 10,000 spectators. A special train was run but, despite high hopes, the match was lost by five goals to one. A supporter's view of the match is on page 103.

Salisbury players study good luck telegrams including one sent by the Mayor before the F.A. First Round Cup game with Peterborough United. Brian Stevens, ever the comic, helps Phil Gilbert with a bit of hair cutting.

Joe Stocks (near line) turns away after scoring the first goal in the F.A. Cup 1st Round tie versus Peterborough United. Bernie Pask (No. 9) raises his arms in celebration.

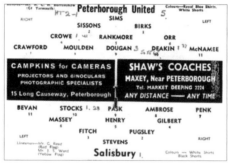

A different view of the first goal.

MEMORY LANE

Derek Dougan meets 'Stevo'

Peterborough United v Salisbury 14th November 1964

This was Salisbury's first return to the First Round Proper of the F.A. Cup since the Barnet/Newport matches of 1959. The city was again awash with hopes of the big-time as the Third Round was just around the corner. The first hurdle was a big one. Peterborough United (Posh) who had only entered the Football League in the 1960/61 season had won their division at the first time of asking and were now holding a mid-table place in Division III. They were well-known in the non-league scene having been Midland League Champions from 1955–1960 and looking for the necessary votes needed to enter the League proper.

I, along with 400 others boarded the 'Special Train' that Salisbury had put on to take us non-stop to the match. The talk all the way there was of Salisbury having a team that would at least bring 'the Posh' back for a taste of Victoria Park, which seemed possible for the first 30-mins as we more than held our own. Brian Bevan had a good run at the Peterborough defence which nearly resulted in a goal. We then forced the first corner of the match when Bernie Pask's fleet of foot surprised their defence. A goal was not long in coming as a cross from Harry Penk saw Joe Stocks score with the Peterborough defence vainly protesting for off-side. Unfortunately, by half-time, Peterborough's position in League Football told on Salisbury's Western League status as we were by then 2-1 down, their equaliser coming about when McNamee lobbed Brian Stevens and Deakin ran through to score.

Their centre-forward Derek Dougan was a player with the same attitude to life as our own Brian Stevens. His manager had doubts about playing him, wondering whether he would take the game seriously. He did enough to score a hat-trick, but one scene from the the match I'll always remember. Derek Dougan was just about to shoot only to be stopped in his tracks by

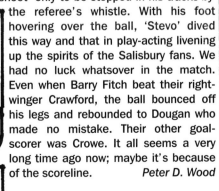

the referee's whistle. With his foot hovering over the ball, 'Stevo' dived this way and that in play-acting livening up the spirits of the Salisbury fans. We had no luck whatsover in the match. Even when Barry Fitch beat their right-winger Crawford, the ball bounced off his legs and rebounded to Dougan who made no mistake. Their other goal-scorer was Crowe. It all seems a very long time ago now; maybe it's because of the scoreline.   *Peter D. Wood*

F.A. Cup Results 14/11/64

Peterborough Utd	5	Salisbury	1	Bournemouth	7	Gravesend	0
Canterbury	0	Torquay Utd	6	Colchester	3	Bideford	3
Q.P.R.	2	Bath City	0	Kings Lynn	0	Shrewsbury	7
Port Vale	2	Hendon	1	Welton Rovers	1	Weymouth	1

The end of the 'Reg Broom era' dawns

Reg Broom

This achievement was not enough to still the clamour for change and on 18th January Reg Broom informed the committee that he would retire at the end of the season. He suggested that the new manager be appointed without delay so that he could assess the playing strength in readiness for the next season.

In the event, Cyril Rutter was appointed from 20th February 1965 and Reg Broom, to his credit, took on the secretary's role until the end of the season in order to finalise all extraneous financial matters and give the new man a clear start to his career. For the record the club's assets stood at a little over £13,000. Cyril Rutter was 30 years old and had made 171 appearances for Portsmouth at centre or wing-half. He was an ex-England youth international and one of his former positions was as Director of Football for the U.S. Forces in Europe.

On the field the Whites finished tenth in the league and Reg Broom's comments on the controversy over the future of the club, based on his programme notes, were, *inter alia*:

> In my 44 years of soccer in Salisbury I have always tried to give the supporters first class football. When this club was formed, I stated that this new club MUST be a success and I would do all in my power to see it.
>
> It now appears that some of the supporters think a change would be best for the club and that Southern League with another manager would be the best thing. Little thought do these supporters think (sic) where the money is coming from, in fact some supporters have said to me 'with the money we have let's have a fling, even if it costs us all the money that we have'. That is not my policy.

His final words following his retirement were:

> During my office as Secretary-Manager, I made some mistakes in some of the players that I signed, but what Manager is perfect? I think that the supporters must agree that good players were brought to Salisbury and that they saw some first class football.

The club won every competition for which it entered at some time or other with the exception of the F.A. and Amateur Cup.

We did not win the Wiltshire Senior Cup because of the rules that a player must live or have been born in Wiltshire. We did however, supply Wiltshire with eight County players.

To all players, Supporters of the club, Officials and Committees of the Football Club and Supporters' Club that have helped me during the period, I wish to offer my sincerest thanks.

If I may respectfully offer a word of advice. May I suggest, Please build a good team to represent S.F.C. before spending money on floodlights. Supporters wish to see a good team on the field, but lights will not give you this.

Thus concluded the career of the man who might well be called the 'Father of Salisbury F.C.'. Modern day readers will have their own views on the changes made in the years following his reign.

The 1965–66 Season — Peter J. Waterhouse

Manager
Cyril Rutter

New manager Cyril Rutter axed nine players and issued a retained list of 11. He now had 28 signing on forms completed and the Salisbury team appeared strong in all departments. Among the new signings were local lads, John Foyle, Brian Pearce, Terry Ling, Mike Miller, Ken Skutt and Steve Donnelly.

The first game in the 1965–66 Western League campaign was at home against Exeter City Reserves. Player manager Cyril Rutter scored Salisbury's first goal of the season from the penalty spot and the team then went on in emphatic fashion to record a 4-0 victory. On the 28th August Salisbury made the journey to Weston-super-Mare and returned home 5-2 victors. In a F.A. Cup 3rd qualifying round tie at Victoria Park against Portland United, a gate of 1277 witnessed the Whites suffer a 3-0 defeat in a bruising encounter. Eight Salisbury players were injured in the game, with only Fitch, Gilbert and Tout fit at the end.

First set-back for floodlights

With regard to the installation of floodlights the City Council turned down the club's application due to the height of the pylons. These would have cost £4250.00.

The Whites unbeaten Western League record went when they lost 1-0 at home to Weston-super-Mare. It was not entirely unexpected after the injuries sustained in the previous week's cup tie against Portland United but the defeat was a set back to their Western League aspirations.

On Saturday 16th October, they made the journey to Glastonbury, looking for their first away win since the 28th August, but it was not to be as Glastonbury ran out 3-0 winners. Salisbury's third defeat in a row saw then slip to 14th position in the league.

The sequence of defeats was halted on the 19th October when Frome Town were held to a draw at Victoria Park. On the following Saturday, Salisbury gave maybe their best performance of the season, shattering Bideford's unbeaten home league record with goals from Knight, Harley and Tout.

Supporters Club come up trumps again

Salisbury Football Supporters Club made their third £2000 donation of the current financial year to the club at a social evening held at the Supporters Club's headquarters.

Football Club Chairman, Mr L. C. Brown, who received the cheque from Supporters Club Chairman, Mr H. Abel, praised the tremendous amount of work which the Supporter's Club was doing for Salisbury F.C. (one could buy a three-bedroom, semi-detached house with garage in Laverstock for £4000).

Further delay on lights

The installation of floodlights was again pursued but was halted when the District Council voted 16-12 to defer a decision until the club's future location had been settled. This referred to the possible use of the land at the Butts (alongside the River Avon near Ashley and Butts Road). Some people believed the deferment was more to do with the opposition of some residents in the Castle Road area to any expansion of the football club's activities. One councillor stated 'if we once allow the lights we shall never get the soccer club away from Victoria Park'.

An extract from the Salisbury Journal on 10th November:

Professional football pitches need the right amenities. A grandstand, covered dressing rooms, a car park, a boundary fence or wall, are all necessities which must be installed before one could even dream of such a luxury as floodlights.

Let us be realistic about this, Salisbury Football Club had something like £13,000 in the kitty at the start of the current financial year. It would cost them probably more than £30,000 to do all the work needed. Had the ground been for sale rather than on lease it would have been easier, but what security is there in a piece of ground which could be taken back by the City Council on the expiry of the clubs lease?

At present we understand that the club pay £500 a year for the use of Victoria Park, where the amenities are not exactly in the realms of perfection, but they have proved highly satisfactory for Western League football.

Returning to football matters, the Christmas period saw a 1-1 draw at Torquay United Reserves followed by a 2-0 home victory over Taunton Town and a 3-4 loss at home to Weymouth Reserves on Boxing Day.

Looking back over 1965, it was the year that Salisbury Football Club appointed their first ever player manager in Cyril Rutter, tried to have floodlights installed and began seriously to consider a move to a new ground. At the end of the year they were in 10th position in the Western League.

Lack of consistency

The New Year started promisingly with a 5-0 victory away to Bristol City Colts. Jimmy Tout scored twice and had a hand in the other three, but the Whites were still finding it difficult to string together a winning sequence. At the home game on the 9th January they went down 2-1 against Bridport, followed by a 1-1 draw away to Minehead, then an away defeat at Frome 2-0.

The next game at Victoria Park saw Salisbury gain their second biggest home win of the season brushing aside Dorchester Town 3-0 with goals from Harley, Knight and Davidson. Terry Ling had an outstanding game in mid-field. Alas the Whites were hit for six at St James' Park, where they suffered a 6-1 defeat against Exeter City Reserves.

Beaten in injury time

In an amazing game played at Victoria Park on Saturday 19th February, 702 supporters were cheering Salisbury to what looked like being their best victory of the season against championship contenders Welton Rovers. Leading 2-1 on 90 minutes, Welton snatched victory by scoring two goals just before the final whistle.

They were to remain unbeaten in the league throughout the

season. A regrettable sequel to this match was the F.A.'s decision to require Salisbury to post warning notices at Victoria Park for four weeks. The incident that caused this action occurred when a well known Salisbury supporter claimed he was offering his friend a pork pie just as the referee was passing inadvertently hitting him (the referee) on the nose! !

Carry on floodlighting

The floodlight issue was again raised and the following report appeared in the Salisbury Times on 4th March 1966:

> *The Club are asking the City Council to take another look at their decision not to permit floodlights at Victoria Park. It seems that the Club will not be moving to the Butts for at least three years and they are to ask the City Council if they will permit the installation of floodlights at Victoria Park for a three-year period.*

This brought a most welcome reaction when, at a City Council meeting held at the Guildhall it was recommended that while Salisbury Football Club wait for the Butts site to be developed as a soccer ground, floodlights be allowed at Victoria Park until the end of the 1967/68 season.

The club agreed in principle to the proposal to move their matches from the Park but said that it would be some time before the final details were discussed by the City Engineer and the club, after which the whole matter would have to go before the City Council. In the event permission was given and if the Butts ground was not ready for use by the end of the 1967/68 season the club could continue to use the floodlights.

Honoured by Referees Association

Mr L.C. Brown, Salisbury F.C. Chairman received the Referees Association's Meritorious award for 20 years service at the 35th Annual dinner of the South Wilts Referees Society at the Red Lion Hotel, Salisbury.

On the football front Salisbury's lowest attendance of the league season (276) on the 26th March saw the Whites defeat Bristol City A, 2-0. The small attendance was probably due in part to the Grand National and the Boat Race being shown on television.

On the second of April only 194 attended the testimonial game when Salisbury paid their final tribute to former Secretary Manager Reg Broom. The game ended with Salisbury defeating

Maurice Owens XI, a team of former Swindon professionals, by 5-1.

Club at the cross-roads again?

Obviously the club did not hide its disappointment with the pathetically low turnout. A Salisbury supporter penned his thoughts in a letter to the Salisbury Times & South Wilts Gazette in the issue of 15th April 1966. Here are some points from his letter:

> *Every Saturday evening the public wants to know how the team got on during the afternoon. But they are not keen enough to go the match and watch a side which have poor results and poor players.*
>
> *Days of Dennis Rogers, Dave Abbott, Tommy Williams and Len Scullard seem to have gone for Salisbury, but sides like Yeovil and Weymouth can still gather teams like this, year after year, why not Salisbury.*
>
> *The club now seems to be at the cross-roads. Either they can have success or failure. I think and hundreds more will agree, that support will not come if we are asked to watch the same dull teams in the same uninteresting league any longer.*   *A supporter (just)*

No doubt his comments reflected the thinking of many Salisbury supporters.

Mr L.C. Brown the Chairman of Salisbury Football Club responded immediately to the letter and his response was published the following week in the Salisbury Times:

> *The Western League we admit is not attractive, but there is little we can do about this at the moment. Those who advocate a switch to the Southern League don't know the full ins and outs.*
>
> *We have gone into this question and have discovered that it would cost us an extra £2000 alone in travelling expenses each season. Many of the away matches are to far-off places and quite often we would have to play mid-week matches in these areas.*
>
> *This would involve accommodation and meals for the players and this coupled with the higher wages we would have to pay — the minimum in the Southern League at the moment is £15 per man, would make such a move completely out of the question for Salisbury Football Club.*
>
> *We sympathise with our supporters who at the moment have little to cheer. We feel just as anxious as they are, but we would ask their patience. We are confident that the name of Salisbury will again soon be making an impact on football in the south west.*

Returning to football the mediocre season continued. The Easter programme gave some hope with victories over Barnstaple at Victoria Park and Weymouth reserves away but the Easter bonnet lost its glitz when the Barnstaple return match was lost by the only goal. A poorish season ended with the Whites in tenth place. Ironically the Welton Rovers side which won the league contained five former Salisbury players ! !

Turning to football away from Salisbury Mike Channon from Orcheston made his debut for Southampton against Bristol City and scored a vital goal for the Saints in a drawn game and at Wembley in July 1966 England, roared on by an ecstatic crowd at Wembley Stadium, beat West Germany 4-2 in extra-time, with Geoff Hurst scoring a hat-trick to win football's World Cup. Team: Banks, Cohen, Wilson, Stiles, Moore, Charlton, J., Peters, Charlton, B., Hurst, Hunt, Ball.

Geoff   Hurst, was England's hat-trick winner.

The 1966–67 Season — Peter J. Waterhouse

An Illuminating Season

Salisbury F.C. long term commitment was achieved when the club installed floodlighting at Victoria Park.

The Whites first official floodlight match at Victoria Park has Chris Waters for Salisbury on the ball with Micky Cave for Weymouth in close attendance. Just behind left, the Salisbury captain Phil Gilbert watches anxiously.

Although the club had previously played a few games under the new floodlights, the Salisbury supporters were looking forward to the official ceremony of 'switching on the floodlights'. The match chosen for this important occasion was the Western Counties Floodlight League match against old friends Weymouth.

Weymouth responded to the importance of the occasion by fielding one of the strongest teams outside league football. They were going through a purple patch having won the Southern League Premier Division for the past two seasons.

The Right-Worshipful Mayor of Salisbury, Councillor W.S. Biddle, performed the official ceremony. He also wrote the following in the S.F.C. programme:

> *It gives me great pleasure to be here this evening to perform the ceremony of 'switching on' the floodlights. I wish the club every success in this new venture and I trust that they will go from strength to strength.*
>
> *You, the supporters of the club, will probably be aware that during my year of Office as Mayor, I have decided to support what I am sure you will all agree are most worthy and deserving causes, viz: the Salisbury Division of St John Ambulance Brigade and the Salisbury Unit, Sea Cadet Corps. During the course of the evening the Football Club have very kindly agreed to take up a collection in aid of my appeal on behalf of these two organisations and I trust that you will give generously.*
>
> *I hope that you will all enjoy what promises to be a good and entertaining match between the 'City' and Weymouth Town Football Club, who have been Champions of the Southern League Premier Division for the past two season.*
>
> *W.S. Biddle, Mayor*

Over the years the Weymouth and Salisbury supporters had witnessed many epic and close encounters and this match was no exception. In an even game Weymouth won by the only goal, which came from the ex-Plymouth Argyle player, Dudley Barry in the first-half.

Short interest
The Whites sojourn in the F.A. Cup did not last long. After beating Cowes 4-1 with goals from Harley(2) Allen and Hodgkins and an away victory against Waterlooville 2-0, Salisbury went out of the prestigious competition under the floodlights at Victoria Park to Fareham 2-1 after holding them away 2-2.

F.A. Cup Results 1/10/66

Fareham Town	2	Salisbury	2	*replay* Salisbury	1	Fareham Town	2
Poole Town	1	Dorchester	0	Minehead	5	Bideford	0
Trowbridge Town	0	Welton Rovers	3						

A commendable season

The league season started unpromisingly. After 12 matches, only four had been won and it was widely believed that Cyril Rutter's introduction of the 4-3-3 system was at the root of the problem. The final match of the twelve was lost 6-1 at Bridgwater following which, on 9th November, the management committee terminated his contract. His playing registration was retained although he did not appear again for the Whites.

The management committee took control and continued to do so until new manager Alan Grant, a former White's goalkeeper signed before the 1968/9 season.

There was no immediate improvement following Cyril's departure but, after a 5-3 defeat by Plymouth Argyle reserves, the team embarked on a 15 match unbeaten run. This came to an end when Dorchester Town took the honours at Victoria Park on 15th April. This was the final home match of the season and saw the Whites finish in a very respectable fourth place in the table.

The season ended with the winning of the Wilts Premier Shield for the fifth time.

Prolific goal scorer Jeff Hodgkins in action. Jeff along with Alan Tyler signed for Salisbury in the 1966/7 season.

The 1967–68 Season — Peter J. Waterhouse

The Whites faced one of the busiest seasons in terms of fixtures to be undertaken. They were involved in the Western League, Hampshire League, Western Counties Floodlight League, F.A. Cup, Wiltshire Professional Cup and the Hampshire Senior Cup.

There were 31 players on the books including new signings, (goal) R. Dennison, (half-backs) P. Languish, A. Williams, R. Handford, (forwards) E. Ashe, R. Donohoe, E. Hall and R. Saunders.

The first Western League match was against last season's Somerset Professional Cup winners, Frome Town at Victoria Park on Saturday 19th August. Goals from Alan Tyler (2) and Barry Pearce (1) saw Salisbury winning 3-0.

Alan Tyler scorer of 2 goals V Frome Town.

Winning ways continued with four straight Western League victories, with the first defeat at Victoria Park on Saturday 23rd September against Bath City 0-2.

SWINDON TOWN
football club

official programme 6d

Onward march to 1st Round Proper

Salisbury's F.A. Cup campaign commenced with a 1st Qualifying Round tie away to Fareham. After drawing 2-2, the team ran out 5-1 winners in the replay at Victoria Park. In the 2nd Qualifying Round, after another draw away to Cowes, the 1st Qualifying Round score was repeated at home 5-1. The next round Newport I.O.W. were defeated 3-0 at Victoria Park.

In a close 4th Qualifying Round encounter at Dorchester Town, on October 14th, the Whites won by the odd goal in three, with goals from Dick Donohoe and John Phillips (penalty). This brought the First Round Proper clash against Swindon Town at the County Ground, Swindon on Tuesday 12th December.

The match should have been played on Saturday 9th December but was postponed because of heavy snow on the Friday much to the disappointment of Salisbury fans – see page 118 for a supporters view of the day and game. *continued on page 115*

Swindon Town
V
Salisbury F.C.
F.A. Cup 1st Round
Tuesday 13th
December
1967

Right: Salisbury F.C. captain, Phil Gilbert shakes the hand of the Swindon Town captain Stan Harland, with the young mascot in close attendance.

Above: Salisbury players in the foreground of the crowded goalmouth are Gilbert (no 6), left, Phillips, (no. 7) Saunders and (in flight) Collins.

F.A. Cup Results 12/12/67

| Swindon Town | 4 | Salisbury | 0 | Yeovil Town | 1 | Margate | 2 |
| Guildford City | 2 | Brentford | 1 | Weymouth | 0 | Leyton Orient | 2 |

Phil Gilbert the Salisbury captain's sliding interception just fails to stop the Swindon attack.

A dejected seated Keith Dyke and Tony Bichard maybe wondering how that went in. Note the snow in the goalmouth beside the ball.

The following is an extract from a report that appeared in a later 'City' programme:

After the anticipation of the previous few days, it was an anti-climax for all connected with Salisbury when the game was called off on the Saturday morning. Supporters from both sides had been guessing whether the match would be on or off and some Salisbury players had a nightmare trying to make the team coach.

Salisbury citizens awoke on Friday to the first winter snow and blizzard conditions were affecting many towns, although Swindon was not too badly affected which set-up the guessing game of whether the match would be played

Three of Salisbury's Portsmouth-based players set out for the City on the Friday evening. At 1.45 in the morning they arrived exhausted. Jeff Hodgkins, Salisbury's centre-forward had been working for his firm in Southampton during Friday and found the way back to his home in Portsmouth blocked. He decided instead to make for Salisbury, but outside of Southampton his car got stuck, so he abandoned it and walked back through a blizzard to spend the night in Southampton. In the morning he caught a train to Salisbury with no car or coat but raring to go.

Salisbury secretary, Ivan Crockett had umpteen problems trying to find the team. Ernie Ashe had rung up to say he was stranded without a train at Yeovil. Fortunately he and other passengers were transferred to Yeovil Junction and along with Ernie Hall, Peter Langrish and Malcolm Ambrose arrived at Salisbury station about 12.30 only to find that the game had been called off.

Swindon had been quite willing to play, even though Don Rogers was out with flu. Phil Gilbert summed up the very disappointed Salisbury players feelings when he stated that 'in the conditions we thought we had a good chance as anything can happen'.

The match was played on Tuesday 13th December and details of the teams were:

Swindon team:
Downsborough, Thomas, Trollope, Butler, Nurse, Harland, Heath, Dawson, (sub Penman, 45), Terry, Smart, Walker.

Salisbury team:
Dyke, Bichard, Fitch (sub Langrish 75), Phillips, Collins, Gilbert, Saunders, Pearce, Hodgkins, Hall, Ashe.

The attendance was 12,193 with gate receipts of £3,118.

Back to earth

After beating Andover Town in the Western League local derby at Victoria Park on Wednesday 1st November with goals from Jeff Hodgkins (3) and Dick Donohoe the Whites moved up to third place in the league.

Top three in league	P	W	D	L	F	A	Pts
Bath City	15	11	1	3	38	16	23
Bridgwater Town	12	7	4	1	34	17	18
Salisbury	**9**	**8**	**0**	**1**	**41**	**10**	**16**

Unfortunately, the following Saturday their title aspirations suffered a set back when they lost 2-0 at Victoria Park against Plymouth Argyle.

Devizes make history

For the last match of 1967 Devizes Town were welcomed to Victoria Park for their first appearance as a Western League side. With goals from Hodgkins (3), Saunders, Gilbert and Pearce(2) Salisbury ran out easy winners 7-0 and this consolidated their third place in the league, just three points off the two pace-setters.

Many of supporters were now convinced that the club should apply for membership of the Southern League, a massive step into uncharted territory.

A warning appeared in the programme at the Dorchester Town home game on Saturday 10th February as follows:

> *On Wednesday evening our lads did well to beat Weymouth by 1-0 in the Western Counties Floodlight League, the biggest disappointment being that only 577 turned up to see this match, – if you want Southern League football you will have to treble this gate before anyone can start to think on these lines.*
>
> *It is up to you the public who can decide our future by backing us whether we win or lose and turning up in the rain, shine or cold. Think this matter over seriously.*

The Whites went on to beat Dorchester Town 1-0 with Ernie Ashe scoring the only goal. On the last Saturday of February they went down 1-0 away to Plymouth Argyle. Plymouth paid Salisbury the compliment of fielding a very strong side with at least seven players who had played in their first team that season.

Excellent news arrives

At the game against Portland United at home on Wednesday 13th March, two players made their debuts, Mike Whitehouse (centre-half) and Graham Muxworthy (wing). Both of these went on to become household names for the Whites.

Salisbury beat Portland United 4-0 with 2 goals apiece from Donohoe and Hall. Their confidence was high going into the Easter games having, over the last two weeks, gained nine points out of ten.

They commenced the programme at home on Good Friday winning 4-0 against Torquay United but lost 1-0 at Bridport on Easter Monday. However the following Saturday at Victoria Park with Phil Gilbert getting a brace they turned the tables on Bridport to defeat them 2-0.

The season ended with Salisbury in the runners-up position and they also retained the Wiltshire Premier Shield.

However the news supporters had been waiting for arrived:

Salisbury F.C. were to play in the Southern League next season.

Roll on August 1968.

MEMORY LANE

The match that never was – F.A. Cup 1st Round

Swindon v Salisbury 9th December 1967

Ken Skutt, Ron Jefferies and myself had arranged to meet in the pub for a pint before the off to talk about the journey and Salisbury's chances, but pulling back the curtains on the Friday morning, I saw a scene that probably had all the children of the City excited but not Salisbury F.C. supporters, snow and lots of it. We then met next day at my house, and after many phone calls our disappointment set in as the news came through that the game was postponed until the following Tuesday. We felt that if we could have played on the Saturday (and it was not as bad snow-wise at Swindon), we might have, at least, scored a draw and, who knows, maybe pulled off a shock win.

It's only when you see your team up against full-time professionals that you appreciate the gulf that is between them. Salisbury were magnificent in a first-half defensive action, with Dyke in the Whites goal seemingly unbeatable. Pat Terry, the Swindon centre-forward, must have thought so. I likened Terry to the cobra, as when he headed the ball, he arched his neck right back before he attacked. In Salisbury's defence, Fitch, Bichard, Collins, Phillips and Gilbert gave as good as they received in that first half, surprising all present. Although the forwards did not get much sight of the opposition's goal, (I cannot really remember anytime that I thought that we were bound to score) a chance did fall to Hall when he seemed clean through, but he was tackled by John Trollope before he had time to shoot.

Swindon, for all their superiority, in the first-half failed to score, so did we dare hope for a shock in the second-half as our hosts were clearly rattled by the lack of goals. We, like all teams, needed that bit of luck, but Swindon broke the deadlock through substitute, Willie Penman. Swindon supporters went mad, we fell silent. Like a great dam bursting, from then on, it seemed as though they were here, there, and everywhere.

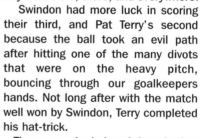

Swindon had more luck in scoring their third, and Pat Terry's second because the ball took an evil path after hitting one of the many divots that were on the heavy pitch, bouncing through our goalkeepers hands. Not long after with the match well won by Swindon, Terry completed his hat-trick.

The way we had played them in that first-half, we all agreed if only we had played Saturday,.......if

Peter D. Wood

4

southern League

The 1968–69 Season — Peter J. Waterhouse

Manager
Alan Grant

Salisbury's introduction to Southern League football was put to a severe test with two away games. At the opening match the Whites were the guests of Brentwood whose main Director was Jimmy Greaves. They were very unfortunate not to share the points, losing 2-1 with Donohoe scoring. On the following Thursday evening they were in action at Gloucester where they won 2-1 securing their first Southern League victory.

No goals in historic Victoria Park first

Saturday 17th August 1968 saw their first Southern League home match at Victoria Park versus Dunstable. A hard fought game finished goalless. Incidentally season tickets were £5 and half that for O.A.P.s. The following Saturday they travelled to Gravesend and picked up all the points with goals from Foley, Hodgkins and Donohoe in a 3-2 scoreline.

Unfortunately supporters would have to wait a little longer to witness their first Southern League victory at home, losing 2-0 against Cambridge City on the last day of August.

On the Monday following, Gloucester City visited Victoria Park and although the hosts had beaten them away only a few weeks previously they could not repeat the performance and went down 1-0. Saturday 7th of September saw the Whites away to Dunstable and despite a creditable defensive display they could not hold out for the 90 minutes. Dunstable scored twice late in the game, without reply.

The supporters had their first sweet taste of victory at home on Saturday 14th September with an emphatic 7-1 win over Tonbridge, with Tyler on the rampage netting four goals with one apiece from Gilbert, Muxworthy and Hodgkins.

The following Saturday they were on the F.A. Cup trail again. Victories were gained at Ryde Sports and then at home to Thorneycroft. They progressed to the 3rd Qualifying Round with an away tie at Waterlooville on October 19th. Sadly they met their 'waterloo' going down 4-2.

F.A. Cup Results 19/10/68

Salisbury	2	Waterlooville	4
Bridgwater Town	0	Frome Town	1
Ashford Town	3	Canterbury City	4
Poole Town	1	Gloucester City	1
replay Gloucester City	1	Poole Town	2

Going into late autumn they were beginning to settle into the Southern League style of football with a string of good results. Wins were gained at home to Gravesend & Northfleet 2-0, Ramsgate 2-0, Wisbech 1-0 and Merthyr Tydfil 3-0, away at Bexley 3-0 and a 2-2 draw at Dartford.

First win in local derby

On Saturday 28th December they started the second-half of the league programme, meeting their nearest Southern League opponents, Trowbridge Town at home. This was the first time that Salisbury had met Trowbridge as members of the Southern League and goals from Hodgkins and Ashe gave them a 2-1 win after being level on 1-1 at half-time.

Salisbury make the 'Sunday Nationals'

After losing two games in early January 1969 the first win of the New Year was a 6-1 victory against Ashford Town. Alan Tyler was in devastating form scoring all the Salisbury goals, including two penalties. The Sunday Express recorded that 'John Charles

Tyler's diving header makes it 5-0 for Salisbury v Ashford. Gilbert, Hodgkins and Muxworthy look on.

scored all four Hereford goals but this was not the best score of the day as Alan Tyler had scored all six of Salisburys'. The programme notes for the next home game against Bexley United, stated that:

For those of you who were at the Victoria Park, it must have been a long time since you saw a Salisbury player score all six goals, as Tyler did. Naturally Alan receives our congratulations, but one must remember football is a team game and without the other players support, no player would score at all, well done lads, keep up the good work.

Salisbury won the game against Bexley United 4-0, with Graham Muxworthy getting a hat-trick and Alan Tyler the other goal. On January 25th they won away to Canterbury, a game which saw the two full-backs scoring. First Tony Bichard equalised an early Canterbury goal and then Barry Fitch scored the winner just minutes from full-time to gain two very valuable points.

After two successive Southern League defeats away from home

Jeff Hodgkins scores the first of his two goals in the 3-0 win over Corby Town on 8th March 1969.

against Banbury and Crawley, both by 2-0 scorelines, the Whites hit winning form once again at Victoria Park. On 8th March a 3-0 victory over Corby Town with goals from Hodgkins (2) and Tyler (1) was followed up with two more home wins; Canterbury City 1-0 (Tyler) and the same score against Hastings United on the last day of March, with Muxworthy scoring. However, their remote promotion chances ended when they were defeated 1-0 away to Corby on 29th March.

On Good Friday 4th April, the Easter programme began at home to Bath City, the promotion favourites, but they could not hold their west country rivals losing 2-0. On Easter Saturday they played away to Tonbridge (won 3-0) and the return game with Bath City on the Easter Monday was lost 3-0.

Salisbury finished a very creditable eighth in the Southern League Division I at their first attempt.

The 1969–70 Season — David Thear

In 1969 Neil Armstrong described the moon landing as 'one small step for man, one giant leap for mankind'. At the risk of being frivolous the Whites had taken the giant leap last season by entering the Southern League. The big question for the fans was 'was it the right thing for the club and could last season's success be sustained?' The season started with high hopes. Teams were playing in the Southern League Div. I and the Hampshire League Div. I. Last year's efforts were thought to have provided a sound basis on which to build and the probable first team squad of J. Phillips, C. Smith, E. Ashe, T. Foley, K. Dyke (goalkeeper), T. Bichard, M. Whitehouse, G. Muxworthy, B. Sawyer, B. Fitch, P. Gilbert and A. Tyler, was considered to be quite capable of achieving success.

Local lads sign on

Manager Alan Grant was confident, and, additionally there were promising players signed on for predominantly Hants League action but who, undoubtedly, had the ability to progress to the first team. Chief of these were Derek Viney and Sean Jordan, both local boys, plus Brian Marwood and Dave Husbands.

Salisbury fall at fourth hurdle

F.A. Cup success was achieved when Ryde were beaten 3-2 in a replay at Victoria Park in the final Preliminary Round. Thorneycroft were then beaten 4-3 away in the 1st Qualifying round, followed by Fareham 1-0 at home and Andover 3-0 in the 3rd Qualifying Round replay at Victoria Park, in front of 2144 spectators.

Old rivals, Weymouth came to Salisbury in the 4th Qualifying Round and won by a single goal,

B. Bevis

M. Whitehouse

D. Husbands

T. Bichard

Salisbury V Weymouth FA Cup 4th Qualifying Round

P. Gilbert

P. Smith

Salisbury expect a gate of 2000 plus for the F.A. Cup 4th Qualifying Round versus Weymouth. Although beaten twice this year by their opponents Manager Alan Grant stated in naming his 13-man squad that this is our finest squad and I am sure we can rise to the occasion. Stan Charlton the Weymouth manager said that he was not underestimating Salisbury and named his strongest squad as follows, previous teams in brackets: J. Clarke (*Newport County*) B. Glover (*Coventry*) D. Barry, K. Etheridge, A. Jackson and T. Rounsevell (*Plymouth*) G. Muir (*Yeovil*) T. Hobson (*local boy*) R. Hall and J. Dixon (*Bournemouth*) J. Ryder (*Swanage*) P. Kearns (*Lincoln*) and T. Allen (*Poole*).

C. Harding

G. Moxham

B. Sawyer

F.A. Cup Results 1/10/69

Salisbury	0	Weymouth	1
Minehead	0	Yeovil Town	0
Glastonbury	0	Cheltenham Town	0
Oxford City	2	King's Lynn	0

B. Fitch

A. Tyler

J. Hodgkins

G. Muxworthy

before nearly 2500 fans. Salisbury were unlucky to lose especially as Weymouth drew Northampton, a League team, in the 1st Round proper.

In the F.A. Trophy, in its first year, the Whites beat Lower Gornal Athletic from the West Midlands League, 4-2, then Lockheed Leamington from the Midland Counties League 4-0 away.

Manager Alan Grant commented on the large amount of space allowed them by both these teams compared with their Southern League counterparts. In the 3rd round they lost away to Poole 1-0 after a 1-1 draw at Victoria Park.

In the Wiltshire Premier Shield, the final was reached by beating

Chippenham Town 2-0 although Trowbridge Town triumphed 3-1 in the two leg final.

For six months the team were unbeaten in the league. This run ended with a defeat by Tonbridge who, at the time, were bottom of the league.

Some changes in personnel had taken place with goalkeeper Dave Bevis (ex-Ipswich) signed from Andover, while Ernie Ashe, now at the veteran stage, left the club on the 18th September to eventually sign for Andover.

Dave Husbands replaced John Phillips who had suffered an injured leg. What Dave lacked in skill he made up for in his enthusiasm, determination and pure effort. Mike Whitehouse, at centre-half, continued to be the lynch-pin of the defence.

Financial worries for the Whites?

What was worrying was the fact that despite a top-half position in the league at New Year 1970, the Whites had played none of the top sides. These were due to be played in January and February, so by early March the chances of promotion should have been more clearly defined.

On the financial side there was worry over the gates at Victoria Park. By mid-December the average gate was 818 compared with the previous seasons' 1018. The Chairman, Len Brown said that 1200 was needed to pay all expenses home and away for both teams. In addition the contribution from the Supporters 'pool' was just a third of that it was in 1947!!

There were also continuing doubts about the suitability of Victoria Park as a playing venue. The location of the children's play area within the football arena, together with the inadequate perimeter fence enabled people to watch matches without payment. In addition the increase in rental fees for the park from £5 per match in 1965 to £15 in 1969 was seen to be exorbitant and represented 20% of the average gate.

New ground the answer?

The club produced evidence to the Council that other Southern League clubs who used council owned facilities were far better treated than it was. The 30/- (£1.50) hire fee for the training facilities per evening at the Sheep Fair field in Castle Road was also thought to be exorbitant.

Unfortunately the Council declined to reduce either amount and talk again turned to the possibility of building a stadium elsewhere in the city area. Newly drained land at the Butts again came under consideration and the club asked about the possibilities of using land at the back of the Friary development. Any decision was deferred however until the Lands Committee had made further enquiries. In the meantime the club formed a special committee to engage in fund raising and £50 was raised almost immediately by three of the club's ladies through a sponsored walk.

In the New Year results did not go Salisbury's way and by the end of January they were in mid-table. Chris Harding, a mainly second team player and Graham Muxworthy were transfer listed. Colin Holder was signed from Rugby, another Southern League club.

Pete Burden, a member of a well-known local football family made his debut against Ashford playing at right back, while Mick Crook, who ran a grocery store in Durrington with his father-in-law, was showing promise.

Manager throws in the towel

In March the club was hit by a double bombshell. The first was Alan Tyler's 28-day ban, meaning he missed seven matches, the second the resignation of manager Alan Grant. He had been away for a few weeks as a result of a serious knee operation during which the team had dropped down the league and was seen to be without rhythm or fitness. His return was expected to put matters right and his resignation was a great blow. His reasons were chiefly financial, 'the money didn't warrant the worry it involved' and, of course, living in Portsmouth cannot have helped.

Monies raised on three fronts

On a more cheerful note donations to the 'New Ground' Fund were arriving from local traders and 14 young lads from Bemerton Heath were sponsored for £300 to walk from Warminster to Salisbury. Equally encouraging was the agreement by the Council's Lands Committee to meet a club delegation to address the possibilities of purchasing suitable land for conversion into a sports stadium.

Sidney Chaplin, a former police Detective Chief Inspector and secretary of the Fund, set a target of £5000 before the end of the year. The Mayor, Mrs Jo Benson, also lent her support and Salisbury's goalkeeper, Dave Bevis, was appointed as a Sales Representative to boost the sagging membership of the Supporters Club Pool competition. A lucky programme was introduced on 31st January.

On the playing side the optimism engendered at the New Year by a reasonable league position and some success in the F.A. Cup and Trophy was entirely misplaced. A dramatic collapse had seen the team drop down the league table, games in hand had turned into defeats, the injury list had grown longer and longer, top goalscorer Alan Tyler had been banned and wanted a move, the manager had left and crowds had slumped lower than ever.

What should be borne in mind is the fact that this was only the second season in the Southern League. The club was very much 'the new kid on the block'. There was, however, a need to learn from the season's events and hope that the new manager would be appointed in good time to decide on the retained list and prepare for next season's challenge.

The 1970–71 Season — David Thear

Manager
Ian McNeill

The new season opened with considerable optimism. The club was in good heart and the new manager, Ian McNeill, appointed in April, had had success at his previous clubs, Ross County of the Highland League and Wigan of the Northern Premier League. Although Jeff Hodgkins had left for Andover and Chris Harding for Gosport, the nucleus of last year's side was retained to which could be added the new manager's signings. Of these John Stevens from Gloucester and a former Swindon Town player stood out. He was a big man, some fourteen stones in weight with a good goal scoring record. He was joined by Ralph Norton from Cheltenham, Cliff Balsom from Poole and Bob Walker, a former Crewe player who was signed on a year's contract following a four-week trial. Unfortunately expectations were not realised and, of the the first seven games only one was won.

The F.A. Cup brought some relief with a 3-0 win over Portland United but it was clear that changes needed to be made. After the game against Rugby which Salisbury lost 1-0, the side were 16th in the table, the lowest position since joining the Southern League.

New Manager set his store on local young talent

The manager had had success with young players in Scotland and said that he was determined to add more local youngsters to those already on the books. One local schoolboy, Sean Jordan, had already shown promise and was substitute for the Rugby match. Most supporters, at that time, felt that the club was on the right lines and when a full strength side was available, success would follow. The suspension of centre-half Mike Whitehouse and the injuries to goalkeeper Dave Bevis and top scorer Alan Tyler had not helped the cause. Also wingers Graham Moxham and Brian Marwood were out of form.

One ray of hope came from the Folkestone manager Dennis Hunt, whose side had just beaten the Whites 4-0, when he tipped Salisbury for promotion. A pretty encouraging remark to a team who were third from bottom of the league, but who, it was considered, had played most of the better sides in the league.

'We wuz robbed'

There was no respite in the F.A. Cup. The reward for beating Portland was a home tie against Poole of the Southern League Premier Division, which, if won, would have resulted in a home tie against Bath City that could have packed in a 5000 crowd. Unfortunately and, despite dominating most of the match, Salisbury lost 1-0. They were the better team throughout, had two appeals for goals disallowed in the second-half and were beaten by a goal against the run of play. It was certainly not their day.

F.A. Cup Results 1/10/70

Salisbury	0	Poole Town	1	Bath City	3	Trowbridge Town	0
Glastonbury	1	Welton Rovers	0	Newport I.O.W.	2	Basingstoke Town	2

Early season blues

Manager McNeill, worried by the start to the season, signed

Jimmy Dixon from Weymouth on a month's trial and he scored in his first match at home to Banbury, which resulted in a 1-1 draw and the following week Stevenage were beaten 1-0 away. In the next fixture Salisbury overcame Frome at Victoria Park.

From the Managers desk

The lot of the part-time football professional can be extremely tiring. Take the case of our players Ralph Norton and John Stevens. On Wednesday 26th August they left home at Bristol and Wootton Bassett respectively, at around mid-day to reach Salisbury by 1.30 p.m. After a coach journey lasting 4½hrs they took part in a hard grafting 90-mins football at Hastings.

On reaching Salisbury at approx. 2.45 a.m. they still had another car journey to make, getting to their respective homes at approx. 4 a.m. on Thursday morning. After a luxurious 3½hours sleep, both reported for their everyday jobs. They were excused training Thursday evening. Friday evening both left home again to come and stay the night in Salisbury in readiness for the 7 a.m. start to Ramsgate. On completing a 6½hour coach trip (holiday traffic) and a 90-min game followed by another long coach trip they arrived at their homes at approx. midnight.

Monday evening it was back to Salisbury for the 2nd leg of the Southern League Cup game with Hastings. This meant leaving home at around 5 p.m., and, after the match, the journey home again, arriving home at around 11.30 p.m.

All one can say is 'a really trying holiday period and thank goodness for understanding wives'.

Local lad makes good

In local football David Syrett, playing for Laverstock Youth, scored a hat-trick in each of the first eight games of the season and in two of these he scored five! He went on to play in over 300 Football League games and scored 90 goals with Swindon, Mansfield, Walsall, Peterborough and Northampton. Bemerton Athletic lost 4-1 to Swaythling in the F.A. Amateur Cup.

For Salisbury, league form continued to disappoint, including a 5-1 defeat at Gravesend, who were generally considered to be a poor side. Bevis, Balsom and Walker were transfer listed and Dixon, who had played well throughout his trial, was given a year's contract.

In league table terms, from 13 games played, three had been won and six lost (goal difference was 13 for, and 22 against) with ten points. At the same time the previous year the team had 15 points with a goal difference of 15–12. With virtually the same players in defence ten more goals were conceded this year compared with the previous and two less goals were scored.

New leagues afoot?

Around this time it became known that the Southern League were considering a geographical split of Division I, into either northern and southern or eastern and western sections. This would mean an increase in the number of clubs (which would help Andover, Basingstoke and Winchester's ambitions), reduce travelling costs and increase the number of money spinning local derbies!

Salisbury continued on the F.A. Trophy trail with a 5-1 home win over Bodmin Town and then a 2-0 away win in the league at Canterbury. One of Ian McNeill's signings Ralph Norton, had his contract cancelled which meant that only one player, John Stevens, retained the confidence of the manager after three months of the season. Meanwhile Derek Burns from Bournemouth was well into a three months trial.

An earlier Salisbury team comprising: *Left/right, back row:* Phillips, Hall, Ashe, Dyke, Collins, Hodgkins, Muxworthy, Whitehouse, C. Smith *(coach),* I Crockett *(sec.). Front row:* Fitch, Bichard, Sawyer, Gilbert. Mascot not known.

At last the team began to blend with Phil Gilbert playing at right-back instead of Tony Bichard, Tony Blackwell, an ex-Old Manor player, taking over from Dave Bevis in goal and playing well and both Mike Whitehouse and Barry Fitch hitting top form again. The midfield comprised Mick Crook, from Durrington, Derek Burns and Graham Moxham with John Stevens, Alan Tyler and Dixon up front. The league position was still worrying, 15th out of 20th, but signs were thought to be encouraging.

Trophy blues again

Unfortunately this encouragement did not extend to the F.A. Trophy when once again Salisbury outplayed their opponents,

Bilston from Staffordshire, only to lose at Victoria Park 1-0.

League form improved a little with wins over Stevenage and Cheltenham but defeats against Burton, Trowbridge, Hastings, Gravesend and Banbury produced considerable gloom. In the Wilts Premier Shield, Trowbridge were beaten 5-2 away. The match was played on a Sunday because Trowbridge had no floodlights!

Two new players were signed, Bob Wakerly an ex-Saint, and Tim Soutar from Gravesend. Locally Old Manor beat Chippenham Town, then of the Hellenic League, in the Wilts Senior Cup.

Too much football played in the city?

Salisbury's poor season was causing financial concern due to diminishing crowds. Crowds were well below what was needed, the average Southern League gate being 684 although all home matches yielded an average of 737. However midweek matches were better supported with an average of over 900. This led to the view, echoed by Ian McNeill, that the proliferation of local leagues was to blame. There were seven divisions in the Salisbury and District Saturday League and more on Sundays. In addition there was the Nadder Valley League and innumerable cups and knock-out tournaments and it was considered by some to deprive Salisbury of support.

This view was not shared by the Salisbury and District League Chairman, George Williams. He pointed out that those involved in local football represented a 0.5% of the population in the Whites catchment area and, in any event, the league was the size it was because that was the number of teams needed to cater for those who wished to play the game. Furthermore it was highly unlikely that if all local football ceased, those involved, or even a reasonable number of those, would support Salisbury instead.

Results continued to disappoint although the Hampshire League side were finding their feet after an indifferent start to the season. Local players in Ron Emm, Malcolm Musselwhite, Bernie Sainsbury and Phil Beattie had proved their worth. It was, therefore, disappointing to learn that the Reserves might have to be axed at the end of the season for financial reasons.

New leagues are put in place

In March the Southern League announced the reorganisation into a Premier League supported by two First Divisions divided geographically North and South from season 1971/72. Thirteen new clubs were elected to the new leagues and these included Andover, Basingstoke, Winchester and Waterlooville. Dave Husbands was voted 'Player of the Year' and Alan Tyler was sold to Guildford. Brian Marwood, Tony Bichard, Derek Burns, Bob Wakerley and Bob Walker were not retained at the end of the season and the reserve side was duly axed.

Ian McNeill leaves early

To cap it all Ian McNeill asked to be released after one year of his three-year contract and duly returned to Ross County. It is fair to say that he was a knowledgeable manager and showed the ability to organise the club on the right lines. The manager's problem was his lack of knowledge of the league and area resulting in a final league position of 14th. Cup results were also disappointing although the Wiltshire Premier Shield was won with an aggregate 4-2 win over Chippenham Town.

So Salisbury finished the season with no manager, nine players retained for the next season and no reserve side. Not surprisingly the average Southern League home gate of 623 meant that the new manager would have to rebuild on a shoe string budget. All in all a season to forget. Roll on 1971/72.

The 1971–72 Season — David Thear

If 1970/71 was a season to forget what were the Whites supporters to think of this one. From the outset the club Treasurer, Peter Wrigley, spelled out the financial situation. He said that:

> On the field mediocrity over the past three seasons has resulted in dropping gates and reduced receipts causing the reserve team to be axed and results had to improve if the club were to thrive.

Only 12 professional players, including Kenny Wrintmore from Trowbridge, Dave Bennett, a veteran but a proven goal scorer from Weymouth, and John Parker from Bath, had been signed and a new manager had taken over.

Because the Southern Division this season yielded only 30 matches against 38 last year the Southern League's annual meeting had agreed that the League's Cup competition be organised into five qualifying leagues, geographically based, for the 34 teams in the Northern and Southern Divisions. The top two teams of each league would be placed in the hat with the Premier Division Clubs for the competition proper. These leagues would be played out at the start of the season.

Manager
Wilf Carter

Wilf Carter takes charge

The new manager, who was third choice behind Ron Gingell of Minehead and Bournemouth scout Tony Nielson, was Wilf Carter, formerly second in command at Bath following a playing career with West Bromwich Albion, Plymouth Argyle and Exeter City. Salisbury was his first post in sole management charge. He wisely, and prophetically, promised 'no miracles'.

Club secretary has doubts about new cup competition

The new league set up was roundly condemned by Salisbury secretary Derek Sharp. He said the Southern Division had been extended with some poorly supported clubs joining, resulting in low gates and receipts and that the new 5/- (25p) ground entry charge was a contributory factor in reducing attendances. There was also the risk of playing some teams too many times and the reorganisation of the Cup competition had been scrapped two years ago for this reason. He felt the competition was neither a league proper nor a Cup competition with the added spice of sudden death.

All these factors could have been tolerated if there had been some success in the 'mini league' but points were few and far between. Salisbury came second to bottom and had no further interest in the competition. To rub salt in the wound, Basingstoke and Waterlooville qualified in first and second place respectively.

No early success

The Southern Division programme itself started on September 11th with a 2-1 defeat at Winchester. Further defeats followed and it was 16th October before the Whites gained their first point in a 1-1 draw at Ashford.

In the F.A. Cup 1st qualifying round Westbury were beaten 4-0 leading to a home tie against Bath which was won 2-1. This was a pleasing result as Wilf Carter came from Bath and three players, John Parker, Kenny Wrintmore and Mike Whitehouse had played for the club. The resultant away tie against Basingstoke (Third Qualifying) brought gloom and despair to White's fans. The 1-1 half-time score was a fair reflection of play but the change in formation from 4-3-3 to 4-2-4 resulted in a defensive collapse with Basingstoke scoring four times against Salisbury's one.

F.A. Cup Results 27/10/71

Basingstoke Town	5	Salisbury	2	Fareham Town	5	Thornycroft Ath.	1
Bideford	4	Wadebridge	1	Bridgwater Town	2	Trowbridge Town	1

This decision by the manager and his failure to bolster a ailing team was bringing criticism from both inside and outside the club. Andrew McCluskey from Yeovil was only his second signing and he soon departed after failing to turn up for a match at Welton resulting in a fine of two weeks wages.

> **Significantly the Supporters Club handed over £6,000 to the Club this season.**

In the F.A. Trophy, Andover were beaten 4-3 at Victoria Park after a goalless draw away and on the 13th November, Welton were beaten 3-1. Old Western League rivals Dorchester were the opponents in the next round. A goalless draw at Dorchester was followed by a 2-0 replay defeat at Victoria Park.

Demonstrations at Victoria Park

This, together with the fact that Southern League results had not picked up and the team were bottom of the Division resulted in angry demonstrations by 200 fans against the committee and manager after the Dorchester defeat. This pressure resulted in a packed protest meeting at the Guildhall on 3rd January 1972. In a reversal of the stance taken after the Dorchester game the meeting laid the blame for the team's situation squarely on the previous manager and gave Wilf Carter a pat on the back and a free hand for another 12 months after his contract expired in May.

Ivan Crockett puts his faith in the youth

Rumblings about the management committee were aired but any question of replacement or re-election was ruled out of order by the Chairman. Club vice-Chairman, Ivan Crockett, said that there was the possibility of money being available for new players and consideration was being given to restarting the reserve side in the Wiltshire Combination. In addition there was a real chance of setting up a youth team.

In the meantime, three new players had arrived on trial, Pete Arrowsmith from Poole, ex-Saint Kevin Hancox and Melvyn Simmonds, an ex-Manchester United player and schoolboy international from Guildford. John Stevens went on the transfer list and eventually returned to his former club Gloucester City.

The Whites still bottom

In the league there was some improvement with three draws since the January meeting. On the 5th February, Salisbury lost 3-1 at Woodford at which point they had not won a Southern League game since November 29th and were still bottom of the league.

On 19th February Salisbury beat Ashford 1-0 and then came off the bottom of the league with 0-0 draw at Ramsgate followed by a 2-2 draw at the Park against the same team.

Technically the team had now become very defensive, but this paid off when Maidstone were beaten 1-0 and Canterbury held to a 2-2 draw. Further good results followed and on 8th April it was virtually certain that re-election had been avoided. Derek Norman, a significant signing from Winchester, was made captain and played a major part in the improved position.

Interestingly the new youth team made its debut under Cyril Smith against Bath (lost 6-1) on 19th March.

The final league placing was 13th and the Wiltshire Premier Shield Final against Swindon was lost 7-2 on aggregate.

About half the playing staff were not retained leaving the manager with plenty of room to manoeuvre in the close season. Those not retained were Tony Blackwell, Tim Soutar, Mike Crook, Melvyn Simmonds, Ken Wrintmore and John Parker. Top scorer was Dave Bennett with 24 goals and 'Player of the Year' was Phil Gilbert.

Cyril Smith who captained Salisbury's youth team, aged 49.

While playing results had been, to put it mildly, disappointing, a bigger disappointment had occurred off the pitch.

Club dealt serious blow

The club's long standing discussions with the City Council over the purchase of land on which to build a new stadium had collapsed in one swift and uncompromising blow. The club were told that the newly drained land, known as the Butts in Ashley Road, would cost £6,000 per acre, meaning that the total cost of a completed stadium would be at least £65,000. While no figure had been quoted during the period of negotiation, past experience had led the club to believe £300 per acre was the likely asking price.

While an appeal to the Council was considered it was accepted that the club's attempt to move to its own premises had foundered and this proved to be the case. It would be 1997 before the dream was realised and the club had the fine Stadium it now plays in.

The 1972–73 Season — David Thear

After last seasons traumas season 1972/73 opened with some trepidation, but not a little hope. Manager Wilf Carter had been given a vote of confidence by the general meeting in January and the league was not thought to contain any exceptional teams.

New signings were Ken Wookey (Yeovil), Ray Elliot (Cambridge City), Tommy Taylor (Poole), Benny Glover (Weymouth) and Bob Duncan (ex Raith Rovers). Unfortunately work commitments had caused the loss of Phil Gilbert who returned to Kent.

The reserves were entered in the Wiltshire Combination. Contenders for the first team were expected to be:

Goal:	Mike Dixon, Malcolm Price (a local policeman)
Backs:	Keith Trowbridge, Benny Glover, Barry Fitch, Mike Whitehouse, Dave Husbands
Midfield:	Bob Duncan, Derek Norman, Tommy Taylor, Graham Moxham, Melvyn Simmonds
Forwards:	Dave Bennett, Ken Wookey, Ray Elliot, Derek Viney

In all, 14 professionals were signed.

The season opened well. Of the first five matches in the league four were won and one drawn and at the end of August the Whites were on top of the league.

Been here before

In the F.A. Cup Westbury were beaten 9-1, and Andover 1-0 before the ghosts of last season reappeared when, having drawn 0-0 at Frome in the next round, the Whites lost 1-0 in the replay at Victoria Park in front of a crowd of 860.

In the F.A. Trophy Premier Division side Guildford City were beaten 1-0 but in the next round Bletchley were too good at Victoria Park after a draw away.

F.A. Cup Results 21/10/72

Frome Town	0	Salisbury	0	*Replay* Salisbury 0	Frome Town	1
				Saturday results:		
Devizes Town	1	Cheltenham Town	0	Barry Town	0	Taunton Town	0
Bideford	1	Barnstaple Town	2			

In the League Cup the Whites reached the final after beating Minehead, Andover and Cheltenham. They subsequently lost to Weymouth after a replay.

At the year end Salisbury had the best away record in the league having lost only once to Bath. At home, however, five league matches had been lost and this, coupled with the F.A. Cup and Trophy defeats, caused alarm and frustration among the fans.

Perhaps the best result of the season thus far was away at Crawley when, due to illness and traffic delays, manager Wilf Carter had to play himself to put eleven players on the field. Crawley were one of the stronger teams but the Whites triumphed 2-0.

50 not out!

On the same day Cyril Smith turned out for the reserves at the age of 50 and they won 4-3 against Old Manor. He turned out four times altogether during the season.

There were pluses on the playing side. Local boy Mick Presley, deputising for the injured Mike Whitehouse, had been a revelation and Derek Norman and Dave Husbands had been solid and dependable. All in all, at the turn of the year, there was optimism and a feeling that, if home form improved, promotion was a distinct possibility.

Prophetic words, but they couldn't have been further from the truth; Manager Wilf Carter was sacked on 6th February following a string of poor results. As at 27th January the team had played nine games since a win and most of these had been defeats, bringing a real threat of relegation.

Cyril Smith and the management committee took over the running of the team and immediately results improved. Dave Bennett, Graham Moxham and Tommy Taylor withdrew transfer requests and altogether a new mood prevailed.

Manager
Robin North

Local man takes the reigns

The search for a new manager brought a sizeable list of candidates and, for a time, Graham Carr from Poole appeared favourite. The management committee were, however, very conscious that the two previous managers, Ian McNeill and Wilf Carter, had lacked local knowledge and this, no doubt, was a prime reason for their final choice. At the end of March they announced the appointment of Robin North, a former Salisbury player and the manager of Andover. His playing career had started at Andover as a 15 year old, then Southampton, at reserve team level, followed by Winchester, Bournemouth, Salisbury and Andover where a broken leg ended his playing career in 1966.

His first foray into management was with Sutton Scotney, then Winchester City and in 1968 he took the reins at Andover who were then in the Western League. From the bottom of the table he took them to the runners-up spot for two successive seasons and then into the Southern League. In the two years in that league they established themselves as a strong outfit on a budget, arguably, considerably less than Salisbury F.C.'s

Relegation avoided

He immediately set about assessing his playing strength. He also concentrated on communicating with all those in the club, as a result of which morale rose. While it was too late to do much about the league position, nine points were gained from his first six games in charge and the final league position was 18th out of 22, much better than had been anticipated.

The Wiltshire Premier Shield final was lost 3-0 to Trowbridge and the reserves lost the Hospital Cup Final 2-0 to Bemerton. Dave Husbands won the Player of the Year Trophy for the second time and Alan Lake was pronounced the best amateur in the club.

Of the most significance was the handing over of £9000 by the Supporters Club which, without doubt, enabled the club to keep going when results were poor and crowd numbers falling.

The 1973–74 Season — David Thear

Once more there was optimism at Victoria Park as the season opened. Manager Robin North had been busy during the summer and there were many new names on the playing strength. These included Trevor Morris, a 34-year old goalkeeper from Bideford, Colin Eyden (Poole), Terry More (Guildford), Peter Burden (Amesbury), David Lock and Keith Smart (Winchester), Jimmy Loughran, a soldier serving at Tidworth and Alan Smith (both Andover), Barry Cook (Waterlooville), Chris Weller (Yeovil), Malcolm Williams (Devizes), Peter Syrett (Swindon), Kevin Kelly (Totton) and Kevin White.

Park veteran seeks pastures anew

Of last season's team, Dave Husbands and Barry Fitch went to Basingstoke where they were joined by former White Alan Tyler, from Guildford. Mick Presley joined Poole, Graham Moxham, Bideford and Mike Whitehouse, Odd Down, then in the Somerset County League. Only Tommy Taylor and Derek Norman remained on the Whites books.

Off the field there had been a backroom revolution. Plans were put in place to become a limited company and to sign a 21 year tenancy for Victoria Park at £25 per annum. The long standing dream of a new ground had been shelved as ever soaring costs had put the prospect out of reach. The tenancy at the Park meant the club would have an incentive to keep both infrastructure and pitch up to scratch. In addition the facilities could be used for training nights.

Excitement in short supply

So what happened on the field? At Christmas, the Whites were at the bottom of the league. In the League Cup Dorchester triumphed 9-2 on aggregate, Weymouth knocked them out of the F.A. Cup 2-0 (in 17 matches over five years Salisbury had beaten Weymouth once) and in the F.A. Trophy Basingstoke were beaten 3-0 after a draw away. Interestingly the Basingstoke manager labelled the team 'the worst Salisbury side I have ever seen' after the draw and this, Manager North believed, gave the players the incentive to win the replay. In goal that day for the Whites was Steve Tilley and his performance was widely praised as was that of Peter Syrett. Unfortunately Kent League Chatham prevented further progress with a 2-0 win in Kent on November 10th.

Of the new players generally, only four were thought to have been successes, namely, Trevor Morris, Peter Syrett, David Lock and Terry More. Colin Eyden, the replacement for Mike Whitehouse, was, unfortunately, like him in temperament as well as footballing ability and by Christmas was serving his second suspension of the season. The others had been disappointing.

In the league, Christmas and New Year brought some welcome relief with five points from four games. Waterlooville and Basingstoke were beaten, the latter by 4-1 in front of the biggest home crowd of the season. Dorchester forced a draw and Andover won 2-1.

Hardened supporters still hoping

This was, however, a false dawn. Thirteen consecutive matches were played without a victory before a late revival at Easter avoided the embarrassment of seeking re-election.

One bright spot was the performance of the reserves who challenged for the top spot in the Wiltshire Combination League. Three of the team, Mark Huckle, Paul Fairclough and Steve Tilley (goal) had played for the first team and indeed, it seemed likely that Steve Tilley would be first choice next season following Trevor Morris's release to become player/manager of Barnstaple Town.

So, once again, a Salisbury manager reached the end of the season under a cloud. Without doubt the team was not good enough and this was confirmed when he released all but six of his professionals. Once again the summer would be spent seeking fresh talent and again the fans would be seeing many new faces next season.

As something of an antidote to the dreadful season Salisbury had suffered, one record was set at Victoria Park. Salisbury's first ever Sunday match was played on 13th January 1974. Opponents were Bognor Regis and the result was a 1-1 draw.

Admission was by programme because fans could not pay cash on a Sunday in those days. The kick-off was at 11.15 and the crowd of over 500 was many more than would have been expected for a Saturday match. Derek Sharp, club secretary, said that anything in excess of 350 would be a bonus but he didn't expect the concept of Sunday football to be particularly successful in Salisbury.

The reason for the switch was, of course, the 3-day working week imposed by the government as a result of industrial action in the power industry.

Another interesting decision by Robin North was the termination of the 'Player of the Year' award. This was because previous recipients of the Trophy considered themselves worth more money and when this was rejected, transfers resulted.

The 1974–75 Season — David Thear

Once again Salisbury's long suffering fans began a season with a much changed complement of players and a sincere wish for better results.

Only six players were retained as professionals from the previous year, namely Keith Weller, Peter Syrett, David Lock, Colin Eyden,

Steve Tilley and Brian Hunt who had joined in February 1974. To these were added Mark O' Connor from Bexley, Dave Hibberd and Ray Keeley from Andover, Paul Christopher and Alan Green from Mansfield and Colin Guy and Brian Crosby both Dorchester.

Alan Green was a 22-year old who lived at Woodfalls, near Salisbury. He played for Bournemouth and then Mansfield until he suffered a blow in the chest in a Division IV match, after which the doctors diagnosed heart trouble. Following a long rest he was passed fit to play again and was signed, initially on a monthly contract. It was to prove to be one of the better signings.

Financial state of Salisbury F.C. disclosed

An AGM was held in the autumn to show the club's financial position before the first meeting of shareholders in connection with the plan to become a limited company.

Henry Abel

The meeting was held at the Supporters Club premises in Stratford Road and a deficit of £800 was disclosed. This was said to be due to the cancellation of floodlit matches and earlier kick-offs, brought about by the power crisis. Gate receipts had reduced by over 50%. The Club Chairman, Mr Les Whitmarsh, was delighted, therefore to receive a cheque for £3000, from the Chairman of the Supporters Club, Mr Henry Abel, putting the finances firmly in the black. Derek Sharp reported that this meant the Supporters Club had given the Whites a total of £194,500 since inception — a truly phenomenal figure in today' s prices.

Bring on the 'heavy roller'

At Victoria Park the club now had its own tractor, gang mower and roller, so no longer did it have to rely on Council contractors for any of the pitch maintenance. The improvement in the playing surface was there for all to see.

Off the pitch activities looked in good shape and it only remained for the footballing side to deliver the goods. Recent history had not prepared the fans for optimism which was just as well because another disappointing season was about to commence.

The first win was in December, when Bexley United were beaten 3-0 at home. Two new signings, Mick Iles from Mansfield and

Dave Lock

Steve Tilley

Chris Weller

Brian Hunt

Colin Eyden

Peter Syrett

Alan Green

Above: The six players who were retained for the 1974/75 season plus Alan Green *(left)* one of seven new players that joined Salisbury.

Graham Thomas, both played in the match.

The F.A. Cup promised well with wins against Cowes, Basingstoke and Alton, until a comprehensive defeat 4-1 by Cheltenham, a Division I (north) side. In both the F.A. Trophy and Wilts Premier Shield they were beaten by Chippenham Town, then in the Western League. The League Cup produced two wins before a loss to Bedford Town.

So the club were free to 'concentrate on the league'. How many times over the past few years had the fans heard this and how many times had the concentration brought them beneficial results? Would it happen in season 1974/5?

Manager calls it a day

Well it didn't happen in January and in February, Robin North resigned. The renewal of his contract was to have been discussed at the February management committee meeting but this never happened. Selby Dando, a Salisbury player in the 1950s, became caretaker manager on 27th February and after 12 games in his charge 14 points were achieved saving the club from the humiliation of seeking re-election. In due course the list of retained professionals for the season 1975/6 included all but three of the present complement. Those not retained were Mick Iles, Keith Weller and Brian Hunt. Barry Fitch, who had rejoined the club after spells with Basingstoke and Frome, re-signed and was retained. The appointment of a new manager had not been made, but clearly, the committee had seen the problems which occur if there is a wholesale clear out of players as had happened in the past two seasons. They now wished to hand a nucleus of players over to the new manager, their fifth in seven years, whoever he might be.

New man to the helm

There was a feeling that Selby Dando might well get the job on a permanent basis. He had sparked a revival and his happy-go-lucky attitude and predilection for attacking football had endeared him to players, club officials and fans, but it was not to be. The latest recruit to the post was 33-year old ex-Torquay United Coach Mike Hughes, who had previously spent three successful seasons as player-manager with Yeovil Town during which they won the SL Premier Division Championship.

Whether this was the right appointment only time would tell. Two things were certain however, the decreased level in real terms of Supporters Club contributions and the falling attendances at matches. So far as the the latter was concerned the average attendance at home matches was only just over 200. The best turn out of over 600, at Victoria Park was when the Conquered Moon, a pub side from Bemerton Heath, lost to Newton Tony in the final of the Wiltshire Sunday Cup!! Bob Burden who had played for the Whites at full-back, played centre-forward for the village side and scored a goal.

The 1975–76 Season — David Thear

Manager
Mike Hughes

The Southern League season opened with the new manager in charge. Again new players were signed and the manager, who was a qualified F.A. coach, was still young and fit enough to play in the defence. Training at Victoria Park became much more professional which may have been an unpleasant shock for some players.

The new players were Glen Stride (Bournemouth), Bev Dixon from the Royal Navy and therefore an amateur; Marvin Gavin (Bristol City) who lived in Birmingham and stayed with the club for barely a month; David Hookway, a goalkeeper from Torquay to provide cover for Steve Tilley and David Loney (Dorchester). In due course a number of local players joined. Bobby Andrews was signed in

November from Shrewton United. He had previously played also for Salisbury Sunday League team Conquered Moon. Then Terry Plank and Andy Strange, both members of Amesbury's Wiltshire Combination League winning team from season 1974/5 joined Dave Selby. Mick Presley, a former White re-signed and was a prolific scorer for the reserves in the Combination.

On the playing front, league form was disappointing with the Whites at or near the bottom of the league for the first three months of the season. Injuries and suspensions played their part and nobody could have blamed the fans for thinking that this season was going the same way as others. There was no money to spend on new signings and at one point, this seemed likely to cause a rift between the management committee and manager.

Keeping the supporters awake

The F.A. Cup provided some relief with wins over Trowbridge 3-1, Swaythling 1-0 and Frome 1-0. Retribution arrived, however, when old enemies Weymouth beat the Whites at Victoria Park 5-4, in one of the best matches ever seen there. Geoff Astle, the England centre- forward in the World Cup in Mexico in 1972 played for Weymouth and scored twice.

F.A. Cup Results 1/11/75

| Salisbury | 4 | Weymouth | 5 | Falmouth Town | 1 | Yeovil Town | 5 |
| Wimbledon | 6 | Kingstonian | 1 | Crawley Town | 0 | Dover Athletic | 0 |

Ironically, this defeat was to prove a turning point in the season. The players realised they could compete against a quality Premier League side and league results improved dramatically. In the F.A. Trophy Salisbury beat Wokingham 2-0 before losing to Fareham Town after a replay.

Somewhere in the top eight?

From then until the New Year 13 points were taken from 10 matches leaving the club in mid-table with everything to play for. Manager Hughes was quoted in the Southern Evening Sports Echo ('The Pink') as saying 'My target is to finish somewhere between

4th and 8th'. The fans would have been delighted with that but in previous seasons it was the months of January and February which had yielded the least success. Would 1976 be different?

On the move again?

Away from the playing arena the Southern League management were considering yet another reorganisation. Basically their plan was to split Division I into three regions covering the north, south-east and south-west, with 16 clubs in each. The Premier League would be reduced by two to 20 clubs. Bridgwater and Taunton were expected to be two of the four extra clubs to join. Salisbury anticipated being in the south-west region meaning more awkward travelling to away games, while losing, possibly, the popular local derbies at Basingstoke and Andover.

Secretary Derek Sharp was entirely opposed to the plan although indications were that it would be adopted in the season 1976/7. The Kent clubs formed a strong nucleus of support seeing the proposal as as a means of avoiding their lengthy journeys to the west of England.

Returning to the league, results continued to improve as did the attendances at Victoria Park. There were 335 paying customers to see Waterlooville beaten 3-0, 100 more than at early season games despite wet and blustery weather. Within 10 days, 453 fans paid to see Dorchester defeated and the club rise to eighth in the table. Bobby Andrews scored two goals in 45 seconds and became a firm favourite with home supporters. Both he and Dave Selby were playing well and earning praise from the Salisbury manager.

To the joy of the fans, league form continued to flourish and at the end of the season 4th place was achieved. Only Minehead, the eventual Champions had a record to compare with the Whites since their recovery after Christmas. They were third highest goals scorers behind the two promoted clubs, Minehead and Dartford and the top scorer in the league was Colin Guy with 20 goals.

They reached the final of the Western Counties Floodlit Cup losing narrowly to Bath City. In the Wiltshire Premier Shield they held Swindon's Third Division team to a draw at the County Ground before losing 1-0 in the replay at Victoria Park in front of a crowd of 953.

Hopes were high for next season. Mike Hughes contract was extended and he travelled the length and breadth of the West Country seeking the three or four players he felt were needed to complete a promotion winning team. Two professionals were not retained, Mike O'Connor, whose season had been severely constrained by injury and Dave Loney. Both the outstanding amateurs, Bobby Andrews and Dave Selby, were re-signed on professional forms with the hope that there were more like them in the local leagues.

It was the Whites best season since joining the Southern League and all connected with the club were, for once, awaiting the next season with genuine hopes.

Moving away from events at Salisbury Football Club this was the season when Southampton won the F.A. Cup by beating Manchester United 1-0 at Wembley, an event which provided a major boost for football in the area. Many Salisbury fans were also Saints supporters and local boy, Mike Channon, was one of the stars of the team as well as being a regular England international.

One time Amesbury schoolboy – Mike Channon.
photo David Bull

A very good season!!!

The 1976–77 Season — David Thear

The first piece of good news for the club was that the proposed reorganisation of the Southern League was not now to be implemented. It would seem that the Kent clubs realised that the new South Eastern Division would result in an almost continual round of matches against their near neighbours with next to no variety. Salisbury heaved a sigh of relief!!

At Victoria Park new trainer's boxes had been installed and the stand re-decorated with the legend 'Salisbury Football Club' across the top in the club colours of black and white. Two new professionals had been signed, Dave Verity from Weymouth and Cliff Myers (Torquay). In due course another former Torquay player, centre-half Derek Harrison, was to sign although his reason for coming to Salisbury was, in part, due to a persistent leg injury which prevented him from playing professional football on a full-time basis. This was to prove more and more of a handicap as the season progressed.

How much at today's prices?

On the down side there was a real risk that the Whites would lose the services of Alan Green, a regular scorer. He was the subject of regular transfer talk and both Millwall and Swindon made offers around £5000. Fortunately he elected to remain. Also the manager was reputed to be interested in an 18 years old centre-half playing for Newport I.O.W. His name was Ricky Haysom and he was,

Alan Green

eventually, to play a significant part in the fortunes of Salisbury Football Club – see page 293.

Turning to the playing side this season's achievements were in marked contrast to the more recent ones. In these seasons, league results had not picked up until Christmas or thereabouts while there had been some success in the major cups in the autumn. In 1976/77 league results were excellent with the club on top of the Division on 8th January 1977. The first defeat had not occurred until Boxing Day at Trowbridge.

Only dipped a small toe in

In the F.A. Cup, Farnborough, then an amateur side from the Athenian League, won 4-0 at Cherrywood Road in the preliminary round. Complacency seemed to be the trouble and having Colin Guy sent off for dissent did not help. In the F.A. Trophy, Bideford from the Western League, won 2-1 so interest then ceased in the two major cup competitions.

F.A. Cup Results 4/9/76

Farnborough	4	Salisbury	0	Penzance	2	Yeovil Town	7
Gloucester City	1	Trowbridge Town	1	Glastonbury	1	Barry Town	0
replay Trowbridge Town	1	Gloucester City	2				

Well done that man

The league success was, however, to bring 'off the field' progress. The Supporters Club donated £4000 up to December with the possibility of more to come and the club's Christmas raffle netted a profit of £200. One ticket seller, John Head of Fairfield Road Salisbury, sold 1091 books which yielded £400.

So the New Year began with high hopes. There were niggling doubts in some quarters because of disappointing home form. At 29th January, of the 10 home games played only four had been won (six were draws) while the nine away games had yielded 14 points. Remember in those days it was two points for a win and only one for a draw.

Disappointingly the second-half of the season failed to yield the points necessary to be seriously in contention and, following a disastrous Easter, when only one point was gained from the three games, they had to settle for fifth position, one place worse than the previous season. Barnet and Hastings were promoted and Salisbury were left to ponder on what might have been.

The 1977–78 Season — David Thear

This was the club's 10th season in the Southern League. Fortunes had been very mixed with poor results in the early 70s, regular changes of managers and a reducing supporter base. The decline was arrested with the arrival of Mike Hughes as manager at the end of the 1974/5 season. Decent cup runs were experienced and the team threatened to achieve promotion in his first season in charge. Crowds were increasing and in August 1977, there was a feeling that this was the promotion season. On the social scene the man recognised as giving all teenagers a new lease of life in the pop music world, died. He was Elvis Presley.

Seasons comings and goings

Firstly, the manager recognised that defensive frailties had cost the club promotion the previous season and set about remedying this by signing highly rated goalkeeper Bob Wiltshire from Trowbridge; Roger Fry a full-back with a lot of Football League experience with Southampton and Walsall; Terry Cotton, a centre-half from Yeovil; Dave Husbands a former White from Basingstoke

Bob Wiltshire

and Bob Andrews, a defender from Swindon Town. Dave Hibberd had left the club and was eventually to sign for Fareham Town. To replace Colin Guy, who was transferred to Weymouth for £1000, Andy Marsh, a schoolteacher, was signed from Poole.

Colin Guy

The wisdom of signing players to provide defensive cover was proved during the opening weeks of the season when injuries reduced the availability of players such as Peter Syrett, who had difficulties after a cartilage operation. In fact, for the opening match only Barry Fitch, of last season's back four was available and Peter Syrett's injury was to restrict his appearances for a large part of the season. In addition the strikers were unable to replicate 1976/7 form. Despite these difficulties league form was very encouraging and by early March the team were second in the table. Margate were on top but Salisbury had games in hand. Mike Hughes was endeavouring to strengthen the team for the run-in but failed in his attempts sign Kevin Griffin from Bath. He went to Yeovil for £750 and Bill Beaney, an ex-Saint from Poole went to promotion rivals Dorchester who also signed John O'Rourke a former Coventry and QPR centre-forward. These players were just the sort that Salisbury needed to provide impetus for their promotion bid and so far as Dorchester were concerned it was money well spent as they achieved, with Margate, a coveted promotion place. The Whites faltered at the same time as last season, losing two games at home in March and at the end of the season had to settle for third place.

Fell at the final hurdle

In the F.A. Cup they were unlucky to lose 2-1 away to Minehead in a Fourth Qualifying replay. The fixture at home had brought a crowd of well over a thousand to Victoria Park. In previous rounds Cowes, Hungerford and Frome had been beaten. Victory over Minehead would have meant meeting Wycombe Wanderers in the next round.

F.A. Cup Results 5/11/77

Salisbury	1	Minehead	1	*Replay*	Minehead	2	Salisbury	1

Saturday results:

Worcester City	2	Weymouth	2		Bideford Town	1	Banbury United	0

In the F.A. Trophy, Wokingham, managed by former Salisbury goalkeeper Mike Dixon, were beaten 2-1 and after a drawn game away, Boreham Wood were beaten 1-0. Cheltenham, however proved too good for Salisbury at Victoria Park.

Club 'Stalwart' parts company

Fans were saddened by the departure in the New Year of Barry Fitch for alleged 'breach of contract'. He had been with Salisbury for nearly 14 years except for short periods at Basingstoke and Frome. At 34 years of age, although not a regular in the side, particularly after the loan signing of Geoff Chalkin from Cheltenham, supporters would always remember his whole

Barry Fitch

hearted displays even when the team were in the doldrums in the early 70s.

On the financial side the AGM in October heard that the club had shown a profit after a loss the previous year. Sponsorship was also an issue engaging the management committee's minds. The F.A. had given official approval to clubs consolidating their financial position through commercial channels and this, it was hoped, would open new avenues for financial support by local companies sponsoring matches, programmes and match balls. In return advertising and loud-speaker announcements and advertising hoardings would be available to sponsors.

Locals come on board

Mike Hughes meanwhile, was still on the look-out for local talent and in November, Roland Bletsoe, who had scored 14 goals in 11 games for the reserves in the Wiltshire Combination, played well against Tonbridge and Steve Slade, the 23-year old Bemerton centre-forward and a prolific goalscorer played in a Western Counties cup match. His record in local football, was 135 goals in 140 appearances for Porton in the Salisbury and District League, 168 in 120 matches for 'Conquered Moon' in the Sunday League and 36 in 60 games for Bemerton. Steve went on to manage Bemerton Heath Harlequins when his playing career ended.

Pyramid on a distant horizon!

Fans of non-league football will be interested to learn that the first tentative moves toward the 'pyramid' structure were mooted in November 1977. The Southern League management were canvassing all their clubs for views on a blue-print for non-league football in the 1980s with a National League, automatic entry to the Football League and some amalgamations. The aim was to boost the status of senior non-league clubs while at the same time trimming costs. Although this sounds familiar it seems to be the first step towards the structure which is now in place.

The most successful season Salisbury had enjoyed in the Southern League so far, now drew to a close. Two decent cup runs, a nail biting end to a league campaign which almost brought promotion and financial stability were the outcomes. There was no silverware except for the Wilts Premier Shield, which was won when a strong Swindon Town side were beaten 2-1 over two legs.

The 1978–79 Season — David Thear

The previous season had been the best since joining the league and although some of the stalwarts of that team had moved on, Alan Green and Peter Syrett to Andover; Terry Cotton to Yeovil and Dave Husbands to Basingstoke, there was no reason to believe that manager Hughes would not be able to attract suitable replacements.

Dave Husbands

However this was not the case. Although over the season a number of players were signed they were not, generally speaking, of the required quality and this coupled with injuries, resulted in mediocre performances, poor results and falling gates.

First stones laid

The biggest factor influencing the Southern League in 1978/79 was the suspension of promotion for the season in order to facilitate the introduction of the Alliance Premier League which was to become what we now know as the Nationwide Conference. This was to comprise the leading clubs in the Southern League and the Northern Premier League with the remaining clubs in those leagues reorganised into new geographical divisions depending upon their final placing in the tables.

The suspension of promotion in the Southern Division of the Southern League however, brought apathy and Salisbury were one of the chief sufferers. A final position of 15th in a table of 21 says it all and, in addition, there was little to enthuse about in the major cups. Bath City knocked the Whites out of the F.A. Cup after Welton Rovers had been beaten and Taunton prevented further progress in the Trophy after wins in three rounds.

Derek Sharpe

Promotion for local stalwart

One hopeful sign was the appointment of Ray Long as commercial manager. His brief was to raise funds principally through a fortnightly lottery to give the manager the means of signing better players in the seasons to come. Also secretary Derek Sharpe's appointment to the Southern League management committee meant that the club now had a voice in the corridors of power.

The 1979–80 Season — David Thear

Manager
Dave Lennard

The season opened with a new manager in charge. Mike Hughes had left to join Taunton and Dave Lennard, a former Bolton, Blackpool and Bournemouth midfielder with 550 league and Cup appearances to his credit, took over.

It was to be a season of extreme contrasts. The final league position was second to bottom despite regular changes in personnel including the re-signing, towards the end of the season, of former favourites Alan Green, Colin Guy and Bobby Andrews. There was no indication in the first half of the season of the dismal outcome, and indeed at 24th November the Whites were in mid-table with 14 points from 13 games. In fact, on that very day the club and its supporters were enjoying one of the highlights of its existence.

F.A. Cup 3rd Qualifying Round.   F.A. Cup 4th Qualifying Round.

Paul Christopher (out of picture) makes it 3-0 for Salisbury as his shot beats the desperate dive of Peter Manuel the Poole Town goalkeeper.

Jim Cumbes the Worcester 'keeper, is beaten by Paul Christopher's second and winning goal. Worcester players look on in despair as the Whites celebrate.

The 'Lions are out of The Den'

In the F.A. Cup Salisbury had beaten Newport I.O.W., Horsham YMCA, Poole Town and Worcester in the Qualifying Rounds with a crowd of over 1500 at Victoria Park for the Worcester match.

Reserves played on!

This brought a 1st Round F.A. Cup tie against Millwall which was played at the Dell, Southampton, in front of nearly 9000 people. It was a 'home' tie for Salisbury but the police, probably correctly, could not guarantee crowd safety and the advantage of playing at Victoria Park was lost. The city itself was consumed with Cup fever and it was estimated that 5000 travelled by car, train and bus to support the Whites. The Salisbury and District Football League postponed all matches that day to allow maximum attendance although the Wiltshire League still expected the reserves to fulfil their fixture at Bromham.

Les Whitmarsh the Chairman of Salisbury gave a message to all supporters in the souvenir programme that stated:

> As chairman of Salisbury Football Club, may I extend a warm welcome to all of you who have come to watch this afternoon's historic match at The Dell.
>
> Of course it is disappointing that we were unable to stage the game ourselves at Victoria Park, but Southampton F.C. have done everything they

could to make us feel at home and I would like to express my sincere and heartfelt thanks to Lawrie McMenemy and his board of directors.

A big thank you, too, to our own secretary Derek Sharp and to the members of the management committee for all their hard work in preparing for today.

I would also like to take the opportunity to congratulate our manager Dave Lennard and all the players on their magnificent achievement in reaching this stage of the competition. Whatever the result today, I am sure the game will be remembered by our club and supporters for the rest of their lives.

Everywhere you looked, information was on hand to keep the fans thirst for information satisfied. Jon Hancock (who at the time was the Salisbury Times & Salisbury Journal soccer writer) interviewed the Millwall manger, George Petchey and a sample of some of the questions he put to him follows:

JH: *What were your first reactions to the cup draw?*

GP: *No great surprise, really. At this stage of the competition you are almost bound to meet a typical non-league side like Salisbury.*

JH: *So how much did you know already about your opponents?*

GP: *They were almost a complete unknown to me, and the longer you spend in the Football League, the more you realise that an unknown quantity is more frightening than a known one.*

JH: *Did you make immediate plans to watch Salisbury?*

GP: *Not personally, although I have obviously ordered reports on them. Funnily enough, the last time Millwall looked at Salisbury was two years ago when we were checking on your striker Alan Green.*

JH: *Finally, the inevitable question. Will you be disappointed if you fail to finish the job at the first attempt this afternoon?*

GP: *There's no way we are going to take this game lightly. As far as I am concerned it's a tough match and if we take Salisbury back to The Den for a replay I will be just as happy as if we beat them well today.*

Pen Pictures of the Whites and the Lions teams:

Salisbury:

Dave Lennard (34) – midfield: Fully qualified F.A. coach who took over as player manager this summer after a distinguished professional career spanning 550 league and Cup games over 17 years at all levels. Past clubs: Bolton, Blackpool, Halifax (where he played alongside Dave Verity) and A.F.C. Bournemouth. Fitness fanatic Dave divides his time between management and a teacher training course.

Dave Verity (30) – midfield: Club captain a former Halifax, Yeovil player. Dave recently shrugged off a long bout of Achilles tendon trouble to re-establish himself in the side. A butcher by trade.

Bob Wiltshire (26) – goalkeeper: Bob measures up at 6ft 4ins as the tallest goalkeeper in the Southern League. Now in his third season after signing from Trowbridge Town. Had trials at Malcolm Allison's Man. City. Customs officer.

Salisbury F.C. 1979–80

Mike Hibbs (22) – utility: Versatile performer who joined the club last month from Amesbury. A Wiltshire county player, he has spent most of his career in central defence or midfield, but his impressive record of 57 goals in fewer than 200 games for his former club has prompted Salisbury to try him in attack. A charge-hand in the NAAFI.

Ken Hallam (28) – centre-back: In his second season with Salisbury, having gained league experience with W.B.A., Notts Co., Sheffield Unt. and Torquay before moving to Worcester, Bath and Trowbridge. Sales rep.

Dave Lock (29) – centre-back: Longest serving player on the clubs books. Left Salisbury for Winchester after his testimonial but rejoined to play whenever his duties as a fireman permit.

Brian Ashton (22) – striker: Talented forward of great potential who was spotted playing Western League soccer for Westlands (Yeovil). Signed last season and obliged with a string of brilliant goals to finish top scorer. Mushroom farmer.

Paul Christopher (25) – midfield or attack: Buccaneering, attacking linkman who arrived at Salisbury via Bournemouth and Mansfield and whose loyalty over five years has been rewarded with a testimonial. Top goal scorer so far this year with six goals, including the two that beat Worcester City in final qualifying round. Civil servant.

Steve Cox (24) – striker: Former Andover and Basingstoke player signed during the close season. Has recently been converted to a target man with considerable success. Telephone engineer.

Tim Coak (22) – left-back: Diminutive but tigerish former Southampton player. Instant hit when signed earlier this year. Signed apprentice professional forms at the Dell in 1974 and was a regular reserve team member. Works with P.&O. shipping.

Roger Fry (31) – midfield: Played 30 matches at full-back for Southampton during their last First Division spell before moving onto Walsall where he made 150 league appearances. Has established himself at Salisbury as a stylish left-side midfielder and an expert from the penalty spot. Welder with Vosper Thorneycroft.

Millwall:

John Jackson (37): John signed as a professional in 1962 and made his league debut two years later. Ever present member at Orient who he joined in 1973. Signed for Millwall this season.

Mel Blyth (33): Won a Cup Winners medal with Southampton. Started his career at Scunthorpe before joining Crystal Palace. Joined Millwall from Margate F.C. in 1978.

Dave Donaldson (25): Signed from Arsenal F.C. in 1973. Made his debut for Millwall at the age of 18. A former English Schoolboy International whose total appearances now total over 230.

David Gregory (19): Joined Millwall in June 1978. Before leaving school achieved a remarkable total of 16 'O' Level Passes. In first season with club he played 23 games.

Tony Tagg (22): Joined QPR as an apprentice in 1972, made four 1st Division appearances during the 1976/77 season. Signed for Millwall in July 1977.

Nicky Chatterton (25): Joined Millwall from Crystal Palace who he joined on leaving school playing in their youth squad and gaining a place in the F.A. Youth Team. Became a permanent member of the Palace first team which won a place in the 2nd Division.

David Mehmet (18): Joined Millwall straight from school. Became a full professional on his 17th birthday. Selected for England Youth v Norway in 1978.

John Seasman (24): Started his career at Tranmere Rovers before joining Luton Town for a transfer fee of £14,000. Joined Millwall in 1975 for a £10,000 fee, he has made over 150 scoring 40 goals.

Tony Towner (24): Joined Millwall from Brighton in 1978. Has over 175 league appearances and 25 goals to his credit, the vast majority with his previous club.

John Lyons (22): Signed from Wrexham for £50,000. Under 18 Welsh international making his debut in the under 21 squad against Scotland. Played in the European Cup Winners Cup for his former club Wrexham.

John Mitchell (27): Signed from Fulham for a club record fee of £90,000, where he made over 150 appearances scoring 64 goals. Played in the 1975 F.A. Cup Final at Wembley.

Local lad scores at The Dell

Mike Hibbs, beats John Jackson the Millwall 'keeper to score Salisbury's only goal.

The Football Echo reported that the first-half was mostly Millwall's with winger Mitchell scoring after 15 minutes. There was a considerable gap in class between the two teams but Salisbury had chances with Christopher being particularly effective. It was a little against the run of play when Donaldson scored the second just before half-time with a speculative 25 yard shot which slipped through Wiltshire's hands. The second half started in sensational fashion when, after just 30 seconds, Mike Hibbs, Salisbury's former Amesbury centre-forward scored from 12 yards, after good work by Lennard and Christopher. City supporters were now in full voice willing Salisbury to score a second goal but unfortunately the scoring

Mike Hibbs makes his presence felt in the Millwall defence.

F.A. Cup Results 24/11/79

Salisbury	1	Millwall	2	Swindon Town	4	Brentford	1
Enfield Town	0	Yeovil Town	1	Wealdstone	0	Southend	1
Fareham Town	2	Merthyr Tydfil	3	Minehead	1	Chesham Utd	2

ended there. The Cup run was over for another year. They had played with great enthusiasm but the result was fair.

The decision to transfer the match to the Dell was vindicated when, before the game, Millwall fans rampaged through Southampton city centre, before attacking Saints supporters in the Warren pub resulting in injuries. By mid-afternoon, six people had been treated in hospital and more were expected.

Salisbury fans were naturally buoyed up by the occasion and the spirit with which the team had played. They had every reason to think that the enthusiasm would be translated to league matches. Nothing could have been further from the truth. The rest of the season was a disaster with only a brief flurry of good results at the end to keep the side in touch with Basingstoke in 22nd place.

The F.A. Trophy failed to provide any relief either with Oxford City winning 1-0 in the 2nd Qualifying Round. One cheerful outcome of the season was Ray Long's continuing success with his fund raising.

MEMORY LANE

I (and many others) ran onto the pitch
Salisbury v Worcester City 3rd November 1979

As always excitement and expectations were high for both teams at this stage of the F.A. Cup, as todays winners would be going into 'the hat' for that all-important 1st Round Proper. The official attendance for the match was 1512 but it looked more like 2000 to me.

We took to the field as underdogs but from the kick-off and throughout it never showed. Dave Lennard, Salisbury's player-manager was first to get into goal-mouth action with a rasping drive, quickly followed by my favourite Salisbury player Paul Christopher whose 20-yard shot on goal warmed Jim Cumbes the Worcester goalkeeper's hands. Just as we were thinking that Salisbury were bound to score, their right-back Graham Selby put over a inch-perfect pass and Kenny Lawrence headed a great goal. I can't say that the ground fell silent as Worcester seemed to have as much support as us. They now took control with Salisbury seemingly unable to get to the ball. Malcom Phelps had the ball in our net again, but thankfully for us it was ruled off-side. Now with the opposition completely in command they so nearly scored a second goal, which surely would have done for Salisbury. We had our goal-keeper Bob Wiltshire to thank as his acrobatic save from Norman Pembroke stopped him from scoring just before half-time.

In the second-half I left my usual spot on the terraces, firstly because my usual friends were getting despondent and secondly I thought if I went and stood behind the Worcester goal Salisbury might score. Ten minutes gone saw Dave Verity unleash a tremendous volley from 25-yds. Then Cumbes had to hurl himself full-length to keep out another goal-bound cracker from Paul Christopher. Brian Ashton slumped to the floor after his shot on goal from only eight yards grazed the bar, when it seemed easier to score than miss. Battling through their defence the same player had his next shot charged down, but Paul Christopher coolly slotted in the rebound, angling in a low drive to the far

corner of the net. Now the Worcester contingent fell silent and tempers were starting to fray. I for one had no nails left. A second Worcester player was booked for an off-the-ball incident which allowed the referee to play a bit of injury time and in the 94-min. an astute pass from Salisbury's skipper saw Christopher cut inside and slide the ball past Cumbes from the tightest of angles. Who cares, I and hundreds of others ran onto that sacred turf. Marvellous feeling!

Peter D. Wood

The 1980–81 Season — David Thear

Manager
Dave Verity

If 1979/80 was bad, worse was to follow in 1980/81. The final league position was 20th out of 24 and the F.A. Cup run which did much to boost interest the previous year, was three days. A draw at home to Trowbridge resulted in a 2-1 replay defeat. F.A. Trophy interest lasted for five matches until a visit to Bridgend in the 3rd Qualifying Round brought a 2-0 defeat. The league season had started promisingly with wins over Dover and Andover in August and Margate in September. Other than these, results were disappointing to put it mildly and in January the management committee lost patience with Dave Lennard. He was replaced by Dave Verity and for a while there was some improvement but it didn't last and the end of the season was greeted with relief.

The only cause for optimism was the average crowds for matches at Victoria Park. The figure was almost 300 which took the club near the top of the attendance table and seemed to indicate that, if the team were successful, there was encouraging potential for the future. The big question was 'How do you provide a successful side?' and would 1981/82 be the occasion?

The 1981–82 Season — David Thear

The short answer was 'No'!! but once again the season's efforts were governed by yet another re-organisation of the Southern League. This time a Premier division was to be formed from the 10 top teams in the existing Midland and Southern Divisions. The task was consequently very clear. Salisbury had to be in the first ten places to be promoted.

Dave Verity, therefore, assembled a 16-man squad with the intention of providing depth of cover to cater for any injuries or suspensions which the season might bring.

Formidable signing obtained

Ted MacDougall

Principal signing were Ted MacDougall, a scorer of over 250 league goals with Manchester United, West Ham,

Southampton, Norwich and Bournemouth, Steve and Ricky Haysom (£1750) from Andover, Ken Thompson (£1000) from Poole, Sean Harvey from Melksham, Colin Tavener, Mike Harrison from Bath, Peter Tindall from Yeovil and Barry Andrews (£750) from Basingstoke.

Ted MacDougall only played five games but scored four times. He eventually returned to Southern League football with Poole. Crowd favourite Alan Green departed for Andover for £875.

The most significant new face was, however, that of Ray McEnhill a local millionaire, who took over as Chairman of the club. More will be heard of him as our narrative unfolds.

Turning to the playing side, the team was bedevilled by injuries and bad weather. At Christmas only three players, Ian Thompson, Colin Tavener and Mike Harrison had avoided injuries and consequently the mid-table league position with 19 points from 20 games was not a bad effort. Unfortunately the Whites were defeated in the opening rounds of both the F.A. Cup and Trophy.

Ray McEnhill

In the F.A. Cup, Wealdstone who included Stuart Pearce, the soon to become England International in their line-up, won 4-0 and followed this up one week later with a 4-1 win in the league.

No Premier for Salisbury next season

By late February the Whites had achieved only three wins in the last 21 games and were well off the target of a top ten finish. Some improvement occurred as injured players returned but by the end of the season they were still seven places away from Premier Division qualification. Nonetheless, Manager Verity's retained list included most of last season's squad and word within the game was that Salisbury would be one of favourites for promotion next year.

A familiar but sad item of news was the decision for financial reasons, to dispense with the reserve side. There had been regular problems in fielding a team in the Wiltshire League and for one match at Sanford, committee man John Topp, Cyril Smith and assistant secretary Alan Hunt had to turn out.

As a little light relief older readers are asked to recall the memorable rugby match at Twickenham, when one Erica Rowe achieved national fame, having displayed, for one and all to see, her two most outstanding attributes! In January 1982, she was at Dean Court to present the 'Cherries' 200 club draw prize, when Bournemouth were playing Southampton in a friendly. The referee was *Mr Cliff Topliss* ! ! !

The 1982–83 Season — Peter J. Waterhouse

A completely new ball game

Salisbury faced the new season with one of the worst injury lists in the club's history. This was particularly unfortunate because this season relegation would become automatic for the teams in the bottom spots whereas previously there would have been a re-election process. A reasonable season was, therefore, essential. For all sides there was the attraction of a competition offering genuine promotion and relegation incentives.

The financial position

It was reported that the the Whites made a loss of more than £9100 on the 1981/82 season as the recession in both the national economy and their own playing fortunes hit them at the bank. The deficit – nearly double the loss on the previous season – was suffered even though costs were pruned by more than £3000 to £48,602. Revenue slumped from £46,862 to £39,479 with a sharp fall-off in proceeds from the lottery which was the dominant factor in the club's finances. Commercial Manager Ray Long revealed that profits were down nearly £8000 to £19,276. The lottery was the club's lifeline, with only the £18,000 proceeds from the one-off sale of the property in Albany Road rivalling its earning power.

Gate receipts slumped by 20% to just over £4000, although the club managed to cut back its wage bill.

The 1982/83 campaign commenced on Saturday 21st August at Victoria Park. The result was a 2-0 defeat by Woodford Town followed by another 1-0 defeat at Hillingdon Borough the

First goal in the net in the 2-0 win over arch rivals Andover Town. *photo: Paul Dible*

following Saturday. About 150 supporters witnessed the first
league victory of the season with a 5-1 win at home on the 25th
September to end Ashford's unbeaten league record. After a 2-2
draw at Dover the team occupied 3rd from bottom place in the
league with four points. October 17th saw them move up to 11th
in the league with a morale boasting 3-1 away victory at Ashford
Town and then, with a convincing 2-1 home win against Erith &
Belvedere, they leaped up the table to fourth place. A 1-1 draw at
Hounslow followed.

The 11-week unbeaten league run ended in a disappointing
defeat at Fisher Athletic which came hard on the heels of an
unfortunate 4-2 Southern League Cup exit at Waterlooville.
Salisbury's defeat at Fisher sent the club five places down the
league to mid-table anonymity.

Meanwhile, a few miles away, Saints' loyal player Nick Holmes
was enjoying a well-earned testimonial year at the Dell. Peter
Chubb was the Saints supporters local Chairman at that time
arranging the event detailed above. Peter was later to become
Mayor of Salisbury and now, in retirement, can be found helping
out behind the scenes at the Raymac.

Once again the Whites moved up to third position in the league
by hitting Thanet United for six at Victoria Park, but the season
started to nose dive with a 3-1 defeat away at Folkestone followed
by 1-0 home defeat to Houslow. The see-saw season continued as
they slipped from third to tenth position in the league.

'Improve or I'm off'

Disillusioned Salisbury manager, Dave Verity put his job on the
line when he told officials he would leave the club unless his side

showed a dramatic improvement . Over the Christmas holiday programme the black December continued with a 3-2 defeat at R.S. Southampton followed by a 4-1 defeat in the return game at Victoria Park on New Year's Day.

Dave Verity, true to his word, resigned. Derek Sharp, the Secretary, said 'Dave worked particularly hard for the club and we are deeply sorry to see him go'.

Meanwhile dependable clubman Cyril Smith took charge of team affairs on a caretaker basis. Struggling Salisbury were rocked by a second resignation within days of the manager's resigning. Club trainer, Barry Fitch quit. As a player he made a record 713 appearances. In all probability the 38 year old left the club in disappointment at being overlooked for the caretaker manager's job. The previous season he had taken over on the trainer's bench as Dave Verity's right-hand man.

Cyril Smith's first game in charge ended in a 4-0 defeat at Canterbury. The Whites then gave their supporters hope when they defeated Tonbridge A.F.C. 3-2 at Victoria Park followed by 1-1 draw at home to Dover. In the next game they came from behind twice to defeat Cambridge City away 3-2. They had taken seven points from nine under Cyril Smith.

It was announced on 14th February 1983 that the club had appointed their ninth manager in 14 years, Geoff Butler.

Manager
Geoff Butler

ALPHA
The beginning of the 'Geoff Butler Era'

Geoff Butler arrived at Salisbury Football Club in February 1983, with a 'curriculum vitae' that many league managers would be proud to possess.

He was born in Middlesbrough on 26th September 1946 and signed professional forms for them in May 1964. As a left-back his promise and skills developed in the club's junior and reserve sides under the watchful eye of manager Raich Carter.

The 'Real Stuff'

The 1965/66 season saw him break into the Middlesbrough first team and, the following season, he played 41 games which saw Middlesbrough gain promotion to Division II. The 1967/68 season proved to be the last that he would play for his local club. In the second round win in the League Cup over Chelsea, their Manager, Tommy Docherty was so impressed by his performance that he paid £57,000 to acquire him.

In his career at Middlesbrough he made 55 appearances. Just days before his 21st birthday he made his debut for Chelsea in a 3-0 defeat at Nottingham Forest. Seven days later he made his home debut against Coventry City. Alas, Geoff proved to be Tommy Docherty's last signing for Chelsea; he was replaced by Dave Sexton who started the task of rebuilding the team with experienced players. Geoff took the opportunity to return to his native north-east when Sunderland paid £65,000 for him. Unfortunately, the Sunderland manager, Ian McCall, who signed him was replaced by Alan Brown, resulting in him making only a few first team appearances. He then embarked on an illustrious career with Norwich City who had come in with a £28,000 offer. His time there saw him make 196 appearances over seven years.

Under the management of Ron Saunders, the Canaries occupied the top perch and when they were defeated by Tottenham Hotspur in the final of the League Cup at Wembley, Geoff won a runners-up medal. In 1976 he headed south to Dean Court, Bournemouth. March 1976 to the 1980/81 season saw him make 119 appearances for the Cherries also becoming the club's reserve team manager leading them to the Western League Division I Championship. The 1981/82 season saw him joining Peterborough United as first-team coach and making 30 appearances for the club.

Is this 'IT' for Salisbury F.C.

Would Geoff Butler's considerable football experience transform the fortunes of Salisbury Football Club and awake one of the 'sleeping giants' of non-league football, to win the hearts of the Salisbury faithful and bring back the glory days of the past?

The team welcomed the new manager with 90 minutes of total commitment to take a richly deserved point off promotion hopefuls Dunstable, followed by a 1-0 victory away to Thanet.

The next scalp was against the league leaders Fisher Athletic at Victoria Park, with a 3-1 win. The Fisher boss stated, after the game, that Salisbury were far superior and probably the best team they had played all season. Geoff Butler said he was aiming for a

Ian Thompson's penalty against Basingstoke.

top-six position in the league and, after the 3-1 home victory over Canterbury, the Whites moved to 9th position. His first defeat as manager was away to Tonbridge.

Salisbury entered the Easter programme with a 0-0 draw at Andover on Good Friday. In the return match at Victoria Park, they beat their old rivals 2-0. A string of encouraging results followed, starting with a home draw against Crawley Town, another draw away to Woodford Town, two home wins against Hillingdon Boro. and Cambridge City, backed by a draw away at Erith & Belvedere. Salisbury's glittering spell saw them holding second placed Folkestone to a 3-3 draw at Victoria Park in the last game of the season, a game in which Geoff Butler's target of sixth position was achieved.

In May Salisbury striker Ian Thompson was about to be transferred to Manchester City but this fell through when they had a managerial change. Bournemouth & Boscombe then offered £18,000 and he was transferred to them to begin a full-time career in the league.

The 1983–84 Season — Richard J.A. Walker

Geoff Butler was to start his first full season and Nev Beal, a leading light in the resurrection of Salisbury City some 20 years

later joined in the summer, as a player, from Bemerton. He scored the first goal of the season in the home defeat by Gosport in the Southern League Cup.

Salisbury entered the F.A. Cup at the preliminary round stage with a home game against Flackwell

Nev Beal at the age of 21.

Heath; a 93rd minute penalty saw Salisbury make progress in a very poor game.

Absolute disaster was to follow in the next round with a totally unacceptable defeat away at Hampshire League Sholing Sports by 2-1.

F.A. Cup Results 17/9/83

Sholing Sports	2	Salisbury	1
Romsey Town	0	Gosport Borough	2
Bath City	4	Shepton Mallet Town	0
Dorchester Town	0	Eastleigh	0

In the meantime the club announced a record loss of £18,000 for the previous season. The F.A. Trophy saw a win over Maesteg Park after a replay; Nev Beal scored two with the opener coming in 43 seconds. In the league fixtures the club was embarking on an eight match unbeaten run when they were beaten at Canterbury. The day was more than a disaster on the pitch, when the dressing room was broken into and a number of players had their wallets stolen. Further progress in the F.A. Trophy came at the expense of Western League, Weston-super-Mare who were dispatched 4-2 at Victoria Park. Salisbury had now found some form and Premier League Gloucester City needed two replays before the Whites were beaten.

Nev Beal (pictured) scored two goals and Tommy Paterson one, in the Trophy replay at home versus Maesteg Park.

Where are they now?

Inevitably, league fixtures seemed a bit drab after exits from both major cup competitions and gates at Victoria Park suffered although the team kept on the fringes of the promotion race. A good win at the start of 1984 against Peter Price's Road Sea helped the cause and the 1-0 win was the visitor's first league defeat of the season. Local interest in the match was enhanced by players such as Bennett, Blochel, Dawtry and Earls who appeared for the visitors. They all had strong connections with Southampton.

Salisbury were now three points behind the leaders. Hopes of winning the league receded when they lost at Crawley on 17 January. The attendance at Town Mead was only 254, which proved it was not just Salisbury who were suffering low gates. The team stuttered along without finding any real form. Points were dropped where they were expected to be won. Goals were hard to come by but this appeared to be the same for all teams as defences were taking control of the games. March saw Salisbury in the top third of the league but thoughts of promotion faded quickly. Road Sea Southampton were striding towards the championship although they had a particularly unnerving experience on a trip to Ashford when their coach window exploded. They were able to continue after their driver recovered his composure although he was temporarily disorientated by the incident. They won the match 2-1.

Road Sea were finally to lead the table at the beginning of April when they caught up with their fixtures. They went on to beat Salisbury in the return fixture at Marchwood, winning 1-0 with a Dean Mooney goal in the 88th minute. The crowd was all of 252!

It was during March that Salisbury lost the services of their secretary Derek Sharp who was admitted to hospital with a heart attack from which happily he made a full recovery.

April also saw Geoff Butler extend his duties to take over from Ray Long as Commerical Manager, alongside his existing duties as Team Manager. Ray Long moved to Road Sea as their first Commercial Manger.

The finish of the season was an anti-climax. A tenth away defeat at Chatham in the last game condemned Salisbury to another ordinary season and they finished in ninth place. Once again the away record proved very disappointing and was principally responsible for their poor position. In preparing for the following year, Geoff Butler released Battams and Frost.

The 1984–85 Season — Peter J. Waterhouse

This was the season which, at times, looked very promising but was marred by unexpected defeats against lower placed opposition.

The season opened at Victoria Park with a win against Canterbury City. The first away league game saw a 2-1 reverse at

A visit to Andover's now defunct Walled Meadow ground on the 1st April 1985 resulted in a 2-0 defeat for the Whites. This picture shows how the two clubs easily swopped players. Andover in stripes (all ex-Salisbury), *l/right:* no. 9 – Jack Howarth, no. 10 – Pete Chisholm and with the ball Barry Andrews. Salisbury, *left/right:* Lee Frost, Ian Thompson and Bob Diaper.   *Photo by Paul Dible*

Dorchester in front of only 92 spectators. The Whites picked up their first away point of the season at Thanet on September 8th with Dawtry scoring. The next away game was to result in a 3-1 defeat at Poole whereupon they were 15th in the league.

A dramatic transformation then followed with six consecutive wins scoring 14 goals against five. This exciting run of good results propelled the club to fourth position in the league and optimistic supporters were even discussing promotion! Geoff Butler promptly scotched the idea saying 'The word promotion is pie in the sky, we are just taking each game as it comes'.

This prophetic comment was soon vindicated when Sheppey United, who had been beaten in eight of their first twelve games, won at the Park and this was followed by a defeat at Andover.

Same match as above. From a Salisbury corner, Ricky Haysom heads for goal in a crowded Andover goalmouth.   *Photo by Paul Dible*

After Christmas the league programme was badly affected by severe winter weather leading to cash flow problems.

The Supporter's Club eased these difficulties and the following report appeared in the Salisbury Journal on 28th January 1985.

Supporters Club Chairman, John Harvey, presented a cheque for £1000 to the Salisbury vice-Chairman Ivan Crockett, who said: 'We are extremely grateful for such a handsome donation. The timing is perfect after the frozen spell and the money will certainly ease our cash flow problems.'

John Harvey

Despite the re-arranged programme the Whites remained in contention for promotion and Easter saw a draw at Cambridge City and a win at home to Thanet. On April 14th they were 4th in the league, vying with Hillingdon Borough and Thanet, but with no chance of overtaking leaders Basingstoke.

Runners-up give Salisbury a thrashing

In the run-in Salisbury lost at home to old rivals Andover Town 2-1, followed by a 2-1 away win at Ashford. However, bottom of the table club Erith & Belvedere held them to a 2-2 draw at Victoria Park and the sky blues from Tonbridge ended the promotion dreams at Victoria Park returning home 3-0 victors. Gosport inflicted Salisbury's biggest league defeat of the season 5-0 and this clinched their promotion to the Southern League Premier Division.

Only 111 spectators were at Victoria Park to witness the Whites go down 3-1 to Woodford. This was the lowest ever home league gate in their 17 year Southern League history.

Unfortunately, throughout the season Salisbury lacked the financial resources to boast a strong squad. At full-strength they were a match for any side in the league, bar perhaps, the champions, Basingstoke, but there was no strength in depth.

'Not a lot of people knew that'

An intriguing article was written by Dave Eidlestein of the Southern Evening Echo for inclusion in one of the 1984/85 programmes. It emerged that, since joining the Southern League in 1968 the club had played in all competitions getting on for 1000 matches. Those games, whether in league, Cup or friendlies, had

Salisbury losing 3-0 to eventual league champions Basingstoke Town at Victoria Park in 1984/85. Jack Howarth Salisbury's no. 9 sees this attempt punched clear by the Basingstoke goalkeeper with Paul Christopher in close attendance.
Photo by Paul Dible

been against at least 130 different teams. It further disclosed which opponents we had played most – not surprisingly the answer was our neighbours from Andover. The club had met 'the Lions' in one tournament or other no fewer than 47 times. Joint second on our most-often-seen opponents list came Poole Town and Trowbridge with 39 each, then Basingstoke 38 and finally Dorchester with 37.

F.A. Cup and F.A. Trophy sojourn

At Victoria Park Salisbury commenced the 1984/5 F.A. Cup

campaign on 1st September with a Preliminary Round win against Marlow Town. In the First Qualifying Round Newport I.O.W. were beaten to set up another home tie, this time against Hungerford Town.

Unfortunately for Salisbury, Hungerford held them to a 0-0 draw at Victoria Park and, at Hungerford, won 3-0 in an almost full ground to end the Whites F.A. Cup dreams for another season.

F.A. Cup Results 29/9/84

Salisbury	0	Hungerford Town	0	*Replay* Hungerford Town	3	Salisbury	0
Totton	1	Fareham Town	1	Chippenham Town	2	Road Sea	2
				Wimborne Town	1	Frome Town	3

F.A. Trophy

Salisbury drew Weston-super-Mare away in the First Qualifying Round of the F.A. Trophy on 15th October and came away with a 1-1 draw, thanks to a Cranmer goal. In the replay at Victoria Park they ran out 3-0 winners, with goals from Paterson, Slade and an own goal. Salisbury then beat Taunton Town 7-0 in the Second Qualifying Round at Victoria Park but this triumph was soon forgotten whey then suffered the humiliation of a 7-1 defeat at the hands of Frome Town, at Badgers' Hill.

The club and it supporters were saddened by the death of Ron Lemon in October 1984. A stalwart of the Supporters Club from its inauguration in 1947 he had served with distinction as Secretary for many years.

Ron Lemon

The 1985–86 Season — Peter J. Waterhouse

Ambitious plans for Salisbury F.C.

This was the season when ambitious plans for a £1 million sports and leisure complex development at Victoria Park were presented to a working party of councillors. The enterprising proposals were at the instigation of Salisbury F.C., the principal users of Victoria Park, which they rented from the District Council.

The inventive scheme involved the construction of a three-storey complex, providing facilities for the Football Club and the Supporters Club. It was planned that the building would cover the area occupied by the children's play space and the football grandstand would include a restaurant, coffee bar and lounge bar, together with sunbeds, massage, sauna and jacuzzi facilities. Additionally it was envisaged that it could incorporate a roller skating rink, which could also be used for indoor tennis and badminton and a new jogging track around the football pitch.

The scheme also included:

- Improved facilities for the disabled.
- New Tennis Court facilities.
- Exhibition and Conference facilities.
- Better car-parking facilities.
- A keep-fit gymnasium.

Drama was to unfold when the club's plans were scotched. A well organised resident's group had opposed the proposals and, despite the club's counter campaign, the Charity Commissioners advocated in their favour quoting an existing by-law which prevented commerical use of the Victoria Park.

Two 'wide boys' joined the club

Peter Johnson

It appeared that the 1985/86 team had all the components to launch a serious promotion challenge. In a strategy to score more goals that season, Geoff Butler adopted a 4-2-4 formation with new signings, Pat Russell and Peter Johnson playing wide. In the line-up were Mark Barber and Tommy Paterson the front runners. Geoff Butler stated 'The flexible system is 4-2-4 when we're going forward'. He went on to say, 'goals ultimately cost the side promotion to the Premier League last season (1984/85). Then again if we are to go up this time, we must tighten up at the back and it helps considerably to have four men in midfield on occasions to prevent other sides developing attacks.'

The new attacking system proved an instant success when the Whites defeated Ruislip 5-1 at Victoria Park on the opening day of the season. Mark Barber, making his debut for the club, crashed in the first goal in only four minutes. The first set-back occurred when he arrived at the club on the following Monday on crutches and with his leg encased in plaster. The injury resulted in him undergoing a cartilage operation, which kept him out of action for some weeks.

Salisbury's first away game of the season was against Erith & Belvedere. They came away with a point in a 0-0 draw; Dave Hookway, the 'keeper, proved to be the hero by saving a well placed penalty shot from Erith's David Beagley. It only took 60 seconds to open the score against Corinthians at Victoria Park on the 14th October.

The first league defeat was suffered at Sheppey United but the team bounced back when Tommy Paterson scored in just 20 seconds in the 4-0 victory over Thanet.

Unfortunately Pat Russell's stay at Salisbury was very brief when he decided to join Weymouth. Another disappointment was the low gates of under 200 despite some very entertaining football.

On the 9th November the team were in third place in the league. They consolidated their position with a fine away victory at Dover 3-2. Then Waterloville were entertained in a league match at Victoria Park on a Sunday in front of 433 spectators. This was more than double the average home gate and the icing on the cake was that they conquered their opponents 2-0.

They missed a golden opportunity to lead the table when they lost 5-3 at Hastings despite a hat-trick from Peter Johnson, his first for the team. Four goals were conceded in the final 14 minutes! Salisbury lost their 100% home league record when Trowbridge Town held them to a 2-2 draw on Boxing Day. Geoff Butler expressed his dissatisfaction with no fewer than five members of the team for producing sub-standard performances!! They slipped to fifth position when Cambridge City secured maximum points at Victoria Park and although Chatham Town were defeated 2-1 at home, their flagging promotion hopes took a nose dive when they went down 2-0 away to Burnham & Hillingdon on Saturday 25th January. The Whites were definitely not firing on all cylinders.

Barry Cranmer scores Salisbury's first goal in the 2-0 win over Waterloville, Tommy Patterson added the second.

When the 'north wind doth blow'

Salisbury took maximum points from Sheppey United at Victoria Park on 1st February with only 139 spectators to witness a game played in inclement weather. The club then had a five week lay-off from competitive action until the 8th March when they won 2-0 against Burnham at Victoria Park. With manager Butler's sedulous planning and, maybe, a degree of dressing-room cajolery, the club then achieved a sequence of outstanding results which included excellent outcomes away to Waterlooville and Chatham Town. After the Chatham victory they were steeling themselves for three matches in four days over Easter.

In a disappointing match at Victoria Park on Good Friday, Andover Town held the Whites to a 1-1 draw. The following day, at home again, Hastings led 2-0, but Salisbury fought back to take a 3-2 lead only to concede another goal, to finish 3-3. The Easter programme was concluded with a fine win away at Dorchester 2-0.

The big push?

With draws away at Cambridge City, Canterbury City and a home draw with Erith & Belvedere, Salisbury faced the daunting task of winning six of the remaining seven matches and drawing one to be assured of promotion. They took maximum points from promotion rivals Dunstable at Victoria Park after a hat-trick of away wins at Ashford Town, Ruislip and Thanet.

Salisbury then faced two vital home games; this was not a time for the faint-hearted. An 11-minute purple patch in the first-half saw three goals from Kevin Dawtry (penalty), Ricky Haysom and Derek Courtney beat off the challenge of Woodford. With two superbly taken goals by Barry Cranmer and Grant Orchard, one in each half, Salisbury defeated Poole Town 2-0.

Off to an early start with Barry Cranmer

In the last game of the season Salisbury travelled to Woodford with the knowledge that promotion to the Premier Division was in their own hands. They had a dream start to the game with Barry Cranmer bundling in the ball from close range in the third minute.

They were virtually assured of promotion at 3.37 p.m. when Kevin Dawtry tucked away a penalty-kick; this was his sixth successful spot-kick in nine matches. Tommy Paterson netted the

Tommy Paterson who scored Salisbury's third goal at Woodford.

The 3-2 win at Woodford saw 'the Whites' win promotion to the Premier Division of the Southern League for the first time in the Club's history. Here they celebrate with their medals. *Left to right*: E. Lisle (assist. manager), T. Paterson, K. White partly hidden by G. Butler (manager), P. Russell, P. Johnson, M. Barber behind D. Hookway, S. Haysom, B. Cranmer, M. Bailey, R. Haysom, D. Courtney, D. Barnes hidden behind B. Chambers, B. Diaper. *Front row*: G. Orchard, K. Dawtry, S. Newark.

third goal. Although Woodford scored twice the Whites did not look in any danger throughout the match. This was the conclusion to a very successful season with the team finishing in the cherished promotion position after an electrifying sequence of exceptional results. The club could now bask in a glow of triumph.

Salisbury's F.A. Cup and F.A. Trophy excursions

Salisbury's F.A. Cup 1st Qualifying Round tie took place on September 7th at Cams Alders, Fareham, where missed chances cost them the game. The replay at Victoria Park saw Fareham Town inflict a 5-0 defeat on a hapless team to put a early end to their F.A. Cup hopes for the season.

F.A. Trophy

Salisbury marched on to the F.A. Trophy 2nd Preliminary Round by defeating Maesteg 4-1 at Victoria Park on the 5th October. The next round saw them 2-0 victors over Bideford Town. They then travelled to Methyr Tydfil to earn a creditable 1-1 draw and in the replay in front of a 372 gate at Victoria Park, goals from Kevin Dawtry and Tommy Paterson set up a First Round tie away to Worthing on the 21st December.

Unfortunately, they lost the game by the only goal to signal the end of their F.A. Trophy excursion.

The 1986–87 Season — Richard J.A. Walker

The second step on that long ladder

After their triumphant finish to the previous season it was difficult to judge how the club would be equipped for their first season at Premier Division level. Money, as usual, was in short supply and most of the previous years team were re-signed.

The first game was at home versus Fisher Athletic and the Whites were soundly beaten 5-1. Ian McGregor, a new centre-forward, scored their only goal in front of a crowd of 257 who clearly did not find prospects encouraging. Some comfort might be obtained later in the fact that the visitors won the Championship on the last day of the season.

Promise was shown by a young soldier, Matt Carmichael. It was his late goal that beat Bridgend Town on 13th September in the F.A. Cup. He was later to make over 70 appearances for Lincoln City in the league. At that date Salisbury had gained only two league points and were already three points away from relegation safety.

Things were going from bad to worse, Kevin Dawtry one of their best players and a regular goalscorer left to join Fareham Town and

McGregor was not available as he had joined the fire service. Tommy Paterson and Calvin Cranmer were suspended and the squad was now wafer thin. Geoff Butler said there was no shortage of players happy to join Salisbury but he was unable to afford their wages. The middle of October saw only two points from 10 games and by this time the club was out of the F.A. Cup and F.A. Trophy. The die was now cast: it was to be a long hard season.

F.A. Cup Results 27/9/86

Trowbridge Town 2	Salisbury 0	Wimborne Town 1	Chippenham T. 1
Forest Green 4	Dorchester Town 2	Devizes Town 0	R.S Southampton 2

The team that had won promotion and had been given a chance at the higher level started to show many changes; Chambers and Orchard had moved on and John Wilson had come in to partner Barry Cranmer in the centre of defence. The bottom of the table on 8th November looked thus:

	P	W	D	L	F	A	Pts
Dudley Town	11	3	6	2	12	23	11
Corby Town	12	2	4	6	12	19	10
Bedworth Town	11	2	3	6	16	20	9
Salisbury	**12**	**0**	**3**	**9**	**6**	**30**	**3**

This was the day the club finally won their first match beating King's Lynn at Victoria Park 5-2. The next game away to Crawley found Nev Beal and Barry Andrews missing through injury and illness and leading scorer Carmichael didn't arrive at the ground until 3.10 p.m. after being stuck on a train from London for an hour. Down 3-0 after 30 minutes the Whites battled back to 3-2 but precious points had escaped although there were definite signs of improvement.

Consistency was still lacking and Salisbury remained bottom of the table on 17th January 1987.

	P	W	D	L	F	A	Pts
Salisbury	**23**	**3**	**5**	**15**	**22**	**52**	**14**

'Goal-machine' returns

Signs were still not very encouraging but Ian Thompson had just rejoined having had to give up a full-time career with Bournemouth because of a pelvic injury. With 13 games to go Salisbury were 10

Geoff Butler welcomes back Ian Thompson after his return from Bournemouth AFC.

points away from safety but Thompson had scored three goals in his first four appearances. It now needed a miracle to ensure survival. They duly tried their best obtaining 25 points from the last 39 on offer to leave thoughts of what might have been if more time had been available. To drop back after one season in the top-flight was a massive disappointment but as Geoff Butler stated in his programme notes for the last match:

> It was obvious to everyone who watched our games that some of the players who started the season were not good enough. It was not their fault it was simply that at that time I could not afford the expense involved in bringing a better class of player to the club. Only when the 'Supporters Club' made available extra funds was I able to sign the likes of Ian Thompson, Barry Mundee, John Bailey, Dave Eddie and Dave Hookway.

Indeed, there had been many changes as is evidenced by the teams themselves. For the first match, the team was:

Hookway, Chambers, Diaper, Haysom, Cranmer B., Andrews, Dawtry, McGregor, Courtney, Orchard, Russell; *sub*. Cranmer, C.

The last match team consisted of:

Hookway, Cranmer B., Diaper, Bailey, Wilson, Mundee B., Newark, Thompson, Cranmer C., Mundee D., Andrews. *sub*. Carmichael.

Salisbury F.C. 1985-86

b/r; Barnes (trainer), Russell, French, Watson, Hookway, Cranmer B, Haysom, Barber, Diaper, Butler
f/r; Groves, Johnson, Cranmer C., Smith, Paterson, Dawtry, Orchard, Newark

5

Beazer Homes Southern

The 1987–88 Season — Richard J.A. Walker

The Passing of a Friend

Salisbury started life again in the Southern Division with a home game against Sheppey United. There were high hopes that it would be possible to mount a serious promotion challenge.

There were several newcomers in the team as Geoff Butler continued his rebuilding programme. Paul Bennett arrived from Road Sea and played in the centre of defence alongside Barry

David
Fretwell

Cranmer. David Fretwell arrived at right wingback and Ian McGregor returned in attack.

Arriving on loan from Brighton was their third choice 'keeper Barry Wood. He had an outstanding season until recalled. City fans were to follow his later career with Port Vale and in the Irish League.

Ian
McGregor

On a sad note, Supporters Club Treasurer, Fred Trowbridge, passed away before the season started. He had put in over 30 years service during which time many thousands of pounds were raised in support of the club. There was a minute's silence at the first game of the season.

Salisbury sitting on a lofty perch

Initial league form was very good, four straight wins put the Whites at the top of the table on 12th September and this position was to be maintained throughout the autumn months.

Short stay in premier competition

There was disappointment in the preliminary round of the F.A. Cup when Barry Town, the Welsh League Champions won 1-0 at Victoria Park.

F.A. Cup Results 1/9/87

Salisbury	0	Barry Town	1
Torrington	3	Glastonbury	0
Gloucester City	7	Westbury Utd	0
Frome Town	1	Poole Town	0
Ottery St Mary	1	Chippenham Town	0

Promising league form was maintained. Salisbury were still four points ahead of the pack on 24th October with a record of:

P 8   W 7   D 1   L 0   F 20   A 5   Pts 22

but cup-ties again brought disappointment. In the F.A. Trophy, after a narrow win over Dorchester Town, Witney Town, who were proving something of a bogey side, won 2-1 at Victoria Park.

Keith Brooks   Sean Sanders   Chris Shaw

This game marked the debut of Chris Shaw, a diminutive but talented, left-sided midfield player. The side was further strengthened with the signing of Keith Brooks from Andover Town.

December saw the arrival of Sean Sanders for a small fee. He, too, came from Andover Town continuing the traffic of players between the clubs. He turned out to be a most loyal and versatile player who had an outstanding career with Salisbury. When Thanet United arrived for only the second ever Sunday fixture at Victoria Park on 13th December, Salisbury were still unbeaten at the top of the table, a draw keeping that record intact.

The first day of the New Year brought the first defeat of the league season when Salisbury succumbed at home to Waterlooville 3-2 in a pulsating match. This was to prove significant at the end of the season when the visitors were one of the two teams to gain promotion. At this stage the club were still in a very handy position with a record of

P 17   W 11   D 5   L 1   F 34   A 13   Pts 38

Matt Carmichael's Army posting meant he was unable to play further matches for Salisbury and he signed for Wycombe Wanderers.

Results take a tumble

It was at this time things started to go wrong with defeats at Dunstable and home to Erith & Belvedere. The club were still in the promotion frame but Dover Athletic had an unassailable lead, with Waterlooville and Gravesend coming up on the rails. By March, Salisbury had slipped to third place as the pace at the top continued to be unrelenting. Defeats by Dover and Waterlooville at home together with a couple of draws against mediocre opposition meant that the club could not quite achieve their ambition of an immediate return to the top flight. It had, however, been an excellent season and Salisbury could consider themselves unlucky. Never before had a team gone through a season with only five defeats and not obtained promotion. Such was the form of the promoted teams, however, that they played 80 games between them and only lost a total of five!

For Salisbury in all matches Dennee Mundee was top scorer with 22 and Calvin Cranmer had 11, although significant contributions were made in all departments. Most appearances were made by Ian Thompson with 48, Barry Cranmer with 47 and Paul Bennett with 46. Despite ultimate disappointment, fans had seen excellent

Ian Thompson

Dennee Mundee

football and much success provided by a team that was strong in most departments, particularly in goal, the centre of defence and in attack.

The 1988–89 Season — David Thear

Maybe this season!

Last season's very creditable third position in the league gave the Whites supporters every reason to be optimistic for 1988/89. There were new signings in Mark Wright, Mike Kilgour and Ian Harris, all from Trowbridge, Ian Chalk and Mark Shergold, while Dennee Mundee had moved to A.F.C. Bournemouth. The loss of Ian Thompson to Merthyr due to a move of job in January was a blow.

The Southern Division itself had been expanded by one bringing the number of clubs participating to 22. The newcomers were Chelmsford City, Trowbridge, Witney and Buckingham.

The league season opened with three wins against Thanet, Poole Town and Canterbury. These were immediately counter-balanced by three defeats, against Burnham, Bury Town and Hounslow. The team for the first home game against Poole Town was: Harris, Cranmer, C., Diaper, Kilgour, Cranmer B., Shaw, Chalk, Thompson, Platt, Wright and Sanders with Rayfield and Shergold as substitutes.

Barry Cranmer gets into the attack in the match versus Corinthian.

Between these opening games came the F.A. Cup Preliminary Round tie against Newbury, which resulted in a comfortable 4-2 victory at Victoria Park. This led to a match against Pagham, a village side from the Sussex County League, in the 1st Qualifying Round. On paper this should not have been a particularly difficult match for them, although in season 1987/88 Pagham had defeated Worthing from the Vauxhall Opel League 2-0, before losing somewhat unluckily, to Tooting & Mitcham.

However, theoretical results are one thing, reality can be quite different. With five minutes to go the Whites were leading 2-1 with goals from Kilgour and Dawtry only for Pagham to score twice more to go through to meet Bashley in the next round. Geoff Butler summed it up in the Football Echo saying, 'This even beats the disastrous run in the Premier Division and I don't know where to turn next just at the moment. I have never witnessed a back-four concede so many chances in my life. We can't defend. The basic rudiments are beyond us'. In the last five matches the team had lost four times.

F.A. Cup Results 17/9/88

Salisbury	2	Pagham	3	Newport I.O.W.	1	Bashley	1
Worthing	3	Totton	2	*replay* Bashley	1	Newport I.O.W.	0
Waterlooville	2	Chippenham Town	0				

Action was taken to strengthen the defence by the signing of Kevin Mulkern from Bournemouth Poppies and Nick Flower from Bashley. Mulkern proved an able replacement for Barry Cranmer who had injured his shoulder against Canterbury and Nick Flower took over from Ian Harris in goal.

Better progress in the next cup competition

Mulkern's first match was away against Bridgend in the F.A. Trophy which was won 6-1. Andover were beaten 5-2 in the next round resulting in Salisbury travelling to Merthyr where, in appalling conditions, the Whites lost 5-0 in front of 863 spectators. In the league, Gravesend, who were then top of the table, were beaten 5-0, but a poor Buckingham side triumphed at Victoria Park 1-0.

Late December, January and February brought the best league form of the season with an eleven match unbeaten run and six wins in a row taking the Whites to fourth place. Promotion had become a possibility but three successive defeats soon brought everyone down to earth. Barry Cranmer's return to fitness had brought a measure of confidence to a side that had been bedevilled by injuries and inconsistency. On the plus side Ian Chalk's transition from Wilts League football augured well for the future and his 16 goals made him the highest goal scorer for Salisbury in the league. The final league position of ninth was probably a fair reflection of the standard of football provided but the fans were disappointed because the previous season's efforts had seemed to point to a much more promising outcome.

Sean Sanders made the most appearances with 52 in all competitions. Home gates for league matches were still less than the club would have liked, the highest of 328 being against Trowbridge Town and lowest 126 against Bury Town. Only sponsorship and the generosity of Chairman Ray McEnhill, permitted the running of a Southern League team.

'Barmy Army' + four !

On a lighter note, as I write, the current team enjoy quite fanatical and boisterous support with a considerable number travelling away to follow their favourites. Even their enthusiasm, however, cannot match the loyalty of four Gravesend supporters who came to Victoria Park to support the Whites in their victory over Bury Town. This result meant Gravesend needed only one point to obtain promotion to the Premier Division, which they duly accomplished!!

The 1989–90 Season — David Thear

Geoff Butler summed up the previous season in the programme for the opening home match of this season by saying:

> *If I had to use one word to summarise our performance it would be inconsistent. We proved many times we were capable of beating the best but let ourselves down on several occasions by dropping points and playing badly against sides we should have beaten comfortably. Obviously we were not quite good enough although you have to remember that losing club captain Barry Cranmer for half a season did not help.*

Most supporters would have had doubts that this inconsistency had been addressed by the transfer activity in the close season.

David Platt was transferred to Poole, Mike Kilgour to Stroud (now known as Forest Green Rovers) and Clive Green to Gosport with David Green (no relation) joining from Swanage. Keith Williams, who had played for Northampton, A.F.C. Bournemouth and Colchester came as player-coach with, in September, Darren Lush signing, in part at least, to cover for Barry Cranmer's absences through injury.

Salisbury to visit new grounds

In the Southern Division itself there were four new clubs. These were Fareham Town who had been relegated, Bashley from the Medisport Wessex League where they had been champions for the past three seasons, Hythe Town who scored 133 goals in 36 matches in the Kent League and Yate Town from the Hellenic League. Thanet United had been renamed Margate.

The first match was away to Sheppey United and was won 4-2. The team was: N. Flower, K. Smith, B. Diaper, K. Mulkern, R. Haysom, K. Williams, C. Shaw, K. Dawtry, I. Chalk, S. Sanders and D. Green. The subs were C. Cranmer and R. Trim. Away league form then proved to be reasonable for a team aiming for promotion, but there was to be no win at home until 29th October when Corinthian were beaten 2-0.

Third family member joins the club

Clearly Geoff Butler had diagnosed the problem and the Corinthian match saw the debuts of Kenny Allen, a tall and agile goalkeeper from Torquay who had previously played for Bournemouth & Boscombe and Dave Syrett, the Laverstock lad who had gone on to play for Swindon, Northampton and Peterborough. He has been mentioned previously in this history as has his father Tony, who held the club's goal-scoring record (72) for a season in Western League days and brother Peter who played with distinction for the club in the seventies.

The victory over Corinthian was the start of a 13-match unbeaten run in the league (10 wins, 3 draws) for which a considerable amount of credit must go to goalkeeper, Allen. His efforts and Barry Cranmer's return from injury, steadied the defence and enabled the rest of the team to express itself more effectively.

Tim Gregory of Sholing Sports this time clears the ball from Kevin Mulkern in the F.A. match that Salisbury won 6-0.

Revenge

Before the unbeaten run began, however, Salisbury had their annual joust with the F.A. Cup and Trophy. In the former, Sholing Sports were beaten 6-0 at Victoria Park thus avenging Sholing's win in a similar round six years before. In the next round Poole Town were held to a 1-1 draw at home, but despite having most of the play, the Whites were beaten 3-1 in the replay.

F.A. Cup Results 16/9/89

Salisbury.	1	Poole Town	1 *(replay)* Poole Town 3	Salisbury	1
Swanage Town	4	Melksham Town	1	Romsey Town 1	Fareham Town	1
Chard Town	0	Dorchester Town	2	Taunton Town 3	Bideford	0

In the F.A. Trophy the first two matches were against Lewes of the Vauxhall Opel League and were drawn. A 4-4 draw at Victoria Park was followed by a 1-1 draw at the Dripping Pan. The second replay, in front of 289 spectators, saw Salisbury triumph by 4-2 despite being 2-1 down with 17 minutes to go. Shaw, Dawtry, Chalk and Sanders scored the goals. This brought an away game at Staines which the Whites lost 3-2 despite, in Geoff Butler's words:

out-playing them but giving away two goals which should've been avoided if defenders had done their job.

In November Dave Fretwell, who had been Assistant Manager for two years, resigned and Eric Lisle took over.

So the New Year saw Salisbury out of the two main Cup competitions but lying second in the league. The 4-3 win by Folkestone at Victoria Park, which saw the end of the unbeaten run triggered an uneven spell of form. Defeats by Burnham, Witney,

Chris Shaw who has just scored for Salisbury in the 1-1 draw with Bury Town receives Dave Green's congratulations.

Erith & Belvedere, Corinthian and Folkestone were offset by wins over Canterbury, twice, Witney, Yate, Trowbridge, Hythe and Erith but the impetus towards promotion was waning.

On the 13th March the Whites were second with 60 points, the same as Buckingham Town. Ominously Trowbridge, Dunstable, Poole and Bashley were all in the promotion frame but with games in hand.

Departure of goalkeeper

Efforts to strengthen the squad had been made with Grant Orchard signing from Winchester, Sean Newark travelling from Devon to help out, Mike Hurdwell came from Thatcham, Richard Thompson from Trowbridge and Karl Bayliss from Sharpness. On the debit side Dave Syrett's bad back prevented him from playing every match, Calvin Cranmer had gone to Downton in order to get regular games and Kenny Allen had been sacked by Geoff Butler following the 5-1 defeat (three down in seven minutes) at Hythe. Derek Douch from Andover took over the goal-keeping spot for the rest of the season.

However these changes were to no avail. Of the last seven matches only one was won, three drawn and three lost. The Whites finished in fifth place leaving the honours to Bashley and Poole who were duly promoted. In addition any last chance of silverware ended with a 3-0 defeat at Downton by Swindon Town in the Wilts Premier Shield.

Local rivals Bemerton Heath Harlequins (under ex-White Steve Slade) had had a memorable first season in the Medisport Wessex League finishing fifth having, at one time, been on top!

Barry Cranmer's testimonial against the Saints first team was a great success despite a 9-0 defeat. The match was watched by over a 1000 spectators in atrocious conditions and Geoff Butler said in the Football Echo:

Southampton were absolutely fabulous, both on and off the pitch. They were tremendous ambassadors for the club. Their players happily signed autographs, fielded their first-team and really turned it on. They could have done it at half-pace and beaten us by five but they did it properly. They didn't take the micky - - - -. It was the best coaching session they (the Whites) could get.

Returning once again to the perennial problem of Victoria Park's suitability for Southern League football, the club's plans to bring

the venue up to scratch were rejected by the Council which placed promotion aspirations in jeopardy and, perhaps, its future existence.

There was, however, some hope when local M.P. Robert Key offered to see if M.O.D. land at Old Sarum could be made

Chris Shaw is Salisbury's Dunlop Hi-Flex Player of the Year. Presentation by Douglas Ferraro on 26th April 1990.

available at a reasonable price. If this was successful the club might be able to do just enough at Victoria Park to satisfy promotion criteria. In the event there was eventual success despite various alarms and misgivings, most of which are too numerous and complicated to detail. The transfer in the intervening years to Old Sarum took place after the 1996/7 season (see page 230 onwards).

The 1990–91 Season — Peter J. Waterhouse

Great team — pity about the ground

The impressive start to the new season with victories away to Erith and Belvedere and at home to Yate Town came to an end at home to Bury Town on 25th August 1990. Salisbury found themselves 1-0 down at half-time but managed to salvage a point in the second-half with Jimmy Smith netting from the penalty spot.

F.A. Cup encounters began with a home preliminary tie against Uxbridge, who drew 1-1 at Victoria Park. In a far from classic replay at

Uxbridge, Salisbury came away 2-1 winners to book a place in the next round at home to Hungerford. A brace of goals from Jimmy Smith saw them move into the second qualifying round where a 4-0 victory was gained at the expense of Bournemouth Poppies in front of a home gate of 501. Dreams ended with a 3-0 defeat at home to Farnborough in front of the largest crowd in a competitive match in eleven years, the gate being 937.

F.A. Cup Results 13/10/90

Salisbury	0	Farnborough Tn	3	Bashley	2	Weymouth	2
Tiverton Town	1	Liskeard	0	Andover Town	0	Marlow	1

Jimmy Smith going great guns

Salisbury suffered their first league defeat of the season away to Sudbury Town on 27th October. Up to that time Jimmy Smith had netted 17 goals from just 16 appearances.

The First Round Proper of the F.A. Trophy was reached after a replay away to Barry Town, following a 0-0 draw at Victoria Park. Geoff Butler was nominated Manager of the Month for November and the Christmas/New Year programme yielded 10 points from a maximum of 12.

On the 12th January 1991, Salisbury welcomed V.S. Rugby in the First Round of the F.A. Trophy and they proved to be worthy winners by four goals to one.

By the end of February the Whites occupied 3rd position in the league and the top four read as follows:

	P	W	D	L	F	A	Pts
Baldock Town	27	16	5	6	48	35	53
Trowbridge	24	15	4	5	42	18	49
Salisbury	**24**	**13**	**7**	**4**	**38**	**24**	**46**
Buckingham Town	22	13	5	4	46	31	44

Double disaster – dismal day

The fans were in for a shock on Saturday 2nd March 1991, when the basement club, Corinthian, won 1-0 at Victoria Park, it being their first away victory. They had gained only one point from their previous twelve away games.

On the following Wednesday, 6th March Salisbury entertained Andover in the Beazer Homes League but the programme for that match printed the news that everyone connected with the club had half expected but dreaded:

All the other news this week is overshadowed by the decision of the Beazer Homes League, that Salisbury will not be promoted this season even if the club finished in the top two of the Southern Division. The league's grounds committee rejected the planned temporary arrangements, which would have enabled the Whites to compete in the Premier Division next season pending Salisbury District Council's acceptance (or otherwise) of the Victoria Park redevelopment proposals. So to the bitter disappointment of all involved with the club, we're in for another enforced season of Southern Division football. It's not much of a consolation, but there are several other clubs in the same situation, which means promotion and relegation at the end of this season will have less to do with footballing ability than the state of the club's ground. Buckingham, for example, are extremely unlikely to be granted promotion with their present facilities, Trowbridge are faced with a huge amount of work they may not be able to complete in time and as many as five current Premier Division sides may suffer automatic demotion to their respective regional divisions. Also, midland section pace-setters, Tamworth have said that they have neither the time nor money to upgrade their ground to the required standard.

To quote Geoff Butler from his programme notes:

Well what a weekend. I had my most difficult task to carry out since I became a manager on Saturday when it was my unfortunate duty to inform the players that we would not be playing in the Premier Division next season no matter where we finished in the league.

Time and our substandard facilities have finally caught up with us as we have been informed by the BHL that the temporary improvements we were intending to carry out at the Park would not be acceptable.

Even if they had been, it is extremely doubtful as to whether we could have got the permission of the City Committee, the approval of the Charity Commissioner and carried out the work before 1st May. All of which had to be done to satisfy the league's Grading Committee.

It is a morale shattering experience for everybody connected with the Football Club and it will take time to come to terms with the situation – if in fact we ever do.

The Football Club, like others, have been under threat for two years that this could happen, well now it is not a threat any more. It has happened. The second threat is that we will be thrown out of the league altogether at the end of next season unless facilities can be greatly improved at Victoria Park. Make no mistake, that will happen if they are not.

I therefore urge all of you loyal Salisbury supporters to voice your opinion towards the right channels. There are lots of people residing locally who are making their objections known to the Council and Charity

Commissioners that they do not want the Football Club to be allowed to improve the facilities at the Park. I think it is about time that the voices of the people who do not want to see an end to Salisbury Football Club playing Southern League Football here at the Park should be heard and heard loudly. May 1992, is looming fast and we all know what that will mean.

One could not doubt the manager's commitment to the club.

In the meantime old rivals, Andover Town had a new face at the top, acquiring a new Chairman in Mr Ken Cunningham-Brown. According to the Salisbury programme notes:

Mr Cunningham-Brown, a wealthy local businessman with keen horse racing related interests, says he intends to assist the club financially but will not be a fairy godfather' who can solve all Andover's money problems at a stroke.

More will be heard of Mr Cunningham-Brown in relation to Salisbury later in this history.

After the initial shock of being told that the club could not play Premier division football next season, the team appeared to have come to terms with the situation, by achieving back-to-back wins against Andover and away to Dunstable.

As promotion was out of the question Geoff Butler said he did not intend to stand in the way of any player seeking to play at a higher level and was renumerated accordingly if that club was prepared to pay what the player was worth.

Geoff was adept at recognising a player's potential and the 1990/1 squad had its share of players who had the ability to progress.

Jimmy Smith v Gosport (*left*) and Margate (*right*) scored 34 goals in 37 games.

Top scorer on form

Baldock Town, the league leaders, visited Victoria Park on Saturday 16th March 1991 and were beaten 2-0 with Jimmy Smith again netting a brace. After this win the Whites gained 13 points from a maximum of 15 just dropping two away to Baldock. On the 6th April the top four of the league table read:

	P	W	D	L	F	A	Pts
Salisbury	35	21	9	5	56	31	72
Baldock	35	20	6	9	59	44	66
Buckingham	29	19	5	5	63	34	62
Trowbridge	29	18	6	5	52	23	60

With games in hand Trowbridge and Buckingham looked the favourites to win the league.

Another team staying put

On Monday 8th April championship contenders Buckingham Town visited Victoria Park. They, like Salisbury, could not be granted promotion from the Southern League that season. Their plans to have moved to a new location had fallen through and although they had plenty of developers queuing up to buy their ground, they had published proposals to stay where they were and improve Ford Meadow to Premier Division standard by the start of the 1992/93 season.

Salisbury beat their fellow Championship contenders 2-0, with two goals from Martin Dowding. Their hopes of the Championship plummeted, however, when they went down 3-1 away to Canterbury who were third from bottom of the league.

Missed by one point

The last home game of the season, saw two more points dropped, this time to mid-table Sudbury Town. Stuart Thomson equalised for Salisbury to make the score 1-1.

The sceptics who had predicted a rapid descent in the league table after the 2nd March 1991, proved to be incorrect. Every credit must be given to the magnificent team effort and Geoff Butler's motivational skills to get the team back on course for the Championship. The top four of the final league table for 1990/91 read:

	P	W	D	L	F	A	Pts
Buckingham Town	40	25	8	7	73	38	83
Trowbridge Town	40	22	12	6	67	31	78
Salisbury City	**40**	**22**	**11**	**7**	**63**	**39**	**77**
Baldock Town	40	21	9	10	66	52	72

Jimmy Smith was named Supporters Player of the Year. He was also top Southern League scorer with 35 goals in all matches.

The 1991–92 Season — David Thear

Because it had not been possible for Salisbury to be promoted for ground grading reasons manager Geoff Butler referred to this as a 'get by' season and so it proved to be so far as league results were concerned. A final position of 12th out of 22 was the outcome. The season was bedevilled by injuries and, on occasions, it was difficult to turn out a full quota of substitutes. On 16th November they were bottom of the league which Geoff Butler put down to defensive frailties and switched to a less attacking style.

There was considerable activity in the transfer market between then and the end of the season with fans' favourite Jimmy Smith moving to Cheltenham for £5000, Barry Cranmer to Basingstoke for £3000 and Chris Shaw to Poole for £4000. Salisbury signed David Payne on loan from Bath, Gerry Pearson from Yeovil, Lee

Darby who had played for Portsmouth, Nigel Tripp from Gloucester, Gordon Hobson a former Saint, from Farnborough Town and Dave Maskell on loan from Basingstoke.

The line-up for the first home match of the season against Newport I.O.W. which was drawn 2-2, was: Mark Coombe (goalkeeper), Russell Fishlock, Kevin Mulkern, Pete Loveridge, Barry Cranmer, David Green, John Woods,

Mark Coombe

Sean Sanders

Sean Sanders, Ian Chalk, John Gomershall and Brett Phillips on loan from Bournemouth.

So far the league itself was concerned there were four new teams in the Southern division. These were Havant from the Jewson Wessex, Braintree (Jewson Eastern), Sittingbourne (Winston League, Kent) and old enemies, Weymouth who had been relegated from the Premier Division.

Attendances shrinking

On the playing side league matters improved in the New Year and the final position was probably what the club deserved. What was more disturbing were the attendances at Victoria Park. The average was less than 200 per game with only 96 watching the Hythe Town match and 97 for the Bury Town fixture.

These gates probably had a bearing on the rift in the boardroom which saw Tony Baker, Derek Drake and Tracy Paton resign. The reason given was the belief that Chairman Ray McEnhill worked with only manager Butler and one or two committee men rather than with the whole board. Wendy Gee's article in the Sports Echo of January 18th refers to differences of opinion between Derek Drake and the manager over reducing the wage bill and quotes the former as saying that Geoff Butler had been warned that the club was heading for financial disaster but had failed to come up with ways of cutting costs.

This news was refuted by Keith Miller, a committee man and the club press officer who stated Geoff Butler had done all he could to cut the wage bill but this did not include shedding all the best players. He referred to the sales of Cranmer, Shaw and Smith as evidence that progress had been made. In the following week's Sports Echo Geoff Butler was quoted as saying he believed the spirit of the club had improved immensely since the financial situation had been discussed at the committee meeting which had precipitated the resignations.

First steps in quest for new ground

Throughout the season there were negotiations for the purchase of M.O.D. land at Old Sarum and in March there was good news. Agreement had been reached for the purchase of the land at half the original asking price.

The next move was to be a joint planning application with Bloor Homes to Salisbury District Council. Bloor already had permission to build 40 homes on land adjacent to the site and were then seeking permission for a further 60 homes. If this was successful they would assist financially in the building of the new stadium.

Closely related to the move to the new ground was, again, the suitability, in the interim, of the Victoria Park for Southern League football. Rumours were rife throughout league circles that at least four grounds did not meet grading standards and because there had been more criticism of the Park's facilities by some visiting officials there was a fear that the Whites were among them. New Vice-Chairman Keith Miller refuted this referring to the repair of the barrier around the pitch, the creation of a Director's area in the stand and the covering of all concrete seating with wood. He also said he had spoken to the grading committee who seemed perfectly happy with the work. Disappointingly there were reports of vandalism to the new work which was hindering progress.

To finish the footballing side to the season there was good news. In both the F.A. Cup and F.A. Trophy Salisbury had success.

Record defeat?

In the F.A. Cup Thatcham were beaten 3-0 after a replay, followed by Poole 2-0 in torrential rain at home and Thame United 4-0 away. The 4th Qualifying Round played on 26th October brought Farnborough, top of the Vauxhall Conference, to Victoria Park and in front of over 800 people they won 7-1 with Simon Reed scoring four.

F.A. Cup Results 26/10/91

Salisbury	1	Farnborough	7	Worcester City	1	Marlow	2
Weymouth	1	Sutton United	1	Tiverton Town	1	Dover Athletic	0

Geoff Butler in the programme notes for 2nd November match against Hythe Town wrote about Farnborough as follows:

Everything about them was professional. Their touch, passing, movement, support play and effort were a lesson for all non-league players to learn from and their finishing was as clinical as you can get. Having said all that we had our moments and if we had got a goal during the first half when we had them wobbling a bit the score could have been a lot closer.

Success was also achieved in the F.A. Trophy with a win over Cwmbran, a home win against Taunton with eventual Premiership referee Paul Durkin in charge and a home win over Wokingham. For this latter achievement Salisbury were awarded £250 as 'team of the round'.

Future England player sees off Salisbury

Retribution however was around the corner. The next round saw a journey to Wycombe to play the then holders of the Trophy. The match drew a crowd of 2917 and a goal in each half saw the home side triumph 2-0. The Whites were not disgraced. Wycombe were clearly the better side and, in Steve Guppy, later to play for England, they had a match winner.

Away from Victoria Park there were a number of events which would be of interest to present day supporters. The first was the surprising triumph of Bashley Youth team over Portsmouth in the F.A. Youth Cup. Bashley's leading light was Paul Sales. Secondly Andover paid £8000, a club record fee, for a young centre-half from Newbury. His name was Roger Emms. Thirdly, Wimborne Town beat Guiseley in the F.A. Vase final. In the winning team and later to become Non-League Player of the Year was one Tommy Killick. (In addition to winning the Vase, Wimborne won the Jewson Wessex League and the Dorset Senior Cup). Sales, Emms and Killick were to become Salisbury regulars.

There was also a report in the national press that Geoff Butler had been appointed manager of the South African national team. It turned out to be Jeff Butler who had been coaching in South Africa for several years but who had been on Norwich City's books as had the Salisbury manager.

What would it have done for the Whites if this report had been true?

The 1992–93 Season — David Thear

What It All Boils Down To

There were four distinct issues running throughout this season, the first and foremost being the desire for a successful football team.

Last season had seen considerable progress in both the F.A. cup and Trophy; the club and its fans wanted more of this. The second issue, intrinsically linked to the first, was the belief that the club had to advance its status by achieving promotion to the Premier Division. Manager Geoff Butler believed that he had built the foundations and, with signings he had made during the summer break, there was every reason to be optimistic. The third issue was the perennial problem of the suitability of Victoria Park for Southern League football. Cosmetic changes had taken place during the close season in that a Director's 'box' had been created in the main stand and access to the upstairs bar in the Pavilion was to be via the pathway in front of the tea hut. In addition, the Pavilion and the area surrounding the dressing rooms and boardroom became restricted to players and officials only. These measures were imposed to conform with league regulations but it was known, of course, that if promotion were achieved more fundamental changes, difficult to attain at Victoria Park, would be necessary. This leads to the fourth issue which was the new stadium.

Nice to see return of old face

Turning first to football issues, there were four new clubs in the Beazer Homes League (Southern Division) namely Wealdstone, Poole Town, Fisher Athletic and Gravesend & Northfleet. Geoff Butler's new signings were Chris Shaw who, was a former White, free from Weymouth; Roger Emms also free and Kevin Bale, both from Andover; Mark Payne from Hungerford and David Fry, a goalkeeper with Football League experience with Crystal Palace and Millwall, from Yeovil.

This latter signing was to replace Mark Coombe who had been sold to Dorchester for £5000 plus a percentage of any fee if he moved on. In due course Dave Maskell was signed, again free, from Basingstoke; Brian Mundee from Bashley and Paul Thompson, a goalkeeper who had played for Swindon.

Nigel Tripp, Lee Darby, Brett Phillips, Terry Arnold and Simon Pope left the club, the latter two to Waterlooville. Assistant Manager Eric Lisle departed and Gordon Hobson became player/coach.

The first match, at home against Buckingham was disappointingly lost 4-1 with John Wilson scoring. The team was

Fry, Fishlock, Loveridge, Emms, Payne, Fletcher, Shaw, Wilson, Hobson, Chalk and Sanders with Gomershall and May as substitutes. This was followed by two draws and a defeat away to Dunstable. then two wins against Havant and Newport I.O.W. A fairly ordinary start!!

Old rivals trounced

Thoughts of an F.A. Cup run as last season were encouraged by a 6-2 home victory over Trowbridge Town who were, at the time, second in the Beazer Homes League Premier Division. John Gomershall scored a hat-trick and Geoff Butler attributed the victory to improved work rate, pressurising the opposition and Gordon Hobson's coaching. The crowd of 425 was more than double the attendance at league games so far that season.

Salisbury's next visitors to Victoria Park were Thatcham Town, whose defeat gave the hosts an away trip to Brockenhurst, resulting in a 3-1 victory before a crowd of 451. The 4th Qualifying Round sent the Whites to Witney and there a battling

Salisbury's second goal v Thatcham Town.

performance resulted in a 2-1 win, Bale and Loveridge scoring.

The all important 1st Round Proper draw brought a trip to Marlow. The match was played on November 14th in front of 940 spectators and the Salisbury team was Simpkins, Payne, Green, Loveridge, Emms, Fletcher, Gomershall, Shaw, Sanders, Chalk and Bale. Hobson and Maskell were substitutes. John Simpkins, on loan from Bashley, was in goal in place of David Fry who had broken his leg against Witney Town in the league match on 27th October.

Too much excitement for some!

The match took pride of place on the front page of the Sports Echo and Wendy Gee reported that opening pressure resulted in a Pete Loveridge goal after 11 minutes. Over enthusiastic away supporters behind the goal clambered over the fencing and Geoff Butler went round to appeal for calm. After further pressure during which Gomershall hit the post, Salisbury were stunned when John Simpkins let a Mark Watkins lofted shot slip through his hands and David May scored. A period of indiscipline followed with Kevin Bale booked for dissent and two near misses by Marlow forwards. However, on 30 minutes, Roger Emms' free-kick was headed square by Ian Chalk to Sean Sanders who stroked the ball home, half-time 2-1 to

Happy Peter Loveridge at Marlow. Away photos: T. Mardell, Sports Echo.

Salisbury.The second-half opened with two Marlow bookings and then on 55 minutes Gary Fletcher picked up a headed clearance to hit a first-time shot in off the post for a 3-1 lead. Another Marlow player was booked shortly afterwards and then, in the 64th minute, Watkins scored for Marlow.

In the last 20 minutes both goalkeepers saw considerable action and after 82 minutes Marlow's Tony Dell was sent off for a second bookable offence. On 84 minutes the Whites' resistance was broken when Kenny Glasgow blasted in the equaliser for Marlow. Three minutes later Sean Sanders was cautioned to become the sixth player disciplined in a frenzied cup-tie.

The replay was finally played at Victoria Park on Saturday 5th December after postponements due to torrential rain. The crowd of 1854 was treated to a roller coaster ride of a game which could be summed up no better than in the performance of Sean Sanders. His 63rd minute goal brought the score to 2-2 which is how it stayed until the end of extra-time. The resultant penalty shoot-out saw the same player fire over the bar

Salisbury players (and fans) celebrate as Sanders (hidden) scores their second.

The F.A. Cup 1st Round Proper replay against Marlow at Victoria Park was even more dramatic than the first game ending with a penalty shoot-out, which Salisbury unfortunately lost. Here some of those moments are captured.

Above: Ian Chalk crashes in goal No. 1 putting the Whites into the lead.

After Marlow had equalised, Sean Sanders (far left) turns away after slotting in the second goal. (more pictures in 'Football Extra').

to leave Marlow winners by 4-3. To rub salt in the wound he had had an 88th minute 'winning' goal disallowed for offside (not him, but a player standing out near the corner flag not interfering in *anyway* with the play). Salisbury, who were far from disgraced, could take heart from the way they played against higher league opposition and it is true to say that this match proved to be a turning point in their league form.

F.A. Cup Results 14/11/92

Marlow 3	Salisbury	3	*replay* Salisbury 2 Marlow 2	*Marlow won on pens* 4-3
Torquay United		2	Yeovil Town 5	Dorking 2 Plymouth Argyle 3
Dagenham & R'bridge		4	Leyton Orient 5	

Marlow played and beat VS Rugby in the next round and drew Tottenham Hotspur in the 3rd Round Proper. They lost and Salisbury were left to lament what might have been.

The other competition for which there were high hopes was the F.A. Trophy. They were drawn away to Worcester City and, although they had most of the play, lost 2-1. Geoff Butler said, 'playing with only one man up front gave them too much respect'. If there was anything to be gained from this defeat it was the clearing of the decks for an assault on the league table. The team was in mid-table with 15 games played and 22 points gained.

International signs on for the Whites

Hung Dang

Promisingly, there were games in hand over most of the clubs above them. Also, there were new signings in addition to John Simpkins already mentioned. Richie Paskins, on a month's loan, Mark Boulton came from Bashley and Hung Dang from Yeovil. Hung Dang had an interesting background. He was Vietnamese born and had won 10 England schoolboy caps. In an international against Denmark he scored both goals in a 2-1 victory. Previously before Yeovil Town, he played for Exeter City, Chard and Poole Town before becoming a very popular and talented member of the Salisbury squad.

At the New Year they were 10th in the league, 14 points behind the leaders Gravesend with two games in hand. Sittingbourne lay in second place, seven points behind Gravesend but with four games in hand. Geoff Butler's view was that the team was coming good and so it proved to be. From 1st January until 1st May Salisbury had played 24 league games, winning 20 of them setting up a nail biting last day decider at Baldock which was drawn to secure the point necessary for promotion. The principal achievement was a 1-0 win away at Sittingbourne in front of 1167 spectators although this was counterbalanced by a 2-1 defeat at home by the same club.

Gravesend had lost their way leaving Sittingbourne who were regarded, in financial terms, as the Chelsea of the league to take top spot with 90 points. The Whites were second with 88 points, Witney third with 84 points and Gravesend fourth with 79.

Geoff Butler's prophecy of an interesting second-half to the season was fulfilled and promotion was achieved – or was it?

Steve
Weaver

Simon
Browne

It is worth looking at the changes to, and strengthening of, the team which took place after Christmas. Crucially, Paul Odey signed from Basingstoke in exchange for David Green and John Gomershall. He was a proven goalscorer who netted twice in his opening two games. Brett Phillips returned to Salisbury from Bournemouth although he was soon released, Steve Weaver, a goalkeeper came from Weymouth and shared duties with Paul Thompson and Simon Browne signed from Dorchester. Dave Maskell was released and subsequently played for Downton, Andover and Bashley.

The Whites scored 87 league goals, an average of just over two a game. Sean Sanders was top scorer with 22 in all matches and, in addition, won the 'Players Player of the Year Trophy' donated by keen supporter Tony Waite.

Promotion denied for runners-up

So much for the good news. The bad news was that the team would not be playing in the Premier Division in 1993/94. It was well known throughout the season that the ground was not up to scratch and the lease expired at the end of the following season anyway. To meet this situation, outline agreement had been reached to ground share with Bashley while the purchase and building of the new stadium at Old Sarum was finalised. The crux of the issue hinged on the motives for ground-sharing. The League management claimed they would be 'bed-hopping' merely to obtain their Premier Division place. Salisbury argued that they were well on their way to getting their new ground and needed a little breathing space and, in any event, a precedent existed with clubs like Solihull Borough who played all their home games at Moor Green. The league did not accept these arguments and the Whites remained in the Southern Division.

It only now remains to see how matters were with the Old Sarum purchase. The position was fully explained in the match programme of 17th October 1992 thus:

> *By now you will all have heard or read of the latest developments regarding the Football Club's proposed move to Old Sarum. On the eleventh of March we applied for planning permission along with Bloor Homes for a new football stadium and golf-*

driving range for us and extra houses for Bloor Homes. The extra revenue generated from the sale of the additional houses was to go to providing access to the new football stadium through Bloor Homes land plus £200,000 for the club. After many meetings between Salisbury District Council, Bloor Homes and officials of the club planning permission was granted subject to the governments Secretary of State Department not feeling it necessary to hold a public inquiry to the development. The relevant papers have been with that department since the last week of July and only on 6th October did we hear that they were not taking any further action. This obviously leaves the door open for Salisbury District Council to grant us the necessary permission to develop a new ground etc.

Unfortunately this has been too long a delay for Bloor Homes to wait and just before the Secretary of State gave his blessing Bloors reverted back to their original plan which did not include facilitating the Football Club.

All is not lost however as negotiations are still taking place between Salisbury District Council and Bloor Homes to open the way for a secondary plan which will allow the Football Club to move as hoped. Obviously it is a disappointment to have permission for a new ground granted with facilities that would secure the long term future of the club and at this stage not be able to take advantage of it but I remain optimistic that this is only a hiccup and better news will follow shortly.

I urge everyone connected with the club at all levels, be it committee members, officials players, staff and supporters to remain optimistic and positive and together we will achieve our goal.

Supporters, still smarting from the decision to stop the club taking up its place in the Premier Division, could only wait and see what the future held.

The 1993–94 Season — Peter J. Waterhouse

So Near, Yet So Far

Another white knuckle ride of a season beckoned the Salisbury City supporters; a season when the Whites were to go tantalisingly close to securing a promotion position in the Southern Division.

In the close season they had to come to terms with the loss of the authoritative captain Peter Loveridge who, with Gary Fletcher, moved to Wimborne Town. In addition Hung Dang and Paul Thompson left the club. New signings were Neil Wickens and Barry Blankley. Also welcomed back was David Platt.

    Garry Fletcher   Peter Loveridge   Barry Blankley

On the F.A. Cup and Trophy trail

Any hopes of replicating last season's epic F.A. Cup run vanished as the Whites faced a tough 1st Qualifying Round away tie to Beazer Homes League Premier Division side Waterlooville at Jubilee Park on Saturday 11th of September. Thanks to an impressive display by Waterlooville goalkeeper, Mark Golding and, with a replay imminent Duncan Burns slotted home a late penalty to put the home side into the next round.

F.A. Cup Results 11/9/93

Waterlooville	1	Salisbury	0	Trowbridge Tn	1	Newport A.F.C.	1
Chippenham Tn	0	Weymouth	5	Frome Tn	0	Moreton Tn	0
Bashley	2	Abingdon Tn	1	Brockenhurst	1	Eastleigh	4

The F.A. Trophy

Just one week after the exit from the F.A. Cup, the team were in action in the 1st Qualifying Round of the F.A. Trophy away to Poole Town. With a goal from Paul Odey they were leading 1-0 at half-time. They had a terrible second-half conceding three goals. A dressing room disagreement after the match resulted in influential captain, Kevin Bale, playing his last game for the club.

Kevin Bale

The Southern League Cup

Salisbury embarked on an exceptional League Cup run on Monday 4th October, again facing Poole Town at Poole Stadium. A much improved performance saw them take a 5-1 lead to Victoria Park for the 2nd leg, which was just as well as they went down 1-0.

The Whites travelled to Weymouth for the 2nd Round tie, where the home side took a 2-0 lead inside the first 11 minutes. Thankfully, Sean Sanders bagged a brace in the second-half to force a replay at Victoria Park, where goals from Chris Shaw, Gordon Hobson and

Chris Shaw

Sean Sanders, resulted in a 3-1 win. This

Sean Sanders

Paul Odey in action.

Gordon Hobson

set up a 3rd Round encounter against our old rivals Trowbridge Town when a Paul Odey goal settled the result at Victoria Park. Another home tie beckoned in the quarter-finals, this time against Dorchester Town on Wednesday 26th January. The Whites were in fine form and a brace of goals apiece from Sean Sanders and Gordon Hobson saw off the opposition.

Virgin territory

They were now in the semi-finals of the League Cup for the first time in the club's history. Supporters' hopes were high when they learnt that they would be meeting Sudbury in the semi-finals. They had previously beaten them away 3-1 in the league that season and recorded a 1-0 home league win just a few days previously. In theory, optimism should have been justified.

With a goal from Sean Sanders and a Gordon Hobson equaliser on 90 minutes, the Whites returned from Sudbury with a 2-2 draw but this was more than cancelled out by a 4-1 defeat at Victoria Park. A week after the exit from the League Cup, Trowbridge Town put paid to their Wiltshire Premier Shield ambitions at Frome Road, by winning 2-0.

Meanwhile back In the league

Salisbury started the season like an express train, winning their first league game at Victoria Park on Saturday 21st August against Fisher Athletic '93 by six goals to nil. The goals were scored by Sanders(3), Odey(2) and Emms(1). The following Wednesday they travelled to A.F.C. Tonbridge, returning home five-nil victors with goals again from Odey(2), Wright(1), Sanders(1) and full-back Bale. August ended with a 1-1 draw at Victoria Park against Canterbury City followed by a creditable draw at Gravesend, and a 3-2 win at home to Poole Town. Paul Odey obtained a brace and Ian Chalk the other goal.

Another goal bound shot from Paul Odey.

Salisbury's first game of October was at home to Wealdstone — the game which saw Barry Cranmer playing again after a two season spell with Basingstoke Town. They duly beat Wealdstone 3-2 and followed this with the same scoreline against Fareham Town. The fine run of league form ended on the last Saturday of October away to league leaders Baldock Town where an under strength Salisbury team went down 2-0.

Paul Odey hits the top spot

Paul Odey headed the list of Southern Division top scorers at this time. There were also physical signs of improvement at Victoria Park with the moving of the barriers at both the city and Park Lane ends.

November started in style with a 1-0 victory away to Buckingham Town, thanks to a Roger Emms' goal. This was followed by a 6-1 win against Bury Town at Victoria Park. With Paul Odey netting his first hat-trick of the season, the Whites moved into second place. The run of success ended in a 1-0 defeat at Witney.

Future captain enlists

Geoff Butler made another astute signing by recruiting Sandy Baird from Bashley.

'Plan B' – Chalkie, Sandy Baird, Puckett and Preston, just like in training.

The strong constructive player settled into the team quickly and went on to win the supporters 'Player of the Year' award.

For the first time in the season, Salisbury lost two league games in succession when the defeat at Witney was followed by the first home defeat against Ashford. However, they soon got back to winning ways by picking up maximum points from six games, which included a 2-0 victory over promotion rivals, Baldock Town. Geoff Butler was named the Beazer Homes League Southern Division, 'Manager of the Month'.

Salisbury's straight six tally ends

This impressive run came to an end at Victoria Park when Gravesend won 4-1 and just three days later at the Poole Stadium, they again tasted defeat at the hands of Poole Town, 1-0. Then there were eight consecutive matches all resulting in victories until, on April 4th, they dropped two points at Weymouth. The Braintree Town game saw the debut of Martin Blackler.

Martin Blackler

Anxious April approaches

The Whites celebrated their eighth league win in succession with a victory over Havant, thanks to a debut goal from ex-Pompey striker Nicky Morgan. However, promotion hopes took a jolt with a sequence of four draws which was broken by a vital win

Roger Emms never one to worry about the odds, doing his best to score in a match versus Poole Town.

Sean Sanders here scoring one of his two goals in the 5-1 beating of Braintree.

at Erith & Belvedere. Then a brace of goals from Paul Odey saw them lead 2-0 against Margate at Victoria Park only for the visitors to get back into the game to make the final score 2-2. Sadly they lost 1-0 at Havant, which was their only defeat in the last 21 league games of the season. They were still in the promotion race with a fighting chance after a home win against Buckingham Town 2-1 which saw them gain third place.

Promotion rivals Witney Town visited Victoria Park and supporters witnessed a tense 1-1 draw. With Sandy Baird getting a late equaliser, the final day of April saw a 1-1 draw at Dunstable.

At the beginning of May victory at Fareham could have kept them in the promotion race but a game which should have been won comfortably, again ended 1-1 and promotion ambitions disappeared. Salisbury finished the season with successes at home over A.F.C. Tonbridge 2-0 and away to Canterbury City by the same scoreline.

The team had faced a debilitating congestion of fixtures in April having to play 14 league matches in just over a month. This was probably a major factor in the dropping of crucial points and one win instead of a draw would have meant a promotion place.

Paul Odey was the leading goal-scorer with 35 goals in 49 appearances, including eight as a sub. Sean Sanders reached a total of 341 appearances and Ian Chalk also passed the 300 mark.

The mighty Spurs visit Victoria Park

Salisbury supporters had the opportunity of seeing a strong Tottenham Hotspur side in action at Victoria Park in October 1993. Ian Walker, a future England goalkeeper featured for the Spurs and the match was watched by 726 spectators, the biggest gate of the season.

A clash of colours for the visit of Tottenham Hotspur to Victoria Park.

The 1994–95 Season — Peter J. Waterhouse

Salisbury's summer signings

After the bitter disappointments of the 1992/93 campaign and the near miss of last season, manager Geoff Butler had been busy in the transfer market. He had assembled a very capable looking side which promised to have the ability to take top Beazer Homes League Southern Division honours. The signings included Jason Lovell from Wimborne £3500, Paul Batty from Bath City for £2000, Duncan Burns and Kevin Clements (Waterlooville), Gareth Hughes (Bashley) and David Coleman (Dorchester).

During the close season a notable departure was that of the previous season's top marksman, Paul Odey, who moved to Weymouth. Also joining him at the Dorset club was midfielder, Barry Blankley. Two popular Salisbury players moved to Poole, namely Barry Cranmer and Chris Shaw and the highly experienced and popular ex Saint, Gordon Hobson left to concentrate on his business.

Here we go!, here we go!, here we go!?

The 1994/95 league campaign commenced with an away match at Tonbridge on Saturday 20th August. The Whites found themselves 2-0 down after 60 minutes, but with a Jason Lovell goal they started to get back into the game. Although they dominated the last 30 minutes, they could not score again.

After the upset at Tonbridge, Salisbury started to play to their potential. Four days later they secured their first victory with a 1-0 success at home to Fisher, with Jason Lovell hitting the back of the net. Roger Emms made his 100th appearance for the club and celebrated by scoring twice in Salisbury's 5-0 home victory over A.F.C. Totton in the Preliminary Round of the F.A. Cup. The bad news for the club was that prolific striker, Jason Lovell, had sustained an injury and would be out of action for up to four weeks.

Salisbury recorded their second league win 1-0 away to Yate Town on August Bank Holiday, with an Ian Chalk goal. He was again on the score sheet when Salisbury defeated promotion favourites, Baldock Town 1-0 in the important league match at Victoria Park. They kept up the pressure on the league pace-setters with an excellent away performance at Bashley. Ian Chalk continued his good form with another impressive goal and then a superb last minute free-kick from Paul Batty saw them bag all three points in a 2-1 victory. This moved them into second position in the league table.

Meanwhile back in the Cup

Worcester City from the Beazer Homes League Premier Division visited Victoria Park for a 1st Qualifying Round F.A. Cup tie. With goals from David Coleman and Ian Chalk, his 100th goal for the club, Salisbury saw off the visitors' challenge. They then faced Poole Town in the next round at Victoria Park and duly won 3-2, with goals from Batty, Clements and Sanders. Unbeaten league leaders, Waterlooville were the next opponents in the 3rd Qualifying Round, at Victoria Park and, in a typical cup tie,

the match see-sawed 1-0, 2-1, 3-2, in the visitors' favour. With goals from Ian Chalk and Paul Batty, Salisbury pulled themselves back into the game and, five minutes from full-time, were awarded a penalty. Skipper Paul Batty made no mistake to send the Whites to Jubilee Park,

Martin Blackler and a Waterlooville player not seeing quite eye-to-eye, as some of the visiting supporters prepare to join in.

photo Daily Echo Sport

Waterlooville for the replay the following Wednesday.

Then he put them into an early lead with a superb free kick and a fine team effort earned them a 4th Qualifying Round clash at home to Ashford Town. Unfortunately, the Whites did not get into this game until deep into the second-half. From being 2-0 down they drew level with Ian Chalk scoring in the 74th minute and Jason Lovell in the 81st. With five minutes to go they had a penalty appeal turned down and, on full-time, Ashford had the final throw of the dice when they scored the decisive goal to take them through to a F.A. Cup 1st Round Proper tie with Fulham.

F.A. Cup Results 22/10/94

Salisbury	2	Ashford Town	3	Yeading	1	Telford United	0
Cheltenham	1	Bashley	1	Newport I.O.W.	1	Trowbridge Town	1
replay		Bashley 2		Cheltenham 1			

The 'Bread and Butter' league returns

Geoff Butler signed Darren Taggart from Witney Town to further strengthen the team who gained their fifth league win in succession when they defeated Witney Town 3-0 at Victoria Park. Jason Lovell came off the bench and soon got back to his goal scoring ways after being out of the team through injury. He netted the second goal after Kevin Clements had opened the scoring and this was followed by a splendid headed goal by Paul Batty.

In the F.A. Trophy the Whites had early success with a fine win away at Newport I.O.W. 4-2. Inexplicably results then started to go wrong. Bognor Regis Town were the visitors to Victoria Park in the 2nd Qualifying Round which ended in a 0-0 draw. The following Wednesday they made the trip to Bognor for the replay and after leading 2-0 they had a dreadful second-half going out of the competition 4-2.

The malaise carried on throughout October with a defeat at Weymouth and on the last day of the month they suffered a 2-1 defeat at home in the Wiltshire Premier Shield against Warminster Town. They got back on track with a convincing 2-0 win at Margate, but, the following Tuesday, in the 1st Round of the League Cup second leg tie at Bashley went down 2-0 (4-2 on aggregate).

Seventh Heaven for Salisbury

Salisbury put all their cup woes behind them for the visit to promotion rivals Baldock Town and achieved their biggest ever away victory in the Southern League. New signing Robbie Carroll, making his debut for Salisbury, must have thought that he was playing for Real Madrid. The team was firing on all cylinders, playing sublime football. The scorers for Salisbury were striker, Jason Lovell (3), his first hat-trick for the club and one each for Paul Batty, Simon Browne, Roger Emms and Robbie Carroll. Future England international Kevin Phillips, then playing for Baldock, was sent off.

Jason Lovell

Salisbury followed up this great victory by beating Yate Town at Victoria Park the following Wednesday. Jason Lovell scored his second hat-trick in successive games and Ian Chalk netted Salisbury's fourth to record a 4-2 victory. They travelled to Clevedon Town on Saturday the 19th November, recording a 1-1 draw and once again Jason Lovell was on target.

Promotion hopes received a set-back, when the league leaders, Waterlooville took all the points at Victoria Park, winning 2-0 on Saturday 26th November.

The Whites made an impressive start to the crucial December games with a 5-2 home win over Margate and this was followed by another home victory, Ashford Town being the victims, with a brace of goals from Jason Lovell and a Robbie Carroll goal. On the Saturday before Christmas, Salisbury were once again on the rampage this time hitting Erith & Belvedere for six. The game saw Jason Lovell netting his second brace in successive games, with Clements, Carroll, Chalk and Guy all getting on the score sheet. They then defeated Fareham Town 2-1 at home on Boxing Day, with goals from Emms and Carroll. The final day of 1994 ended disappointingly, when Newport I.O.W. won 3-0 at Victoria Park.

When the going gets tough, the tough get going!

The New Year commenced with a tough away draw against Weston-super-Mare, followed by a journey to Wealdstone, the game finishing 2-1 in Salisbury's favour. After the victory at Wealdstone the team hit a purple patch, going on to win five games without conceding a single goal. This included a fine away performance against promotion hopefuls Havant Town. A worrying feature was the injury list which included club captain Paul Batty, who was out of action with a serious knee injury. Newcomers who made their mark with the club were Paul Morrell, who was signed from the Hong Kong club Sing Tao and Gary

Manson from Dorchester Town. Also welcomed back by Salisbury was Mark Payne after business commitments had ruled him out for the first-half of the season.

At the beginning of March the promotion race was hotting up and the top four positions as at 11th March 1995 read:

	P	W	D	L	F	A	Pts
Salisbury	**28**	**19**	**5**	**4**	**62**	**26**	**62**
Waterlooville	27	19	4	4	54	18	61
Baldock Town	28	18	6	4	59	33	60
Havant Town	25	17	3	5	50	19	54

Salisbury continued their march to Championship honours. Their determination was emphasised in the game against Tonbridge. With the visitors building up a 3-1 lead at Victoria Park, they fought back with goals from Sanders and Chalk to share the points.

Wasted journey match
An impressive run of 18 consecutive games without defeat came to an end at Braintree Town on Tuesday 11th April. The match should have taken place in January when the team travelled all the way to Braintree only to have the game called off 45 minutes before kick-off because of a frozen pitch.

After this set-back, they commenced the vital Easter programme with a fine 2-0 win away at in form Fareham Town with 'keeper Steve Weaver saving a penalty. They then saw off Erith & Belvedere 5-1 at Victoria Park, and this was followed by wins over high-fliers Waterlooville away and Havant at home. They were in superb form at Waterlooville and with goals from Jason Lovell and Ian Chalk returned home 2-0 winners.

Hearts in mouth time
Salisbury's biggest gate of the season was on Monday 1st May, when 1054 flocked to Victoria Park to see the Whites defeat Havant Town in an emotionally draining game. There were no goals going into the final minute when Havant were penalised. Up stepped specialist Simon Browne, who executed a precise free-kick with his left foot to score and send the Salisbury supporters into ecstasy.

Simon Browne

Coming up to the last game of the season it was still possible that Baldock Town could snatch the Championship away from Salisbury. The Whites had to slip up at home to Wealdstone and Baldock had to win by a big enough margin at Margate. Ian Chalk scored first in the 25th minute and then added a second on 41 minutes, but Wealdstone got back into the game with a second half goal. This did not help the Salisbury supporters' nerves until the home side were awarded a penalty five minutes from time. Once again Simon Browne was the man who calmed the anxieties by slotting home the spot-kick; 3-1 to Salisbury. The match, promotion and Championship had come to Victoria Park

At the whistle, scenes were reminiscent of the first Championship side in 1947/48, when the Whites won Western League Division II. Scores of supporters waited patiently outside the pavilion to greet manager Geoff Butler and his magnificent team.

Many accolades were paid following the successful season; notably Geoff Butler was made Beazer Homes League Southern

Photographer Roger Elliott of the Salisbury Journal and Times captured this scene when Salisbury City F.C. gained promotion to the Premier Division by defeating Havant Town 1-0 at Victoria Park.

Division, 'Manager of the Year'. Also there was a civic reception by the District Council at the Guildhall and the manager was presented with a special community award.

Enthusiastic Salisbury City F.C. supporters greeting the players in the Guildhall Square, following their open top bus tour of the city-centre with the B.H.L. Southern Division Trophy.

Happy Salisbury City F.C. players enjoying the Civic Reception, at the Guildhall Salisbury.

Salisbury City F.C. players and officials ready for the ride around the city-centre

---

The Non-league Club Directory Award

The Non-league Club Directory named Salisbury City as the West of England, 'Non-League Club of the Year' in their awards for season 1994/95. The Directory said 'For much longer than they will wish to remember, Salisbury City have been described as that friendly club that plays in a "Park"! Progress seemed to be limited by this restriction but now another excellent side built by long serving Geoff Butler is actually in the Beazer Premier Division and plans for a bright future are confidently being discussed. Their Championship win was well deserved and their loyal supporters will be thoroughly enjoying the chance to see their heroes taking on the top Beazer sides once again.'

The 1995–96 Season — Peter J. Waterhouse

Back Where We Belong

Would the new summer signings, Matthew Parkin, Robbie Harbut, Richard Paskins and Lee Webb complete Geoff Butler's blueprint for Beazer Homes League Premier Division consolidation? Alas two notable departures during the close season were that of the previous season's top scorer, Jason Lovell and Duncan Burns to Bashley and Waterlooville respectively.

Salisbury's opening league match was away to promotion favourites Rushden & Diamonds, on Saturday 19th August, in front of a gate of 1532.They went down 3-0, but were far from disgraced.

Martyrs escape

The first home game was against Merthyr Tydfil on Wednesday 23rd August; Merthyr had been a Vauxhall Conference side the previous season. The Evening Echo described the game as a '0-0 massacre'. The Whites should have won comfortably but once again they could not convert their good approach work into goals and the brilliant form of the Merthyr Tydfil 'keeper, Gary Wager, held the score at the final whistle to 0-0.

Yet another home game, which should have been won after leading 2-1 was against Hastings Town. However, six minutes of defensive mayhem put Hastings 4-2 up. The Whites were still in the game when Gary Manson reduced the deficit two minutes from time and there was more drama with a penalty award right on full-time, but Simon Browne's spot-kick was saved.

On August Bank Holiday Monday, they suffered a 2-0 defeat at Gloucester City. Happily they secured their first home win against Sudbury Town on 2nd September with goals from Paskins (2) and Harbut. The following Tuesday they lost 2-0 at Crawley.

F.A. Cup rounds beckon

Saturday the 9th, saw the team on the F.A. Cup trail once again, with a home tie in the First Qualifying Round against Hungerford Town. Goals from Harbut, Manson, Browne, Guy and Chalk saw them through with another home match this time against Newport I.O.W. In a disappointing and inept performance their F.A. Cup hopes ended with a 3-1 defeat.

F.A. Cup Results 23/9/95

Salisbury	1	Newport I.O.W.	3	Welton Rovers	1	Trowbridge Town	2
Workingham Town	1	Aldershot Town	2	Bideford Town	4	Taunton Town	2

On the last Saturday of September the Whites commenced a run of seven matches undefeated. In the game against Gravesend &

Northfleet, they secured their third league victory, with a brace of goals from Gary Manson. Away from league action, they defeated Poole Town 5-0 in the first-leg of the Dr Martens Cup, and a 2-0 home win against Fisher '93, saw them into the F.A. Trophy Second Round.

High football drama at Victoria Park

Two remarkable games took place at Victoria Park. The first, on Wednesday 25th October, was when Gloucester City were the visitors and for 85 minutes the Whites were totally outplayed. The most ardent Salisbury City supporter must have marvelled at the scintillating football displayed by the opposition; they did well just restricting Gloucester City to three goals.

With only five minutes to full-time, Gary Manson suddenly developed a voracious appetite for goals, with first what was thought to be was a consolation goal. Pushing forward, he then got Salisbury right back into the game with goal number two. With Gloucester rocking and home supporters shouting themselves hoarse, Matthew Parkin hit a tremendous shot from 30 yards which smacked against the Gloucester cross-bar. On 90 minutes, Manson levelled the score 3-3, to complete his incredible hat-trick; the opposition supporters looked to be in deep shock as they left Victoria Park.

The second dramatic game was on the following Saturday (28th October) when Cheltenham Town were the visitors. They made a great start to the game, when the ex-Salisbury striker, Jimmy Smith, lobbed the ball over the goalkeeper, Steve Weaver from 15 yards just 19 seconds into the game. However, the Whites never lost confidence in themselves and on 20 minutes got back on level terms with a Simon Browne free-kick from fully 20 yards. They found themselves 3-1 down in a five minute spell in the second-half; Wayne Noble then brought them back into the game after 59 minutes with a stinging shot that took a slight deflection before hitting the back of the net to make the score 3-2. Once again the never-say-die spirit prevailed when they were awarded a free-kick in injury time. Martin Blackler's ball was only half cleared and it was left to Kevin Clements to score with another 20 yard shot to make the final score 3-3.

Salisbury had then completed two remarkable come backs

against two classy sides in just four days. A word of advice to new supporters, never leave the ground early.

In the F.A. Trophy Second Qualifying Round clash versus Sudbury Town at Victoria Park on Saturday 4th November, they were held to a 2-2 draw, after making all the running. Noble (penalty) and Chalk were the scorers. In the first replay at Sudbury on Tuesday 7th November, after extra-time the scores were locked at 2-2. Unfortunately the Whites lost the toss for choice of venue for the second replay and Sudbury won 3-2 to progress to the next round.

How did they get on? – Don't ask

For the first time in 11 Saturdays Salisbury played away when they travelled to Hastings Town on Saturday 11th November and lost 6-2. The following Saturday Halesowen Town were the visitors to Victoria Park and as the game entered its final minute the City looked to have the three points. Then they were punished twice from corners, the first a header from a flick-on. From the kick-off they gave the ball away immediately and Halesowen swept back down the field, won another corner resulting in the ball being

scrambled in again at the far-post. The final result was 3-2 leading to another thoroughly depressing weekend for the club and its supporters.

Salisbury notched up league victory number four against Atherstone United at Victoria Park on Saturday 2nd December with goals from Manson and Clements. The following week saw them make the long journey to Stafford Rangers. Stafford had gone 19 league games without success, but by the law of averages would have

Robbie Harbut giving it some in the game versus Halesowen.

to win sooner or later. Unfortunately for Salisbury, their losing sequence came to an end when they won 2-1.

Supporters were given an early Christmas present with a win at home 1-0 to V.S. Rugby, on 16th December with Paul Masters scoring. They remained on the winning trail with their first away victory in the league in the season, gaining three precious points at Burton Albion, thanks to a Gary Manson goal. They failed to make it three straight wins going down 2-1 at home to Baldock Town on Saturday 23rd December but made amends by beating Dorchester Town 2-0 at the Wessex Stadium on Boxing Day with goals from Sandrey and Masters before losing at home to Gresley Rovers 4-1 on 13th January 1996.

Further into the New Year Salisbury went five games unbeaten. Of these, three were in the league at home to Crawley Town 2-1, Burton Albion 2-0 and away at Cambridge City 3-1. Then after drawing 1-1 at Trowbridge Town in the Dr Martens Cup 3rd Round they progressed to round four of the competition by winning the replay at Victoria Park on 21st February. They marched on in the Dr Martens Cup, beating Newport A.F.C. away 2-1 on Monday 26th February. Ironically, Newport defeated Salisbury two days later in the league game at Victoria Park 3-1. However, the next Saturday, at home, the Whites got back to their winning ways with a 1-0 victory over Cambridge City, with Carroll netting.

They now faced a sequence of seven away games, resulting in three draws versus Gravesend & Northfleet, Sudbury Town and Chelmsford. This was followed by three defeats against Ilkeston Town, Worcester City and Baldock Town. An solitary away win at V.S. Rugby completed the seven.

City on wrong end of 'away goal rule'

Salisbury were now steadily picking up points and, as at the 2nd April, they occupied 13th position in the league with 43 points, just seven points off the 'magical 50 points' for virtual safety. After the 0-0 home draw on 30th March against Chelmsford City, they made the journey to Baldock Town on the following Wednesday for the first leg semi-final clash in the Dr Martens Cup, which ended 0-0. In the second leg at Victoria Park, the game ended 1-1, which meant the Cup run ended on the away goal rule.

Above: Roger Emms although a centre-back, was still among the goals which included getting on the score-sheet at Fisher (F.A. Trophy), Burton Albion and Hastings Town at Victoria Park plus making sure City did not lose with a good strike at Cheltenham Town.

In the final league run-in the Whites secured Beazer Homes League Premier Division status for another season by a draw away to Gresley Rovers 2-2 (13th April) and a 3-1 home victory against Worcester City (27th April). At home they lost 2-0 to Ilkeston Town and the league Champions, Rushden & Diamonds again by the same score-line on 24th April. The campaign concluded with a very creditable draw away to third placed Cheltenham Town 3-3.

They won the Wiltshire Premier Shield for the first time since 1978/79, when they defeated Chippenham Town in the final at Westbury United F.C. football ground on Wednesday 1st May, thanks to a brace of goals from Robbie Harbut.

Manager Geoff Butler ably supported by assistant manager Gordon Hobson, had skilfully guided the Whites through the trials and tribulations of Premier Division Football and the supporters could now look forward to next season with renewed confidence.

Gordon Hobson.

6

Dr Martens southern

The 1996–97 Season — Peter J. Waterhouse

Last Season at Victoria Park

Summer signings

The sound Salisbury squad was further strengthened by the summer signings of Mark Smith from A.F.C. Bournemouth, Jonathan Preston from Bournemouth Sports and Peter Conning from Trowbridge. Chris Shaw returned to the club for his third spell and Micky Spencer had now signed on a permanent basis having spent the end of the previous season on loan from Bath City. In addition goalkeeper John Simpkins who also spent the end of the previous season on loan became a permanent signing. Robbie Carroll left the club in the summer to move into the ICIS League with Basingstoke Town. Robbie had scored 16 goals in 71 appearances.

Salisbury City's first league match of the 1996/7 campaign was away to Gravesend & Northfleet. Just three minutes of bad defending denied them a winning start to the season. Simon Browne, the free-kick king, hit home a 21st minute drive from 20 yards to give Salisbury the lead and Micky Spencer's brave header thirteen minutes later restored the advantage, just after the home side had levelled the score. That lead was held until the 78th minute when Gravesend's Mark Mundy drifted in at the far post to head

223

home. Two minutes later the same player's head did the damage again when he rose unchallenged to score from a free-kick to make the score 3-2 to the home side.

Salisbury riding high

With the disappointment of the first league game behind them, Salisbury hit top league form by going nine matches undefeated including away wins at Merthyr Tydfil (3-2), Chelmsford City (2-1) and a superb victory at Cheltenham. In this match they opened the scoring in the 82nd minute with a magnificent Robbie Harbut strike. Cheltenham were awarded a penalty late in the game which could have robbed them of victory but John Simpkins made a brilliant save diving low to his left to keep the ball out. Matt Lovell eventually sealed the points with a well struck free-kick over the Cheltenham wall into the far corner of the net.

Dr Martens League Premier Division positions at 9th October:

Top 4	P	W	D	L	F	A	Pts
Gresley Rovers	10	7	3	0	18	5	24
Gloucester City	10	7	1	2	22	10	24
Salisbury City	**10**	**6**	**3**	**1**	**18**	**11**	**21**
Halesowen Town	11	6	2	3	18	11	20

The impressive run of league results came to an end on Saturday 12th October when Ashford Town won 1-0 at Victoria Park, and this was followed by another defeat at home to Cheltenham Town 2-1 the following Wednesday.

   The Whites picked themselves up after the two home defeats by defeating Halesowen away 2-1 and drawing away to King's Lynn 1-1. The run of eight unbeaten away wins in the league came to an end when they went down 2-1 at Sittingbourne on 28th December and, sadly, on the following Wednesday (New Year's Day), they were beaten at Newport A.F.C. 3-1.

Trying to keep the ball rolling

There was a somewhat indifferent second-half to the season and sustaining the momentum of the opening months of the season proved difficult. The team encountered a catalogue of injuries and suspensions which took its toll.

The depletion of the team was so grave that there were six senior players missing for the away game at Nuneaton which resulted in a 4-0 defeat. Nevertheless, the Whites recorded away victories at Sudbury (1-0), Ashford (1-0) and there was the match at Gloucester on the last day of the season, which saw an incredible drama unfold. Gloucester City needed the three points from the game to secure promotion to the Vauxhall Conference. They began the match with confidence and found the back of the Salisbury net within minutes, only to have the goal ruled offside. On 21 minutes they took the lead when they hit the ball from the left into the Salisbury goal-mouth and found the outstretched leg of a Salisbury defender who turned the ball into his own net.

The scores were levelled in the 13th minute of the second-half. Ian Chalk put the Gloucester defence under pressure causing the ball to break loose to Lee Webb who slotted home from six yards. Then, 13 minutes from full-time, a Gloucester defender was sent off for a professional foul on Robbie Harbut. The Whites quickly capitalised on their one man advantage. A Simon Browne corner was headed towards goal by Roger Emms for Lee Webb to net from close range for his second goal of the match. With only two minutes remaining Robbie Harbut crashed in goal number three from 18 yards.

Salisbury players and supporters run the gauntlet

A section of Gloucester City supporters could not contain their disappointment and frustration when they spilled onto the pitch and the referee withdrew the players. When the two sides returned they proceeded to play out the final few minutes which saw the second-half ultimately ending just over one hour after it began. The Salisbury victory opened the door for Gloucester's near neighbour and rival, Cheltenham Town, to gain promotion to the Vauxhall Conference as runners up. In a few seasons they were to make a meteoric rise from Dr Martens League Premier Division to Nationwide English League Div. II to be an inspiration to all ambitious non-league clubs.

It was imperative that Salisbury retain their Dr Martens League Premier Division status prior to moving to the Ray McEnhill Stadium at Old Sarum. They finished the season in a mid-table position proving that they were a match for virtually any team in the league by beating all the top five teams apart from the Champions, Gresley Rovers.

Manager Geoff Butler used the adjective 'satisfactory' in describing the season.

Good-bye to Victoria Park

As the season drew to its conclusion it was time to bid a fond farewell to Victoria Park, the ground that had served the club since 1947 but ultimately scuppered the Whites promotion in 1993. The bitter disappointment and frustration this had caused has already been documented in this book.

Looking out over the ground from the old stand, just like many of the supporters who witnessed the final game Salisbury were to play at Victoria Park, was a time for reflection. There were memories of the many F.A. Cup and league encounters which had taken place there over the past 50 years, especially the local 'derbies' against Andover, Basingstoke, Dorchester, Trowbridge, Yeovil and Weymouth which had attracted gates of thousands. A few supporters would still have recollections of the wonderful Weymouth epic of 1947.

The old ground was undoubtedly showing its age with the ancient pavilion being nicknamed the Wendy Hut and the pitch suffering the indignity of being named the cabbage-patch.

Known by some as the 'Wendy Hut' but fond memories prevail of the pavilion to all officials, players and Salisbury City F.C. supporters.

The Last Game at Victoria Park

A gate of 1024 witnessed Salisbury's last ever game at Victoria Park on Thursday 1st May 1997 when old friends Dorchester Town were the opposition. The supporters circulated with the players before the kick off and the young supporters had the opportunity for communal photo-shots with all the players, management and directors before the kick-off.

Although a sense of sadness was felt at the occasion, a carnival atmosphere prevailed together with a positive outlook for the future at the Raymond McEnhill Stadium.

Both teams pull-out all the stops

After a three match losing sequence Salisbury were anxious to bow out of Victoria Park with a victory and their hopes were raised when they were awarded a penalty after 35 minutes. Sandy Baird stepped up to take the spot-kick but the Dorchester goalkeeper made an excellent save by palming the ball over the bar. At the other end Salisbury City's outstanding goalkeeper, John Simpkins, pulled off a point-blank save from Dorchester forward Tommy Killick.

Then Paul Masters created a moment of football magic when he acrobatically hit the ball on the volley towards the top corner of the Dorchester goal, but the goalkeeper, Paul Gadsby made a remarkable save to prevent a score. On 85 minutes, Dorchester's Martyn Sullivan hit a brilliant shot from 10 yards to beat John Simpkins but the ball clipped the crossbar and the score remained 0-0 at the final whistle at Victoria Park.

Salisbury City F.C. quest for Cup glory

The quest for F.A. Cup glory season commenced on Saturday 14th September against the Combined Counties League side, Godalming and Guildford in a dire struggle at Victoria Park. The Whites were rather fortunate to settle for a 0-0 draw, with two superb saves goalkeeper John Simpkins to save their blushes.

In the replay the following Tuesday they were boosted by the return of Ian Chalk and Paul

Masters and won 2-0, with goals from Simon Browne (penalty) and Lee Webb.

See-sawing up and down

When the Whites travelled to Cheltenham Town for the 2nd Qualifying Round match on 28th September the team were understandably confident thinking a repeat of the league game a few weeks before would be very welcome. In a thrilling encounter they had a dream start when Robbie Harbut pounced to fire home into the top corner of the Cheltenham net after only seven minutes. Cheltenham got back into the game on 13 minutes when Darren Waight hit a shot just inside the far post. Salisbury were back in the lead after 25 minutes, Roger Emms powerfully heading home a Chris Shaw cross.

On 39-minutes Cheltenham were level once again when Jason Eaton bundled the ball over the goal-line. Eleven minutes into the second-half the home team were in front for the first time when Eaton headed past the Salisbury goalkeeper. Salisbury threw caution to the winds by pushing Roger Emms up front and the strategy paid off very quickly, with the same player nodding the ball onto Lee Webb who scored from a tight angle.

Unfortunately, within two minutes Cheltenham were back in the lead when Jason Eaton completed his hat-trick with another header to make the score 4-3 to Cheltenham. Salisbury laid siege to the Cheltenham goal and Dave Boyce hit a fierce shot only to see the goalkeeper tip the ball over the crossbar. The home side were very pleased to hear the referee blow the final whistle.

F.A. Cup Results 28/9/96

Cheltenham Tn.	4	Salisbury City	3	Weymouth	1	Abingdon Town	0
Bashley	4	Thame United	3	Witney Town	2	Wimborne Town	2

F.A. Umbro Trophy

With victories against Witney Town at home in the 2nd Qualifying Round, and a 2-1 win at home to Harrow Borough after a 2-2 draw at Harrow in the following round Salisbury progressed to the 1st Round Proper with an away tie at Hastings on Friday 17th January 1997. They trailed 1-0 at half-time through a goal on 30 minutes but, once again, they used the tactic of pushing Roger

Three scenes from Salisbury's F.A. Trophy games. *Top:* Lee Webb centres from the wing in the Witney game.
Centre: Matt Lovell on the ball in the Harrow Borough game.
Bottom: Simon Browne who scored for Salisbury in the 1-1 draw versus Dorchester.

Emms up front and this paid dividends within 10 minutes when Ian Chalk and Roger Emms got on the score sheet in the 55th and 58th minutes. The Whites were then in control and the match was settled when Lee Webb turned in a cross

from Mark Smith at the far post. This was the signal for Roger Emms to return to the centre of defence and Salisbury had little trouble holding their advantage.

They had reached the 2nd Round Proper of the F.A. Trophy for the first time in their history. They faced Dorchester Town at Victoria Park on Saturday 8th February in front of a gate of 727 but had to settle for a 1-1 draw after scoring first through Simon Browne. In the replay, played at Dorchester on Tuesday 11th February, substandard defending contributed to their downfall. They found it difficult to cope playing into a strong wind in the first-half and in the 22nd minute, Craig Wilkinson opened the scoring for the home side following a goalmouth scramble. They increased their lead on 30 minutes when they were awarded a penalty. Craig Taylor made no mistake from the spot to put Dorchester 2-0 up. Just minutes later the Whites got back into the game when Ian Chalk rounded the Dorchester goalkeeper. Salisbury were then applying the pressure and Roger Emms knocked down a Simon Browne free-kick for Barry Cranmer to tuck the ball in at the far post. They failed to capitalise on the high wind to their advantage and, cruelly, just two minutes from full-time Owen Pickard hit home Dorchester's winner.

A victory would have meant a prestigious and financially rewarding home game against the Vauxhall Conference side Woking in the 3rd Round. The only crumb of comfort was that they would have had to play Woking without seven senior players due to suspensions and injuries.

New shape appears on Old Sarum skyline

To help the finances involved in building the new stadium the club gave supporters the opportunity to purchase a building block which was to be used in the construction of the new stadium.

Throughout the 1996/97 season work at the new stadium at Old Sarum had been gaining momentum week by week. Many enthusiastic Salisbury City supporters made regular visits to the ground to view the development and construction taking place.

Buy A Block!

Salisbury City Football Club is offering YOU a unique opportunity to help finance the new stadium at Old Sarum. The club's asking individuals and local businesses to contribute by buying a block used in the construction. In return your name will be engraved on a plaque and displayed at the new ground for evermore. The cost of this once in a lifetime opportunity is £15 for individual supporters and £58.75 for businesses (incl. V.A.T.).

To show our appreciation, all participants will receive a complementary ticket for any home league game at the new ground during the opening season. Any business playing £60 or more will also receive a £10 reduction on a programme or pitch-board advertisement for the 1997/98 season.

It has taken the football club fifteen years to get this far. Now the finishing line is in sight. With one final push we will achieve our goal of owning a stadium with superb facilities that we can all be proud of.

If you would like to participate, please return the application form with your remittance, making cheques payable to Salisbury City Football Club. Further application forms will appear in the Matchday Programmes over the next few weeks. You can also pick one up at the office at 38 Endless Street, or from the Pavilion on match days.

Many thanks, Geoff

Although the above photo was taken before the final game at Victoria Park this was the squad for that day (versus Dorchester Town).
Back row l/r: G. Butler (manager), S. Baird, B. Cranmer, R. Emms (*capt.*), S. Mildenhall, J. Simpkins, S. Browne, G. Fletcher, D. Rofe, M. Guy, M. Lovell.
Front row: L. Webb, R. Harbut, M. Parkin, (Cranmer, T. *mascot*), I. Chalk, P. Masters, J. Preston, C. Shaw and unknown trainer.

Some of the early work taking place at the new ground and stadium.

The Raymond McEnhill Stadium

It was a very popular decision when the club decided to name the new stadium after the highly respected Chairman Raymond McEnhill.

The following statement appeared in the club programme of 22nd March 1997.

OUR NEW STADIUM

AN IMPORTANT ANNOUNCEMENT

On Thursday it was officially announced that the football club's new stadium at Old Sarum would be called the Raymond McEnhill Stadium after our chairman.

Ray has been chairman at the football club for 15 years and without his support during this time there would be no football club at all by now. I think it is a fitting tribute that we should name the new stadium after him.

The board of directors were unanimous in their support of such a decision, which was taken without consultation with Ray.

He was slightly embarrassed and reluctant to agree at first and wishes to stress that he had no part in the decision.

I can think of no better way of showing our gratitude than by naming our new home after him and I hope you all agree.

Geoff

Roger's final goodbye to 'Vicky Park'

Club captain Roger Emms wrote a very good article in ' *The Captain's Corner*' feature of the programme.

Here is an extract from his column:

> It will feel strange leading the team out tonight, hopefully in front of a few more people than we've been getting lately. There's no doubt about it, that tonight is a sad occasion as well as a momentous occasion and we mustn't forget that Victoria Park doesn't just belong to us. Anyone can take the mickey out of the pitch and facilities in this world of super-stadiums. But it has also belonged to those who have played here over the last fifty years, when things were very different.

Many clubs sent messages of good wishes prior to the move to the Raymond McEnhill Stadium. Here is a selection of them:

A few words from our friends in football.......

'Farewell to Victoria Park. We shall miss the old ground, the scene of many battles and we shall certainly miss the splendid hospitality and friendship we always received there. Hope to see you at the new stadium!'
Peter Faulkner, Chairman, Waterlooville Football Club.

'Like you, we are moving ground, but you have beaten us to it! In a way it is a shame that we are both leaving grounds with character, but if we are both to progress we have no choice but to move to grounds with superior facilities. Even though you are leaving your Victoria Park base, the memories of it will remain with you all for the rest of your lives.'
Brian Spare and all your friends at Gresley Rovers.

'R.I.P. Victoria Park and may your resurrection at the Raymond McEnhill Stadium be happy and successful'.
Bob Twyford, General Manager and all at Bath City F.C.

'We at Manor Park wish the Club all the best for the future as you leave Victoria Park for pastures new. Personally I have visited the ground on many occasions, especially during my years at Weston-super-Mare, when we always seemed to be drawn together in the F.A. Cup or Trophy!'
Phillip J. Wright, Commercial Manager, Nuneaton Borough A.F.C.

'I think the Worcester City fans will remember the sunshine, daisies on the pitch and the open goal which Ian Scott missed in our last game at Victoria Park. Those with longer memories will no doubt also look back on our F.A. Cup defeat in 1979. A trip to Salisbury was always something a bit different and we hope Old Sarum proves to be the same. We're hoping to move too before long — memories are important, but so is the future. Best wishes.
Julian Pugh, Worcester City F.C.

I was pleased and delighted to have been asked to write these notes for the last ever Matchday Programme for 'the Whites' at Victoria Park. It will remain a collectors item not only for myself and 'Whites' fans, but for many football enthusiasts from all over the country and possibly even further afield.
We are privileged that Geoff Butler wanted Dorchester Football Club to play the last game at Victoria Park. The next question is will 'the Whites' last season at Victoria Park end without a win over their nearest rivals 'The Magpies'. If it is, it will be the first for a long time and my first as manager of Dorchester Town F.C. In fact, I think it would be my first ever as player and manager....winning here has been as difficult as anything.
Many congratulations on everything you have achieved at Victoria Park and I wish you all, (as much as my own team), every success at Old Sarum. With very best wishes.
Stuart Morgan, Dorchester Town F.C.

The club produced a special Souvenir programme to commemorate the last match at Victoria Park. It featured a number of special recollections and observations by players, ex-players and supporters. The very much missed, Cyril Smith, one of the city's greatest sportsman and ambassadors, made this contribution to the programme.

'This 50 years for me means the very beginning, because your mind always goes back to the beginning of your career. The memories of the first season will always stick in my mind, because you always remember everything that was happening at the time. We had a little bit of success too, winning the Western League Div. II, which made it all the more recognisable.

It was a very good team for the time, bearing in mind WWII had just finished and everyone was a little bit starved of entertainment. We had gates of 5000 plus on Bank Holidays, it was marvellous. I remember all the trailers and horse-carts that we had to hire in for the Weymouth and Newport County games. As you know before all that I had been "on call" for Arsenal, especially in the two years from 1944 while WWII was on. I used to get a telegram from them when they wanted me to play and I was all ready to move to London in Christmas 1946. Unfortunately I

Photo Roger Elliott,
Salisbury Journal.

was called up for National Service! Of course, I was very glad when Salisbury got up and running and I signed for them in the summer of 1947 and in August we kicked-off.

Of course we've had some good runs since with different teams and I don't think anyone will forget the F.A. Cup against Millwall at the 'Dell'. I know we lost, but I don't think we were outplayed on the day in anyway at all.

As for 1997, well it's a big step to go forward and think about Conference football, but if the team are good enough and their ambitions are big enough, then good luck to them. We must all pay tribute in the meantime to Ray and what he's done for the new stadium, because without him, I don't think it would be possible even to think that far.' <u>Cyril Smith was talking to Kevan Gover</u>

The 1997–98 Season — Peter J. Waterhouse

The First Season at the Raymond McEnhill Stadium

All's well that ....

At last the great day had finally arrived – Saturday 16th August 1997 – almost 50 years to the day since the first fixture away to R.A.F. Locking. It was Salisbury City F.C.'s first league game at the Raymond McEnhill Stadium Old Sarum. The curtain raiser was against the reigning Dr Martens Premier Champions, Gresley Rovers, who had been unable to take their place in the Conference due to their ground not meeting the Conference criteria.

A good crowd of 574 spectators cheered the captain, Roger Emms and his team down the stand steps onto the playing pitch. Brian Carter and his team of dedicated groundsmen had produced a playing pitch of outstanding quality. From the stands the pitch had the appearance of a lush cricket outfield.

Brian Carter

Red tape abounds

The club had endured an anxious wait after the Dr Martens League grading committee's inspection revealed that the plumbing work was incomplete in the temporary changing rooms. Thankfully, they gave the club an extra 24 hours to carry out the necessary work by a 5 p.m. Monday deadline. Just prior to the opening pre-season friendly against A.F.C. Bournemouth the club had to satisfy the Wiltshire County Council's safety team on the same day.

The green light was given just hours before the evening kick-off. In the worst scenario, they could have been fined £15,000 and even expelled from the Dr Martens League if the deadline had not been met. This was certainly a nail-biting 24 hours for the normally unflappable manager, Geoff Butler and his management colleagues.

Etched in history for ever – Simon Browne

A bumper gate of 876, saw Salisbury entertain A.F.C. Bournemouth in a pre-season friendly. They went down 3-1 with Simon Browne scoring the first ever Salisbury goal at the new stadium.

The Whites prematurely celebrating Dave Puckett's 'goal' disallowed for hand-ball.

Authors note: The Ray McEnhill Stadium became known to the supporters as the Raymac. and it is this name that we will use from now on within this book.

Ian Chalk falls to the ground after scoring the Salisbury winner against Gresley.

The opening league match proved to be an absolute cracker. The hero of the day was Ian Chalk, the hard-working mid-fielder. From a Lee Webb pass inside the penalty area he coolly feigned to shoot twice and then flicked the ball to the side of the Gresley goalkeeper and this goal, six minutes from full-time, ensured the Whites maximum points.

Throughout the season the club faced a catalogue of injuries resulting in difficulty in fielding a settled side. The first setback suffered was losing the services of the promising and dependable goalkeeper, John Simpkins, through illness. Geoff Butler drafted in the Swindon Town 'keeper Steve Mildenhall, on loan, but he was not allowed to take part in F.A. competitions. Throughout the season the Whites saw seven different goalkeepers perform for the club. By the end of August they had played five league games, winning twice, drawing once and losing twice, which included a fine away win at Atherstone United 3-0, with goals from Webb(2) and Preston(1). They occupied 10th position in the league.

Autumn dawns on an indifferent 'City'

The month of September saw Salisbury go down 3-0 at home to Dorchester Town on Wednesday 3rd, followed by a 2-0 defeat at

Worcester City the following Monday. Thankfully, they bounced back with a 3-0 victory at Sittingbourne, with goals from Sandrey, Puckett and Chalk. Nineteen-year old Joe McCormack, transferred from Fareham Town, made his debut in goal and faced a baptism of fire in the match at home on Wednesday 24th September against Merthyr Tydfil. The Merthyr strike force were on fire as they hammered home five

Kevin Braybrook

goals to win 5-2 in an action packed game. Other players making their debuts in that game were Chris Male from Newport I.O.W. and Kevin Braybrook, the former under 18 Northern Ireland International, from Yeovil Town.

October saw just three league matches due to the F.A. Cup commitments. To Salisbury's credit the team took seven league points out of a possible nine, although the team was plagued with injury problems. The home game against Tamworth, with goals from Whale, Finlayson and Braybrook, saw a 3-2 victory. A very good point was picked up at Ashford Town with an Ian Chalk strike. This match saw Matt Lovell making his 100th appearance. The last home game of October saw Hastings Town beaten 2-0 with Whale and Finlayson on the score-sheet.

Matt Lovell who played his 100th league game for Salisbury against Ashford Town.

The first day of November saw them at home to King's Lynn, the team that ended the F.A. Cup run seven days earlier. Salisbury found themselves without the entire back four through injury and, they went down 3-2, with goals from Holmes and Braybrook.

They endured an agonising November gaining just one point out of a possible 15. The point was gained in the home draw against Worcester City on Saturday 22th November from a Holmes goal. Salisbury saw defeats at home to Burton Albion 2-0, away to

Nuneaton Borough 2-1 and Halesowen Town 4-1. The home game against Burton Albion saw Dave Mogg in action in goal; the experienced goalkeeper was signed from Forest Green Rovers.

Winter skies darken

Salisbury opened the busy December period with a well-earned point away to Gloucester City on Tuesday 2nd December, thanks to a 89-minute strike from Scott Bartlett. The following Saturday 6th December, Ashford Town were held to a draw at the Raymac. Again Salisbury returned with another well earned point from Bromsgrove Rovers. They

A later photo of Scott Bartlett who scored away to Gloucester.

were 2-0 down on 54 minutes, but their fighting qualities prevailed and goals from Puckett on 55 and Housley on 76 minutes, saw the score at 2-2. The Saturday before Christmas, 20th December, the Salisbury supporters were treated to a Christmas feast of four goals, Emms, Preston and Browne(2) scoring against Sittingbourne at Old Sarum. On Boxing Day, they made the unsuccessful journey to Dorchester Town, losing to a Tommy Killick goal in the seventh minute.

Salisbury returned to action at the Raymac. the following day against St Leonards Stamcroft. Here maximum points were secured with goals from Puckett and Whale. They entertained Forest Green Rovers for the New Year's Day fixture at Old Sarum.

Forest Green had been promoted from the Southern Division of the league in the previous season. Their home ground was The Lawn, which is situated in Nailsworth, a small market town with a population of 6000 on the edge of the Cotswolds in south Gloucestershire. They went on to gain promotion to the Conference, a remarkable achievement in all circumstances.

Injuries take their toll again

In the match the injury jinx which had dogged the team all season struck again when club captain, Roger Emms, sustained a nasty injury to his ankle which would keep the tough centre-half out of action until the end of February. In a hard fought game the Whites went down 2-0 to the Championship contenders.

The following Saturday a crowd of 1314 witnessed the away game at Crawley's superb £5-million stadium. Salisbury's injury crisis was accentuated when no less than eleven changes to the team were announced at the match. Sadly, Crawley's Simon Ullathorne scored the only goal of the game. On Saturday January 17th Salisbury made the journey to St Leonards Stamcroft where they lost 6-2, with Bright and Chalk getting on the score sheet.

Saturday 24th January they entertained Nuneaton Borough at the Raymac. This was the match that saw Ian Chalk, one of the most outstanding players in the history of the club celebrate his 500th game. Manager Geoff Butler paid this tribute to Ian Chalk in the programme notes that day.

Ian Chalk

Loyalty is a word seldom found these days in football, but today Ian celebrates his 500th game for the club. This really is a fantastic achievement by a player who is loved and respected by supporters and team mates alike. Ian has been a pleasure to manage over the years and I consider myself fortunate to have had the pleasure of his services. He should feel extremely proud of his achievement, not just in terms of games and loyalty, but also his magnificent contribution over the past 10 years to the progress and success of the Club. Well done Ian. Thanks for everything.

Enjoy the game.   *Geoff*

David Bright opened the scoring on 25 minutes but two goals from Nuneaton on 36 and 37 minutes put the visitors into the lead. However, three minutes later Kevin Braybrook hit the Salisbury equaliser and the game ended 2-2.

Salisbury secured their first league victory of 1998 when they defeated

Halesowen Town on the 31st January at the Raymac., with Ian Chalk scoring the all important goal in the 86th minute. The fans were further heartened that Gordon Hobson had returned to assist Geoff Butler until the end of the season.

Club captain, Roger Emms's reaction was summed up in the programme for the Halesowen match.

> *It's brought a smile to my face, because everyone knows what Gordon can do in terms of motivation and being in and around the players. Both Geoff and Gordon have different strengths and as a team they work very well together. It's the first bit of encouraging football news I've heard all week. Gordon does get close to the players, especially when dishing out instructions. He's a very good motivator and very encouraging. I've got a lot of time for him and so have the players and so it can only be good news for the Club.*

Following the Halesowen match, their manager put 14 of his players on the transfer list. Alas, the following Tuesday, the Whites took a 5-0 hammering away to Bath City. The month of February saw them take just two points from three games, losing away to Hastings, drawing at home with Cambridge City and, on the last Saturday, drawing away at Rothwell.

The 'evergreen' Gordon Hobson playing for Salisbury at Victoria Park in a match versus Halesowen.

John Harvey, left and above the sponsor board with John's name at the top. Below a minutes silence is observed.

Sadly the club lost one of its most loyal supporters when, just hours before the match against Cambridge City, John Harvey died. The Club stated in the following match programme:

It was with deep sadness that Salisbury City Football Club lost one of its most loyal friends just hours before the match against Cambridge City. John Harvey died in the early hours of Saturday 21st February, 1998. Ironically, he was the match-ball sponsor for that day. A minute's silence was observed by both teams before the kick-off.

Ian Chalk said of John:

I've known John for the ten years I've been here and he was a stalwart of the club. He travelled to all the away games. It's a big shock. You need people at the club who do the work that John did and he will be sadly missed.

Geoff Butler added:

John was a wonderful dedicated servant to Salisbury City Football Club and the Supporters Club since 1947. He raised an absolute fortune for the Club through a variety of fund-raising activities. His wife Jean along with John ran the refreshment hut at Victoria Park for several seasons. They were a devoted couple and John will be sadly missed. Our sympathy goes out to Jean and the family.

The first Saturday of March saw the return match of the 'Battle of the Cities' – Salisbury City versus Bath City. The 5-0 hammering at Bath was still fresh in the minds of the Salisbury players and there was great relief when a Robbie Harbut goal secured all three points.

Salisbury's precarious league position was eased by picking up precious points with a 1-1 draw at Tamworth which saw the debut of 17-year old Kevin Bush. A 2-1 victory was secured at home to Atherstone United but a reversal was suffered at King's Lynn, in a 3-0 defeat.

Nail-biting time begins

Salisbury went into April with just six league games to play – three at home and three away and they occupied 18th place in the league, just one point ahead of Bromsgrove Rovers and in a dreaded relegation position.

The first home game of April, a six-pointer, was indeed against Bromsgrove Rovers and this was won to take a massive step towards securing their place in the next season's Premier Division, thanks to goals from Ian Chalk and 'Man of the Match' Leroy Whale. Ian Chalk moved into second place in the leading 'All-time' goal-scorers for the Club, just 16 goals behind Roy Watts (180) and a goal ahead of Roy Fisher.

After the crucial win against Bromsgrove Rovers, Salisbury faced a daunting away game against table-toppers Forest Green Rovers, on Good Friday 10th April. Although they had the majority of the play and were leading by 2-0 at 70 minutes they went down 3-2 with Bright and Thompson getting on the score-sheet.

One moment your up, then ....!

On Easter Monday, they were at home to Gloucester City. Losing by 2-1, super-sub Gordon Hobson levelled the score in injury time but just 30 seconds later the Salisbury supporters joy evaporated into total heartache when Gloucester's Andy Tucker curled a superb shot into the top corner of the Salisbury net to settle the score 3-2 to Gloucester.

They procured a priceless point away to Gresley Rovers on Saturday 18th April with a 1-1 scoreline and the last home game of the season was played on Wednesday 29th April. The stakes could not have been much higher and a victory would have lifted Salisbury clear of the drop zone. The hard-fought match against Rothwell Town which was played in driving rain produced only a 0-0 draw which meant that Salisbury had to win their last match of the season away to third placed Burton Albion on the following Saturday.

All's well that end's well

Salisbury left their best performance of the season to that last game of the season and in doing so avoided the dreaded drop.

They pressed forward from the start; Simon Browne hit a 30 yard shot beating the Burton 'keeper only to see the ball crash against the post. They then took the lead on the 14th minute. Neat play saw David Bright smack a right-foot volley at the Burton 'keeper – the ball swerved to the right leaving the alert Mark Thompson to slot home. Burton got back into the game after being awarded a penalty when their top scorer, Andy Garner, placed the spot-kick into the bottom of the Salisbury net.

The set-back only served to instill more resolve and, just before half-time, the never-say-die attitude of Ian Chalk prevailed when he pursued a long ball out of defence. The gifted mid-fielder held the ball up before playing it back to Danny Holmes whose first-time cross found the head of Dave Bright. He nodded the ball into the far corner of the Burton Albion goal.

The second-half of the match saw the Whites maintain their grip

Team captain, Roger Emms and Simon Browne celebrating along with some of the young joyful Salisbury faithful.

on the game and at the final whistle the score was 2-1 in their favour.

Did the Salisbury supporters dance a gig in Gigant Street, not quite, but the 'Toast of the City' that night was to Geoff Butler/Gordon Hobson's, plucky players.

final bottom 6 places:	P	W	D	L	F	A	Pts
Gresley Rovers	42	14	6	22	59	77	48
Salisbury City	**42**	**12**	**12**	**18**	**53**	**72**	**48**
Bromsgrove Rovers	42	13	6	23	67	85	45
Sittingbourne	42	12	8	22	47	66	44
Ashford Town	42	8	5	29	34	85	29
St Leonards	42	5	10	27	48	97	25

What happened in the Cups?

The F.A. Cup campaign for 1997/8 commenced on September 13th with a home win against Chard Town. Although they enjoyed home advantage again for the 2nd Qualifying Round, against Weston-super-Mare the visitors from Somerset held on for a 2-2 draw. The replay at Weston saw the score deadlocked again at 2-2 after extra-time. Salisbury won the dreaded penalty shoot-out.

A score-line to forget!

On Saturday 11th October, Taunton Town made the journey to Old Sarum for the 3rd Qualifying Round tie. The visitors went down 3-0, which meant the Whites had progressed to the final Qualifying Rounds with a difficult away tie at King's Lynn on the 25th October. Regrettably they were stopped in their tracks going down by 5-0 thus ending their hopes of going into the hat for the 1st Round Proper.

Ian Chalk scored in the game against Taunton.

F.A. Cup Results 25/10/97

King's Lynn	5	Salisbury City	0	Tiverton Town	5	Sudbury	0
Basingstoke	5	Braintree	1	Staines Town	0	Margate	3

F.A. Trophy

Salisbury slumped out of the Trophy at Berkhamstead Town on Saturday 29th November, losing 2-1. Their opponents went into the hat for the 1st Round Proper and were rewarded with an away tie at Kidderminster who won the Trophy in 1987 and were runners-up in 1991 and 1995.

Royal tragedy

After the ups and downs of this season, one event will probably stay in people's minds for many a year and this was marked with two tributes that appeared in the next match-day programme:

Following the weekend's tragic events, Salisbury City Football Club would like to pay its own tribute to Diana, Princess of Wales this evening.
There will be one minute's silence just before kick-off.
Please remember in your thoughts Diana, her family and especially her two sons.
Thank you

It just brings home how unimportant football is when something like this happens.
We're all in deep shock — the whole nation is.

Geoff Butler
Salisbury City Football Club

Danny Rofe climbs high for Salisbury versus Buron Albion in March 1997.

The 1998–99 Season —   Peter J. Waterhouse

The Whites Peaks and Trough Season

Supporters were given the opportunity to see Geoff Butler's new summer signings in action at the pre-season friendly games. The new players included goalkeepers Jason Matthews and Nick Stone, Lee Dyson and Lee Whittle in defence, Adrian Randall, Neil Housley and Tyronne Bowers in mid-field and the prolific goal-scorer Paul Sales. The latter two players became firm favourites with the Salisbury faithful. Paul Sales netted 75 goals for the Whites in 135 games before returning to Bashley. Later he was transferred to the ambitious Eastleigh F.C. before returning to the Raymac in 2005. Tyronne Bowers also joined Eastleigh at a later date.

Tyronne Bowers   Jason   Adie Randall   Paul Sales
                    Matthews

Geoff Butler secured the signature of Adie Randall, arguably one of the most gifted players ever to wear a Salisbury shirt. Unfortunately the Salisbury supporters only had the chance to marvel at his accomplished skills for one short season before he was transferred to Forest Green Rovers for a record fee of £20,000. Details of his career are shown on page 299.

The Whites commenced the new season taking seven points from the opening four games, with two home victories against Tamworth and Weymouth, an away draw at Crawley and an away defeat to Grantham Town. The latter was to signal a losing sequence of five league matches.

Invitation accepted

After the Wednesday evening game against Crawley Town on September 16th, which was lost two-nil, Geoff Butler took the highly unusual step of inviting a Salisbury supporter, Trevor Savage, into the dressing room to question the players on performance and attitude. This may well have been an attempt at amateur psychology but the following makes interesting reading. It appeared in the next matchday programme.

My name is Trevor Savage. As a person who has worked in the sports and leisure industry for the last 23-years as both a sports coach and in managerial roles, I will not criticise the players of our team on their ability. If a player can't perform at the standard of Dr Martens League Premier Division, he should not feature in the team. Players should never be put in a position where they are destined to fail and the management and coaching staff should ensure this does not happen.

My main complaint was the lack of desire and commitment the team has shown at recent home matches. Football is a game of passion, with success only coming from individuals hard work, supported by total teamwork.

Once in the dressing room, I asked the team if they really wanted to play for Salisbury City. Were they really committed to the Club, did they really want to win. Unfortunately, I was greeted by a general silence. This might have been as a result of embarrassment, or perhaps they were told to sit and listen. I then asked the team if they were happy with the performance, and pleased with our league position. At this point, Roger made it quite clear he was very unhappy with the whole team's recent form. I went on to ask the team what the supporters could do to help the team improve, as the last thing many of us want to do is get on the player's backs. Chalkie took the opportunity to say that the supporters are doing all the team expects by turning up each week. It was now up to the players to put things right on the field.

Having had the chance to talk with and meet the players in unusual circumstances, I would like to thank Geoff and the players for listening and particularly Roger and Chalkie for their responses. I wish there had been a few more comments from the others, but perhaps they will let their feet do the talking on the pitch.

I would like to call on the supporters of the Club to look for the positive aspects of the team's future performances, because in sport, 90% of success comes from positive support and encouragement, not criticism.

COME ON CITY – three points will do nicely!

From being one of the Premier Division's early pace-setters, the Whites then plummeted to the third from bottom position in the league table. Up to and including Saturday 13th October they had only taken 12 points from 13 games.

The campaign got back on track on Saturday 7th November when Grantham visited the Raymac. Adie Randall hit the winner to secure a 1-0 victory. The mid-fielder had now scored 11 goals in 18 matches. By the end of the year, Salisbury were regularly collecting league points and the only downside to December was the 4-0 defeat away at Dorchester Town.

Cutting ones teeth at Dr Martens

The side was further strengthened when Geoff Butler's connections with A.F.C. Bournemouth paid dividends. The English League Club agreed to loan their promising young striker, James Hayter and he made his debut at the away match at Halesowen and scored in the 3-3 draw.

An outstanding partnership developed between Paul Sales and James Hayter in the eight games they played together. It was to yield nine goals from Sales and seven from Hayter whose short stay with Salisbury produced five wins and three draws.

James Hayter

Paul Sales

A few years later in his career with A.F.C. Bournemouth he recorded the fastest hat-trick in the history of league football coming off the bench for a league game and hitting three goals in 2 minutes 20 seconds.

Better late than never

Salisbury gained their first league away win of the season at Cambridge City on Saturday 2nd January with a 3-1 victory. Roger Emms, Paul Sales and Adie Randall (penalty) got on the score-sheet. Seven days later they made the journey to Merthyr Tydfil when, thanks to James Hayter's goal they returned with the points. The City's next away game was to the runaway league leaders Nuneaton, on Saturday 23rd January. Nuneaton had yet to lose at home in the league that season. The Salisbury team, now playing with great conviction, did not appear to have any apprehension regarding this impressive home record. After surviving early pressure they became the first Premier Division side to win at Nuneaton, with another James Hayter goal.

Hayter to Hayter

James Hayter in conversation with Alec Hayter (Salisbury's Press Officer) after the outstanding win at Nuneaton:

> I don't care how close in they are, as long as I'm scoring and we're winning, Neil (Housley) did well down the left and I just followed it in like you should do. Paul (Sales) is very good in the air and I try to feed-off his flicks. He holds it up well and I just look to play-off him. It was a pretty good standard today and we more than held our own – its a decent standard and I'm enjoying my football at the moment.

Another view as told to Alec Hayter by Adie Randall:

> Everyone was superb today. We could have had four of five and they're running away with the league. That just shows how we've come on. We surprised everyone here.

Robbie Harbut:

> We've only been beaten once in the league since October and we've had a great run. The way we're playing at the moment I'm feeling very confident and it's brilliant playing for the team. We're looking forward to every game.

Spectacular Salisbury were then ascending the league table. The home win against Bromsgrove Rovers saw James Hayter playing his last game before being recalled by AFC Bournemouth and, naturally, he signed-off with the only goal of the game.

The following recognition appeared in The Daily Echo, on his return to Bournemouth:

> Cherries' boss, Mel Machin paid tribute to young striker James Hayter after he admirably filled Mark Stein's boots during his sides 0-0 draw against promotion rivals Manchester City. Machin hailed the young striker saying 'I thought James was absolutely exceptional considering he is still a teenager' James said 'It was a fantastic atmosphere'

The club's fourth away win in succession was at the expense of

Burton Albion, goals from Paul Sales and David Bright assuring maximum points in a 2-1 victory. Merthyr Tydfil were welcomed to the Raymac. on Saturday 13th February and although the Whites were not at their best, they took all three points thanks to a Robbie Harbut goal. This was an entertaining game with both goalkeepers making excellent saves. Adie Randall then held joint

third place in the Premier Division's goal charts with 13 goals.

Success on the field was reflected by the bumper home gates the club were now experiencing, proving that a successful Salisbury team would considerably swell the gate receipts.

Robbie Harbut who scored Salisbury's winner at Merthyr and their fifth at Bath City.

Paul Sales who scored at Burton was also among the goals at Bath City.

The two cities do not disappoint

The Whites looked forward to the tough away game at Bath City with relish. Over the years this fixture had produced many enthralling contests.

The match, played at Twerton Park on Tuesday 16th February, proved to

Adie Randall scored at Bath.

Tyronne Bowers hit two in same game.

be no exception. Playing with the slope in the first half, the visitors built up a three goal lead, Paul Sales, Adie Randall and Tyronne Bowers all getting on the score-sheet. In the 59th minute, Bath found a life-line to make the score 3-1. Salisbury came back on 68 minutes when Bowers netted for his brace. To their credit the home side responded by pushing men forward looking for a break-through, but the Whites were still goal-hungry. Sales launched a bullet-header at the Bath 'keeper, who could only parry the ball into the path of Robbie Harbut, 5-1 to Salisbury. Bath City scored twice inside two minutes in the closing moments of the game to bring to an end a thoroughly enthralling match which was a credit to both sides.

Dr Martens League Premier Division

Top four including 16 Feb.	P	W	D	L	F	A	Pts
Nuneaton Borough	30	20	6	4	66	23	66
Gloucester City	29	13	9	7	41	35	48
Bath City	28	13	7	8	42	26	46
Salisbury City	**28**	**13**	**7**	**8**	**39**	**39**	**46**

The following comments about the game by the Salisbury City captain, Ian Chalk were reported in the programme of 20th February:

It was an unbelievable result tonight. Despite finishing 5-3 we were 5-1 up at one stage. Its just great for everyone at the Club. We're not really disappointed we let three in. I think at the beginning of the game we would have been happy with 5-4! I mean, at the end they were playing 7 or 8 up front and we had to defend against it. They broke us down a couple of times but at the end of the day we could have had another couple at the other end, so we can only be happy with 5-3. I thought everybody was magnificent – we did ever so well in the first-half and used the slope and the wind to our advantage which we're probably guilty of not doing sometimes. It was just a different class of performance today.

The magnificent unbeaten run was eventually terminated at the Raymac. on Saturday 20th February against Halesowen Town. Uncharacteristically, the Whites found themselves 2-0 down but a goal from Paul Sales raised hopes. Unfortunately missed chances meant the result was a 2-1 defeat.

The impressive away form continued at Bromsgrove with two goals in three minutes in the final stages of the game. Again they secured all three points and this victory moved them into third place in the table. The run of away matches continued at King's Lynn and Worcester City. In the former, Salisbury went ahead for the first time in the 77th minute. King' Lynn them pushed everyone forward in a attempt to salvage something from the game and this paid off when, after a full scale brawl between the two sides, they scored their final goal on 92 minutes to achieve a 3-3 draw. The Worcester game was drawn 0-0.

City succumb to last kick equaliser

On Saturday 13th March the scene was set for the runaway league leaders, Nuneaton Borough's visit to the Raymac. The highest league gate of the season, 1050, saw Salisbury take the lead on 34 minutes when a Tyronne Bowers cross found Neil Housley seven yards from goal and he made no mistake. The visitors were handed a life-line on 87 minutes when they were awarded a free-kick for a controversial hand ball decision. Nuneaton's Gavin O'Toole floated the ball over the defensive wall and beyond goalkeeper Jason Matthews, for the equaliser.

Neil Housley scored for Salisbury against Nuneaton.

The following Monday, March 13th, the Whites succumbed to their first away league defeat of the year to Atherstone United, going down 2-0. They also lost at home in the following league match 2-0 against Rothwell Town. Thankfully, Salisbury gained a victory in the home match against old rivals Bath City on Saturday April 3rd. They found themselves two goals down at half-time but a goal from Eurshell Fearon playing his second game for the club and a brace from Ian Chalk saw the game swing in the home team's favour.

An agonising April

Sadly the season took a nose dive after this. They lost away to Hastings Town 3-2 on Monday 5th April and this was followed by a home draw against Boston United. The poor run persisted, with defeats at Tamworth 2-1, and at home to Burton Albion. The last home game of the season was played on Wednesday 28th April against relegation candidates Gresley Rovers. It ended in a 2-2 draw.

The Premier Division campaign reached its conclusion on Saturday 1st May at Gloucester City. The Whites produced a champagne performance to deny Gloucester City the runners-up position. The travelling Salisbury supporters were treated to another virtuoso performance from Adie Randall. Salisbury went into the lead from a Tyronne Bowers strike on the 14th minute and went further ahead when they were awarded a penalty on 41 minutes – up stepped Adie Randall to slot the spot-kick home, his 16th goal of the season. The club would sorely miss the exceptional midfielder in the following season. Gloucester City scored a consolation goal on 86-minutes: the final score Gloucester City 1, Salisbury City 2.

Parachutes needed?

The old proverb 'What goes up must come down' proved to be correct when the Whites fell from the lofty heights of third place in the league table at the end of February to a mid-table position at the close of the season. At the beginning of March it looked a distinct possibility that the club would finish in a top-five position so the descent was a disappointment. However to be realistic the majority of the supporters would have settled for mid-table respectability at the beginning of the campaign and an F.A. Cup 1st Round Proper encounter against Football League opposition.

The Whites F.A. Cup Expedition

Salisbury's splendid F.A. Cup run got underway with a difficult away tie at Dorchester Town in the 2nd Qualifying Round. It looked a very tricky prospect as Dorchester Town had held Salisbury 3-3 at the Raymac. before the F.A. Cup clash. However any pessimism was unfounded when the Whites booked their place in the 3rd Qualifying Round with a 3-0 victory with goals from Ferrett, Randall and Sales. Again the Whites faced an away tie, this time against Hungerford Town. Danny Rofe scored his first goal to earn a replay at Old Sarum the following Wednesday.

The visitors gave Salisbury one almighty shock, when Simon Sly scored after 30 minutes following a lively opening. Paul Sales equalised before half-time and Robbie Harbut gave them the lead from close range after the 'keeper failed to hold a fierce shot from Adie Randall. The lead lasted two minutes when poor defending let David Toomey level the score. The deadlock was only broken in injury time when, after a Hungerford defender had been sent off, Paul Sales hit the winner with a sensational overhead kick.

Unbelievably, Salisbury City met Carshalton Athletic twice in succession in major F.A. competitions. They won 2-1 at Old Sarum

Neil Housley who scored a hat-trick in Salisbury's 6-0 win.

in the First Round of the F.A. Trophy on Saturday 24th October and a week later travelled to Carshalton for the important F.A. Cup 4th Qualifying Round tie only for the referee to call off the game shortly before the kick-off as the ground was waterlogged. The game was put on hold until the following Tuesday when a relentless Salisbury hit them for six, with goals from Paul Sales, Robbie Harbut, Adie Randall and a hat-trick from Neil Housley.

The Whites could look forward to the F.A. Cup First Round Proper match against Hull City on Saturday 14th November.

Bring on the 'Big Boys'

A then record gate of 2573 at the Raymac. witnessed a close encounter in which underdogs Salisbury had opportunities to cause

Below: Sees a clash of stripes as Adie Randall powers through the middle of the Hull defenders.

Above: the Hull goalkeeper, Steve Wilson saves from the diving Salisbury striker, Paul Sales.

an upset. They enjoyed a fair share of the play in the first-half and after only eight minutes Ian Chalk unlocked the offside trap to race clear only to see his effort blocked by the Hull goalkeeper with his knees. Just before half-time the supporters hopes were high when Chris Ferrett's exquisite through ball put Paul Sales away but the 'keeper, Steve Wilson, came to the rescue again by courageously diving at his feet to cancel out the threat.

Not to be..............again!

Moments later the Salisbury faithful suffered heartache as Hull's Steve Hawes and Matt Hocking linked-up to feed the ball to Greg Rioch who executed a brilliant shot to score from 22 yards. Hull made the score 2-0 with 12 minutes of the game remaining when the ball was flicked home from an inswinging corner. Naturally the Salisbury supporters went home disappointed, but they were proud of the team and the club who made the day such an exceptional experience.

F.A. Cup Results 14/11/98

Salisbury City	0	Hull City	2	Worcester City	2	Torquay United	1
Basingstoke	1	AFC Bournemouth	2	Yeovil Town	2	West Auckland T	2

Yet another important Cup tie, was the 2nd Round of the F.A. Trophy, just seven days after the Hull City match. Salisbury made the journey to the Conference side Woking and lost 2-1. The final stages of the game saw them pushing forward looking for a winning goal instead of settling for a draw and they were punished by a late Woking strike.

Salisbury's last game of the season was the final of the Wiltshire Premier Shield. They triumphed for the 11th time in their history by defeating Swindon Supermarine 2-1.

The 1999–2000 Season — Richard J.A. Walker

After the usual round of friendly matches, the most interesting of which involved Yeovil Town who sent a strong side to Salisbury on 7th August and won 2-1, City travelled for their opening fixture to

Boston the following week. Boston and their controversial manager, Steve Evans, had made no secret of their aim of reaching the Conference this year.

Four added to the squad

Salisbury had new faces in their squad. Paul Myers was in goal, and Martin Shepherd, from Dorchester, in attack. Nick Miles and Dominic Bartley arrived as the season got underway.

Boston gave due notice of their intentions by thrashing the Whites 6-0 in what was the first part of a double in a triumphant season. The club had to wait until their third game before securing their first victory, beating Halesowen Town 2-0 at the Raymac. Geoff Butler had made prophetic comments in the match programme:

> *Believe me when I tell you that this football club is desperate for funds to enable us to compete at this level of football. I do not believe that enough people in the city realise the situation regarding the finance of the club. It is imperative that the income generated by the football club increases considerably if we are to survive at this level.*

Salisbury then had a mini-run of success with three wins out of four games. This was a turbulent season for goalkeepers. No fewer than eight were to appear in the one season. Steve Mildenhall returned again on loan from Swindon Town in the third game but left after a month, Simpkins then played from September until being injured at Dorchester in November. Others to appear were Edmonds for two games then Shuttleworth for a further seven. Potter and Price then took over the No. 1 jersey until Matassa arrived in March until the end of the season.

Wins over Crawley at home and Worcester away lifted spirits but consistency was lacking and two successive defeats brought the fans back to earth.

F.A. Cup and F.A. Trophy

The opening fixture in the F.A. Cup was a tricky game at West Clewes against Welton Rovers then riding high at the top of Western League First Division. Salisbury negotiated this with some comfort although the hosts drew level in the first-half. Maidenhead United away were next up and again Salisbury triumphed with a

Salisbury City's goalkeeper Simpkins, whose long punt enabled Sales to put the Whites in the lead at Maidenhead.

remarkable Paul Sales goal, back heading the ball in the net first bounce after a long clearance. Another away draw at Oxford City was the 4th Qualifying Round obstacle. On the eve of the fixture news broke of the club's severe financial difficulties, hardly an ideal preparation for a match Salisbury were expected to win. In the event this was perhaps the most disappointing performance of the season. Losing 2-0 just after half-time strenuous efforts were made to redeem the position but in vain as Oxford City held on, Martin Shepherd's goal proving insufficient.

F.A. Cup Results 16/10/99

| Oxford City | 2 | Salisbury City | 1 | Lymington & NM. | 1 | Aldershot Town | 3 |
| Yeovil Town | 2 | Witney Town | 1 | Bath City | 1 | Stevenage Town | 0 |

In the F.A. Trophy progress was short-lived. Tonbridge were beaten at home but Sutton United were far too strong. They won 5-2 with five different scorers to expose the Whites defensive frailties. Salisbury had a very heavy injury list at the time but there was absolutely no excuse for the defeat at Devizes in the Wiltshire Premier Shield. This competition seemed to be downgraded in importance each year; was it any wonder the players lacked interest? Coupled with a Southern League Cup defeat at home to Newport I.O.W., Salisbury had been put out of three cup competitions in 11 days.

An award for Paul Sales

League results were very patchy until the end of January culminating in a 5-1 defeat to a relegation threatened Grantham, another extremely dismal performance. This was particularly disappointing as the home fixture had been won by 5-0. The 5th of February saw a brilliant 4-4 draw at Twerton Park against Bath City, followed by three consecutive wins and then five consecutive

Paul Sales, won the 'Salisbury Football of the Year, award which was presented by the Salisbury Journal.

defeats which severely imperilled the clubs ability to stay in the Premier Division. The spectre of relegation was only banished by wins at Atherstone and Cambridge City at home followed by draws at Gloucester and at home to Weymouth.

Jimmy Smith had returned from Gloucester City at the end of March following their financial troubles. Paul Sales was chosen by the Salisbury Journal as 'Salisbury Footballer of the Year'. He had had an outstanding season. At this time Matt Lovell, Darren McCluskey and Tom McMemeny left, the latter on a scholarship to America.

The last three matches had yielded but one point, and only one team had let in more goals and they were relegated. Salisbury, however, had reached safety and would compete in the top flight for a further season. It had all been too close for comfort once again.

The 2000–01 Season — Peter J. Waterhouse

This season was to become one of the most turbulent in the history of the club. On the pitch matters would pale into insignificance compared with the activities behind the scenes. It was to see the end of Geoff Butler's reign as manager and threaten the very existence of the club as a force in non-league football.

Two young academy players join the Whites

But all this was in the future. The close season saw three new signings. Lee Bradford, from Weymouth brought welcome experience while Wayne Turk and Phil Corcoran joined from Cirencester Academy. While the latter two swiftly made their marks Lee Bradford suffered a cruciate ligament injury as did Kevin Brabrook.

The new season commenced with a win at home to Halesowen, the team being: Shuttleworth, Bartlett, Andy Cook, Braybook, Emms, Lush, Bowers, Sales, Turk, Smith and Shepherd with substitutes, Miles, Corcoran and Simpkins and, after 10 league games, of which six had been won, Salisbury were in fourth place:

Top 4	P	W	D	L	F	A	Pts
Crawley Town	10	7	2	1	24	10	23
Burton Albion	10	5	5	0	17	9	20
Welling United	10	6	2	2	15	11	20
Salisbury City	**10**	**6**	**1**	**3**	**21**	**17**	**19**

The Weymouth game on August Bank Holiday Monday, had drawn a crowd of 617 to the Raymac. and this proved to be the second highest league attendance of the season. The result was a deserved 3-2 win with Phil Corcoran scoring a cracking goal.

Salisbury lose out of F.A. Cup and Trophy financially

On 30th September the Whites played away at Clevedon in the F.A. Cup 2nd Qualifying Round. A good cup run was imperative in order to bolster the club's financial position.

They made a dream start when, with only 33 seconds on the clock, Roger Emms met a Scott Bartlett free-kick to propel the ball into the back of the Clevedon net. From poor defending, Clevedon's Andy Mainwaring drilled home a 13th minute equaliser and just before half-time, Dave Mehew put the home side into a 2-1 lead. What Geoff Butler said to his players at half-time one can only guess but Salisbury's attitude completely changed in the second-half. A superb free-kick found Paul Sales who squared the ball across the face of the goal for Jimmy Smith to finish off the move on 49 minutes to level the score at 2-2. They took the lead on 52 minutes

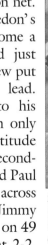

Martin Shepherd whose skill and passing resulted in a goal.

Salisbury's lead came by way of a volley from Tyronne Bowers.

Jimmy Smith scorer of two goals at Dorchester.

when Tyronne Bowers volleyed the ball home from a Martin Shepherd cross. Victory was sealed in the 80th minute when Jimmy Smith converted a penalty making the scoreline 4-2.

3-1 up with only 20 minutes to go

On Saturday 14th October, Salisbury travelled to Dorchester Town in the next round. They took the lead on 19 minutes when Jimmy Smith chested the ball onto Paul Sales for the striker to tuck the ball into the back of the opponents net. Four minutes later Jimmy Smith doubled the score. The Dorchester manager then brought on a third striker in an effort to get back into the game. Salisbury took their foot off the pedal and Dorchester saw a chance with a set-piece goal on 27 minutes. The second-half saw Salisbury getting back on the attack and, after several near misses, Paul Sales netted a loose ball. Once again a casual Salisbury allowed Dorchester to get back into the game on 68 minutes with a goal from a nod by Matt Lonnon.

Dorchester were now playing with confidence and, on 76 minutes, they got their equaliser with Lonnon scoring again, his goal going in off the post. Seconds later Dorchester's Pickard tapped the ball home from an O'Hagan pass, to put Dorchester Town into the next round.

Salisbury's frustrations continued when they went out of the F.A. Trophy 1-0 away at Bashley on 4th November.

F.A. Cup Results 14/11/2000

| Dorchester Town | 4 | Salisbury City | 3 | Tiverton Town | 1 | Gloucester City | 3 |
| Bath City | 3 | Sutton United | 0 | Dartford | 0 | Havant & W'Ville | 4 |

'Golden Nugget' match approaches

Returning to league fixtures Salisbury were at home to local rivals Bath City on 7th October. Historically this fixture had produced a banquet of goals and this game was no exception. I had the privilege of viewing the match as one of the guests of life-long

Wayne Turk scored a brace in the draw with Bath City.

Salisbury supporter, Tony Rattue, who was celebrating his 60th birthday. His match party took place in one of the club's superb executive boxes. A neutral watching would have returned from the game delighted. At half-time City found themselves 2-1 down after Wayne Turk had put them in the lead. Martin Paul had levelled the score for Bath and on the 44th minute they were

Scott Bartlett's corner resulted in Salisbury's fourth goal.

awarded a penalty. From the spot-kick the same player sent the Salisbury goalkeeper, John Simpkins, the wrong way to take the lead.

In the second-half, on 64 minutes, Wayne Turk scored to level at 2-2. Bath substitute Sam Allison then restored the visitor's lead but on 81 minutes Paul Sales found the target from a Jimmy Smith pass and two minutes later from a Scott Bartlett corner a Bath defender sliced the ball into his own net and it looked as if the Whites were on the way to victory.

However, with four minutes of injury time played Kevin Lloyd headed the ball into the Salisbury net from a Mike Davis corner to make the final score 4-4 to the delight of the travelling supporters.

Paul Sales draws first blood against the 'Hammers'

The following Monday supporters, 2196 of them in all, were treated to a feast of exhibition football when Harry Rednapp brought a star-studded West Ham United side to play a testimonial match to commemorate Geoff Butler's service to the club.

The Premiership noblemen went a goal down when West Ham's Michael Feriante handled the ball inside the area and Salisbury's Paul Sales scored from the spot.

Harry Rednapp

Unfortunately, three minutes later, the referee spotted an infringement by a Salisbury player at the other end and former

Bordeaux, Blackburn and Arsenal striker, Kaba Diawara beat the keeper from the penalty spot – the first of a hat-trick for the striker, which saw the Hammers win the game 3-1.

League matches probably seemed a little dull after the West Ham visit and this was reflected in the results. It was nearly two months before the next win and that was against Moor Green at home. The Christmas/New Year period also had little to get excited about with two draws and a loss. Things picked up however when one of the pace setters, Worcester City, were beaten on 16th January.

Reaching dizzy heights

Next up was the visit of Stafford Rangers, a game dominated by Salisbury who were 3-0 up in the first 10 minutes. On-loan player Dave Wakefield scored a brace and Martin Shepherd one. Paul Sales netted the fourth goal at the final whistle to make the score 4-1.

Salisbury recorded another double when they defeated Moor Green away 2-0 with on form Paul Sales and Jimmy Smith on the score sheet. They were now riding high and after 25 games were in third position in the Premier Division.

Top 4	P	W	D	L	F	A	Pts
Burton Albion	25	13	12	0	48	24	49
Margate	23	15	3	5	44	18	48
Salisbury City	**25**	**12**	**5**	**8**	**47**	**42**	**41**
Welling United	27	10	11	8	34	32	41

Progress came to an unanticipated end on 3rd February when they lost 4-1 at Tamworth which turned out to be the start of a losing chain of five matches, scoring only twice but conceding twelve. One of these matches was against eventual champions Margate.

CD not out for Roger

The Whites, who were missing several key players, were far from disgraced in losing 1-0. It was also Roger Emms' 400th appearance for the club.

On 24th February Salisbury lost 1-0 at Merthyr and this proved to be the last match in charge for Geoff Butler.

Salisbury's ex-captain Roger Emms, still going strong.

For most of the season there had been concern among supporters over the financial well-being of the club. Chairman Ray McEnhill, who was in failing health, had, warned of losses that he would not meet and ultimatums had been lodged some twelve months previously. However there had been some hope when Geoff Butler reported in the match-day programme on Saturday 10th February that he had identified a number of local people who would definitely be prepared to invest in the club if the terms were right. However this venture did not bear fruit.

Salisbury's Chairman Ray McEnhill.

Newsletter explains some facts

Numerous Salisbury City supporters had become very frustrated by the off-field happenings and this prompted the S.C.F.C. Fanzine to publish an unofficial emergency newsletter which was distributed at the home match against Tamworth on Saturday 3rd March. Although Salisbury were a non-league club, many City supporters followed their beloved team home and away and were as passionate for their team as any Premiership Club supporter.

These supporters were in for a shock when the crisis reached a climax as Geoff Butler was made redundant.

The following report by Wendy Gee appeared in The Daily Echo on Wednesday 7th March 2001:

Geoff Butler is in a state of deep shock today after losing his job as manager of Salisbury City after 18-years in charge.

The longest serving one-club manager in the upper

Geoff Butler

echelons of the non-league pyramid, Butler was yesterday summoned by the solicitors representing chairman/main shareholder Ray McEnhill and told his post as full-time team/commercial manager had been made redundant.

'I'm just shocked at the moment,' said Butler, struggling to conceal his emotion after returning to the Club to start clearing his desk.

'I've just made the club £10,000 from a sportmen's dinner and recently took them to the highest (third) they've ever been in the Dr Martens Premier Division – and that's my reward for 18-years service.'

Ex-Saints and Pompey defender Andy Cook, who doubles-up as team captain and Football to the Community Officer, will take charge of the side for tonight's Premier Division trip to Newport County and is favourite to take the job on permanently.

Speaking on behalf of the McEnhill family, Sue Wharmby of In-House Public Relations said ' The operation at Salisbury is going to be restructured because it is not working financially. Geoff's position will not be refilled in its current capacity. It is hoped that a player-manager can be put in to save the Club some money'.

She added, ' Geoff has done a great job and the McEnhills would like to thank him for that.'

Cook admitted there was a 'state of disbelief' that the man whose name has been inextricably linked with Salisbury City F.C. for nearly two decades had been shown the door.

The Club had yet to break the news to the rest of the players, but Cook said: 'Everyone here is devastated, the office staff can't believe it.'

The shock turn of events follows a turbulent five weeks at the Club that started when McEnhill's representatives called for Butler, the then Managing Director and six of his fellow Directors to stand-down due to City's 'continuing financial losses.'

After strong resistance, all seven finally quit the board at midday last Friday having been warned the Club would be in serious jeopardy if they did not resign by the noon deadline. Until yesterday, however, Butler

remained a full-time Club employee.

Ironically for the Middlesbrough-born former Boro, Chelsea, Norwich City and A.F.C. Bournemouth defender, this was Butler's testimonial season and a crowd of 2196 turned out in his honour to watch the Whites take on West Ham United in October.

Geoff Butler's input to the club over many years was colossal and several disillusioned people severed their connections with Salisbury City F.C. after his dismissal. One thing to be sure about 'there's only one Geoff Butler'.

Andy Cook

Andy Cook took charge of the team after the manager's departure and immediately the Whites beat Newport County 1-0.

'City' take on a player-manager

Taffy Richardson
player-Manager

Taffy Richardson then took on the role of player-Manager and his first game in charge of the team was away to league leaders Margate. Taffy appointed former team-mate Tommy Killick as his assistant.

Although Margate took the lead, a late equaliser from Martin Shepherd after good work from Tommy Killick secured a well-deserved point.

Quite naturally the upheaval at the club had unsettled the players and, from Taffy's introduction as player-manager for the Margate game, only four more league games were won, the final match being a 2-1 win over Cambridge City at the Raymac.

Reflecting on the season as a whole 13th place in the table was a fair position considering the off-pitch circumstances.

The following account, written by the recently appointed Director of Operations,

Tommy Killick

Mark Groves, appeared in the match-day programme for 7th April 2001:

I want to look forward – the past has happened and there is nothing that we can do to alter it regardless of what various thoughts may be. I make no apologies for having accepted the position of Director of Operations offered by the McEnhill family with the brief to ensure that the Club reaches the end of the season and looks at the way forward thereafter. Believe me, this Club has enormous potential if we go forward as a unified team – on and off the field.

My first job was to ensure that the Club had an immediate future following the departure of so many people who were instrumental in carrying out the administration and compliance that is necessary for any football club at this level. We would not have been able to stage the game at Newport without the help of Andy Cook, who took on the role of caretaker-Manager and Allan Finch who took over as Club Secretary. We are thoroughly indebted to Judy Maffey, our Secretary/Office Manager who has turned her hand to everything that has been thrown at her and, I can assure you that the tasks that she has carried out have been many and varied – all with a smile on her face. I must also mention Dave Beaven who has taken over the safety certificate – a vital role to ensure that home matches can be played. People like these are the life-blood of the Club. It has been extremely encouraging to see so many people who have not previously been actively involved in the Club willing to help.

The emphasis in the future will be on the POSITIVE in all aspects. Everybody and that means everybody, will need to work together to ensure not only the immediate future of the Club but a structure that will enable a move forwards. It is my very firm belief that the appointment of Taffy Richardson is a major step towards achieving these ambitions. You will have seen Taffy's uncompromising style of play and I can assure all of you that he is no less positive off the field. Taffy's first job was to appoint Tom Killick as our assistant-Manager. Tom's approach to the game is similar to Taffy's and that is apparent as soon as you meet him. I have spoken to all the players individually and collectively and their attitude towards the future is first-class.

This attitude has been reflected on the pitch and there is far more of a collective spirit than there has ever been before. Those people at the games against Newport, Ilkeston, Margate and Welling will have seen how the 'new era' is developing on the pitch. I cannot emphasise enough that the Club will go forward on the basis that it is more important than any individual. We will not always get things right but I can assure you that the attitude will always be POSITIVE.

At the end of the season we will be looking at the future structure of the club and finalising a business plan to take things forward. This will involve all those people who want to see the Club prosper and will determine how we progress.

Get behind the Club and give us POSITIVE encouragement, after all, we should all have the same objectives at the end of the day.

Mark Groves: Director of Operations

Well, what were the fans to think? It was clear that changes had to be made if the club were to exist on a sound financial footing. Would this mean a lower standard of football? There were no ready answers and the next season was approached with some trepidation.

The 2001–02 Season — Richard J.A. Walker

The season was to prove one of the most disappointing ever. Not only were results some of the worst experienced, but the very future of the club continued to be at stake due to financial problems.

'Chalkie' calls it a day

A sad start was the news that Ian Chalk had decided to leave the club. He was the very epitome of everything one hoped for in a player at this level; loyalty, tried 110% in every match, and more skill than he was ever given credit for. A dedicated professional, he made 684 appearances and scored 183 goals.

On reflection it was an omen that the end of an era was coming. What a pity he has had no Testimonial.

Of the opening five fixtures, four were drawn and

Ian Chalk in action versus Havant.

the other was a defeat at Folkestone. The first Bank Holiday fixture saw Newport I.O.W. draw 1-1 in Salisbury in a very entertaining game. They had to come from behind and Sales scored one of only two goals he achieved in the whole season. City played Weymouth on 4th September losing at home 3-2. Speakman scored his second goal in two games but his star was soon to wane and he left after three months.

Injuries forced the club to field perhaps their most inexperienced ever team in the away game at Hednesford and a 6-0 defeat came as little surprise. Alarm bells were now ringing at the way the club was regressing.

Trying to take our minds off a new grim world

Tuesday 11th September was a day of infamy that will be remembered in history for many decades and it had nothing to do with the first league visit of up and coming Tiverton Town. A very subdued atmosphere existed but the visitors, ably led by the quicksilver Ovans, won comprehensively and Salisbury were now anchored to the bottom of the table, a position they were to retain throughout the season.

F.A. Cup

Tiverton Town visited the Raymac. for the second time in a month. The Whites held a relatively comfortable half-time lead but only drew 3-3 with a late Roger Emms goal after the visitors had scored three quick goals in the second-half. The replay saw Salisbury ahead at the interval before the opposition again scored three without reply to end local interest in the competition.

F.A. Cup Results 29/9/2001

Salisbury City	2	Tiverton Town	2 *replay*	Tiverton Town	3	Salisbury City	1
Bath City	1	Bideford Town	3	Christchurch	1	Cirencester Town	3
Highworth Tn	0	Weymouth	3	St Blazey	3	Chippenham Town	1

Narrow defeats against Welling and Weymouth followed. By the end of October Tony Malessa became the sixth goalkeeper as a result of injuries although he was not at fault in a sixth consecutive defeat. City's record was now:

P 14   W 0   D 4   L 10   F 6   A 32   Pts 4

At this stage relegation was virtually inevitable and nine straight defeats were recorded.

City break their duck in lower league fixture

The reserves fixture against Lymington & New Milton in the Wessex Combination was taken by the first team and a cheap 12-0 victory followed. One has to ask what this did for the morale of the normal reserve team who went to the top of the table as a result. Nevertheless the first victory of the season in the Southern League followed when fellow basement club Hednesford Town were beaten 1-0 at the Raymac. At this stage the club had played 32 players in the first team. This was a sure sign of problems. Paul Sales had been out injured since the Welling game and would not reappear until the New Year.

Out of all 'trophies'

There were four more consecutive defeats after the Hednesford game and elimination from the F.A. Trophy, Wilts Premier Shield and Southern League Cup followed in quick succession. Fifteen of the last seventeen games had seen defeats and another new 'keeper, James Bittner, had arrived.

Foreboding hangs in the air

By now no-one doubted the club would be relegated. Nevertheless

Latest 'keeper, James Bittner

a victory at home against Folkestone, the second of the season, provided some Christmas cheer and this was followed by four more points from two games including a first away success at Ilkeston. It was all too little and much too late, but it was the long term future of the club that was causing even more concern.

Once again Mark Groves went into print in the programme to deal with the possible involvement of a consortium led by Alan Ball the 1966 England World Cup star and others, but it all came to nothing.

Another Salisbury favourite departs

February saw Paul Sales leave for Bashley for a reported fee of £5000. A move had seemed to be on the cards for some time and the general feeling was that he no longer wanted to play for Salisbury even though contract negotiations had started and he had been offered more to stay. He was reputed to be the club's top earner. He stated he wanted to move back to Bashley; not exactly a career advancement but it forced the club into the only decision they could possibly make which was to take the money before he left for nothing under a 'Bosman'. Injuries had severely limited his appearances and two goals in 15 games was a paltry return for player of his ability. His stay at Bashley proved short lived and he was to move on to Eastleigh for an even higher fee.

Ryan King had arrived from Backwell United of the Western League and was to finish top scorer with 15 goals. He was the one success in a dreadful year. One

Ryan KIng

other highlight took place with the visit of Moor Green on 2nd March when City won 5-0 with Adam Wallace making an appearance and finishing with a goal to his name. Salisbury's season then collapsed with eight further defeats in nine fixtures, the final chapter being provided in Salisbury on the last day when fellow relegation compatriots Merthyr Tydfil won 2-1. The league table said it all. Salisbury used a total of 51 players this season. This was definitely a year to forget.

Adam Wallace

The 2002–03 Season — Peter J. Waterhouse

Has it all gone?

During the close season discussions had taken place to find someone to take over the financial responsibilities of the club and Mr Cunningham Brown, the Andover F.C. Chairman, had become involved. Unfortunately this did not produce a mutually satisfactory solution and, in due course, the club released the following press statement:

> The directors of Salisbury City Football Club Limited (S.C.F.C.) have completed a detailed review of its financial position. The directors and Mr Ken Cunningham Brown had been negotiating arrangements for the coming season, and were encouraged by the positive response that Mr Cunningham Brown's proposed involvement had generated.
>
> The projected full year cash deficiency for the coming season is approximately £100,000. Unfortunately this has proved to be an insurmountable hurdle to overcome within the resources that could be committed.
>
> The directors of S.C.F.C. appreciate the time and effort given by Mr Cunningham Brown.
>
> In the absence of any other realistic proposals to continue football at the present level, the directors have concluded that S.C.F.C. will be unable to play in the coming season. It is hoped that the club can be reorganised during this period so that it can recommence competitive football in the season after that, but on a more viable basis.

In the meantime, the directors wish to make the stadium facilities more widely available for sporting activities for schools and others. They have already taken steps to take this forward, and invite any interested parties to contact them.

The club tried to resign from the Southern League but this was not accepted because the resignation was not written on official headed Salisbury City F.C. paper. This gave breathing space for a consortium to be formed by two local businessmen, former Whites player Nev Beal and David Harrold who appointed Saints favourite Nick Holmes as General Manager.

When the 'Saint' comes marching in

Manager
Nick Holmes

This consortium convinced Mr Wike that they could successfully take over the club and, with the new manager began to prepare for the season. Fortunately most of the previous season's players were still available.

The emotion generated by the prospect of losing the club and the events leading up to the successful conclusion were ably described by Gary Richards, one of the Whites most vocal of supporters, in the match day programme for the first friendly of the season against Yeovil Town:

The Longest Night

News spread quickly on Monday evening when a press release was issued by the club owners announcing the withdrawal of Salisbury City Football Club from all competitions and that the club would not be playing football for at least a year, in fact if at all ever.

In a scene reminiscent of the old 'cowboy' movies the Cavalry began to move in to the car park area at the stadium to find out what was going on. As headlights sped down the service road each car and its occupants were greeted with mutterings of disbelief at what was taking place.

For long moments those gathered stood close to tears, wondering if the emotional roller-coaster that had been Salisbury City Football Club for the past couple of years had finally come off its rails.

Inside the ground, the local media, alerted by frantic phone-calls and e-mails, were talking to Club Director, Robert Wike in a bid to find out if there was a way to save the club.

Mr Wike had already spoken at length to representatives of the consortium whose bid to take the club forward had been turned down. One of the consortium had just literally come back from France to come directly to the club.

Discussions, all passionate, were held to try and find a way of stopping the seemingly inevitable happening. Supporters, Shareholders and Committee Members stood by as Mr Robert Wike, the McEnhills' representative and Club Director finally came out to talk to us.

He listened carefully to all comments and suggestions and although faced by a bitterly angry and heartbroken group Mr Wike tried to answer all that he was asked. The emotions were running high within the group but everybody acted with decorum and as Mr Wike left the stadium talk went back to what, if anything, would be done to save OUR club.

As you know now, the Whites are on the pitch in front of you, and this a result of much work by both the consortium and Mr Wike, as well as many others behind the scenes. Let us hope the club now has a way forward and a big thank you to all those who rushed to the Stadium on Monday night to show their undying commitment and support for the club.

Nev Beal	**Gary Richards**	**Darren Blick**
Dave Harrold	**Dave Todd**	**Roger Brocksom**
Derek Melhorn	**Jon Surtees**	**Lisa Brocksom**
Micky Harrold	**Trevor Cross**	**Douglas Ferraro**
Martin Ramm		

Mike Turner (*Salisbury Journal*)
Dave (*Spire FM*)

May I thank you all on behalf of everyone connected with the club, for your shows of support and solidarity at such short notice.

The Yeovil Town match was a testimony to the ethos of non-league football. Supporters from Yeovil and the Whites gave generously to a 'bucket' collection and there was goodwill all round.

Other clubs coming to the Raymac. for friendly matches reacted in a similar manner and led the Whites supporters to believe that there was a future.

Also in the Yeovil match-day programme a page was dedicated to the many welcome messages of support that had been received on the Salisbury City F.C. unofficial web page forum, headed:

The Family of Football Speaks Out

Fans and officials of the following clubs included:

Bashley	**Welling United**	**AFC Wimbledon**
Bath City	**Swindon Town**	**AFC Bournemouth**
Hayes	**Witney United**	**Grantham Town**
King's Lynn	**Crawley Town**	**Tonbridge Angels**
Weymouth	**Worcester City**	**Dorchester Town**
Tamworth	**Boston United**	**Erith & Belvedere**
Frome Town	**Halesowen Town**	**Clevedon Town**
Dagenham & Redbridge		**Havant & Waterlooville**
Yeovil Town		

Plus support from ex-whites in Australia and Taiwan ! !

'Devastated to hear your news, Salisbury City will rise again, it must ! !'

'West Country football can't afford to lose a club of Salisbury's standing'

'I was sorry to see the news, last season you sang your hearts out of "we'll never die", now's your chance to put the words into action.'

'Good luck in the future' 'Hope you pull through and see you at Park View.'

From a Weymouth fan 'From every true Weymouth supporter, I would like to wish all SCFC fans our deepest regrets at what has happened. If there is any help you fans need, be it support at a day of action to protest, or items for fund raising, just let me know and I will do my best to arrange it. All the best and I hope you win the greatest battle of your lives.'

'Good luck in the future from all Tamworth fans. '

From a Welling United fan, 'Whatever you need, whatever support you want, just ask.'

'Good luck with any future plans for football back in Salisbury. The three fans that witnessed a 5-1 hammering at Grantham (yet continued to sing) deserve better.'

'Everyone is with you, remember this the "Heart" of football, we don't need ANY club at this level folding. We need clubs such as Salisbury City to stay alive for the benefit of English non-league football. Long may it continue.'

'As someone who admired the way your fans outsung ours at St. George's Lane (Worcester fan) last season when you were 6-0 down, I am sure your club will rise like a phoenix from the ashes.'

'I am sure all is not lost. Look at AFC Wimbledon. I know they have a bigger fanbase, but building from scratch is possible. Good luck to all you Salisbury supporters.'

Let play commence

Apart from a opening defeat away to Erith & Belvedere and an early F.A. Cup exit at home to Bideford the Whites started to play their football with confidence and style and it was apparent that the players had accomplished a new level of fitness under Nick Holmes and Tom Killick.

Nick Holmes soon sets the pace

After the excellent away win against promotion rivals Banbury United the Whites were moving up the league table but the

  promotion drive was temporarily derailed when they lost 3-1 away to Bashley in an evening kick-off from the fixture that was postponed from a New Year's Day match, due the pitch being waterlogged.

Josh Thomas (*left*) scores the first goal in Salisbury's 3-2 win over Histon (4th January), on-loan Callum Burt (*right*) netted the second.

The club also suffered a set back

due to an administrative mix-up when they fielded an ineligible player who had, ironically, taken to the field as a substitute against Spalding United.

The irony was that the match was effectively won by the time he took to the field. The club was fined and three points were deducted by the league for the error.

However, Nick Holmes's management and motivational skills excelled and the players responded to the points lost with a positive attitude and even greater endeavour. However it was difficult to gauge the psychological impact on the other league pace-setters.

With the benefit of hindsight, in a hyper-critical analysis of the season one could argue promotion was lost due to the fact that the Whites only picked up two points out of a maximum of 12 against the two promoted teams, namely Dorchester Town and Eastbourne Borough. Early in the season they lost away at Dorchester 5-1, but in an exciting return fixture drew 0-0.

The games against Eastbourne yielded one point; Salisbury

shared the points away from home but lost 2-1 at the Raymac. in a contentious and controversial game.

The club had come tantalisingly close to promotion at the first attempt. However supporters could now look forward to the next season with renewed optimism.

The 2003–04 Season — Richard J.A. Walker

This was to be a very important season with restructuring taking place in non-league football. As a result of the creation of the Nationwide Conference North and South it was essential that Salisbury were in the top eight of the Eastern Division if they were to play in the Premier Division in season 2004/5. Although the club had recovered well from the very nadir of despair which had greeted the arrival of season 2002 there was still a lot of work to be done to achieve their ambitions. Money was still tight and disappointingly only one new signing had been made when early season friendlies got underway. Stuart James, who was endeavouring to make a career in journalism, joined as a wide mid-field player from Bath City. None of the other trialists impressed with the exception of Matt Tubbs, who eventually decided to join Premier League Dorchester Town.

Never on Sunday

For the first time the club kicked-off with a Sunday fixture, at home to Burgess Hill Town who had newly arrived from the Sussex County League. The visitors were well up for the match and Salisbury, who missed a number of chances and seemed lethargic throughout eventually lost 1-0. Burnham again proved an unlucky venue for Adam Wallace. For the second year in succession he was injured there, breaking a toe in scoring the opening goal. The team missed enough chances to run-up a cricket score and eventually succumbed to a last minute penalty in losing 2-1. Local rivals, Bashley were early visitors to Salisbury and in a stormy match, three players, Phillips for Salisbury, Connelly and Gee for Bashley were all dismissed. The Whites won convincingly to lay the Bashley bogey with Steve Strong scoring a hat-trick.

Results continued to show the team's Jekyll & Hyde form; there was a magnificent come-back from 2-0 down with a last minute penalty equaliser at powerful Tonbridge who had a 100%

record at the time. This was followed by a home draw and then a 4-0 thrashing by free-spending Eastleigh.

The F.A. Trophy proved its usual disappointment when a dreadfully poor home fixture saw the club exit against Clevedon Town in which Phillips was sent off for the second time in the season.

Start of Memorable F.A. Cup Run

The F.A. Cup run began with home wins against Odd Down and Taunton Town. A third home draw in succession to Western League Westbury United and one began to think that this might be Salisbury's year. As usual however, for the supporters this turned out to be anything but an easy tie, notwithstanding the visitors supposedly inferior status as a Western League First Division side. Westbury, well marshalled by ex-White Darren Lush, did not come just to make-up the numbers although Salisbury again missed enough chances to win several games. They were frustrated at every turn, before Cooper eventually gave them the lead. Home supporters relaxed, but so did the team so much so that Westbury equalised and there was no-way back.

Three off in 'local tie'

The replay was a very different game, a number of injuries causing problems with team selection and there were worrying chances of an upset. Early dominance saw City lead after 15 minutes but eventually the hosts equalised with a penalty. Salisbury's chances became harder when Thomas was sent off but Wayne Turk eventually put them ahead. Wallaces's return from a long injury as a substitute lasted eight minutes before he was also sent off in a spat with a home defender who was dismissed for retaliation. The team held on under pressure and following this scare a trip to Havant & Waterlooville, a powerful Premier League side, seemed a daunting task!

The league season had appeared to be drifting into obscurity but the game at West Leigh Park Havant lifted all the supporters. James Taylor gave the hosts an early lead and current form looked likely to be maintained before Wayne Turk equalised. Surprisingly, after

Havant had regained the lead, Nick Holmes made bold changes taking off Emms, Wallace and Phillips replacing them with Crook, Turner and James. The see-saw second-half continued with the score reaching 3-3, before Crook hit a magnificent winning goal on 86 minutes to send the Whites through to a 4th Qualifying Round tie with local rivals Lymington & N.M. from the Wessex League.

Goalkeeper nets as Wednesday beckons

A crowd of nearly 1200 gathered for this game and Salisbury fell behind in 40 seconds, levelling on seven minutes with a disputed penalty. The second-half saw them comfortably through by 5-1. Kevin Sawyer was possibly the only Salisbury goalkeeper in their history to score a goal for the club when he netted from a penalty in the last minute after regular penalty takers, Funnell and Wallace had been substituted. Crowds gathered in the Sarum Suite to watch the televised draw for the 1st Round Proper. All were desperately hoping to be pitted against the biggest team in the competition at this stage. After nearly every other team had come out of the hat, the commentator

Kevin Sawyer

announced that Sheffield Wednesday will play............ his voice was drowned out by a roar from those present and we knew that it was indeed a trip to Hillsborough that was our reward.

Pinch me I'm dreamin'

Cup fever swept the City. The match was to be played on Sunday 9th November, since Sheffield United had also been drawn at home that weekend and would play on the Saturday. Salisbury were beaten 4-0 but were not disgraced. Suffice it to say that the club probably benefited by a cash injection of up to £50,000 and the lift it gave to team spirit and the profile of the City was clear to see. By this time Matt Tubbs had signed a contract in October following his release from Dorchester and Craig Davis had joined from Bashley for a club record fee of £15,000.

F.A. Cup Results 9/11/2003

Sheffield Wed.	4	Salisbury City	0	Woking	3	Histon	1
Grays Athletic	1	Aldershot Town	2	Bournemouth AFC	1	Bristol Rovers	0

Some of the action captured in pictures from Salisbury City's 2004 F.A. Cup run.

All pictures featured here are with the kind permission of the Salisbury Journal

←   1st Qualifying Round

Andy Cook *(left)* only scores on the big days. Here he fires in his first of the two that opened the scoring for Salisbury in their 4-1 defeat of Taunton Town.

2nd Qualifying Round   →

Centre-forward Leigh Phillips *(right)* in the thick of it again, trying (like all of the Salisbury team) to no avail to score that all important winning goal. Final score in the home fixture against Westbury United was 1-1, Cooper was the only one to find the net for the Whites. Salisbury won 2-1 in the replay at Meadow Lane, Westbury with goals from Wayne Turk and Leigh Phillips.

←3rd Qualifying Round

(left) A delighted Wayne Turk celebrating (along with Salisbury supporters) after scoring his first of two goals at Havant & Waterlooville.   Other scorers for the Whites in the seven goal thriller were Josh Thomas and Darren Crook.

4th Qualifying Round

(*left*) Josh Thomas rises head and shoulders above everyone else as he scores the Whites equaliser from a Stuart James corner in the match against Lymington & New Milton

(*right*) In a match of cracking goals this one takes some beating. Adam Wallace powers in his second of the afternoon past the diving Lymington 'keeper, after a cross-field pass from Darren Crook.

Darren Crook (left) fires in the Whites fourth goal in scintillating style, after Adam Wallace's pass, thus returning the earlier favour.

(*below*) After the match versus Lymington & New Milton at the Ray McEnhill Stadium on Saturday 1st Nov., City players celebrate. From *left to right*, Purches, Killick (*coach*), Wallace, Cooper, Cook, Bartlett, Davis, Funnell, Brown, Crook, Turk, Holmes, Thomas, James, climbing on shoulders are Turner and Strong.

(*above*) The seemingly packed to the rafters Sarum Suite, where the excitement even surpassed that at the game, whoops in delight as the televised draw reveals that *Sheffield Wed.* will play...... *Salisbury City*.........wowww ! ! !

Meanwhile back in Dr Martens

This was three times the club's previous record fee paid for Peter Loveridge in 1990. All in all, it was a far cry from 1968 when Graham Moxham was bought from Bideford for £50. Neither Tubbs nor Davis were eligible for the Hillsborough fixture. Salisbury then embarked on a long unbeaten sequence and 10 days after the cup-tie won the return at Eastleigh in front of a large crowd made up mostly of Salisbury supporters who saw their team play their best football of the season in winning 2-1.

This run continued until a visit to third placed Histon on the 17th January, which resulted in a narrow defeat, due to a late, disputed and controversial penalty. Salisbury were without three players who were suspended, previous indiscipline now having to be accounted for. Ashford were next at home and although Wallace and Turk returned from suspension, all rhythm had disappeared and City were somewhat lucky to win at the death, when the visiting goalkeeper fumbled a shot from Strong which trickled over the line.

November's euphoria a million miles away

This was the start of a very barren period with six of the next eight games away. Only seven points were achieved from these fixtures, which for the most part, were against teams at the lower end of the table. Confidence was at a low ebb, chances were created but the forwards seemed unable to score and the defence were unable to keep any clean sheets. Hopes of a top finish, crucially important in this season receded dramatically, particularly with a tough set of fixtures against all of the top teams, looming.

Although a win at Hastings was welcome, defeats followed in three consecutive away games at Fisher, Corby and Stamford. Stuart James left the club to start a full-time career in sports journalism after the game at Fisher Athletic. A particularly disappointing display at home against a doughty Rothwell side, who equalised in the 90th minute, was followed by another poor display at Burgess Hill which saw the hosts complete a double with another 1-0 win.

At this crucial point Glen Howes joined from Newport I.O.W. and Aaron Cook arrived after a drawn-out transfer saga with Bashley reputedly for a fee close to five figures. The defence improved and the team went on a winning run of four games until they played Tonbridge at home in front of a good attendance of 924. Salisbury played well but again failed to take chances including a missed penalty by Tubbs in the 70th minute when they led 1-0. Eventually they conceded a penalty equaliser in the 94th minute, when Phillips, under a pile of players, was adjudged to have handled. A poor display at Newport and a trip to King's Lynn looked very formidable.

Glen Howes

The Whites starting 'goal' achieved

Wayne Turk scored one of the goals at Kings's Lynn.

This time it was the Linnets who had an off-day and Salisbury won 2-0 in what was their first visiting success at The Walks since 1986. At this point the season declined with the team only able to score three goals in their last six games including a home reverse by 3-0 to King's Lynn. Paradoxically this game saw Salisbury's promotion place secured after other results went with them.

The season ended on a very flat note but the team had managed to accomplish what they had set out to do. The cup run and the visit to Hillsborough together with a top seven finish would have been deemed very satisfactory at the start of the season and both had been achieved.

It was now time to wait to hear who next year's opposition would be, but inevitably it would provide a stern test with many of the old Ryman Premier League sides being involved. It was essential therefore, that team strengthening be carried out with two forwards an absolute priority. In 12 of 21 home games they had not managed to score more than one goal.

Back to the F.A. Cup

The next five pages endeavour to describe the euphoria of the visit to Hillsborough. Those who went will never forget it and will have their own personal memories of that day.

Welcome to Meadow Lane

The FA CUP

Westbury United
vs
Salisbury City

F.A.Cup 2nd Qualifying Round Replay
Wednesday 1st October 2003
kick off 7.30pm

Official Match Programme £1

2nd QUALIFYING ROUND
WEDNESDAY OCTOBER 1st 2003
KICK OFF: 7.30pm

WESTBURY UNITED Green & White Hoops		SALISBURY CITY White & Black
Mark Batters	1	Kevin Sawyer
Mark Pearce	2	Scott Bartlett
Dean Wheeler	3	Andy Cook
Lee Carpenter	4	Michael Cooper
Darren Lush	5	Roger Emms
Nick Beales	6	Matt Davies
Russell Fishlock	7	Wayne Turk
Jerad O'Pray	8	Gary Funnell
Toby Colbourne	9	Leigh Phillips
Wayne Wheeler	10	John Purches
Steve Perkins	11	Steve Strong
Tom Evans	12	Stuart James
Ben Gardner	14	Aaron Turner
Lewis Porter	15	Josh Thomas
Tim Welch	16	Sam Allison
Jamie Bradley	17	Matt Holmes

William Bull - Hampshire

Simon Hooper - Wiltshire
Neil Fautley - Wiltshire

WHITES

The FA CUP
4th QUALIFYING ROUND

SALISBURY CITY
v.
LYMINGTON & NEW MILTON

Saturday 25th October 2003
3:00pm

Matchday Programme Sponsor
FIVE RIVERS LEISURE CENTRE

Main Team Sponsor
IN-EXCESS

2003/2004
Matchday
Programme £1

SALISBURY CITY
(White Shirts, Black Shorts)
V.
LYMINGTON & NEW MILTON
(Orange & Blue)

KEVIN SAWYER		
SCOTT BARTLETT	1	
ANDY COOK	2	ALAN WALKER-HARRIS
MICHAEL COOPER	3	DARREN CURTIS
ROGER EMMS	4	PETER SMITH
MAT DAVIES	5	WARREN KENNA
WAYNE TURK	6	JIMMY SHEPHERD (CAPT)
GARY FUNNELL	7	TREFOR SMITH
ADAM WALLACE	8	JOHN MULHERN
AARON TURNER	9	LEE HODDER
STUART JAMES	10	PHIL STONE
	11	PATRICK JAMES
DARREN CROOK		BEN THOMPSON
JOHN PURCHES	12	
STEVE WITT	14	KEVIN REACORD
STUART BROWN	15	KEVIN JAMES
MATT HOLMES	16	PAUL STURMEY
	17/22	CHRIS SMITH
		JOHN BAILEY

REFEREE: MR A. GRAVES (WESTON-SUPER-MARE)
ASSISTANT REFEREES: MR R. GILLARD (CHARD), MR T. LAWRENCE (BRIDGEWATER), MR S. ROBBINS (BRISTOL)

Sunday November 9th 2003 Kick-off 2.00pm

Sheffield Wednesday		Current Form	Salisbury City	

Nationwide

Wednesday
- Have not won in their last six matches
- Have lost their last two home matches
- Have not won in their last four home matches

Salisbury City
- Lost their last match
- Have won four of their last 5 away matches
- Have lost one of their last 8 League matches
- Have lost three of their last 16 matches

Owlsbet Match Odds

Result
1/8	Wednesday to win
12/1	Salisbury to win
13/2	Draw

Half Time / Full Time
| 9/2 | Draw/Wednesday |

Correct Score
8/1	Wednesday to win 5-0
9/1	Wednesday to win 2-0
12/1	Draw 1-1

To bet now with Owlsbet, call
08000 323 365 and quote Owlsbet
All odds are subject to fluctuation

Manager: Chris Turner

		PLAYED	SCORED
1	Kevin Pressman		
2	Derek Geary		
3	Brian Barry-Murphy		
4	Graeme Lee		
5	Dean Smith		
6	Leigh Bromby		
8	Paul McLaren		
9	Grant Holt		
10	Lloyd Owusu		
11	Paul Smith		
14	Steven Haslam		
15	Chris Stringer		
16	Craig Armstrong		
18	Jon Shaw		
20	Richard Wood		
21	Jon Beswetherick		
22	Ola Tidman		
23	Robbie Mustoe		
24	Terry Cooke		
25	Guylain Ndumbu-Nsungu		
26	Michael Reddy		
30	Adam Proudlock		
40	Adrian Thompson		

Wednesday

v Salisbury City

INTERVIEW
Robbie
Mustoe

INTERVIEW
Richard
Wood

ACTION FROM
Bristol City

Manager: Nick Holmes

		SCORED	PLAYED
1	Kevin Sawyer		
2	Scott Bartlett		
3	Andy Cook		
4	Michael Cooper		
5	Josh Thomas		
6	Matthew Davies		
8	Wayne Turk		
9	Gary Funnell		
10	Adam Wallace		
11	Steve Strong		
12	Stuart James		
14	Darren Crook		
15	John Purches		
16	Roger Emms		
17	Matthew Holmes		
18	Aaron Turner		
19	Stuart Brown		
20	Leigh Phillips		
21	Steve Witt		
22	Craig Davis		

Referee	Ass. Referee	Ass. Referee	Fourth Official
K. Friend	N. Murphy	R. Tiffin	M. Brown

MEMORY LANE

The 'Trip Up North'

Sheffield Wednesday , Sunday November 9th 2003

The big day had arrived and we had travelled from near and far. We were not all regulars and some had not been seen before.

It was dark, very dark and we got up before dawn wondering whether it would all be worth it with at least a five-hour trip each way and the odds obviously stacked against the team we supported so desperately. This just had to be the stuff of dreams but did those who were going realise just how privileged they were.

We travelled through sleepy villages to the Raymac. for our coaches. There were still some philistines who did not realise what this was all about. Arriving before 7 a.m. on a winters morning, a grey dawn was trying hard to appear and yet a great crowd was gathering. Cars were parking and disgorging occupants by the hundred. The Club shop was already open doing great business in selling scarves and all manner of favours. Was this a solstice in disguise!

Wagon trail rolls in

Then they appeared, lights one after another as 16 bright coaches hove into view on time and in convoy all capable of holding up to 50 passengers. Turning smartly and facing north they lined up as an Armada. Just after 7.30 a.m. the convoy took off on a journey that seemed suddenly totally surreal. Salisbury playing at Hillsborough — all these people — where had they all come from? The journey north was without incident save for the sight of motorway services stations being taken over by hundreds sporting Black and White, all well-behaved, perhaps apprehensive in unfamiliar territory.

Outside of Sheffield, the coaches drew up at the roadside as dictated by the local police who provided an escort to the ground. It was as if Real Madrid were in town as we were escorted through red traffic lights to a spot close to

the ground reserved for a vast phalanx of away support such as followers of this tiny Club might never see again. This was the stuff of dreams!

We were at the historic Leppings Lane end which was buzzing with noise. The Stadium was particularly impressive and goodness knows how the players must have been feeling whey they came out to balloons and horns although it was doubtful that this of itself would be enough to swing the match. *continued page 286*

Happy Salisbury City F.C. fans of all ages, wait to board the 16 coaches at the Ray McEnhill Stadium at 7 a.m. on a cold November morning.

☆

☆

☆

A small section of the 2000 Salisbury supporters in full voice out-singing, now and throughout the match, the Sheffield Wednesday supporters.

The famous clock facade at Hillsborough home of Sheffield Wednesday.

Nick Holmes weighing up the odds?

Salisbury's Scott Bartlett emerging from the tunnel alongside Wednesday's 'keeper Kevin Pressman.

Happy families reunited for the big-one awaiting the kick-off. It's all smiles now, hoping that the Whites would be among those `giant killers'

☆

☆

☆

Phil Harding of TVs Time Team, among the 2000-odd supporters who made the trip north, proudly showing his true colours – the Whites.

Wallace *(left)* out jumps his marker in an early battle, while *(right)* Strong cheekily tries to chip Pressman the Wednesday goal-keeper in the Whites very first attack.

(above, left to right) Davis, Cooper, Turk, Sawyer and Funnell easily outnumber the Wednesday attack at the hosts first corner.

James *(left)* tumbles under a Wednesday defender.
(right) Cook showing good control as the Whites start another attack on the Sheffield Wednesday goal.

(*above*) Scott and Turk tussle with a Wednesday attacker.

(*above, left to right*) Funnell, James, Cooper and Thomas can only wonder how Sheffield's fourth goal got by.

We are the 'famous Salisbury'

The match itself started well for our favourites and it is perhaps not being partisan to say that for half-an-hour we gave at least as good as we got and perhaps a little more.

Wallace broke for a close range shot saved by the 'keeper and Strong chipped him from 20-yards but again the goalkeeper was good enough to deny us to groans from the Leppings Lane end. Just before half-time the referee gave a penalty against us for a trip in the penalty area. It looked harsh but we would think that, wouldn't we! Still only 1-0 at half-time and we had done well. The second-half had barely started and we were 2-0 down and in our heart of hearts we knew that there was no fairy tale to come. Although it did not stop any of us from singing, as all of us were singing throughout, easily out-singing the Sheffield support. It was damage limitation now and tired limbs had given their all.

Probably 4-0 was about right but we were not down hearted. The Club so near to extinction just over 12 months previously was now vibrant and alive and although it was a quieter journey home there were no recriminations and all felt that it had been a memorable day.

When again will we hear the like of an F.A. Cup draw that announced:

'*Sheffield Wednesday will play Salisbury City*'............

Richard J.A. Walker

(*below*) Salisbury supporters although losing, still singing.

personalities, past & present

David Thear, Richard Walker, Peter Waterhouse and Peter D. Wood

all photos here are from private collections (except for Reg Broom, Geoff Butler and Nick Holmes)

Reg Broom 1947-1965

★ Reg Broom was in football management for 48 years. He was Salisbury Football Club's original manager who went on to hold the post for 18 years. Reg had previously been in charge of the old Salisbury Corinthians but resigned in 1947. He was the brainchild behind the formation of S.F.C. becoming one of the founder members. Reg also held the post of Chairman of the Western Football League. Under him the Club won all competitions that it entered except for the Amateur and F.A. Cup, although they reached the 2nd round in both of these competitions. Under Reg Broom S.F.C. won promotion in their first season and were judged by the press to be the most exciting team to watch in the southwest. A record surely that Reg Broom will never have taken away from him, is under his management over 8000 spectators were at a Western League Div. II match.

Ray McEnhill 1981-2004

★ Peter Wood reflects: I was at the Ray McEnhill Stadium helping to get it ready for the opening match when a voice I knew from way back made me look around. I walked over to Ray and shook his hand saying, 'In case I don't get another chance I want to thank you for all you've done for S.C.F.C., I've supported them since the mid-50s but if it hadn't been for you Ray, there wouldn't be a S.C.F.C., we'd be doing a ' Poole Town'', 'Just doing my bit for the Club', he replied. That to me summed up Ray McEnhill, a man whose generosity has helped so many. Ray was a local man in a family of five, on leaving school he had many jobs but while working for Johnson Wax saw an opportunity in the cleaning business that would set him up for life. He started a company called ' 20th Century Cleaning' which became his first of many successful businesses. After many years he sold the cleaning company and went into the business of buying up bus companies, from which he formed a successful company, 'Drawline Transport', finally selling this and becoming Chief Executive to 'National Express PLC'. He became Chairman of S.C.F.C. in 1982. Sadly Ray died of a brain tumour in 2004, aged 64.

Geoff Butler 1983-2000

★ After seasons of mediocrity Geoff Butler's arrival at the Club in February 1983 was to herald a transformation in the fortunes of Salisbury City Football Club. Within a few seasons the Whites gained promotion to the B.H.L. Premier Division by finishing runners-up to Cambridge City (1985/86). The team also took the runners-up position again in 1992/93 and in the 1994/95 season became B.H.L. Southern Division League Champions. Geoff Butler was named Manager of the year in that league. Geoff proved to be a superb negotiator and with his powers of persuasion the Club signed many outstanding players the calibre of A. Randall, R. Emms, J. Smith, I. Chalk, and P. Sales to mention a few. If the need arose he brought in players on loan deals, notable players being J. Hayter and S. Mildenhall. Under Geoff's management the Club reached the F.A. Cup First Round on two occasions.

**Nev Beal
2002**

★ Nev Beal – Cometh the hour, cometh the man. Salisbury City F.C. darkest hour saw Neville Beal and Dave Harrold guiding the club from the edge of the abyss on Black Monday. Salisbury City F.C. renaissance commenced that day and under Nev's leadership, hardwork and enthusiasm the club has gone from a position of desperation to inspiration. His first major coup was the astute appointment of Manager, Nick Holmes. Neville a local company director is a Salisbury City F.C. man through and through having joined the club as a player in 1983 and playing over 100 games for the Whites. He is certainly not the archetypical football club Chairman. Instead of sipping a post match Gin & Tonic in the luxury of the club Boardroom, he is to be found helping out at the Sarum Suite bar serving pints of beer to thirsty supporters. Also Nev fulfils a major role in the management of the ladies and girls teams where his young daughter regularly plays for the club.

**Nick Holmes
2002**

★ Any self-respecting football fans will know what Nick Holmes achieved during his playing career with Southampton F.C. and, if they don't the excellent books about the Saints by Hagiology Publishing will fill any gaps. It is what he has done while at the Raymac. that is of importance here. Since arriving he, with the Directors has turned the club into an open and happy one. Early results on the field were mixed but much better than could have been expected given the traumatic events of summer 2002. Season 2003/4 saw promotion and a cup run which culminated in an unforgettable day in Sheffield. The following season Tommy Widdrington was signed to fill the role of player-coach and this turned a relegation threatened team in the Isthmian league into a confident outfit which easily gained mid-table security. Promotion to the National Conference (South) was then achieved following the transfer to the Southern Premier league and the club reached the last eight of the F.A. Trophy. As I write in February 2007 Salisbury have, this season, reached the 2nd Round of the F.A. Cup when they lost to Nottingham Forest in a replay, the quarter finals of the F.A. Trophy and are top of their league. Nick's stated aim is a Football league place and who would argue against this happening. Salisbury City F.C. are very lucky to have such an accomplished and approachable man in charge – long may he remain.

**Peter Yeldon
2004**

★ Peter Yeldon the analytically thinking international entrepreneur brought an extra dimension to the club with his business flair and financial dexterity which resulted in Salisbury City F.C. moving quickly forward with the financing of important high-profile transactions. Whilst watching the Whites with his two young sons he appreciated what he saw then joined the talented Salisbury City Football Club Board of Directors. Peter Yeldon's philosophy of meticulous forward planning is now very evident with the Salisbury City aficionados.

**Mary Case MBE
1924**

★ Mary Case comes from a family who have supported Salisbury City F.C. over several generations. Her father first watched the club in 1893 and she herself followed in his footsteps in 1924. For many years Mary Case has sponsored the club in both the first and last matches of the season and is to be seen at nearly all games both home and away. Her services were honoured in 1990 when she was made an Honourary Life vice-President of the Football Club. Farther afield, in the Queens Birthday Honours of 2006, Mary was awarded the M.B.E.

Stuart McGlashan 1999

★ Stuart McGlashan has been involved with Salisbury City F.C. in one job or another since 1999. His first contact then was watching his son Andrew playing in the youth team. When Geoff Butler started a reserve side in 2000 with Brian O'Donnell as Manager they did'nt have a Physio and as Stuart's son had now progressed to the reserves he volunteered for the job. During this time he did several jobs including designing/producing the programme, Secretary and assistant Manager under Ian Chalk and Clive Bowden when they became reserve team Managers. In those days manager and assistant did it all, open up the stadium, serve behind the bar, provide the refreshments, clear up the dressing rooms after the game and lock-up after everyone had gone. His first involvement with the first team, was to cover for Polly (Conrad Parrott, physio) occasionally, if he got stuck on some far-flung motorway on mid-week games.

In 2000 the family business, McGlashans Property Services along with BM Windows sponsored the start of 'Football in the Community', with Andy Cook, which has been a great success with local schools and youth community. When Salisbury City F.C. and Ken Cunningham-Brown parted company in 2002, Nev Beal and Dave Harrold put together a rescue package and asked Stuart if he would like to be a director.

Stuart says that he cannot put into words the elation he now feels after all those years of hard work by all at the club. As he handed me (*pdw*) the text of this article we were on the terraces at Tiverton F.C.; the date was Saturday 15th April 2006. All around, Salisbury City F.C. supporters, male, female, young and old (including all the directors) and players, were singing, 'We Are The Champions'...................

Paul Orsborn 2005

★ Paul Orsborn, born in Great Yarmouth, Norfolk, has always been a keen footballer and fan of the game but never rose above playing for his local village team of Reedham on the Norfolk Broads. Paul moved to Salisbury in 1977 and two years later started his own graphic design and printing company which, in the mid-nineties, began to print the Salisbury City programme. Soon after he was asked to join the Board of Directors and is as keen as anyone to see the Club progress to bigger and better things.

Derek & Reneé Sharp 1959 & 1967

★ Derek and Reneé Sharp epitomise the true spirit of a football club supporter. It is virtually unthinkable to envisage Salisbury City F.C. without them. Entering the stadium through turnstile D, one is greeted by the genial Reneé selling a selection of fundraising tickets and a few feet away the dapper Derek selling the match-day programmes. They were married in 1967 and it was not long before Reneé started fund raising for the club. She has raised tens of thousands of pounds on match-days with general ticket sales. Derek joined the management committee of Salisbury F.C. in 1959. In 1961 he was appointed assistant-Secretary to the then Secretary-Manager Reg Broom. Due to his business commitments Derek was unable to accept the post of Secretary in 1966 when Reg Broom retired but was elected to the post four years later at the time of Ian McNeil's appointment as manager. The early 70s were unsettling with several changes of manager and in addition Derek was forced to take on the duties of temporary Treasurer without notice. Temporary became 10-years!! In 1977 he was elected to the Southern League Management Board being involved with the joint-Liaison Committee for the formation of the 'Pyramid' for non-league football. He was also the club representative on the Western Counties Floodlight League and in 1982 was elected Chairman. Whilst working for Ray McEnhill in 1982 Reneé introduced him to Derek and as a result Ray became Chairman of the the club later that year.

**Alec Hayter
1947**

★ 'I am told that I've been watching the Whites since 1947, but as I was only three years old then, I did'nt know much about it. Some would say I've not improved!' Many S.C.F.C. supporters describe the dulcet tones of Alec Hayter as 'The Voice of Salisbury City F.C.' The football journalist is well known for his B.B.C. Radio Wiltshire work and football reporting for: Football Echo, Non-League Paper, Southern Echo, Sunday Independent and the Western Daily Press. Alec, for a time was Programme Editor and S.C.F.C. Press Officer, then in May 2006 he took on the mantle of Salisbury City Football Secretary.

He, despite his mature years, has mastered the intricacies of the internet and is a regular contributor to the Club's Forum.

**Dave Todd
1971**

★ Dave Todd has been an avid supporter since his father first took him to see Salisbury F.C. beat Bath City 2-1 in the F.A. Cup match at Victoria Park on the 9th October, 1971 when he was only six years old. At the age of about 10 he started writing down the teams, which he has developed over the years, so much so that for the last 30 years he has facts and figures on Salisbury City F.C. which are second to none.

He was part of the Matchday Programme team from 1988 to 1991, then in 2001 he played an integral part, as Alec Hayter's right-hand man. It all changed again in May 2006 when Paul Orsborn became Programme Editor with Dave and Mike Turner sharing the programme write-ups.

In 2001 he set up an unofficial 'Fans Forum' on the 'web', then a year later along with Darren Blick brought out the Salisbury City F.C. independent web site and together they vastly improved the Fans Forum.

Since a spell away from the area in 1991, he has rarely missed a game and became well-known on the non-league circuit as part of the 'White Army' alongside the likes of Gary Richards and Paul Carpenito.

Reading this you could be forgiven for thinking Dave is just a walking encyclopedia on S.C.F.C., but I can vouch for the man – he's got plenty of soul.

**Joan Wilmer
1947-2004**

★ Supporter par excellence Joan Wilmer began supporting her beloved team way back in 1947. No task was ever too menial for Joan to undertake if it was to benefit the club. One of her roles for many a year was that of S.C.F.C. laundress, ensuring the team kit was always spotlessly clean for every game. Joan was always willing to offer good hearted advice to any linesman (asst. ref) who happened to be within hearing range. There are many anecdotes to be told relating to Joan supporting the Whites. One of my favourite accounts was when an American tourist went to Victoria Park to watch an English 'soccer' game. The American was so impressed with Joan's support for the Whites, that he stated 'Gee man, I've gotta take a photo of the lady'. A personal lasting memory of Joan was when Salisbury defeated Barnet in the F.A. Cup First Round in 1959. Joan stood by the players tunnel congratulating each Salisbury player coming off the park. Sadly, Joan passed away in 2004. The crematorium was packed with her many friends and her coffin carried a floral tribute in the shape of a football in club colours. The service ended with a resounding chorus of 'Up The Whites'.

A commemorative plaque is placed at the Ray McEnhill Stadium in tribute to Joan.

our all-time top 30

David Thear
Richard Walker
Peter Waterhouse
and Peter D. Wood

Roy Fisher
1947–1954

Tommy Williams
1947–1950

Dennis Rogers
1947–1954

Cyril Smith
1947–2004

Roy Onslow
1958–1960

Alan Kingston
1954–59

Terry Compton
1958–1963

Roy (Ginger) Watts
1959—1963

Brian Stevens
1959–1966

Barry Fitch
1964–1978

Alan Tyler
1967–1972

Paul Christopher
1974–1982

Alan Green
1974–1978 & 1979–1981

Ian Thompson
1981–83 & 1986–87

Ricky Haysom
He has been with the Club, intermittently, since
1981 as player, assistant manager and scout.

Barry Cranmer
1981–1991

Sean Sanders
1987–1996

Ian Chalk
1988–2001

Jimmy Smith
1990–94 & 2000–01

Roger Emms
1992–2003

Simon Browne
1992–1998 and 2005

Paul Sales
1998–2001 and 2005

Adie Randall
1998–99

Andy Cook
1999

Scott Bartlett
2000

Wayne Turk
2000

Matt Tubbs
2003

Aaron Cook
2004

Tim Bond
2004

Tommy Widdrington
2005

The thirty players presented here may not be your first choice and arguments will last for maybe the next 60 years as to who are the best who have ever played for the Whites. The present team, at my time of writing these few words is the 2006 side and one would like to include them all after their excellent cup run and season but who knows what is around the corner.

Nearly every season produces popular players and heroes but do they stand the test of time? I thought to myself, when watching Salisbury F.C. in the late 50s, that any team that contained the likes of Ambrose, Ashe, Bichard, Collins, Fitch, Gilbert, Hodgkins, Moxham, Muxworthy, Phillips, Stevens, Tyler, Waters and Whitehouse would never be surpassed — but who of the present age group remembers any of them?

I did not see the very first team play but Fisher, Rogers and Smith I did have the pleasure of watching and I used to hope they would always be playing for the Whites.   *Peter D. Wood*

Roy Fisher (centre-forward) — Native of Southampton, was a member of the 1947 Salisbury team. A prolific goalscorer netting 34 league goals in the 1947/48 campaign. He was on Southampton F.C. books before joining Salisbury and scored 163 goals in his career with them.

Dennis Rogers (right-winger) — His dazzling runs down the right-wing and pin-point accurate crosses made the player a firm favourite with the local supporters. Before joining the club in 1947 he played for the Everton 'A' side, Chester and Peterborough. Dennis rejected the opportunity to join Swindon Town in October 1947, scoring 19 league goals for Salisbury in their first season.

Cyril Smith (inside-right) — Started his football with Pirelli Youth team, joining Southampton in 1939 at the age of 17 and signing for Arsenal in 1944. He was a true gentleman on and off the field, a player of great flair who had an eye for goal as well as a provider for others with his running and carrying. Scored 14 league goals in his first season with Salisbury. Held many posts including Team Manager.

Tommy Williams (centre-half) — Was a very stylish player and an influential club captain. Former Welsh amateur international before turning professional for Cardiff City. He played for the British Army in Italy during WWII Was captain of the Salisbury team which set up a Western League record in playing 19 consecutive matches without dropping a point.

Roy Onslow (centre-forward) — Joining the Whites at the start of the 1958 season, he had had considerable league experience, making over 200 first-team appearances for Swindon Town. Moving to Chippenham Town prior to his move to Salisbury F.C. Roy was a brave archetypical English centre-forward who scored a total of 37 goals for the club. He will always be remembered for the great goal he scored against Barnet at Victoria Park to put Salisbury through to the Second Round Proper of the F.A. Cup in 1959.

Alan Kingston (goalkeeper) — Born in Longparish, Hampshire, he was playing for Andover's Western League side at the age of 15. Had a trial for Portsmouth and when still only 17 signed for Southampton, playing for one season in their Combination side with one game in their Division II side. Opponents for that one game were Swansea. The Saints won 5-2 and scoring both goals for Swansea was Trevor Ford a Welsh international well-known for his bustling style. Alan joined Salisbury for the 1954–55 season. playing in a era where the position did not receive the same level of protection it does today. Played in the successful cup run of 1959–60.

Terry Compton (centre-half) — Joined from Bristol City in time for 1958–59 season. A tall commanding centre-half who had played 44 first-team games at Bristol City. He was to be at the centre of defence for the most successful period in the club's history. Died in 1991 at the fairly young age of 60.

Roy (Ginger) Watts (inside-left) — Joined from Bristol City in 1959 where he made many reserve team appearances. A prolific scorer laying claim to 180 league and cup goals (which is still the club's record); in fact in only four seasons at Salisbury he was the top goalscorer for three. He left to join Welton Rovers in 1963 where he continued to find the net on a regular basis.

Brian Stevens (goalkeeper) — 'Stevo' to all who knew him, big-hearted character, who never seemed to get depressed, no matter the score. Could always be relied on after the game to have everyone laughing within minutes. Started his career in football as a centre-half, playing a few games in goal when the 'keeper was injured. Signed for Salisbury F.C., in the early 60s. All-round sportsman, playing cricket (along with B. Fitch and A. Tyler) for South Wilts. Saints signed him as cover for John Christie, where he played 12 times for the first-team plus a further 67 for the reserves. In 1980 while playing cricket at Hursley for Andover Banks CC, Brian, who was only 46, died suddenly from a heart attack. At his funeral in Salisbury many G.P.O. workmates as well as sportsmen from all parts of Hampshire and Wiltshire attended.

Barry Fitch (left-back) — Signed from Brighton in March 1964 going on to make 713 appearances. Another player who always gave 110% for Salisbury. Terrier-like tackler who played the 'new' role in football as the attacking full-back. Within six months of signing for Salisbury he was playing in the 1st Round Proper of the F.A. Cup at Peterborough.

Alan Tyler (inside-right) — Native of Manchester, said to have cleaned George Best's boots. He was there as an apprentice, making appearances in the reserve side before becoming disillusioned and joining the Army. This was where S.F.C. discovered him and paid for his early exit. Scored all six goals in the beating of Ashford in January 1969. In his career with Salisbury scored 90 goals

Paul Christopher (inside-forward) — Joined from Mansfield Town in 1974 where he made seven first-team appearances scoring one goal. A stylish forward who scored the two goals in the F.A. Cup match versus Worcester City. This event put the club through to visit the Dell to play Millwall in the First Round Proper. Had a joint-benefit with Cyril Smith.

Alan Green (striker) — Joined Salisbury after a long layoff from football, after being injured while playing for Mansfield in a Division IV match. A local lad from Woodfalls he also played for Bournemouth AFC. Very quick and tricky player, he was top goalscorer for the club in the seasons 1976/77, 1977/78 (shared), 1979/80 and 1980/81. Alan remarked recently, that playing at Victoria Park on summer evenings was the best ! His favourite derby games were against Poole Town, with a certain Mr R. Bazeley (Poole Town and Dorchester) having many a challenge with no quarter sought or given. When asked how he managed to jump so high (not being the tallest of strikers), he replied: 'determination'.

Ian Thompson (forward) — Joined from Poole Town for a small fee. A quick and skilful forward he was leading scorer in his first full season with 19 goals. In May 1983 he was transferred to Bournemouth & Boscombe for £18,000, a record fee at that time for a Salisbury player. Injury forced him to give up full-time football and he returned to Victoria Park in 1986/7 before moving to Wales in his job as a schoolmaster a year later. Scored a total of 70 goals for the Whites.

Ricky Haysom (centre-back) — Excellent clubman who joined Salisbury along with his brother Steve from Andover in 1981. Had a good eye for goal, especially at corners and free-kicks. He and his brother belonged to the team that won the Southern League Championship for the first time in the club's history in the 1985/86 season. Still with Salisbury (2007) in a scouting capacity. A formidable figure on and off the field. His handshake (first) I liken to being caught in an animal trap, difference being it comes with a friendly smile. I believe its friendly but of course it's a smile?

Barry Cranmer (defender) — Joined Salisbury with his brother Calvin from Andover in time for the 1981–2 season. A commanding central defender who scored many goals from set pieces. Had he not held a good position outside of football, he would surely have progressed to the Football League. Left to join Basingstoke in 1991, but subsequently returned to Salisbury for two further short spells.

Sean Sanders (forward) — A versatile and loyal player who in his time played in all positions (except goal) for the team. He was extremely influential in the early 1990's and contributed greatly to the successes achieved during a period of attractive football. Following a knee injury was forced to retire from Southern League football and played for a period with Stockbridge. Scored 97 league and cup goals for Salisbury.

Ian Chalk (mid-field or striker) — A highly talented player, whose total commitment and never-say-die attitude made him a firm favourite with the Salisbury faithful. The local born player signed for the club in 1988. He gained considerable experience with Wrexham, Swindon Town and Peterborough United. Incredibly, Ian made over 600 first-team appearances for Salisbury scoring 176 goals, just four short of Roy Watts all-time record.

Jimmy Smith (centre-forward) — The former Torquay United player was a significant signing for S.C.F.C. From his first game for the Whites it was obvious he was a striker of notable skill. His first spell with the club produced over 60 goals in less than two seasons. The prolific goalscorer was transferred to Cheltenham Town for £5000 in 1991 to the disappointment of the Salisbury supporters. He later returned to the Whites.

Roger Emms (defender) — Signed for the Club in 1992 from Andover Town and was a very popular player with the Salisbury supporters. The strong defender virtually won every 40/60 tackle; he was generally acknowledged to be one of the best central-defenders in the region. Hopes were always high when Roger moved upfield to position himself for a set-piece for, not only was he a superb defender he could score goals as well, getting 52 for the club in his long and distinguished career with Salisbury City F.C.

Simon Browne (defender) — The dependable defender rejoined S.C.F.C. in August 2005 from his native Weymouth where he started his career. He has also played for Swanage & Herston and Dorchester Town. Simon left Dorchester Town to first join Salisbury City in March 1992, where he had five satisfying seasons before rejoining Weymouth. He was a member of the 1994/5 Salisbury City team that won the B.H.L. Southern Division Championship. Supporters will remember Simon's magnificent free-kick goal that clinched promotion for the Whites to the Southern Premier Division, in the final minute of the match against Havant at Victoria Park on the 1st May 1995. He rejoined the club in 2005.

Paul Sales (striker) — Born in Southampton on 9th January 1974. Skilful Southampton based striker who signed in time for the start of the 1998 season and scored on his debut versus Tamworth. Was subsequently top scorer in each of his next three seasons with 21 goals in 1998/99, 31 in 1999/2000 and a further 21 in 2000/01. Season 2001/02 was an injury hit season when he only scored two in 17 appearances and in February 2002 he returned to Bashley for a fee of £5000. Subsequently moved to Eastleigh and helped them into the Conference South through the playoffs. Returned to Salisbury for season 2004/2005 and scored 23 goals in all matches.

Adie Randall (mid-field) — Signed from Endsleigh League Division I side Bury in July 1998. Adie started his career with A.F.C. Bournemouth before moving onto Aldershot Town. Figured in six-figure transfers to both York City and Burnley and was later transferred to Bury in 1996 for another £100,000 transfer-fee. Alas this superbly gifted mid-fielder played just one season for Salisbury. In the 198/99 season, a record fee of £20,000 took him to Forest Green Rovers.

Andy Cook (defender) Signed in October 1999 after leaving Millwall, initially on a non-contract basis before becoming Football in the Community Officer. Made his debut on 26 October 1999 at Merthyr Tydifil. He was in the Southampton team that played in Barry Cranmer's testimonial match. Has made over 200 appearances. Andy had just returned to the Salisbury team after suffering a facial injury in a league fixture at Northwood when, on the 25th February 2006 in the quarter-final of the F.A. Trophy versus Exeter, he sustained a bad leg break, which seems to have all but finished his playing of football for Salisbury City F.C.

Scott Bartlett (mid-field) — The Salisbury born and bred Scott Bartlett, started his football career with A.F.C. Bournemouth. He later moved to Cirencester Town before joining the Whites in February 2000. The popular speedy player with his enthusiasm and loyalty, has become a firm favourite with the local fans. Scott is equally at home in midfield or defence and, at the time of writing has made nearly 300 appearances for the club.

Wayne Turk (mid-field) — Born in Swindon on 21st January 1981. Represented Swindon School Boys from the age of 11 through to the age of 16. At the age of 12 he spent 2 years at Oxford United School of Excellence. On leaving school at the age of 16 went to Cirencester Football Academy for two years which included a three year Sports Science course as well as playing football for Cirencester College. While studying at Cirencester College, he was captain of the successful academy football team which won the English School's F.A., 'under 19 Cup' in 1998 and 1999 and the British Colleges Trophy in 1998 and 1999. In 1998 he represented the British Colleges National Team in Florida USA. Signed for Salisbury City F.C. in 2000 from Cirencester Town F.C. Scored his 50th goal for Salisbury v Hayes(a) on 17th Feb. 2007. Played his 300 game v Hayes(h) 27th March.

Matthew Tubbs (forward) — Born in Salisbury on 15th July 1984. Started his career as a Youth Player with Bolton Wanderers and progressed to AFC Bournemouth. Played for Salisbury City F.C. in a pre-season friendly in 2003 before deciding to sign for Dorchester but luckily for Salisbury he was not happy there and in October signed for the Whites. Top goalscorer in his first season and when Paul Sales rejoined the club for the 2005/06 season struck up an instant firecracker partnership, each feeding off each other with an uncanny understanding. Always knowing where the other was or going to be produced some memorable goals. To mention just two, both from 2005/06 season. The first away at Evesham, sprinting out of midfield, not seeming to look at their advancing goalkeeper, with his back on goal flicks the ball up over his head and their static guardian of the net. Second, at home to Grantham. City's third, cutting in from the left he outfoxes the defender then hits the ball with breath-taking power into the top corner of the net.

Aaron Cook (centre-back) — Signed from Bashley in March 2004, Aaron commenced his football career with Portsmouth and has played for Swansea City, Exeter City and Havant & Waterlooville. He took on the mantle of Team Captain in 2005 and is now held in high esteem by the Salisbury supporters.

Authoritative Aaron Cook has established himself as a colossus in the defence.

Manager, Nick Holmes described Aaron in 2006 as the best centre-back in the Southern Premier League.

In the summer of 2006 the defender received the prestigious N.L.P. 'Southern League Player of the Year Award' in recognition of his outstanding season. (2005/2006).

Tim Bond (centre-back) — Born in Carshalton, 29.11.84. Began playing football at the aged of 13 for Chichester City Colts. At the age of 15 moved on to play for Barnham Trojans. During high school represented West Sussex and Sussex schools in which two games were played at Fratton Park and The Dell. He joined A.F.C. Bournemouth aged 16 after being recommended by his college manager Steve Constantine. Played for their under 17's and under 19's also represented the reserve team on a regular basis. Won A.F.C. Bournemouth 'Youth Team Player of Year' in 2003. When they released him in March 2004, he joined Salisbury. Made his debut on 6.3.2004, at home to Hastings United in a Dr Martens League Eastern Division fixture. Studying Exercise and Health Science at Chichester University.

Tommy Widdrington (mid-field) — Has proved to be one of the most influential players ever to wear a Salisbury City F.C. shirt. He joined the club from Port Vale in February 2005 when the club were near the Isthmian Premier League relegation zone. Thankfully the club survived, losing just once in their last 11 games.

The commanding mid-field player has established himself as an exceptional coach with his methodology and attention to detail. The former football league player has now helped the Whites with his coaching and motivational skills gain Nationwide Conference South status.

7

Ryman Isthmian League

The 2004–05 Season — David Thear

Whither shall we wander?

The close season was a period of anxious anticipation for the fans. Last season's final league placing meant that Salisbury would play in the Premier Division of either the Ryman Isthmian or the Dr Marten's Southern League.

The former would mean breaking new ground with unfamiliar journeys particularly in and around London. The latter would entail longer journeys but retaining matches with Chippenham, Bath, King's Lynn, Tiverton and Banbury.

Here lies the answer

In the event the club joined the Isthmian League Premier which comprised:

Eastleigh Folkestone Invicta Salisbury City Tonbridge Angels	}	ex. Dr Martens Eastern Division (4 clubs)
Chelmsford City Dover Athletic	}	ex. Dr Martens Premier Division (2 clubs)
Cheshunt Leyton Wealdstone Yeading	}	ex. Ryman Isthmian League Division I North (4 clubs)

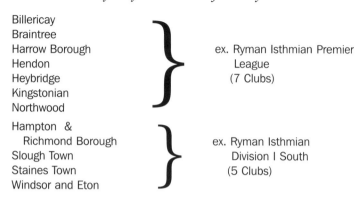

Billericay
Braintree
Harrow Borough
Hendon   } ex. Ryman Isthmian Premier
Heybridge   League
Kingstonian   (7 Clubs)
Northwood

Hampton &
    Richmond Borough   } ex. Ryman Isthmian
Slough Town   Division I South
Staines Town   (5 Clubs)
Windsor and Eton

The only local derby would be against Eastleigh who had made some impressive signings during the close season.

There was a view that the Isthmian League would provide easier access to the Conference than the Southern League and in the past, the Whites had made unsuccessful overtures for a transfer.

The coming season was, therefore, a chance to test this theory, particularly as the minimum stay in the new league was thought to be three years. Quite how this 'undertaking' would be honoured was not clear as the composition of any league, year on year, is determined by the locations of promoted and relegated clubs. If travelling costs are to be contained, one of the determining factors in any reshuffle, then some transferring of clubs between leagues in the same step in the Non-League pyramid would seem inevitable.

The best laid plans......

Having said that the preparations for the new season were complicated by the news that Tommy Killick, the assistant manager for the last few seasons, had left to join Poole Town as manager and Nick Holmes had had to spend a considerable time in Florida in connection with his business there. The stay, due to the affects of three hurricanes in close succession, was extended until the New Year which meant that the close season friendlies and almost half of the league programme lacked his personal supervision.

The friendlies were, as usual, a mixed bag. Three Conference level clubs were played and one, Gravesend, was beaten. Mark Kelly, a former Irish International, took charge of the team in Nick's absence and it was noticeable that he favoured more of a passing game than that employed last season. Gary Funnell had left to join Poole Town and John Purches did not re-sign. Popular local lad Darren Crook went to Lymington & New Milton but Salisbury retained his signature on Southern League forms. Mark Lisk joined from Bashley and Sean Cook from Thatcham. Last season's perceived weakness 'up front' did not seem to have been addressed although the rest of the team seemed strong enough. Adam Wallace, a quality player who had yet to play to his full potential, was suspended for 42 days from 7th September as a result of an incident with the reserves the previous season.

Despite these factors the season opened with three wins and two draws. Folkestone, Kingstonian and Cheshunt were all beaten at home while the Staines and Braintree matches ended in draws. The team for the opening match was: Sawyer, Bartlett, Lisk, Aaron Cook, Thomas, Mat Davies, Howes, C. Davis, Wallace, Tubbs and Bond with Phillips, Matt Holmes, Strong, Cooper and Hedges as substitutes. These players provided the nucleus of the side until changes were made in an attempt to stem a subsequent flow of poor results. After the Cheshunt game the wheels fell off with a 2-0 defeat at home to Leyton and two visits to Stag's Meadow, Windsor, to play Slough Town and Windsor & Eton F.C. brought no reward. There were to be two more abortive trips to Stag's Meadow during the season.

Money-earner beckons again

The first saw Salisbury beaten 3-2 in the F.A. Cup, with Slough scoring the winner in the 87th minute. The victors played and beat Walsall an experienced league team. The second visit was to lose to Slough in the Bryco Cup. Staying with the F.A. Cup, the Whites 3-1 victory at Weston-super-Mare in the 3rd Qualifying Round was arguably their best result of the season.

Weston were eighth in the Nationwide South and were unbeaten at home including a 2-0 win over Grays Athletic, eventual runaway winners of that league and the F.A. Trophy. On the day Salisbury played superbly and could easily won by a larger margin. Acting manager Barry Blankley, who had taken over from Mark Kelly the previous week, must have been mightily impressed by his charges.

F.A. Cup Results 30/10/04							
Slough Town	3	Salisbury	2	Tiverton Town	4	Newport County	1
Lymington & N.M.	1	Woking	1	Thame	0	Forest Green	5
replay Woking	4	Lymington & N.M.	1				

   Unfortunately the team had flattered to deceive. The poor league form which had started with the Slough match on 30th August continued with only four wins in 19 matches to 8th January 2005, at which point, relegation beckoned. Mark Kelly, who had looked after the team until Barry Blankley's arrival, had left for personal reasons and Nick Holmes could only manage a couple of flying visits. The defence, which had been reasonably secure at the start of the season, lost confidence and seemed unable to keep a lead. The match against Hampton & Richmond epitomised the problem when a 2-0 half-time lead was lost with three opposition goals in 20 minutes. Even Alec Hayter, the joint match-day programme editor with Dave Todd, was lost for anything encouraging to say when describing the dismal performances against Harrow and Wealdstone.

No Christmas cheer!

The Christmas/New Year period, when Mitch Blake, the reserve team manager and former manager of Downton was looking after the first-team affairs due to Barry Blankley's pre-arranged commitments, brought a win over a weakened Leyton side in the Bryco Cup and the postponement of the local derby at Eastleigh. This match had been keenly anticipated as hundreds of Salisbury fans had made the journey on a cold but bright Boxing Day only for the kick-off to be first put back and then called off due to a frozen pitch.

   The good news at New Year was that Nick Holmes' business affairs in Florida had been sorted out and he was returning in time for the league match at Leyton on 8th January. Although this was lost, Windsor & Eton were beaten 5-1 at the Raymac. on the following Saturday with Wallace(2), Craig Davis, Tubbs and Matthews scoring. The latter had re-signed for a fee from

Eastleigh in the autumn in an endeavour to boost the strike force. On 2nd January, Yeading who had featured (but lost 2-0) in a televised 3rd Round F.A. Cup tie against Newcastle United on the previous Sunday, were beaten 2-1 at Yeading with goals from Matthews and C. Davis (penalty). The Whites included Sean Hale, a new signing from Fleet with previous Conference level experience, although Adam Wallace was suspended. The way the win was achieved seemed to indicate that the corner was turned but, again, this was not so.

That sinking feeling sets in

The next four league matches were lost with the Whites scoring only twice while conceding nine. (In addition there had been a 3-0 defeat away to Slough in the Bryco Cup). They were back in the

relegation zone, three points behind 18th placed Hendon who had two games in hand. The home game against Tonbridge Angels on the 19th February was, therefore, crucial. They had three points less but with a game in hand. As might be expected it was a scrappy affair with Craig Davis scoring the all-important goal to achieve a 1-0 win. However, it did nothing to convince the Salisbury supporters that

Craig Davis about to score the winner at home to Tonbridge Angels.

their fortunes were to change for the better. It was clear that the defence needed strengthening and the eager running and enthusiasm of the younger players needed controlling and harnessing if the team were to climb out of trouble.

These two issues were addressed when, on 26th February, Matt Jones, a full-back from Winchester and Tommy Widdrington, a midfield player from Port Vale, were named in the side. As Neville Beal said Tommy Widdrington was just the player needed. Nearly

Tommy Widdrington

a hundred games for Saints and many more for Wigan Athletic, Grimsby Town, Hartlepool, Macclesfield and Port Vale gave him the skill and experience so desperately needed. In addition he was a model professional and a talker both on and off the field. Matt Jones, the other new signing proved to be a solid defender and with Tim Bond and Aaron Cook establishing themselves in the centre, the defence was transformed. Mich Blake's specialist coaching of goalkeeper Kevin Saywer was also paying dividends. The game at Northwood was won 3-0 and from then until the end of the season, only one game was lost and this at home to Harrow Borough after the mathematical possibility of relegation had been eliminated.

Unfortunately players had left. Adam Wallace, who had scored 54 goals in 113 matches in his Salisbury career, moved to Basingstoke due to work commitments and Mat Davis to Brackley Town on loan. Josh Thomas was transfer-listed and he and Steve Strong had had loan spells at Bashley. Sean Cook had returned to Thatcham and Aaron Hedges the reserve goalkeeper had moved on. Alan Walker-Harris had taken his place for the home defeat against Chippenham Town in the Wiltshire Premier Shield before Simon Arthur took over as cover for Kevin Sawyer. Richard Gillespie was signed 'on loan' from Bashley to see if he could reproduce his goal scoring form in the Southern League Eastern Division at a higher level. Somewhat unluckily he failed to score in the eight matches, four as substitute, for which he was selected and at the

photo: Sports Echo

Matt Tubbs performing acrobatics in his attempt to score against Eastleigh, on Easter Monday.

end of the season it was decided that he did not warrant a permanent transfer and the fee involved.

There remains only the 4-0 defeat at home to Thurrock in the F.A. Trophy and the less said about that the better.

So how is the season summed up? The F.A. Cup run was good, the F.A. Trophy, a non-event and in the league a comfortable mid-table position was achieved after early scares.

More 'football' played in new league?

What about 2005/06? There is little doubt that the type of football played in the Ryman Isthmian League came as a surprise to all. Even the lesser teams seemed to have solid defences and one, or more likely two, fast raiding forwards. The overall style was different to the predominantly 'long ball' game played in the Dr Marten Eastern Division. In addition each team seemed to have at least one experienced player. It took Salisbury time to learn to live with this and it is significant that Dover Athletic and Tonbridge Angels, old Southern League teams, didn't and were relegated. Folkestone Invicta lived dangerously and only Eastleigh, who were the opponents when the then record gate of 1151 for a league match at the Raymac. was set at Easter 2005, managed to achieve success by gaining promotion to the Nationwide Conference South via the play-offs.

The coming to terms with Isthmian League football was then, hopefully, in the past and the club could look forward to building on the successes achieved in the latter part of the season, or could it?

The bomb was dropped immediately after the end of the season. Salisbury City F.C. were transferred back to the Southern League Premier Division!!! An appeal was lodged but to no avail. The Raymac. would host the following clubs in season 2005/06.

Aylesbury United	Cirencester	Mangotsfield United
Banbury United	Evesham United	Merthyr Tydfil
Bath City	Gloucester City	Northwood
Bedford Town	Grantham Town	Rugby United
Chesham United	Halesowen Town	Team Bath
Cheshunt	Hitchin Town	Tiverton Town
Chippenham Town	King's Lynn	Yate Town

The number of trips around the M25 had been reduced and lengthier journeys to Grantham, King's Lynn and Merthyr Tydfil reinstated. The potentially lucrative visit of AFC Wimbledon, newly promoted to the Ryman Isthmian Premier, with a fan base running to thousands, had been lost but local derbies with Bath City, Chippenham Town, Cirencester Town, Gloucester and Tiverton would be some compensation.

However, whatever league the Whites were to play in the team's needs would be the same. Top priority would be a proven goal-scorer to take advantage of the constructive football being played in midfield, the permanent capture of Tommy Widdrington to marshal the team and the retention of those players who had played a prominent part in the final 12 games of the season.

The astute direction of the Board, which comprised, at the end of the season, Neville Beal, Stuart McGlashan, Peter Yeldon and Paul Orsborn (of Sarum Graphics who print the match-day programme) would be needed to ensure financial stability. The average home attendance in excess of 500 per match, had demonstrated that there was considerable potential support for a successful team.

There was a short period in the season when David Malone, a former director of Winchester City, joined the board but he moved on by mutual agreement. His introduction of 'Fantasy Football' to the fan's website is likely to be a lasting legacy of his time at the Raymac.

There would be a new groundsman in 2005/06 as a result of Brian Carter's retirement. The excellent surface at the stadium owed everything to his and his team's efforts.

There was also a view that a reserve team was essential if the successful youth team players were to be retained. This may be easier said than done if past attempts are anything to go by.

Dedicated supporter now watching from afar!

On a sad note, Joan Wilmer, of whom photographs appear in this book, died not long after the start of the season. She was a life-long supporter and a real local character particularly when urging the team on. She had sponsored Josh Thomas's kit for the season and it was her son's wish that her name remain in the programme after her death.

The end of season awards were organised by Lynn and Martin Robinson who had worked tirelessly for the club and Supporters Trust, organised coaches for away matches and in particular, ran the Club Shop. The winners were:

S.C.F.C. Juniors Player of the Year	Aaron Cook
Media Cup	Sean Hale
Players Player and Away Man of the Season	Kevin Sawyer
Management Committee Player of the Season	Tim Bond
Manager's Player	Wayne Turk
Golden Boot	Adam Wallace (17 goals in all matches)
Supporters Player	Craig Davis (14 goals in all matches)
Clubmen	Alex Hayter and Dave Todd

The last of these awards recognised, amongst other things, the expertise and skill needed to produce the match-day programme which is, without doubt, one of the finest in non-league football circles. In addition Alec was the club's Press Officer as well as Radio Wiltshire's commentator for Salisbury City F.C.'s affairs while Dave is a statistician without equal.

Salisbury's 'Golden Boot Player' Adam Wallace calmly slots in his penalty goal in the 5-1 defeat of Windsor & Eton. Mark Lisk is the other Salisbury player in the background.

photo: Sports
Echo.

Matt Tubbs and Dennis Rofe
having a difference of opinion
during the Eastleigh game –
with Tommy Widdrington
showing a bit of that
'Newcastle tact'.

Adam Wallace congratulated by Mat
Davies, Steve Strong and Josh Thomas after
scoring his penalty, and second goal
against Windsor & Eton.

☆ More memories of the 2004/05 season ☆

photo: Sports
Echo.

Its defence versus defence with Matt
Holmes getting stuck in and winning
the ball in the match versus Billericay.

Andy Cook and Shaun Dyke in a
fair....ish tackle during the Easter
game versus Eastleigh at the
Raymac..

8

southern premier

'Super Leigh' returns to 'the Wessex'

Arrivederci Ryman League, hello Southern League was the message for the new season. There were the usual arrivals and departures amongst the playing staff. Adam Wallace had gone to Windsor & Eton, Mat Davies moved to Winchester City, Josh Thomas to Bashley and Leigh Phillips, a talisman of the terraces had gone with Tommy Killick to Poole Town, newly promoted to Wessex League Division I. Arrivals included the return of old

Paul Sales

Chris Ferrett

Simon Browne

friends, Paul Sales from Eastleigh, Chris Ferrett from Bashley and Simon Browne from Weymouth all of whom had previously played with distinction for Salisbury in the past.

New teams and new grounds were in evidence during the early weeks of the season with first ever visits to Evesham and

Mangotsfield and a visit from Cirencester Town. The team hit the ground running, winning five and drawing two of the first seven matches after the visit of Yate Town for a Friday fixture which drew a crowd of 800. This put Salisbury firmly in pole position in the league with an average attendance of 660. Momentum and expectation were now growing at the Raymac.

The F.A. Cup saw a tricky trip to Clevedon where a tropical downpour and an early red card for Scott Bartlett didn't help so to go through to the next round after a replay was acceptable. The next tie at Yate provided a more comfortable win against a team who come May were to be one of the surprises of the season. Yet another away tie followed when some 250 city followers descended on a wet Pennydarren Park, Merthyr, in a game which saw Salisbury dominate the first half, before going behind. Matt Tubbs equalised and Salisbury looked likely winners before his departure with a nasty leg injury. He was helped off the field by Kevin Bushby who was being groomed to take over as trainer from Conrad Parrott. After his departure, Salisbury lost to a goal scored 2–3 mins from the end. Fortunately the incident involving Tubbs caused him to be out for only a fortnight.

F.A. Cup Results 8/10/05

| Merthyr Tydfil | 2 | Salisbury City | 1 | Chippenham Town | 1 | Sutton United | 0 |
| Weymouth | 1 | Bath City | 0 | Cirencester Town | 2 | Havant & W'ville | 1 |

Next up, a trip to Hardenhuish Park, Chippenham and a first league defeat of the season, in the first Wiltshire derby in a league fixture for many years.

Western League memories rekindled on the Trophy trail

The F.A. Trophy saw a visit to Paulton Rovers, opponents in the early days of the Western League. The trips were never easy then and, with the opposition going well at the time in the Southern League Western Division, an awkward tie was expected.

It went to a replay where the substitute Adam Heath saved the home side's blushes with two goals in extra-time which were to ignite Salisbury's long run in this competition for the first time.

Paul Sales scores the first goal in the 3-0 defeat of Grantham.

It was the league, however, that all supporters felt should be the priority this season. Grantham, Rugby Town and King's Lynn were dispatched; the latter being of significant value later in the campaign. The Whites then held a four point lead at the top of the table and home attendances were threatening to go through the 1000 mark.

A blip at Yate occurred just before a trip to Malta to play Marsaxlokk, a first foreign venture since the 1960s. This excursion

Matt Tubbs scored the winner versus King's Lynn.

was enjoyed by the team and some 30 fans who also visited the island to watch Salisbury win 3-0.

In the Trophy the luck of the draw turned in their favour with home ties against a now struggling Newport County who were overcome 3-0 with Tommy Widdrington's late strike being a candidate for goal of the season at the time. Before

Scott Bartlett wins the ball in the King's Lynn match.

this match took place George Best, arguably the most talented footballer of his generation died. A minute's silence was observed before the game. There were those who criticised his hedonistic life style as being responsible for his early death; others would say he packed more into one life, than many would in three (see photo on page 397).

In the next round Harlow succumbed to a Matt Tubbs penalty.

As in 1947, records tumble

The turn of the year was a time to take stock and the picture facing the supporters was a rosy one. Salisbury were a point clear in the league, with games in hand on their challengers. The home record showed only one goal conceded in the league in 10 games all of which had been won. Paul Sales and Matt Tubbs shared 25 goals and were providing the dual strike partnership every successful club needs. The defence had conceded only eight goals in 19 games and a trip to Canvey Island of the National Conference beckoned in the 2nd Round of the Trophy. This sort of success put pressure on everyone. It was felt that this could be the year when the club could fulfil their dream of Conference South football. The new Directors were certainly building up the momentum and taking the club forward.

City took the field at Canvey to the cheers of over 300 travelling fans in the primitive segregated away Sea Wall end. Without Widdrington, Sales and Tubbs this looked to be a tough task but Aaron Cook turned out to be a colossus at the back. Replacements Matt Holmes, Robbie Matthews and Alex Haddow, in an unaccustomed striking role, rose magnificently as did their team mates to the demands made on them and Alex Haddow's sweet strike in the second-half was no more than they deserved.

There were setbacks, of course. They came with a first home defeat by Team Bath on 28th January. To give the visitor's credit, they passed the ball as well as any team faced during the season and deservedly won 1-0. Interest in the League Cup ceased at home in a replayed tie against Cirencester after a previously somewhat bizarre abandonment. A changed side took the field in front of a small crowd which again reflected the lack of importance given to these fixtures.

A trip north beckons – but it's not Newcastle

All eyes were on the home Trophy tie with Stalybridge Celtic from the Conference North, entirely new opposition for the club. A large crowd saw a draw with Celtic playing for the replay. Over a 100 travelled north on the following Tuesday to see the Whites gain a well-deserved victory. They were, by general agreement, much the better side and a 1-0 defeat flattered the northern team.

This tie secured a visit to St James' Park to play Exeter City who were conceived as being the 'Sheffield Wednesday of the Conference'. In the event the Grecians were unable to live up to that billing.

Only one team in Wiltshire!

Salisbury fans, now cock-a-hoop, turned up en masse for the visit of Chippenham Town, north Wiltshire rivals and fellow promotion aspirants. The biggest crowd (1907) since the Hull City cup tie made for a terrific atmosphere, joined as they were, by many fans supporting the visitors. Paul Sales with nerves of steel hit the winner after Matt Tubbs had equalised with a penalty.

Matt Tubbs who has just scored City's first, shows 'safe hands' with Adam Wilde, in a reference to Scott Bartlett's first born.

The Trophy run was felt to be distracting the players unnecessarily from the principal objective of winning promotion.

A gleeful Matt Tubbs turns to celebrate his equalizer from the penalty spot in the match against Chippenham Town.

Perhaps one should look at this from their point of view in that they naturally wanted to give of their best and, in doing so, they certainly advanced the profile of Salisbury City F.C. earning good money for the club's coffers.

The 'distraction' was related to league form and at the end of February, bitter weather, the lowest gate, the lowest

(*right*) The Salisbury team congratulating Paul Sales (*far left*) on scoring the Whites winner, all of which is told on the up-to-the-minute electronic scoreboard in the background.

temperature and an abject performance was experienced against Banbury, the only team to score three goals in a league game against Salisbury all season. Exeter City, when it came proved a bit of an anti-climax. About 1300 visiting supporters made up a crowd of 3653 on a freezing but sunny afternoon. A number of controversial incidents occurred with Tim Bond's sending off after 14 minutes putting the Whites on the back-foot. The penalty which followed didn't help and neither did a broken leg to the unlucky Andy Cook shortly afterwards. They found themselves 3-0 down after 55 minutes but, when the numbers were evened up by a home player being sent off, they fought back to reduce the losing margin to 3-1.

It was in this match that Tubbs exacerbated the injury he received at Merthyr in the previous Autumn causing him to need a cartilage operation which kept him on the sidelines until 15th April.

Is it Conference South or Southern Premier?

It was now the league or bust! This did not prove to be as easy as it seemed to be before Christmas. Halesowen and Bedford both spoiled the march on the championship each winning 1-0. Mangotsfield would not lie down at the Raymac. Losing 2-0 with 10 minutes to go they fought back to take a point. Salisbury were now down to second place but with games in hand. Gates were holding around the 800 mark although anxious looks were going towards the dreaded play-offs, even when they cruised past Aylesbury and beat Evesham who were struggling at the wrong end of the table.

Coming into the home straight the

Alex Haddow who scored the Whites second goal versus Mangotsfield must have thought he'd secured the points.

Although bandaged Aaron Cook is still in the thick of it along with Tim Bond desperately seeking City's equalizer at home to Halesowen Town.

other challengers seemed to be picking up maximum points. What many think of as a seminal moment occurred on April 1st at Banbury. With the teams level and five minutes remaining a draw looked likely taking Salisbury down to second place but Robbie Matthews on as a sub for newly signed Ashan Holgate from Swindon, scored the winner from Luke Prince's precise pass.

Best team ever? – Yes!

Salisbury won the match 2-1 and never looked back. The fixture list showed there were eight games left to play in April. These

contained away mid-week trips to a rampant King's Lynn, a resurgent Rugby Town as well as Tiverton Town with whom there had been little success recently. Where the adrenaline came from may never be known. Salisbury carried all before them, winning all eight matches. King's Lynn, with a season's best crowd behind them,

Wayne Turk scored the Whites opening goal and third at King's Lynn.

Ashan Holgate who scored City's second at The Walks.

was the toughest task but a Turk goal after two minutes set the seal on a magnificent performance that the home team couldn't quite match in spite of a partisan crowd's support. The 'Towns' of Rugby and Hitchin were swept aside and the stage was set, on 15th

continued on page 319

Luke Prince turns away after scoring Salisbury's first goal in the match versus Hitchin Town.

A determined Wayne Turk beats Richard Wilmot, the Hitchin 'keeper, and scores the second.

All pictures on this page are from the Salisbury City V Gloucester City match.

Paul Sales scored the Whites first goal.

Rennie Regis grabs a slice of the action.

Letting their hair down, Paul Sales and Ashan Holgate.

Second goal scorer Alex Haddow.

Luke Prince tries a shot on goal.

This is only the start of the Champions celebrations.

April, for Salisbury to claim the Championship if they beat Gloucester City at home. Their goal difference was huge, much better than their nearest challengers. A crowd of over 1600 including a goodly contingent from Gloucester contributed to the atmosphere. Paul Sales, who had proved doubters wrong about his long-term fitness, put the City ahead and Alex Haddow hit an absolute screamer into the top corner just before half-time to send the Whites in at the break with a lead which they were to keep to the end. This was the time the club celebrated success at last in their venture to achieve Conference South football for the first time.

Below: Action and goal scorers for Salisbury versus Cheshunt.

The score was 5-0 and it could have been 10 with City at times playing breath-taking football. Wayne Turk above scored two, *above right*: Aaron Cook scored his first of the season, *right*: Tim Bond achieved the same and *bottom right*: sees Matt Tubbs hammer in the fifth. Paul Sales laid on four of the goals without scoring himself.

Left: Tommy Widdrington hit everything but the back of the net with this flying effort.

With Alex Haddow leading, the Whites run out at the Raymac., through an applauding 'Guard of Honour' provided by Cheshunt in the last home match of the season. I don't know about anybody else but this brought tears of joy to my eyes!!

pdw

Before the Cheshunt match (*right*) Lynn Robinson, the Management Committee Secretary, presents Salisbury captain Aaron Cook with the 'Supporter's Player of the Year' Trophy. This was his first of the four accolades he received for the 2005/06 season.

Not 'third time lucky' for Chippenham

For all the remaining matches Salisbury had the customary 'guard of honour', winning them all, conceding only one further goal when Team Bath were avenged at Twerton on the last day.

Supporters could now look on dispassionately as the other four teams had to fight it out through the play-offs. Eventually it was Bedford Town who triumphed over Chippenham Town to join forces in the Conference South next season.

Howzat? – As good as the last 'Ashes series'

This was a season that will never be forgotten by fans, be they young or old. Yes, there were some disappointments along the way but, in taking an eclectic view football fans would expect it no other way. This was a magnificent team effort which surpassed all expectations. The fans responded, the average attendance at home being the highest in the league, 902.

Southern League Shield presented to Salisbury City F.C.'s Aaron Cook

F.A. Trophy 2005/2006
A few memories of Salisbury City F.C.'s magnificent record breaking run – on the following five pages.

2nd Qualifying Round: Salisbury versus Clevedon.

The F.A. Trophy

Circle photo has Paul Sales congratulating Craig Davis on scoring the Whites first goal, while right Matt Tubbs scores the second goal.

3rd Qualifying Round: Salisbury City versus Newport AFC.

Wayne Turk tricks his way through.

Matt Tubbs in action.

1st Round Proper: Salisbury City versus Harlow Town.

The only goal of the match was scored by Matt Tubbs. Here Harlow are defending with Paul Sales attacking while Matt Tubbs awaits the outcome. Also on the scene for Salisbury is the team captain, Aaron Cook.

2nd Round Proper: Salisbury City F.C. versus Canvey Island.

This was the match that started the supporters thinking that the Whites were going somewhere in the F.A. Trophy this time. The game was played with no Tommy Widdrington, Paul Sales or Matt Tubbs all missing through injuries.

Outnumbered, just, Robbie Matthews and Chris Ferrett battle on.

Matt Holmes, head and shoulders above all, nearly scored with this header.

Alex Haddow gleefully slides the ball under the Canvey Island 'keeper from a pass by Robbie Matthews, to put Salisbury in the lead. Celebrations begin.

Oh what a wonderful feeling, for all ! !

3rd Round Proper: Salisbury City F.C. versus Staylbridge Celtic.

Home 0-0 – Attendance 1553

The last few stretches before the match versus Staylbridge who came for a draw. Towards the end City were playing the same game as can be seen above and below, as forwards and defenders were all in the same area. As time got tight even Kevin was sweating on it.

Away up north in Manchester – Staylbridge Celtic 0-1 Salisbury City

At last a goal, its a rain-swept evening, just over 700 stalwarts, excellent ground, does all that faze Matt Tubbs? – no, dummies Paul Pettinger and, goal!

More from Manchester. Top: Stalybridge defend in depth.
Centre: Didn't we do well and rightly so. It's celebration time.

Quarter Final Exeter City versus Salisbury City F.C.

Aaron Cook with Glenn Cronin of Exeter, match officials and mascots.

Matt Tubbs looking to break through with Craig Davis in close attendance.

Kevin Sawyer clutches a goal-bound shot.

left to right: Not seeing eye-to-eye with the referee are Sawyer, Cook, Widdrington, Turk, Bartlett and Beswetherick.

A worried Matt Tubbs looks on as Andy Cook, in pain, is carried from the field of play after breaking his leg.

Simon Browne and Craig Davis salute the supporters at the end of the match.

Letting Paul Jones, the Exeter 'keeper, know he's about ,Salisbury City's, Paul Sales.

MEMORY LANE

The Summit is in Sight

Exeter City v Salisbury City F.A. Trophy Quarter Final Saturday 25th February 2006

So, Exeter versus Salisbury, quarter finals of the F.A. Trophy and the biggest game since Hillsborough.

Tony had decided that his Friday night commitment in Kent could not be shelved, so at 5 o'clock on Saturday morning the alarm rudely awakened us. By six, the three of us, Tony, Alison and son Michael were in the car heading off the Isle of Sheppey in North Kent, heading to Burbage home of the 'Ancient in Years' (otherwise known as my parents!). Arriving we hurriedly made toast and coffee, before being urged out again for the drive to Exeter.

When we arrived in Exeter we found a handy 'Park and Ride' which took us to the city centre, a quick look at the cathedral then off to a pub for lunch. We were greatly heartened to be joined by numerous other black and white scarved individuals, all seeking sustenance!.

Leaving the pub, we dutifully followed the most Ancient in years, confident in his ability to find a football ground. Eventually, asking a friendly local for directions, we discovered that we had walked about 1½ miles in the wrong direction! Never mind, we made our way back up the hill and came across a likely looking crowd, following them to the Exeter ground in St James Park. We waited outside for the gates to open and cheered when the first, second and then third supporters' coach arrived, disgorging its quota of cheery souls.

My first impression of the ground was of a well equipped stadium, sadly lacking facilities for its away visitors. Crammed onto a small terrace facing the wind with no shelter and in the shade for the entire afternoon, I have had more comfortable football viewing experiences. However, due to our early arrival we had a prime spot in the front. It took about five minutes to realise that two shirts, one jumper, one winter coat, hat, scarf and gloves were going

to be of no use against the bitter cold of the away end. My feet had turned to blocks of ice and my hands to a state of total numbness before the teams had left the field after their warm up. It was going to be a long afternoon, but the goals to come would surely generate enough warmth to keep us going. The chants and cheering began and although I was later to learn that not everyone

.......................*continued on next page*

had the same experience that day, from where we were at that time a cheery and welcoming atmosphere prevailed.

The teams came out onto the pitch to cheers and roars of encouragement. Exeter fans seemed somewhat few in number and not so vocal as us. All was set for a fantastic, successful afternoon's football.

Ten minutes into the game and a stunned silence descended as the weather suddenly got colder and the wind more biting. We watched in disbelief as Tim Bond walked off the field in response to the referee's red card. The incident which provoked this happened at the far end of the ground so I have no idea whether or not it was justified, although many (and not all Salisbury fans) have said since that it was a harsh decision. The resulting successful penalty dampened spirits that little bit further. All I can say is that what had seemed a tough but not impossible task had suddenly become very much harder.

Things then became worse as Andy Cook, who had only been on the field for 10-mins or so was carried off with what appeared to be a broken leg. The same move resulted in an Exeter corner from which they scored. Ten men; two goals down; an experienced player injured; what could the fans do?

Well, sing of course! Shout and cheer and galvanise the team. We kept up the encouragement and derived a considerable amount of pleasure from watching the wayward kicks of the Exeter goalkeeper who despite his local knowledge of the effect of the wind at that end, couldn't seem to keep the ball inside the ground (I should add that in the second-half, Kevin had no such difficulty).

Even though things were tough, Salisbury did not seem completely out of the game. We kept cheering and they kept playing. Unfortunately, the third goal for Exeter went in soon into the second-half and we knew that the dream was over.

One of the most foolish acts I have seen on a football field resulted in the departure of an Exeter player. Having at some point picked up a yellow card, he then, right down by our corner flag kicked the ball away from the City player about to take a throw in. The referee pulled out his yellow card, looked at the player's number, looked in his notebook and changed yellow for red. Then Robbie Matthews scored! Joy was unconfined. Could a miracle happen? Liverpool turned it around against AC Milan – could 'the Whites' do the same against Exeter?

Sadly, no. The final whistle blew and Exeter had won. Our players came to our end and applauded the supporters. We cheered back – they had played well and tried hard, but it just wasn't to be. Disconsolately, we left the ground, amazed at the number of police that had gathered around. We headed for our bus stop, returned to the car and headed back into Wiltshire.

The cup run was over. Money had been earned; experience gained and now it was down to the players to focus on the league – a league of which we were top. Could we drown the disappointment by winning promotion? By the time you read this, you will know the answer, but for now, for us, that dream lives on.

Alison Batchelor

The following pictures are of a deservedly happy group of players, officials and supporters of Salisbury City F.C. on their winning the Southern Premier League 2005/06

left to right: Mitch Blake, Matt Holmes, Paul Sales, Matt Tubbs, Ashan Holgate, Aaron Cook, Scott Bartlett, Tim Bond, Wayne Turk, Kevin Sawyer, Simon Browne, Rennie Regis, Alex Haddow, Tommy Widdrington and Luke Prince.

In the Sarum Suite.

Those mighty men with that mighty shield.
Standing left to right: Paul Orsborn, Jimmy Case (ex Liverpool and Saints), Barry Blankley, Nick Holmes, Tommy Widdrington, Peter Yeldon.
Kneeling l/r: Mitch Blake, Nev Beal, Stuart McGlashan.

Thirsty
anyone?

Three pictures of Salisbury City F.C. players and others who are in all sorts of ways connected with the the Club, deservedly celebrating with that mighty Southern League Shield.

MEMORY LANE

Taking the bull by the horns

King's Lynn F.C. v Salisbury City F.C. – Tuesday 4 April 2006

Sixteen of us on a mini-bus 'The Walks' bound – King's Lynn battleground. The whole journey had been score-forecast chatter. All of me seemed to be in my mouth, heart, stomach, finger-nails as I stepped into that immense ground that night. You could hear 'Linnets' greeting each other like long-lost brothers and sisters, so many were coming out of the woodwork for this game. As the teams lined up with Salisbury in near-on white, a roar erupted from us all. Standing there opposite their double-decker stand which covers ¾ of one side it seemed near to bursting. Yet within 5-min of kick-off we were in the lead. A ball into the box by Browne, haphazardly kicked away, returned on the volley by Turk like an exocet, it passed their keeper 'twice' before he moved. We danced like 'puppets on a string', but no time to phone base before a hopeful lob under our cross-bar was dropped by Kevin and they were level. Then 'the Lynn' thumped it non-stop into our box and Aaron, Bondy and all hoofed it out. Sanity returned with a sweet corner from Prince, Sales as a decoy and young Holgate (his second game, wow in this atmosphere) rose and calm as you like, headed in the Whites second. Shortly after this, another pass forward to Ashan resulted in him being laid flat and out of action for 5–10 minutes of the battle. Salisbury were playing sizzling football, Tommy to Wayne, Haddow across to Luke off on a run, another tantalizing cross, panic in their box, who to mark, Salesy, Ashan, Wayne, Tommy? We all needed a drink at half-time, forget the queue. Out they came still playing at a furious pace but still playing football. End to end, back and forth, King's Lynn dug-out trying all the tricks they knew, one, two and three substitutes all used, but they could not break through, we did. Scotty B to Tommy, Sales climbs, still up there when every-one else had come down (like a shirt on a line, he just hangs there) flicks a peach of a ball into the path of Turk, who beats two scurrying Linnets, twists

then thumps an unstoppable shot across their guardian of the net and into it. Can we relax now, just a little? No is the answer, they pile in even more, then its Robbie for Ashan and we nearly make it four; by then we are singing 'We are top of the league, who?, we are top of the league. On the way home at a pub in Wisbech (no friends of 'the Lynn'), when we came out, the landlord, his customers and us were singing 'There's only one team in Wiltshire' ....
the Whites......magic   *Peter D. Wood*

Salisbury City F.C. 2005/06 – Southern Premier League Champions.
GX Soccer Awards: Premier League Club of April, Premier Club of the Season, Southern League Club of the Year.
Left to right, back row: Neil Arnold (fitness adviser), Mike Harris, Jamie Barron, Robbie Matthews, Kevin Sawyer, Peter Yeldon (director), Neville Beal (chairman), Paul Orsborn (director), Stuart McGlashan (director), Simon Arthur, Simon Browne, Adam Jones, Charlie Knight, Conrad Parrott (physio). *Middle row:* Alex Haddow, Andy Cook, Scott Bartlett, Luke Prince, Michael Cooper, Aaron Cook, Mitch Blake (goal-keeping coach), Nick Holmes (general Manager), Barry Blankley (assistant manager), Tommy Widdrington (player/coach), Tim Bond, Chris Ferrett, Wayne Turk, Paul Sales, Gary Horgan. *Front row:* Jamie Dennison, Jon Beswetherick, Rene Regis, James Whisken, Matt Tubbs, Craig Davis, Chris Knowles, Adam Wilde, Matt Holmes, Adam Heath.

9

conference south

The 2006–07 Season — David Thear, Richard J. A. Walker and Peter J. Waterhouse

Civic Pride

Salisbury is a comparatively small city with an imposing world-renowned 13th century cathedral (built 1220–58). It has been romantically entitled 'the English Venice' featuring five rivers meandering through the valleys into the city. In addition, it boasts many characteristics which include a picturesque market square and many historic buildings.

However, overseas' visitors would not associate Salisbury with a thriving and successful football club but this may be about to change. Perhaps the Raymac. will be on future tourist's agendas if the Club's plans for League football come to fruition. In this respect this season could well be crucial if momentum towards the goal is to be maintained.

photo pdw

The centre of the High Street is now a popular traffic restricted zone with none of the businesses from the early 1950s photograph still trading (see page 12).

'Little Venice'
in the
City of
Salisbury

photos
pdw

Last season's success led the recently elected Chairman of Salisbury District Council, the Honourable Mrs Spencer to

'congratulate Salisbury Football Club on winning the 2005/6 season's Southern League Premier Division and gaining promotion to the Football Conference South'.

Furthermore, at the Southern League's AGM held in Torquay, the club was named Premier Division Club of the season and Southern League Club of the Year. Four of the promotion winning squad – Tommy Widdrington, Wayne Turk, Matt Tubbs and Paul Sales were highlighted in the pick of the league side for the 2005/6 season.

The Southern League Shield

The shield which was presented to captain Aaron Cook, was inaugurated in 1895 when the trophy was donated by Mr J. Oliver for annual competition by clubs competing in the Southern League. The first winner of the Shield was Millwall F.C. and, over many years of distinguished history, it has progressively been enlarged with additional surrounds added to record each successive Championship.

The Southern League Player of the Year

Many accolades were paid to Aaron Cook, in acknowledgement of his outstanding season for the club. His reputation was further enhanced when, in the summer of 2006, the Non League Paper presented 'The 2006 Southern Player of the Year' award to the Salisbury skipper.

Sporting pride, at the races

Celebrations continued well into the summer months when our sporting cousins at Salisbury Race Course included a handicap race on the card of the Bibury meeting. The race, named 'The Congratulations to Salisbury City F.C. Handicap Stakes', went under starters's orders at 5.30 p.m. on the first day of the meeting. It was won by ' Katchit' ridden by Tony Culhane, owner Mr Tim Corby and the trainer was the legendary sportsman, Mike Channon.

Preparation for the new season commence

The close season saw six players being released. They were goal-keeper Simon Arthur, defenders Michael Cooper and Ian

It's still only pre-football season 2006-07 but Salisbury City F.C. are already onto a winner.

l/r Trev. Nev. and Paul of S.C.F.C. with race officials and Mike Channon (2nd right) line up for the celebrations.

Richardson, utility men Chris Ferret and Rene Regis plus striker Adam Heath. Adam Wilde, the left sided midfield player, completed a move to Conference Nationwide side St Albans.

In addition the Whites record signing, Craig Davis, was placed on the transfer list at his own request and in due course moved to Bashley. Gary Horgan departed to Mangotsfield United.

Kevin Sawyer was placed on the transfer list after asking manager Nick Holmes to release him from his contract prior to the Southern League 'Challenge Cup' game at the Raymac., on Saturday 5th August. The club reluctantly agreed and, subsequently, he joined his old club Cirencester Town.

Prelude to Conference South

The club signalled their intent to make a significant impact on the Conference South by the signings of the former Bristol Rovers full-back Jonathan Bass whose career included 72 appearances under Trevor Francis at Birmingham City, Irish striker Declan McGregor, the former Cobh Ramblers and Cork City player and 24-year old goal-keeper, Ryan Clarke from Bristol Rovers. He had Conference experience from a loan-spell at Forest Green Rovers. Also, manager Nick Holmes promoted youth team prospect,

Jon Bass   Declan McGregor   Ryan Clarke   Charlie Knight

Charlie Knight, to the first team squad after an excellent 2005/06 season.

Lee Stephens and Gary Middleton joined to provide further depth. Off the field there were other changes. Alec Hayter became Football Secretary (he retained his role with Radio Wiltshire), Doug Ferraro, Assistant Secretary and Mike Turner, Sports Editor of the Salisbury Journal, Press Officer. He combined this with running the official club website and, with Dave Todd, writing the matchday programme.

Perhaps most alarming to Salisbury supporters was the news, in June, that Peter Yeldon had stepped down as director. Rumours abounded but, happily the status quo was restored on August 21st when the club issued the following statement.

> Salisbury City today confirmed that Peter Yeldon has rejoined the club's board of directors.
>
> The businessman unexpectedly declared his intention to resign during the summer break in a move that caught many fans and club officials by surprise.
>
> Yeldon took the unusual step of announcing his decision via the club's 'Fans Forum', fuelling speculation that there had been a boardroom power struggle – rumours that were quickly quashed by Yeldon and fellow directors Neville Beal, Stuart McGlashan and Paul Orsborn.
>
> Yeldon, a passionate City supporter, has now decided that it is time to end the speculation by rejoining the City fold.
>
> He said: 'There was never any falling out. My announcement caused all sorts of mayhem and rumours with some people saying I wanted to be chairman and others saying Neville and I had had a big fight when in fact we've never had a cross word in our lives.
>
> It's pretty hard to fall out with Neville, really!
>
> 'I have obviously stayed involved throughout and in fact, according to Companies House, I have never stopped being a director because my forms were never put through.'
>
> The director is delighted with City's promising start to the season – the club's first in the Conference South – and re-iterated that should the Whites earn promotion in the future, he and his fellow directors were fully committed to ensuring the infrastructure was in place to allow them to move further up the non-league ladder.
>
> Yeldon added: 'We've already got a fan base that would look good in the Conference. If the players get us promoted, then whatever we need to go up, we won't let them down. There would be absolutely no impediment.'

An encouraging sign for the future was the work beginning on the perimeter fence which would enclose the two open sides of the ground. This work was essential to meet Conference criteria particularly if promotion were to be achieved.

Pre-season

There was the usual crop of friendlies and trialists. The game against Woking was significant in two ways. The first was that it enabled the team to be judged against full-time Conference opposition and, secondly, the performance of Liam Cockerill led to him signing 'on loan' a little later. He was, however, only named to play for the Whites in six games, four as substitute, before returning to Woking.

Another pre-season game was against Hitchin Town for the Southern League Challenge Cup (SL Champions v SL Cup winners season 2005/6). Goals by Tubbs two and Sales, (his 100th for the club), saw the Whites win 3-2 in front of 432 spectators.

AUGUST

August saw six league games played. The first, against the bookies promotion favourites Lewes, was a draw at the Raymac. where performance and standard of opposition encouraged the fans to believe they had nothing to fear in the new league and, so it was as the next four games were won. The Newport match, at home, was closely contested between two very evenly matched teams but Thurrock away was a runaway 5-1 victory despite conceding the first goal. A healthy number of Whites supporters made the journey and suffered delays on the M25.

The match at Histon, on Bank Holiday Monday (most people think bank holidays bring local derbies but the Conference South computer thinks otherwise) saw the first defeat. Despite being level at half-time the Whites were beaten by a decent side who took their opportunities well. At the end of the month they were second in the league and Wayne Turk was named 'Conference South player of the Month'.

SEPTEMBER

There then followed a run of five league wins with a total of ten goals for and three against. The outstanding match was undoubtedly at home against Eastleigh. The crowd of 1688 saw an action packed game won 1-0 despite Tommy Widdrington and Matt Tubbs being sent off after a melee in front of the dugouts. The nine men then scored the winner through Tim Bond.

It's nice to know your here

The home matches had seen the emergence of a second very vocal area of Whites support. Traditionally the most noise came from the fans in front of the entry at the country end of the stadium but there was now a growing contingent of younger supporters in the In-Excess stand. They sing, chant and are a major source of support for the team.

Pictured left is The 'Country End' choir in near-on full voice with maybe, 'We are the Salisbury, the famous Salisbury'. This is only part of the travelling 'White Army', who believe it or not we make even more noise on the away grounds.

Right, is just a small selection of 'The Younger Ones', that make all the noise on the terraces behind the goal. It makes no difference which way the Whites are kicking this is their patch, so sometimes a bit of baiting takes place, all in good fun !

photos and words Peter D. Wood

The run saw a marked upsurge in spectator numbers, the September home average being 1342. The month finished with a visit to VT F.C. (formerly known as Vosper Thornycroft FC) in the F.A. Cup 2nd Qualifying Round. VT F.C. play in the Wessex League Premier Division and Salisbury's visit resulted in their best ever gate of 370. A special stand had been erected and their organisation was excellent especially concerning car access. With a former Whites favourite, Tyronne Bowers, in their side they fought valiantly but, in the end, were well beaten. It was good to see two veterans from the first ever Salisbury team, Denis Rogers and Jack Parker, chatting at the game.

Going into October Salisbury were top of the league and had

drawn Eastleigh away in the F.A. Cup. Nick Holmes was named 'Manager of the Month'.

On a sad note Steve Tilley, former Salisbury goalkeeper, died on 12th September.

> *One minute's silence was observed before the kick-off at the Bishop's Stortford match in his memory. The following tributes are taken from the matchday programme of September 23rd 2006:*
>
> *Steve had played for the Whites during the 1970s and was a keen golfer, often supporting charity golf days in and around the Salisbury area.*
>
> *Tragically, his 20-year-old daughter, Jennifer had died in a car accident two weeks earlier and his father had died 12 weeks ago.*
>
> *City chairman, Nev Beal said: ''Everyone connected with Salisbury City FC will be sorry to hear the tragic news of Steve's death. Obviously, the club sends its condolences to his family.''*
>
> *Whites manager, Nick Holmes added: ''I met him a few times. I remember last year at the South Wilts Pro-Am day he holed-in-one. He gave his closest-to-the-pin-prize to the person who was second, which typified him as a character.''*

OCTOBER

The first match was at Basingstoke where away supporters contributed significantly to the bumper gate of 1311. In fact, Salisbury's away support was leading to home clubs, generally, enjoying some of their highest gates when the Whites were visitors. Alec Hayter commented in one of his match reports that those who chant 'everywhere we go' should perhaps add 'gate receipts will show'. The match with Basingstoke was drawn with the home team playing much better than their league position suggested.

Former player turns the screw

The F.A. Cup game at Eastleigh saw Salisbury progress to the final qualifying round when Paul Sales conjured up a piece of football magic with an acrobatic strike on the hour. It was a pulsating match before a crowd of 1402 – a record for a competitive fixture at the Silverlake Stadium. The only cloud on the horizon was the dislocated knee suffered by Tommy Widdrington when celebrating the winning goal.

Paul Sales scored at Eastleigh.
photo Southern Daily Echo

The draw, on the following Monday, resulted in an away tie against Fisher Athletic, a then full-time outfit who were considered to be one of the best sides in the Conference South. The game itself was a classic cup encounter. Two evenly matched sides battled throughout with Aaron Cook scoring the winner in the second-half. The Non League Paper gave it five stars for entertainment. The subsequent draw at last provided a home match with Fleetwood Town, of the Unibond League, the opponents.

Is it just a blip or maybe an UFO?

Meanwhile, league form had slipped with Salisbury's unbeaten home record ending following a lack lustre performance against Braintree. In consequence they dropped from the summit of the table to second with a posse of teams in hot pursuit. The superstitious would blame the dreaded 'Manager of the Month' award.

On October 31st, allegedly, an elderly lady was seen flying on a broomstick in the vicinity of Old Sarum. Air Traffic Control could not confirm the flight path but it was established later that she was a white witch who was to bring good fortune.

NOVEMBER

The month opened away at Eastbourne. Here another poor performance resulted in a defeat with the winner coming in injury time and Matt Tubbs was sent off for the second time this season. Fortunately, the other results had mostly gone in the Whites favour so the one point from the last two games still left them hanging on to second place.

The Kudos of the F.A. Cup

Notwithstanding, the club were in buoyant mood eagerly looking forward to the F.A. Cup 1st Round encounter with Fleetwood. So far, £18,750 had been banked from participation in the competition with a further £16,000 for the winners of this tie.

The beginnings of Cup fever were to be detected. The unofficial fans website buzzed with speculation and there were numerous exchanges with the Fleetwood fans. Many felt that the gate would beat the record of 2168 against West Ham and so it did. There were 2648 present on Saturday 11th November, which coincidentally was Nick Holmes' birthday and Fleetwood contributed a number of good humoured and noisy followers. Salisbury won 3-0 with Matt Holmes scoring one of the goals, his first for the club, which was a nice birthday present for his dad.

However the win was not an easy one. Fleetwood started confidently but, after 10 minutes were undone by a Matt Tubbs special – a powerful shot into the far top corner of the net after gliding past a defender. Ryan Clarke was then called on to make a top class save at full stretch from a 25 yard free-kick. The half-time score was 1-0 and the Whites looked confident.

The second-half started with a penalty appeal being turned down and in the 60th minute Salisbury went further ahead with Matt Holmes scoring after a Tubbs free-kick just outside the penalty area. Nine minutes later he broke free on the left before crossing for Scott Bartlett to rifle the ball home at the far post.

The Whites finished on top but Fleetwood never gave up and left the field to applause from both Salisbury and their own fans.

Salisbury were in the second round for only the second time in their history.

There was little doubt that every non-league club coveted a match with Nottingham Forest which was exactly what Salisbury got at home. The white witch had done her work well.

However, before moving on to the match and its build up, there was a drawn game at Bognor in which Jon Beswetherick sustained a cruciate ligament injury. This, together with the injury to Tommy Widdrington in the Eastleigh cup tie, meant that the Whites would be without two key players for the Forest game. Additionally, Aaron Cook received a yellow card, his fifth of the season, which meant a one match suspension was imminent. In the event this was served with the re-arrangement of the Wilts Premier Shield tie against Swindon Town.

Also, before the F.A. Cup 2nd Round, there was the home F.A. Trophy game against Enfield. On paper, this was not a difficult match nor would it be expected to attract a large gate. The former proved correct with the Whites winning 2-1 in some style. The gate, however, was nearly 1500, the attraction being the distribution of vouchers entitling all who attended to tickets for the Forest tie. The ground limit was set, eventually, at 3100, so even after Nottingham Forest, the F.A., sponsors and players had had their share everyone with a voucher was guaranteed a ticket. This did not stop some hardy souls from queuing at 5.30 a.m. at the Raymac. the following day.

The Salisbury Journal did the club proud with a special supplement and Radio Wiltshire did Whites related interviews throughout the week. One mildly disappointing aspect was the response of the retailers in the city. There was no dressing up of windows as there had been for the Newport County game in 1959.

The icing was put on the cake when the BBC announced they were going to televise the game live on 'Match of the Day' on Sunday 3rd December. Not only would the club receive welcome publicity but the financial rewards, with possible prize money, would provide a sound financial base against further development of the ground and playing strength.

Celebrity status, let's have more

A well used proverb is 'success breeds success' and the quote thoroughly illustrates the new found celebrity status. Never before in its history had the club been in the spotlight of media attention. Ever since the draw for the F.A. Cup 2nd Round was made the Raymac. had been a hive of activity with a procession of local, regional and national T.V. and radio networks seeking interviews with practically every national newspaper taking an interest.

The demand for ground board advertising sites increased spectacularly which saw the club's marketing department working to maximum capacity. In addition there was an unforeseen demand for season tickets.

DECEMBER

This was undoubtedly the most exciting and onerous December Salisbury City F.C. had ever experienced.

The month was dominated by the first game against Forest which was drawn and the replay 10 days later, at the City Ground. This was followed by an F.A. Trophy tie at home to Woking, a match which would normally have been the highlight of the season.

Turning first to the home game on December 3rd, once again the gate and receipts record was broken with 3100 spectators packing the Raymac. Spectators started to make their way to Old Sarum hours before the 1.10 p.m. kick-off. Parking in the main car park was strictly limited owing to the complex logistics of modern broadcasting. After a night of strong wind and storms, as if by magic, the weather changed into a dry sunny day.

Andy D'Urso, late of the Premiership, was referee and the first-half was evenly contested although Forest, perhaps, had the edge. The goal, which gave them a 1-0 lead at half-time, was a well taken angled shot following a corner.

Grown men weep with joy !

Salisbury returned to the field with new found vigour. Wayne Turk came near to levelling the score when a looping volley was headed off the goal line, prior to Salisbury's 'keeper Ryan Clarke, making two inspired saves. On the hour, Jon Bass's hanging cross was knocked down by Paul Sales and, with Forest looking most likely to clear the ball, Matt

Luke Prince dazzles a Forest defender.

Holmes courageously got in a waist-high header. Matt Tubbs pounced, dragged the ball clear of the Forest captain and drove it into the top corner.

The Raymac. erupted. Salisbury fans sensed an upset with their team pressing for a winner. They almost got one after 76 minutes when sub. Robbie Matthews headed on Luke Prince's free-kick to Aaron Cook whose shot was blocked at the near post. Declan MacGregor's run at goal looked promising until he was taken out by the Forest skipper. End-to-end football continued and it took a brilliant save from Ryan Clarke to ensure Whites made it into the third round draw for the first time in history. Celebrations were the order of the day before the draw was made – the winners were to be at home to Charlton Athletic ! !

City make the Nationals again

The following Monday the National and Regional press featured the epic game. Many of the papers ran special articles on the Salisbury players and, naturally, numerous reports gave prominence to Matt Tubbs. The Sun called him a 'Tubthumper ! !'

Their thoughts on the game

Colin Calderwood the Nottingham Forest manager:

> *'There is nothing negative about the way they play, they were efficient and have good players in certain areas. We will have to be better when we face them at the City Ground'.*

Neville Beal Chairman S.C.F.C.:

> *'Before the match, all I wanted was for the players to give their all and do what they do normally and they did that – and more. They didn't take a backward step all game'.*

Nick Holmes:

> *'I hope the result gave the lads belief they can compete at that level. We're not out of it just yet'.*

The BBC commentary team described Tubb's goal as 'pure quality' while he, himself, said it was the 'most important of his life'.

Everybody's thoughts were now on the replay – December 12th at 7.45 p.m. Twelve coaches contributed to the majority of the 1200 or so Salisbury fans who saw the game. The result, which was fair, was a 2-0 win for Forest but the Whites could be very proud of their efforts. The Forest centre-forward, Nat Tyson, was the difference between the sides and Colin Calderwood, the Forest manager, was gracious enough to concede that, over the two games, Salisbury had played the game properly and given them more problems than many a team in their league. Again the Whites were given TV coverage, this time by Sky.

In between the two Forest games, Havant and Waterlooville beat the Whites in the league when, perhaps, minds were elsewhere.

Unfortunately Matt Tubbs was sent off for two offences. This was his third dismissal and would bring a three-match suspension over the Christmas period.

On Saturday 16th Woking were well beaten in the F.A. Trophy. The first-half was, probably, the away teams but Salisbury dominated the second-half and could easily have scored more than the three goals, the final one of which, by Matt Tubbs was as good an effort as you would see anywhere. The reward for beating Woking was a home tie against Southport on 13th January.

The F.A. Cup run and the continuing progress in the F.A. Trophy were causing some fans to worry over possible fixture congestion in the second-half of the season. Before the

Christmas/New Year holiday the Whites had already played less league games than their rivals and this position was further aggravated by the postponement of two home matches versus Dorchester Town on 30th December and Yeading on 6th January due to waterlogged pitches (the 'monsoon' experienced on 30th December was spectacular) and two draws against Western-super-Mare did little to help the team climb the table. Continuing injuries to Beswetherick and Widdrington led some to believe that strengthening of the squad was necessary if the promotion push was to be maintained. Danny Clay had joined from Exeter and Matthew Robinson from Forest Green and this had helped but would there be more? Matt Tubbs tendency to earn suspensions placed doubt over the team's ability to score and there was, of course, the interest of other clubs in his future to be taken into account. As at 7th January Salisbury were ninth in the table, 10 points behind leaders, Histon, with three games in hand.

Two pictures of the tropical storm (in winter) that descended on the Raymac. as the teams were in the tunnel waiting to take the field. I personally have only ever seen rain like this in my National Service days when I was in the jungles of Central America. If it had lasted ½hour instead of five minutes, we would have all had to swim out ! !
Peter D. Wood

Both these photos were taken from the press box left, on Saturday 30th December. Believe it or not they both show the same stands and view. I was in one of them along with 900 or so fans, all of us trying to believe what we were seeing and thinking, that it couldn't get any worse, but it did as the second picture here shows.

F.A. Cup 2nd Qualifying Round – VT F.C. v Salisbury City F.C.
30th September 2006

3-0
Salisbury goalscorers:
Paul Sales
Tim Bond
Declan McGregor

Salisbury team:
Clarke, Bass, Beswetherick, Cook, Bond, Holmes, Turk, Prince, Sales,
McGregor, Haddow.   Subs: Bartlett, Matthews, Cockerill, Brown, Bulman.

F.A. Cup 3rd Qualifying Round – Eastleigh v Salisbury City F.C.
14th October 2006

1-0
Salisbury goalscorer:
Paul Sales

Salisbury team:
Clarke, Bass, Beswetherick, Cook, Bond, Widdrington, Turk, Prince, Sales,
Tubbs, Bartlett.   Subs: Matthews, Holmes, McGregor, Brown, Bulman.

F.A. Cup 4th Qualifying Round – Fisher Athletic v Salisbury City F.C.
28th October 2006

1-0
Salisbury goalscorer:
Aaron Cook

Salisbury team:
Clarke, Bass, Beswetherick, Cook, Bond, Holmes, Turk, Prince, Sales, Tubbs,
Bartlett.   Subs: Matthews, McGregor, Haddow, Brown, Bulman.

F.A. Cup 1st Round – Salisbury City F.C. v Fleetwood Town
11th November 2006

3-0
Salisbury goalscorers:
Matt Tubbs
Matt Holmes
Scott Bartlett

Salisbury team:
Clarke, Bass, Beswetherick, Cook, Bond, Holmes, Turk, Prince, Sales, Tubbs,
Bartlett.   Subs: Matthews, McGregor, Haddow, Brown, Bulman.

Some action and celebrations from the Fisher Athletic versus Salisbury City F.A. Cup match. From the first whistle to the final one, this was a real cup battle.

Peter D. Wood

MEMORY LANE

F.A. Cup 4th Qualifying Round

Fisher Athletic v Salisbury 28th October 2006

It was a cloudy mild October day and, once again, we were on the road. This time we travelled with a perceived sense of injustice since the draw had given us an eighth consecutive away game. Destination: Champion Hill, home of Dulwich Hamlet, which Salisbury had last visited on 28th January 1950. This time the opposition was Fisher Athletic, temporarily ground sharing pending an upgrading of their own facilities at Rotherhithe. The pitch was in perfect condition although the crowd was small with about 200 following the visitors. There was a noisy reception as the teams took the field. Fisher made the early running and Ryan Clarke made an outstanding save from the marauding Damien Scannell on seven minutes. City slowly gained in confidence and Luke Prince and Wayne Turk carved out a close range chance for Paul Sales before a defender intercepted with the 'keeper stranded. More pressure from the hosts kept the defence fully occupied broken by a five minutes delay when a firework was thrown onto the pitch from outside the ground. Several more chances came and went Fisher's way including one where Luke Prince showed his work-rate by being in position to clear off the line. In the second-half Fisher redoubled their efforts with Damien Scannell again taking the eye. After Ryan Clarke had been forced into a headed clearance, Steve Watts just missed with a 40 yard lob and the same player clipped the crossbar from 30 yards with Ryan Clarke beaten. The deadlock was broken when a Salisbury attack was halted by a foul on Matt Tubbs. Luke Prince took the kick, an inswinging left-footer which Tim Bond cushioned over a defender with his head and it fell to to Aaron Cook who scored, to send the visiting fans delirious. With 20 minutes to go it was going to be a battle but every man was up for it and redoubled their efforts. Fresh legs arrived in the forms of Robbie Matthews, Declan McGregor and Alex Haddow. Injury time seemed never ending, seven minutes being added. Salisbury unashamedly celebrated with their fans because they knew they had beaten a very good full-time team. The hosts might argue that we had the luck and, on another day, they might have won comfortably. As far as luck was concerned one might argue that, after eight consecutive away ties, we deserved some and this was not another day. This was Saturday 28th October and the opposition was the redoutable Salisbury City!

Well done City.

Richard Walker

F.A. Cup 1st Round Salisbury City F.C. v Fleetwood Town
In case anyone has forgotton: 1, Nick showing off the prize; 2, Getting down to the nitty gritty as Aaron leads out the Whites; 3, Keeping Salisbury in the competition is Ryan Clarke; 4, Paul Sales doing what comes naturally; 5, No prizes for guessing who scored first, Matt Tubbs; 6, Matt Holmes choose an excellent time to score his first goal for the Club (Dad's birthday); 7, Somewhere in there is Scott Barlett who made sure with Salisbury's third.

Now the whole City's gone ticket crazy and the BBC M.O.T.D. crew move in.

These three lower photos
Peter D. Wood

Salisbury City F.C. v Nottingham Forest – 2nd Round F.A. Cup
3rd December 2006

I don't think anyone who went to this match didn't enjoy it.
It was excitement for the whole 90 minutes, a true F.A. Cup battle !

Peter D. Wood

☆

☆

☆

SALISBURY CITY

NOTTINGHAM FOREST

www.polycomp.co.uk

TRIP HOME. NEXT

Nottingham Forest v Salisbury City F.C. – 2nd Round F.A. Cup (replay)
The 'City Ground' was far from full but, what an atmosphere Salisbury's fans created and what a ground to play on.   *pdw*

F.A. Cup Results 2, 3 & 12/12/06

Salisbury	1	Nottingham F.	1	Aldershot	1	Basingstoke Town	1
Bristol Rovers	1	Bournemouth	1	Swindon Town	1	Morecambe	0
Torquay	1	Leyton Orient	1	Bristol City	4	Gillingham	3
replays Nottingham F	2	Salisbury City	0	Basingstoke Town	1	Aldershot	3
Bournemouth	0	Bristol Rovers	1	Leyton Orient	1	Torquay	2

MEMORY LANE

Centre stage for All to see

Salisbury City F.C. v Nottingham Forest – Sunday 3rd December 2006

The trip to Hillsborough in 2003 had seemed like a 'once in 50 years' experience but, here we were only three years later preparing to play equally high profile opponents, this time on our own ground in front of a live 'Match-of-the-Day' audience. Although Salisbury 'born and bred', I was now living in Chandler's Ford, so it was from there that the day started. First I had to pick up my father from Salisbury and I arrived there just in time to hear his recorded interview on BBC Radio Wiltshire, with his recollections of the team from the first game in 1947.

On from there to the stadium, where the car park looked like it had been taken over by some sort of travelling circus but, it was in fact the vast operation that accompanies a BBC TV live outside broadcast. Inside the ground, various scaffolding gantries had appeared, including one above the seated season ticket holders area which actually caused one of us to have to move seats since his existing one was occupied by a substantial amount of metalwork.

Although we could dream of an upset, the realist inside me was just hoping that we gave a good account of ourselves. A nervous start was inevitable, but amazingly short-lived and, after a lucky escape when Tim Bond sliced the ball over his own cross-bar, the Whites gradually got a toe-hold in the game. Watching the video afterwards, the first-half maybe wasn't a classic for the neutral but, despite being a goal down at half-time, the fans were generally upbeat about the display so far. Expectations rose a notch early in the second-half when a brilliant Wayne Turk volley was headed off the line and that seemed to give players and fans more belief that maybe we weren't out of contention. That was soon tempered by an ominous spell of Forest pressure – we just couldn't get out of our half and a second goal looked inevitable. However we clung on and, in the 61st minute, suddenly we were level. At that time, it looked to most like a scrambled goal – we didn't care but, the benefit

of being able to watch it on TV showed that it was another masterful piece of skill from Matt Tubbs.

Surely Forest would step up a gear or two? No, if anything it was the part-timers who got stronger as the game went on and could even have sneaked an historic win late in the game. I couldn't resist the temptation to watch it all again in the evening and, start to look forward to the replay..................

Martin Smith

JANUARY

Fortunately the Yeading match was re-arranged for Tuesday 9th January. It resulted in a comfortable win for the Whites with Robbie Matthews scoring twice. Perhaps, more importantly, it provided the third match of Matt Tubbs' suspension freeing him to play in the Southport tie. The gate, at 621, was the lowest for a first team match at the Raymac. so far in the season.

The Southport match followed on the following Saturday in front of nearly 1200 spectators, only a few of whom had made the 5/6 hour trip from the northwest.

The best time to score the winner

Hopes were high particularly as Southport were managerless and were near the foot of the Nationwide Conference table. However this was not reflected in their play. Salisbury had the best of the first 20 minutes and Wayne Turk opened the scoring after charging down an attempted clearance. This advantage was soon lost, however, when Ryan Clarke totally miskicked leaving a Southport forward to walk the ball into the inviting net. This inspired them to greater heights and there was nothing much between the teams thereafter. It was in injury time that Turk scored his second and the winner to send the Whites into the next round.

There then followed three league games and, if promotion momentum was to be maintained, these had to yield points. After the Yeading game, Histon were top of the table, seven points ahead of the Whites who had two games in hand. There were other clubs higher than Salisbury, so any slip could prove costly. In the event all three games were won with only one goal conceded.

The local derby at Eastleigh was eagerly awaited. The crowd of 1426 was another record for a competitive match at the Silverlake stadium and at least half of them were supporting Salisbury.

The only goal was scored by Paul Sales although many would have attributed it to a defender. Salisbury were always the better side and the win completed a trio of 1-0 victories over their rivals this season.

The home game against Cambridge City was won despite Matt Tubbs missing a penalty – a rare event. The dismissal of the goalkeeper who committed the foul was very harsh but the resultant ten men battled well. They owed at lot to the substitute 'keeper, Edgar

Mercade, who played brilliantly and it was ironic that it was his venture upfield for a corner in the last minutes that created the opportunity for Robbie Matthews to run virtually the entire length of the field with the ball at his feet before beating a despairing defender on the line.

The third game was at home to Bedford. Again the Whites dominated for much of the game but went in level on 1-1 at half-time.

The second-half was almost entirely Salisbury's but goals would not come. Matt Tubbs had several chances but the Bedford goalkeeper, Ian Brown, performed heroically. Salisbury fans were willing Tubbs to score his first goal since coming back after suspension and this he did in the 75th minute from a header by Robbie Matthews. Alex Haddow made the game safe eight minutes later. New signing Michael Fowler, from Gloucester, came on as substitute for the last five minutes or so.

Robbie Matthews, who scored the second goal versus Cambridge, a goal that nearly brought the house down. Players and spectators alike did not know whether to laugh, cry or applaud. Most probably did all three.

This result put Salisbury in third position in the league, one point behind Histon. Welling, who had played two games more were top, one point ahead of Histon.

Breathing space for league battle

All three sides are scheduled for action in the 3rd Round of the F.A. Trophy on Saturday 3rd Feb. so the battle for league supremacy was held in a abeyance. Salisbury's visit to Kettering (2nd in the Conference North) could well be the match of the round.

Entertainment for all

For the statistically minded, at the the end of January over 20,000 people had been present at the Raymac, for the league, F.A. Cup and Trophy matches. An average of 1255 per game. For the league matches alone the average was 976; a remarkable record compared to just a few years ago.

A thirst for statistics?

The local brewery Hopback, through their Sales Manager, Greg Futcher donate a crate of 'Summer Lightning' every time Ryan Clarke keeps a clean sheet for the Whites. Up to the Bedford game the 'party cellar' for the end of the season knees-up contained 12 crates.

Salisbury's No. 1
Ryan Clarke.

It was also good to see, on 27th January, that work had started on the ground improvements on the open side. The finished product will comprise two 75-seater stands plus standing with four steps of terracing running the whole length.

FEBRUARY

Another busy and eventful month. The emphasis had to be on the F.A. Trophy but the league could not be treated lightly if promotion was to be a realistic prospect.

The next game in the Trophy was against Kettering at Rockingham Road. The hosts were favourites having won this event in the past but this counted for nothing because the result was a comfortable win for the Whites with Matt Tubbs scoring twice. They challenged for every ball and never let their opponents into the game.

Helmets needed?

An excellent result but a game which would be remembered for all the wrong reasons, when the away fans, who were prevented from leaving because of a perceived threat from young so-called Kettering supporters, were pelted with stones and coins from outside the ground. The stewards would not open the gates so the Salisbury fans were sitting targets, nor did they call the police. That was left to a visitor!! Help arrived very quickly and the youths dispersed. There were minor injuries and considerable distress but, thankfully, nothing significant.

The Kettering fan's website was filled with apologies but it seemed that this was not the first incident of this nature at Rockingham Road this season. It is hoped that action will be taken by the club's management to ensure it is the last.

Déjà vu?

This victory produced another away tie. Salisbury would now meet Stevenage Borough, a full-time outfit from the Conference. Not much change here from the quarter-finals of last season. Again there was good support for the team but this was not enough. They were well beaten by a decent side who played the game the right way. Taking nothing from the winners the match was marred by the inexperience of the referee. Both sides suffered from his uneven performance and both sets of supporters were singing 'you don't know what your doing'.

That man in black!

For non-league fans the Trophy is a major event. There are 'old pros' in the teams and it is important that the person in charge commands respect. Fans of both teams would probably hope that the lesson is learnt. Sharp-eyed viewers would have seen the referee acting as the fifth official at the following day's League Cup Final between Arsenal v Chelsea and as assistant referee at the Reading v Arsenal game on 27th February. He may have benefitted from seeing how Howard Webb handled those matches.

Mud, mud glorious mud !

In the league Bognor Regis Town were beaten on a very muddy pitch at the Raymac. when colour was provided by the visiting supporters. There was then a rather fortunate draw at Bishop's Stortford. Aaron Cook equalised with a penalty in the last minute, the third time the Whites scored very late in the last four matches.

The victory over Hayes was very comfortable and brought the number of matches since a defeat to 12.

Nick Holmes's nightmare begins

This run was extended to 13 with the home draw against Dorchester. Salisbury played with 10 men for an hour after Matt

This is the very, very muddy pitch for the Bognor game. Aaron Cook celebrates Salisbury's first goal. For Paul Sales its mud everywhere, nose, eye and you guess?

Tubbs was sent off for the fourth time this season. This would seem to be a record for any Salisbury player over the years and one which he will not enjoy. The team will not enjoy his six-match suspension either. As at 25th February the Whites were lying second in the league, two points behind Histon with both having played 26 games.

A bonus for the end of season 'knees-up' ! !

Returning to the Trophy Salisbury were awarded 'team of the round' for the victory over Kettering. This comprised a plaque from the Mayor, Councillor Sheila Warrander, 20 tickets for the final and four crates of Carlsberg lager.

Receiving the plaque from the Mayor Sheila Warrander, are Salisbury Directors, Stuart McGlashan *(far right)* and Paul Orsborn. Also in the photo is Andy Cook.

The Stevenage contest brought nine yellow cards plus a red and Tommy Widdrington was ordered from the dug-out. The first booking was within two minutes of the start which left the referee with no option but to continue the practice, somewhat raggedly, throughout the game. It was not, by any means, a dirty game and it is likely that the bookings for dissent were borne of frustration.

Non-league fans deserve better than this. It is not acceptable for an inexperienced official to learn his trade at the expense of their enjoyment of the game.

The accumulation of cards will bring suspensions so it was re-assuring to see the signing of Alan Neilson, the former Saints player, from Tamworth. He will provide cover in defence and it is to be hoped that something similar can be done to cover Matt Tubbs and Robbie Matthews whose red at Stevenage was for two offences.

MARCH: In like a lion

Salisbury City reached the penultimate month of the season with their stunning Conference South 11-match undefeated run still intact. It was further extended into the first week of the month with away victories at Fisher Athletic and Dorchester Town.

Up pops the bogey again, or was it a nightmare?

The Whites met Eastbourne Borough at the Raymac. on 10th

continued on page 363

The Whites 2006-2007 F.A. Umbro Trophy venture

☆   ☆

☆   ☆

☆

3rd Qual. Round Salisbury City v Enfield – 25th November 2006

Salisbury won 2-1 with 'Mooncat' scoring both the Whites goals, one a penalty.

1st Round Proper – Salisbury City v Woking – 16th December 2006

The Whites beat Woking with three cracking goals, two from Matt Tubbs (*far left*), one a delicate chip, the other vied with Wayne Turk for power.

2nd Round – Salisbury City v Southport – 13th January 2007

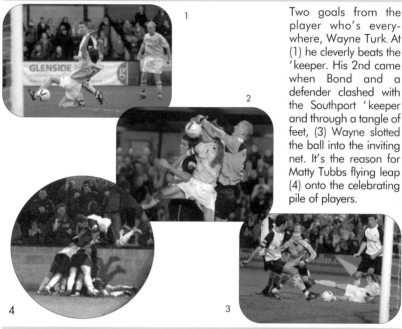

1

2

Two goals from the player who's everywhere, Wayne Turk. At (1) he cleverly beats the 'keeper. His 2nd came when Bond and a defender clashed with the Southport 'keeper and through a tangle of feet, (3) Wayne slotted the ball into the inviting net. It's the reason for Matty Tubbs flying leap (4) onto the celebrating pile of players.

4

3

3rd Round – Kettering Town v Salisbury City – 3rd February 2007

This was a 120% team performance not allowing Kettering a moment in control. Matt Tubbs scored both of the Whites two goal. Above he's just about to score his first and (*left*) he is being chased by Scott Bartlett and Paul Sales for a bit of back slapping.

Quarter Finals – Stevenage Borough v Salisbury City
24th February 2007

Sales(1) has barely landed and he's booked, not long after Clay(2) joins him. Yet Tubbs(3) is sent flying with not a word of warning. Add to that the sending off of Matthews, the forced exit from the dug-out for Tommy Widdrington, which left one to ponder, were we all playing with the same rule book?

March. The sides first met in the Southern League Eastern Division four seasons ago and this was the fourth meeting between the two clubs, with Salisbury yet to taste victory.

The game saw new signing Marvin Brown making a dream start by scoring inside the first five minutes. However, the excellent start developed into a nightmare scenario when the Eastbourne skipper Paul Armstrong's 35 yard volley gave Ryan Clarke no chance. With so many of the City players having an off-day, sections of the Salisbury supporters started to become frustrated and their frustration was compounded when Eastbourne were awarded a penalty mid-way through the second-half, with Simon Browne handling in the box. Scott Ramsey made no mistake with the spot-kick; this penalty was the first the team had conceded for 13

Marvin Brown celebrating with fellow striker Paul Sales after scoring in debut game for Salisbury City versus Eastbourne Borough.

months. Salisbury had a good penalty appeal turned down 10 mins from time. However, they still retained pole position in the table after the 2-1 defeat due to second-placed Histon losing at Lewes. It emerged later that day that Paul Sales had sustained a broken hand in the match and could be side-lined up to six weeks.

Continuation of good away form

City continued to set the pace with a workmanlike performance at Cambridge City the following Tuesday. Luke Prince put Salisbury in front inside the first six minutes. Marvin Brown doubled the lead 23 minutes later with a spectacular scissor-kick. The striker landed awkwardly during another raid on the Cambridge goal and was replaced by Declan McGregor. McGregor later scored his first league goal for the club to secure maximum points.

Vital points lost at the Raymac.

Hopes were high the following Saturday when the club entertained relegation threatened Thurrock at the Raymac. Missing from the team sheet were the prolific strikers Matt Tubbs (suspension), Paul Sales and Marvin Brown (injuries). Alas, Salisbury suffered a serious setback to their title aspirations after being held to a goalless draw in a game which saw the continuation of the poor home form. Histon leap-frogged Salisbury to the top of the Conference South table after their 2-1 victory at Dorchester. The Cambridgeshire side underlined their own title aspirations by demolishing promotion hopefuls Havant & Waterlooville 4-0 the following Tuesday.

Injury crisis deepens

The attacking options caused further concern after Robbie Matthews sustained a thigh strain during the Thurrock game and was extremely doubtful for the Lewes match. It was also reported that Marvin Brown was not going to figure in the match. On the plus side, keeper Ryan Clarke went to hospital after the Thurrock game with a suspected broken finger but fortunately there was no break.

Ex under 19 international joins city on loan

The Club responded positively to the injury crisis by securing the services on loan for a month, of 22 year old Jerome Watt, the Northampton Town attacking midfielder. The player had made more than 12 appearances for them this season in the Coca-Cola League One. Watt, a former England under 19 international, went

continued on page 366

Injury crises and suspensions derailed the Whites spring promotion push ! !

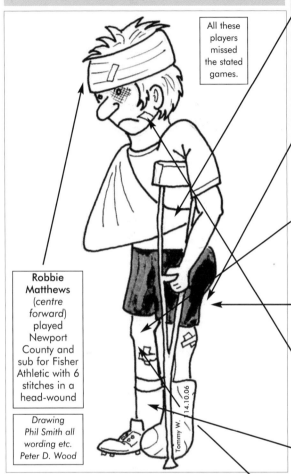

All these players missed the stated games.

Paul Sales
(centre forward)
(broken hand)
Cambridge City
Thurrock, Lewes
Hayes
Farnborough Town
Welling United
Sutton United
Histon
Newport County

Marvin Brown
(forward) (groin)
Thurrock, Lewes, Hayes
Farnborough Town
Welling United
Sutton United, Histon
Newport County

Wayne Turk
(midfield) (knee)
Was injured in the Hayes home match on 27th March. Turk an ever present member of the team then missed the rest of the season.

Tim Bond
(centre-back) (groin)
Welling Utd, Sutton Utd
Histon
Newport County
Fisher Athletic
Braintree

Danny Clay
(midfield)
(40 stitches in his chin)
Histon

Alan Neilson
(midfield) (calf)
Was injured away at Sutton United on 7th April. Then out for the rest of the season.

Michael Fowler
(midfield) (knee)
Bognor Regis Town
Bishop Stortford, Hayes
Fisher Athletic
Dorchester Town (twice)
Eastbourne Borough
Cambridge City
Thurrock, Lewes, Hayes

Robbie Matthews
(centre forward)
played Newport County and sub for Fisher Athletic with 6 stitches in a head-wound

Drawing Phil Smith all wording etc. Peter D. Wood

On Sat. 10th March (2nd match of Matt Tubbs 6-match suspension) Salisbury were top of the league and 2nd to Histon in the form table having P6 W4 D2 L0 F15 A6 GD11. On Tues. 17th April (return of Paul Sales) they were 15th in the form table having P6 W2 D1 L3 F6 A9 GD-3, 2nd in league but 16pts behind 'Champions', Histon.

Matt Tubbs
(forward)
6-match suspension
Dorchester Town, Eastbourne Borough
Cambridge City, Thurrock, Lewes
Hayes

Ryan Clarke
(goalkeeper)
1-match suspension
Newport County

straight into the squad for the game against Lewes and before the kick-off, Robbie Matthews passed a late fitness test. The game saw Salisbury failing to capitalise on a couple of gilt-edged scoring chances. Lewes made the most of their opportunities and scored the only goal of the match mid-way through the second-half.

Histon opened up a seven-point lead over Salisbury at the summit of the Conference South with a 5-0 home victory over Hayes. Having beaten Hayes 4-0 away last month, City supporters carried high hopes that the club would return to winning ways against them at the Raymac. on the Tuesday following the Lewes game. Wayne Turk made his 300th appearance for the club and put the ball in the net on 67 minutes, only to be flagged offside. Again Salisbury had to settle for a 0-0 draw and droves of supporters left the ground in frustration before the final whistle.

The final game of the month at the Raymac. saw Manager, Nick Holmes, making five changes to the team in a bid to hold the club's position in the play-off places. However, the Whites' promotion aspirations received another setback as the rub of the green deserted them. The game saw Salisbury reduced to 10-men 12 minutes into the second-half when 'keeper Ryan Clarke was red-carded for handling outside his area. They battled tooth and nail to get back into the game after Farnborough beat the Salisbury wall from the resulting free-kick. City went close on several occasions but the score remained 1-0 to the 'boro. at the final whistle. No doubt there will be more twists and turns in the race for the play-off places in the month of April. The points yield from the last five home games was just three from a possible 15.

A dejected Ryan Clarke walks from the field of play having handled the ball outside his area. A wicked wind had held the ball up from a overhead kick which wrong-footed him. Helping Clarke in that long lonely walk is Matt Tubbs.

photos and wording pdw

In his cage (turnstile) and sentry box, Ron always has a smile for all.

We only sing when we're winning?

A few doom and gloom merchants supporting the club had been having a field day with their dire predictions over the last couple of weeks coinciding with the Whites loss of form.

At the beginning of the Conference South campaign, manager Nick Holmes stated that a top eight position at the end of the 2006/07 season would not be beyond the City capabilities. Most supporters would certainly had settled for the great F.A. Cup and F.A. Trophy runs achieved this season. Nevertheless doubtful supporters entering through turnstile D will be reassured by Ron Chalk that this spectacular season is still up and running. He has the rare gift of conveying that the most important person in the stadium has just passed through his turnstile.

APRIL

Beleaguered Salisbury took a giant step towards the play-offs with a priceless away victory to fellow promotion hopefuls Welling United on Wednesday 4th April, which marked the end of the four match goal famine.

At this crucial stage of the campaign Histon had opened a formidable 13 point lead over second-placed Salisbury at the summit of the Nationwide Conference South. The following Saturday, City took all three points away to Sutton United thanks to Matt Tubbs third minute goal.

Record league attendance as top two do battle

The Whites met the Champions elect, Histon at the Raymac. on Easter Monday. For the first 45 minutes they matched the opposition in every department, however, Histon broke the deadlock just two minutes into the second-half and were then gifted two more goals from defensive errors. The visiting team and their supporters returned to Cambridge effectively 'Champions'.

Oh what a carve up

On Saturday 14th April, City headed to Wales to take on Newport County who had a dream to get back into the Nationwide Conference via the play-offs. However it was Salisbury that had a dream start. Within the first five minutes they had raced into a two-goal lead but on 20 minutes the hosts got back into the game with a hotly disputed goal. On the stroke of half-time a Matthews 'goal' was ruled out when the player was adjudged to have pushed an opponent. Just after the break Tubbs made the score 3-1, but City then conceded two scrappy goals. There was more joy for Newport when the referee awarded them a penalty and then dismissed goalkeeper Matt Bulman (who was making his first full league appearance for the City), ruling that he had brought down the Newport striker, Charlie Griffin. Mike Fowler took up the goal-keeping role but was sent the wrong way for the spot-kick, resulting in a contentious 4-3 victory for the hosts. The race for the play-off places was beginning to reach fever pitch after the Newport County game with six clubs still contesting the four available places.

Top seven of Nationwide Conference South (14-04-07)

	P	W	D	L	F	A	Pts
Histon (Champions)	38	27	4	7	77	38	85
Salisbury City	38	20	9	9	61	36	69
Welling United	39	21	4	14	62	46	67
Braintree Town	39	19	10	10	46	37	67
Bishop's Stortford	39	19	9	11	66	50	66
Havant & Waterlooville	38	18	11	9	64	62	65
Newport County	36	19	5	12	70	47	62

New sponsors of the Football Conference

It was announced that the new sponsors of the Football Conference for the start of the 2007/08 season on a three-year deal would be the gambling giants, Blue Square. The top division would be known as the Blue Square Premier, while Conference North and

South would become Blue Square North and South respectively. It was stated in the Non League Paper that the Blue Square chairman, Martin Belsham, had revealed that the company had been looking to get involved in football for a long time and felt the Conference represented the perfect opportunity.

Welcomed back by team and supporters alike

Paul Sales returned to the team for the Fisher Athletic game at the Raymac. on Tuesday 17th April, after missing nine matches through injury. Within 13 minutes he was on the score sheet and the prolific Sales/Tubbs combination later doubled the score with an archetypal Tubbs strike. The home side comfortably secured maximum points after a spectacular own goal in the second-half.

The long journey to Braintree on the following Saturday, in hot sunny weather, did nothing to resolve the play-off places contest. The goalless draw, with a predominance of 'big boot' on a bone hard pitch, was probably the only result possible. The teams had, at that time, the best defensive records in the league and the forwards had few chances.

Havant & Waterlooville were the visitors on Tuesday 24th April and, again, a draw was the result. The Whites scored first with the equaliser coming in the 90th minute. This was the day Alan Ball, the youngest member of England's World Cup winning team died. He had been to the Raymac. as recently as the Nottingham Forest Cup tie and Nick Holmes, a colleague of his at the Dell, subsequently dedicated the play-offs to him.

Twenty-eighth April re-visited

Saturday 28th April brought the last league fixture of the season – 59 years to the day after the epic match in 1948 against Weymouth which climaxed the club's very first season.

Basingstoke were the visitors and they were in danger of relegation being fifth from bottom of the table. Salisbury were already sure of a play-off place but wanted to retain second position. Both sides needed at least a point and for the other matches to go in their favour. Before the kick-off the referee called for a minute's silence in tribute to Alan Ball's memory which was greeted by spontaneous applause around the ground. It was a hot day with another

Alan Ball

bone hard pitch and perhaps understandably both teams used long ball tactics throughout. Paul Sales twice went close in the first-half and Ryan Clarke made a superb save just before half-time to deny the visitors the lead. The second-half was mostly played in midfield until Salisbury stepped up the pace in the last 10 minutes when Cook, Fowler and Bartlett all went close to scoring. The result was a 0-0 draw, (the match in 1948 was also a draw) and the sizeable Basingstoke contingent in the crowd celebrated wildly when they knew they had done enough to secure Conference South football for next season.

The result meant the Whites had scored just five goals in the last eight home games but the end had been achieved.

Now for the play-offs ! ! !

The play-off system has been in most senior football leagues for a number of years. It has the great merit of prolonging interest in the season and generating considerable extra income for the participants. Its detractors will say that the second best team, over the whole season, should be the side to gain promotion and not be subjected to a sudden death contest where, surprisingly frequently, the team in an inferior league position triumph. Salisbury were now in this position and promotion to the newly named Blue Square Premier lay in a maximum of three games to be played.

For the four clubs and the supporters involved in these games the matches will be endured rather than enjoyed, with the entire season climaxing over 10 days or so. The games will be a Don't-lose-your-concentration and Don't-do-anything-daft kind of scenario.

Tommy Widdrington may use alternative phraseology. Tense, fingernail-biting days lay ahead but probably not football for the connoisseurs and purists of the game. Nick Holmes used this piece of philosophy in one of his club programme notes: ' If you're scared of losing you cannot win'.

Will the final chapter of the 60 year history of Salisbury City F.C. close with a fairy-tale ending?

Before moving on to the matches it is worth considering how the club has fared over the season. At the start most supporters and probably the management as well would have settled for a mid-table final league position. Runs in the F.A. Cup and Trophy would have been very acceptable but few people would have expected what actually happened.

Firstly in the league the team were potential champions until the Spring when a combination of suspensions, injuries, hard pitches and windy conditions, brought to an end a sequence of results which saw them neck and neck with Histon for the Championship.

In the event Histon ran away with the title finishing 19 points ahead. The Whites had the best defensive record in the Nationwide South and also the highest average home league gate of 1119, nearly 200 more than the next best, Newport County with 932. The best home gate in the league was against Histon. Matt Tubbs was the third highest scorer in the league with 20 goals and this after missing around a quarter of the matches. Salisbury's away support continued to improve substantially the gates of all their opponents.

In the F.A. Cup the previous record run of 1959 was beaten when Nottingham Forest won 2-0 in the 2nd Round replay at the City Ground. In the F.A. Trophy Stevenage won 3-0 in the quarter final at the Broadhall Way Stadium and went on to beat Kidderminster in the final at Wembley.

The Cup and Trophy runs brought big gates as well as publicising the club nationally.

The ground improvements at the Raymac. were passed by the league grading committee so if promotion were to be achieved there would be no difficulties. Indeed only a little more work would be required if the club were to achieve Football League status in the years to come.

Not only did the first team have a successful season but the Youth team won the Hampshire Midweek Cup and, indeed, all the younger teams enjoyed some success. The under 8s won their league in their first competitive season. The ladies team in the Hampshire County League Division I, came a creditable fourth and the other girls teams also had success. Much praise is due to organisers, coaches, parents and all who played. The reserve team had a chaotic season due to poor administration. The Suburban League must be an improvement.

The man with the gloves 'scores' with the fans

The selection of Ryan Clarke as the Supporters' Player of the Year was something of a surprise. Many fans were disappointed when he supplanted their favourite, Kevin Sawyer, at the start of the season but his subsequent performances were a key feature in a successful defence and the award was well deserved.

Play-off semi-final away to Bishop's Stortford
Around 200 Salisbury supporters made the lengthy trip to Hertfordshire on a sunny day and contributed greatly to the atmosphere at Woodside Park. Those who went to the league match there in February had fond memories of the excellent playing surface and they were not disappointed. There could be no excuse for not getting the ball on the ground.

In the event both teams did just that and the outcome was a fast flowing game, considerable skill and a liking for attacking. The first-half was very even with both sides having chances to score. In the second-half the home team took the lead with a well worked goal. The Whites responded when substitute for Paul Sales, Robbie Matthews, equalised from close range. Tommy Widdrington came on with about 10 minutes to go and from then on Salisbury got on top although the winning goal proved too elusive.

The teams were applauded by both sets of fans at the finish. They were a credit to Conference South football and Bishop's Stortford is a club fans would look forward to revisiting. The referee was excellent and there were no serious fouls or incidents in the match.

Play-off semi-final home to Bishop's Stortford
Several coaches contributed to the 200 or so Bishop's Stortford fans who arrived at the Raymac. on the hot afternoon of 5th May. They were confined to the city end of the ground where, for safety reasons, there was no access to the terracing behind the goal or opposite the main stand. Local supporters were crammed into the remaining areas.

The pitch was in better shape than for the Basingstoke game. Salisbury were without Paul Sales who had a hamstring problem and Tommy Widdrington was, again, on the bench.

The match was a thriller. Both teams played decent football with the visitors' neat passing testing the Whites defence. Matt Tubbs scored the first goal after 17 minutes but 12 minutes later Tim Langer and Max Porter combined for the latter to beat Ryan Clarke.

The visitors started better in the second-half and, indeed, probably shaded it throughout. However there were signs that Salisbury's superior fitness was beginning to tell and, in extra time, they dominated and scored twice through Robbie Matthews and Michael Fowler. Marvin Brown who came on for Tubbs showed neat touches.

It was a classic encounter and, like the first tie, was a credit to

(*right*) Tubbs scores the 1st goal for the Whites in scintilating style in the 2nd leg of the play-offs versus Bishop's Stortford.
(*photo with permission of Daily Echo Sport*)

Goal ! ! Matthews (*left*) whoops in delight after scoring Salisbury's 2nd and Fowler (*right*) turns away after slotting in no. 3. Both these goals came from clever passes courtesy of Brown (*top right*) seen with Prince celebrating the win. (*photos permission of Salisbury Journal*).

both teams. There was only one booking and that for kicking the ball away after the whistle had blown. The referee was apologetic when penalising Brown who appeared not to have heard the whistle. It was a match that would have done credit to the final. There were scenes of jubilation after the game as Salisbury fans worked out how to get to Stevenage on a Sunday evening for the final. Coaches would be on offer meaning a busy time for the management and all concerned with travel arrangements.

Braintree, who beat Havant & Waterlooville 4-2 on penalties, would be the opponents. Salisbury have lost and drawn with them this season so a win would round things off nicely.

Agony of it all, it's worse than having a baby – spoken by a man !

Would the final be as good as the semis and would the Whites achieve their highest ever place in league football? An estimated 2000 supporters travelled to the Broadhall Way Stadium to find out. Braintree were well supported although outnumbered. The heavy rain made for a difficult journey and the pitch was a lot softer than of late.

The match was covered by Setanta TV as well as Radio Wiltshire and Spire FM who did full live commentaries. Those who remained at home could patronise the pubs with Setanta facilities and one of these, the Devizes Inn, got into the spirit of the day by decorating its bar in Salisbury colours. The atmosphere was electric and the roar in the packed premises when Matt Tubbs scored nearly blew the roof off. The game itself was evenly balanced with both sides having periods on top and there is no denying that, on the day, Braintree were exceedingly unlucky to lose. It was decided by one incisive movement, six minutes from the end. Robbie Matthews provided a weighted pass to Luke Prince who sped up the wing to fire in a fast low cross. Matt Tubbs saw it coming and his rapier like finish at the near post determined the outcome of the match. The aim had been achieved. Conference (Blue Square Premier) here we come.

Train Dave, a fanatical Whites fan, also known as David Lloyd, contributed a personal view of the day in his own inimitable style but heavily edited to placate the censor. See page 379. At the final whistle it was impossible not to feel sympathy for George Borg, the Braintree manager, his players and their supporters. George, who over the years has had his brushes with authority, is widely regarded as a lovable rascal but a genuine football man.

A pale evening sun shone after the storms and the renaissance was complete. In five years the Whites had gone from the threat of extinction to distinction. When this book was first mooted the authors asked Nick Holmes to arrange a bumper last season to maximise sales and interest. The club has provided just that – in spades.

After the presentation ceremony, the fans celebrated in the ground where players threw their shirts and, in one case, boots, into the crowd. Festivities continued in the car park, on the way home and for some, at the bar at the Raymac. until the early hours.

To sum up. Two good teams, good refereeing, enthusiastic support and a welcoming host club – what an advert for non-league football !

So what does next season mean? Visits to local rivals such as Woking, Aldershot, Weymouth, Oxford and Forest Green as well as lengthy journeys to York, Leeds and Halifax. It means playing against full time clubs and, from being the best supported team in the Conference South, Salisbury could well be in the middle of the pack. Support has to be maintained. Foundations for a successful football club have been laid and the next few years are crucial.

Now to calm down our readers after the excitement of the best ever season we offer a few thoughts and observations as well as, we hope, the stepping stone for the next historian to chronicle the club's activities.

continued on page 380

In a tense fairly even encounter, with Braintree probably having more shots on goal Clarke made another important save (1). Then with only 8 mins to go, (2) Matthews started the move that led to the only goal of the game. A pass out to Prince who took the ball to the bye-line, where he crossed to the goal area (3). Tubbs left his marker for dead and, hit the ball first-time into the back of the Braintree net (4).

(*Below*) Tubbs turns gleefully away and (*left*) it was tears of joy and laughter as the celebrations began for Salisbury City and their fans.

The Salisbury City F.C. express thundered on. After a brief stop in the Ryman League its was non-stop at the Southern Premier and Conference South.....................then maybe a chance to catch one's breath, before..........

If you really, really love them clap your hands,

Princey with his Princess.

Tommy with Theo & Kai his two biggest fans

If you really, really love them clap your hands,

(*above*)
The Nick & Matty Holmes support team,
l/r: Lyndsey, Kim and Carolyn.

Wer'e surrounded by ALL
our No. 1's ! ! !

If you really, really love them.......

really, really love them........

really, really love them, clap your hands.

All words & music 375-378 pdw

(left) Phil Harding with Bronze Age Man.

MEMORY LANE
Conference South Playoffs Final
Braintree Town v Salisbury – 13th May 2007 – Stevenage

Our journey started by coach to Andover, via Grateley, then on the metal tracks to Waterloo. My travel companions were the usual energetic bunch, Toddy, Pinky, Malx and so on and, of course Mrs Train who loves her away-days to watch the Whites, black & white ribbons in her hair. A little celebration was to be had on the way, because Pinky won the forum prediction league and Malx supplied a bottle of champagne. Not bad French fizzy wine, I suppose. On arrival at Waterloo we headed straight to the underground for a muggy and humid 20 min. trip under the earth to Kings Cross, phew. There were loads of trains to Stevenage so we all had a beer in the pub on the concourse – just to put some liquid back into our blood-streams after dehydrating in the underworld. All done and dusted we caught the train and, on our arrival, we took a taxi to Our Mutual Friend, a public house 10 min. away from the Broadhall Stadium, to spend time contemplating what was in store for our team that day. Later, full off beer, we headed off to the ground and what a sight there was to greet us. The stand behind one of the goals was chockablock with City fans and, to the right, there were many more in the seated area – great stuff. The lads came on the pitch with a tremendous roar from the City contingent and my horn as well. The Whites were in for a hard match against the geezers from Essex who were in no mood to mess about. They pushed the Whites from the onset but the lads stood firm and did, occasionally, put the Irons on the back foot. No score at half-time was fair but from the second-half kick-off the country cockneys were in no mood to take prisoners. Things took a turn for the better in the last 20 mins of the game when all the Whites fans were standing and singing together. The lads got all fired up and, with seven mins to go, Robbie 'Mooncat' Matthews fed a neat ball to Princey who raced down the left like a whippet, then a low cross to Tubbsy who blasted it past the Braintree goalie. The Whites fans went ballistic, me as well. It was the longest 10 mins of my

life waiting for the ref. to blow the final whistle. He did and it was all over. City fans poured onto the pitch. Conference proper here we come ! ! !

At the end Tommy Widdrington came over and handed me the empty celebration bottle of champagne with the words 'way eye man Dave, this is far ewe'. Top man is our Thomas.

David Lloyd
(Train Dave)

Then, Now and in the Future

At the beginning of our chronicle, the world was worried about the 'Cold War'. Now, the common enemy is terrorism.

There is a parallel in the game of football. In 1947 parochial leagues provided the competition. Now the pyramid system has opened up unheard of opportunities for travel as well as progression.

Four very much-missed, Club Stalwarts.
left/right:
F.R. (Fred) Trowbridge (Treasurer),
E.T. (Ron) Lemon (Secretary),
John Harvey (Chairman S.W. Division)
making the presentations:
Henry Abel (Chairman Salisbury Supporters Club).

Initially it was Supporters' clubs who raised funds and Salisbury were particularly strong in this area and donated thousands of pounds. Nowadays funds are sought from corporate sponsorships and television which has largely replaced the former method. The Supporters' Trust, which assisted for a brief period, might perhaps be resurrected in the future.

On the pitch no longer do players come out five minutes before kick-off. Today they assemble much earlier to undergo drills and exercises designed to increase their physiological and pschological state. Gone too, are the days when the trainer had a bucket of water and a sponge. Today, both Conrad Parrott and Kevin Bushby are armed with more modern and sophisticated impedimenta.

Ahhhh, I feel better already and the trainer hasen't even reached me yet ! !

What of the future? The costs of running a team in the higher echelons of the pyramid require a marketing strategy, unheard of at the club's formation. There will be many challenges ahead which could include a full-time operation and it is to be seen if they are surmountable.

HERE'S TO THE FUTURE ! !

STOP PRESS !

Matthew Tubbs was selected to represent the England non league team in the summer. (A first time ever for Salisbury City F.C.)

football Extra

peter D. wood

The photos in the following pages were either too large for their relevant chapters or not mentioned as such. They are of 'moments in time' within the 60 years of Salisbury City Football Club. Some show the winning of trophies, others 'a first', there's jubilant supporters and those extra 'star' matches, but all giving us that little bit of 'Football Extra'

Salisbury F.C. V Charlton Athletic – 29th July 1993

Charlton sent a full-team squad for the match. Salisbury were defeated by the small margin of 2-1.

The top photo features Kevin Bale and Simon Browne in action and in the picture right Steve Weaver the Salisbury 'keeper stops a goal-bound shot.

Match attendance 528

Salisbury's team for the match: Weaver, Blankley, Browne, Loveridge, Sanders, Pearson, Payne, Batty, Chalk, Wigley and Bale.

1950/51 F.A. Cup 3rd Qualifying Round, Salisbury 1 Trowbridge 0, attendance 7000. Trowbridge goalkeeper, Vince breaks up a Salisbury attack. Dando (no. 3) was later to join Salisbury.

1953/54 Paddy (Patrick) Hasty collides with the Barnstaple 'keeper suffering a fractured cheekbone. Cyril Smith scored the only goal of the game.

Union Sportive de Torquennoise and Salisbury F.C. 1955
Salisbury won 4-2, scorers: Prentice, Noyce, Clancy, Uren

Union Sportive, *l/r, back*: Oeman, Dumotier, Wielfaer, Maes, Savidan, Billiet.
Front: Dutillent, Allart, Cloet, Lamenw, Sainty
Salisbury F.C., *l/r, back*: Fleming, Weeks, Kingston, Heagren, Tuck, Farrell.
Front: Knight, Uren, Noyce, Prentice, Clancy.

Salisbury don't want cash – just Cup glory!

The above heading and the words below are part of an article by Sam Leitch (*Daily Mirror*). The Salisbury F.C. manager Reg Broom made some interesting comments and threw some light on the age old arguments of how fit the players of those days were compared to their contempories of today.

Reg Broom, 61-year-old manager jammed a balance sheet in Sam's hand.

'Look at the money we've got, £12,355 4s 6d – and believe me when I tell you we are not remotely interested in the cash from the F.A. Cup. We're well off. We want the prestige, the honour and the glory.'

Reg also stated: 'Salisbury are only associate members of the Football Association, but if we beat Newport County that would surely gain us full membership.'

Salisbury according to Sam 'is the richest little soccer gold mine I have ever seen. They must be the envy of every non-League club in the country and a good few fourth division sides. Their supporters' club has poured in £49,000 in 11 years.'

Sam goes on to ask, 'What of the team?' 'A professional organisation run by amateurs and one of the best set-ups in southern England, says Reg proudly. 'I ask for ninety minutes heart and soul from the lads once a week and that's all. They get well paid, training is their responsibility, not ours. The players never see each other from Saturday to Saturday.'

Salisbury
F.C.
V
Newport
County
A.F.C.
2nd Round
F.A. Cup
5th
December
1959

Terry Compton (captain) leads out Salisbury F.C. for the F.A. Cup 2nd Round versus Newport County the Football League side. Following Compton out onto the pitch are Selby Dando and Ian Allen.

Salisbury's captain, Terry Compton and Alf Sherwood of Newport County, shake hands as the referee spins the coin for choice of ends at Salisbury's first ever venture into the 2nd Round of the F.A. Cup. *Note* Press-box, top of stand.

A flying Alan Kingston turns the ball around the Salisbury goal-post, while most of the crowd hold their breath.

Alan Kingston: A cup match versus Gloucester, I came out to punch away a ball and connected with Bob McAlone's chin which laid him out. Tommy Williams our trainer ran on to sort him out. When he was about to leave, I said, 'how about my broken finger'? which was hanging down loose. He wandered around looking at the ground and in the goalmouth found a lolly-stick, which he used as a splint, and bound it with a strip of plaster. 'That's you fixed' he said 'you can carry on the match now'! !

Some of the happy 6000+ crowd (with cheer-leader and bell).

Above and below: Seemingly packed to the rafters are the Whites supporters, complete with bells, rattles, and cornets. It's laughter and thumbs up all-round.

Photo provided by Alan Kingston

Salisbury F.C. 1954/55.
Back row, left/right: Rogers, Williams, Targett, Heagren, Gray, Kingston, Witt, Booth, unknown *Front row, left/right*: Stiff, Prentice, Fleming, Cutbush, Long.

Photo provided by Bill Sainsbury

Salisbury F.C. 1956/57 – Hants League
Back row, l/r: R. Timms, K. Michelson, J. Goodwin, R. Weeks, B. Passall.
Front row, l/r: J. McManus, P. Frost, P. Maunder, N. Mignot, B. Sainsbury, R. Henwood.

Salisbury's Bournemouth League XI (1957-58)

Back/row, left/right: D. Rogers (*trainer*), J. Day, C. Waters, D. Rattue, K Barfoot
M. Lake, R. Knight (*assist. trainer*), C. Rattue (*ass. Manager*) G. Rowden
(Manager)
Front/row, left/right: B. Amey, M. Miller, D. Tuck (*captain*), P. Way, T. Lloyd,
J. Buckley

Above: Cyril Rutter who took over the reigns of Manager of Salisbury F.C. from
Reg Broom, here signs a few autographs for the young supporters. Cyril played
regular football for Portsmouth before taking on management at Salisbury.

1960/61 – Winners of Western League Div. I, Alan Young Cup, Wilts Professional Shield.

back, l/r: P. Rushworth, B. Collins, S. Dando, T. Alexander, J. Cross, K. Prosser, B. McAlone, S. Miles, G. Trise, G. Kaile.

front: R. Sevier, R. Onslow, unknown, I. Allen, R. Broom, T. Compton, A. Sainsbury, B. Clancy, J. McCartney, R. Watts, unknown, D Hill.

behind back: T. Williams, S.D. Morgan, C. Waters, B. Stevens.

Committee members: back right of T. Williams: E. Quinton, right of B. Stevens: R. Owen, R. Read, R. Knight (3rd team asst. trainer), H. Leaver

Middle row far left: S. McKenzie, L Whitmarsh, right of G. Kaile, C. Rattue, F. Elliot

Peterborough United V Salisbury F.C.
F.A. Cup 1st Round – November 1964

The Salisbury captain, Gordon Henry greets his opposite number from the Posh.

Gordon Henry followed by Barry Fitch, run out for the the second-half.

Come on you Whites

This is the opening goal of the match, scored by Joe Stocks of Salisbury (far right), also in the picture for the Whites is no 8, Malcolm Ambrose.

A small section of the 10,000+ crowd.

A determined Bernie Pask tricks his way around a Peterborough defender before crossing the ball.

Salisbury F.C. 6
V
Ashford 0
11th January
1969

In the scoring of these six goals, Alan Tyler equalled a club record set up by Stan Abbott in the beating of Wells 9-0 in October 1955. Ian Henderson scored five against Yeovil in 1963.

Alan Tyler rounds the Ashford goalkeeper Hills for his first of six.

How these goals came about:

7-mins: Whitehouse intercepts a ball in mid-field and sends Alan away with a great through ball. Tyler takes the ball around the 'keeper and scores with a screw-shot past a defender on the line. 20-mins: Hodgkins shoots on goal but his shot is deflected to Tyler who makes no mistake with a left-footed shot into the roof of the net. 35-mins: Muxworthy is brought down in the penalty area and Tyler's spot-kick gives the keeper no chance. 49-mins: Muxworthy floats in a corner kick, Tyler sends a flick-header into top corner of the net. 50-mins Phillips centres from the right, Tyler runs in on the blind side, dives to send another stunning header past Hills. 88-mins: Tyler beats two men in the penalty area but is brought down by a third. He reluctantly takes the kick himself, then sends a wonderful shot into the corner of the net.

Alan Tyler slams in his second.

A rare picture of Brian Stevens the all-round sportsman, seen here as the proud all-round family man.

photo from Hazel Best

Chris Waters: After training we were all in the bath and the gas boiler went out, Stevo jumps out and disappears in search of a light. He walks back into the room with a very large piece of lighted paper. There was a huge flash and a bang, there stands Stevo with singed hair, no eyebrows and the last anyone saw of Bernie Pask that session, was a small naked man running across Hudsons Field ! ! !

Salisbury winners of the Bill Locke Memorial Cup.
Back row, left/right: D. Pugsley, R. Massey, B. Penzer, S. Miles, G. Moody, H. Penk, C. Smith, Reg Broom (secretary-manager)
Front row: T. Palmer, B. Stevens, B. Collins, A. Cranmer

Salisbury F.C. V Millwall
F.A. Cup 1st Round (played at the Dell Southampton)
Saturday 24th November 1979

Salisbury captain Dave Verity shakes hands with the Millwall captain, watched by the referee and line officials.

Salisbury 1980/81

Back row, l/r: J. Topp (trainer), C. Guy, K. Hallam, unsure, M. Hibbs, D. Moss, D. Lennard, R. Haysom, A. Green, T. Coak, M. Oakley. *Front row:* R. Legg, P. Christopher, P. Dowthwate, D. Verity, P. Bishop, P. Tindall.

Alan Green who top scored for this season, was presented with a typewriter by the sponsers (Guarantee Office Equipment) on the pitch at Victoria Park on the following game versus Margate, for scoring a hat-trick in three consecutive games. Andover Town(h) 18th September, S.L.Cup – Ashford(a) 20th September – and Margate(h) 27th September, Beazer Homes Southern.

photo supplied by Robin North

Manager/Coach Robin North at Stratford Road in the early 1970s.

Robin North: Inside five minutes of a match away to Yeovil while playing for Andover, I put in a strong tackle on Kenny Pound. There was a loud crack and I thought I'd broken his leg but looking down I saw it was mine. Dennis Heagren our captain took me to a nearby cottage hospital, then left. I was on a small trolley waiting for some attention. I was still there at the end of 90 mins when Dennis came to see my progress. He offered to take me to Winchester (he ran his own taxi business) so we set off on the long 80-mile journey and I think he found every hole in the road !

Southampton Team 1980-81

photo by kind permission of David Bull

Back row, l/r: Golac, Nicholl, Watson, Katalinic, Wells, Waldron, George, Hebberd.
Front: Boyer, Williams, Holmes, Keegan, Channon, Baker, McCartney

The photograph above was included as it shows Nick Holmes the Salisbury City F.C. manager in his younger days (age 26) when he was a consistent member of Southampton F.C., scoring a total of 64 goals His first team appearances of 539 were only bettered by Terry Paine and Mike Channon (here aged 32).

Paul Christopher and Cyril Smith's testimonial.
Salisbury versus Bournemouth AFC on Monday 25th April 1983.

Paul Christopher and Cyril Smith.

Trevor Morgan scores the opening goal for Bournemouth from a George Best cross.

Bournemouth AFC: *from:* Leigh, I., Heffernan, T., Sulley, C., Spackman, N., Brignull, P., Impey, J., Dawtry, K., Best, G., Beck, J., Morgan, T., Lee, T., Nightingale, M., Graham,. M., Allen, K., Williams, K.
Salisbury *from:* Pullen, C., Cranmer, B., Battams, G., Green, K., Golac, I., Haysom, R., Diaper, B., Frost, L., Hibbs, M., Thompson, I., Christopher, P., Newark, S., Brooks, K., Butler, G.
*Referee:*Glasson, A.R. (Salisbury). *Linesmen:* Tilley, K.R. (Durrington).Nash, A. (Codford)

Right: Guesting for Salisbury was the Yugoslav International, Ivan Golac, seen here with an admirer.

George Best in amongst the daisies at Victoria Park.

The match at Victoria Park, with the magnetism of George Best, pulled in nearly 2000 spectators, Salisbury's best crowd for a decade. Best's girlfriend the former Miss World, Mary Stavin also watched the game. The final score was 2-0 in Bournemouth's favour.

Barry Cranmer's Testimonial 23rd April 1990

Some of the Saints players with Barry Cranmer, *Back row, left/right:* Dodd, Cockerill, Moore, Andrews, Adams, Flowers, Ruddock and Shearer. *Front row, left/right:* Rod Wallace, Case, Barry Cranmer, Rideout and Cherednik.

April 1991

Pictured here is City Mayor Kay Cooper Joel, putting her signature to a Salisbury Football Club petition, which was aimed at defeating the opposition to the proposals for upgrading the facilities at Victoria Park. County councillor Greg Condliffe (*far left*) told a gathering that £500,000 plans to improve sub-standard facilities at the club were essential for its survival in the Beazer Homes League. Geoff Butler the team manager (*centre*) said, 'that when the people of Salisbury learnt of all the aspects of the development and, not the misleading information put through people's doors, that they would choose to back us'.

Marlow 3 Salisbury 3
19/11/92
replay
Salisbury 2 Marlow 2
(lost 3-4 penalties)

John Simpkins

These were the players picked by Manager Geoff Butler for the two games versus Marlow.

Mark Payne

Dave Green

Roger Emms

Gary Fletcher

Kevin Bale

Gordon Hobson

Chris Shaw

Dave Maskell
(sub)

John Gomersall
(sub)

Ian Chalk

Sean Sanders

Peter Loveridge

J. Simpkins from Bashley.
M. Payne from Hungerford.
Dave Green from Swanage.
P. Loveridge fee of £5750 paid to Dorchester.
R. Emms free from Andover.
G. Fletcher small fee paid to Brockenhurst.
G. Hobson player coach, 500 league games, Lincoln & Saints

Geoff Butler

Chris Shaw 2nd spell originally from Bournemouth A.F.C.
S. Sanders from Andover 1987.
I. Chalk local, prev. Wrexham, Swindon, Peterborough.
D. Maskell, Waterlooville, Bashley, Andover and B'stoke. Gomersall from Andover.
K. Bale, Maidenhead, Newbury and Andover.

Salisbury F.C. V Marlow Town 1st Round F.A. Cup (replay) 10th December 1992

Left: Man of the match, Sean Sanders jumps over the 'keeper as he clutches the ball from Salisbury's attacking forward.

Right: Marlow 'keeper is in the net but unfortunately for the Whites the ball is not.

Left: Sean Sanders turns away in delight, after diving full-length where all the boots were flying, believing he had surely scored Salisbury's winner. The 'goal' was ruled offside, not Sean but another Salisbury forward standing out by the corner flag, who was in no-way interfering with play.

Hung Dang (Vietnamese born, won 10 England schoolboy caps) far right, scores Salisbury's first goal in the 4-0 beating of Canterbury City in the 1992/93 season.

PDW: Salisbury are on the attack and Jeff Hodgkins has run out to the wing taking a couple of defenders with him, leaving Alan Tyler free. The ball breaks back and a 50-50 ball falls between Mike Whitehouse and an opposing defender. I close one eye, hardly daring to look...........crunch, the defender sails up in the air and Hodgkins turns to us (spectators) and says 'thank heaven he's on our bl**dy side'.

Hey look that's me at Victoria Park, in the 1992/93 season – but who is me? Do I still follow the Whites, maybe I'm now playing for them, or England even?

Presentation time for the 1992/93 season.

Sean Sanders (*centre*) with three trophies one of which is 'Players Player of the Year' which was kindly donated by supporter, Tony Waite.

Mark Payne receives the 'Supporters Player of the Year' from a proud Joan Wilmer.

Keith Miller presents Sean Sanders with a 'Man of Match' award.

John Harvey is seen here presenting Keith Miller vice-chairman of Salisbury City F.C. with a cheque from the Supporters Club for £1500. This brought the total donated to the Club since its formation in 1947 to £300,000.

Home of the Whites is starting to look its age, as Sean Sanders mesmerises the opposition. Also in the picture for Salisbury are Kevan Bale (*right*) and Roger Emms (*centre*).

The final whistle, May 1st 1993 at Baldock. Salisbury 'promoted'. Sean Sanders shakes the linesman's hand and Mark Payne No. 7 white shirt celebrates. Kevin Phillips (No. 7 dark shirt) walks off. Disappointment was to follow when promotion was denied.   *photo provided by Tom Kelly*

Salisbury clinch the Championship – 11th May 1995
Beazer Homes Southern Division
V
Wealdstone

Salisbury leaving the field at Victoria Park applaud the crowd. The Whites won 3-1 with goals from Ian Chalk 2 and Simon Browne, the match attendance was 627.

Salisbury team: Weaver, Burns, Baird, Blackler, Emms, Morrell, Mulkern, Clements, Lovell, Chalk, Browne,. *subs:* Payne, Manson.

The players decided that Geoff Butler needed an early bath.

Aerial view of Victoria Park the home of S.C.F.C. 1947–1997.

Salisbury F.C. V Tottenham Hotspur – 14th October 1993

The Salisbury team for the match included: Steve Weaver, Mark Payne, Barry Blankley, Simon Browne, Roger Emms, Barry Cranmer, Chris Shaw, Paul Odey, Sean Sanders, Ian Chalk and Brett Ball.

Left: Simon Browne (No 3) is beaten in this Tottenham attack.

Right: The fleet of foot Sean Sanders dazzles a Spurs defender with his ball control.

Left: Salisbury's Brett Ball's shot crashing past the well-beaten Ian Walker and into the Tottenham net.

Match attendance 736

On the 4th of August 1997, Simon Browne leads out the team for the friendly against Bournemouth A.F.C. This was the match chosen for the opening of the Ray McEnhill Stadium. Salisbury lost 3-1 in a entertaining game with Bournemouth showing a good approach throughout. Simon Browne became the Whites first ever goal-scorer at the new stadium.

I remember him – what's his name?

Many, many, many, many, many players have played for S.C.F.C. over these last 60 years. Here are but a few, who are mainly from the 90s + a sprinkling from the late 60s, 70s and 21st century. Can you name any of them. To stop all the arguments (but possibly start a few) and so you can sleep at night the answers are on page 492.

It states within the first few pages of this book, 'a grateful acknowledgement for the use of photos supplied by the Salisbury Journal'. Well a great many of them will have been taken by either of these two lads. David Smith, (*left*) who retired on Tues 6th March 2007 after 42 years and Roger Elliott who is still there and going strong after a mere 35 years.

I do my best to distract Roger from his lens when I see him at the Raymac. by talking about his greater passion, Bob Dylan. Only once did I get close, but the Journal still printed his picture.

They must have many a laugh when they first print out their photographs. I'm still waiting to see the Journal's policy when the Raymac. has its first 'streaker', will it be a 'real swinger', a 'policeman's helmet' or will Roger unfortunately be discussing Dylan's 'Never- Ending Tour' at the time with yours truly !　　　　　　　　*pdw*

A typical day in the life of the travelling 'White Army'

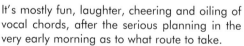

It's mostly fun, laughter, cheering and oiling of vocal chords, after the serious planning in the very early morning as to what route to take.

☆

☆

Bottom five photos pdw.

Some of the journeys are many, many, many miles away, i.e. Histon, Bishops Stortford, Nottingham, Cambridge, Lewes, Braintree, Newport, etc. etc. and yet the ever increasing support is always there. In most cases the good humour and laughter on the outward journeys is matched by the fun and high spirits on the return treks. With the success that the Whites have enjoyed these last few seasons, when they are defeated, no-one seems to dwell upon it for very long. I for one have realised that the world does not revolve round a game of football (put it down to growing older), Nick Holmes is not a `saint', the team aren't ALL Arnie's and finishing in the top six, is not for a place in Europe.................yet........................maybe in 2012 ! ! !

All photos except below from pdw.

What are football matches without supporters. Imagine the World Cup Final in an empty stadium, impossible, could the players even perform? Here are but a few more of that loyal band of supporters that follow the Whites – most games having a good time !

above photo pdw

Remember 2003/04 and the F.A. Cup?
An excellent cup run, which resulted in another visit to a famous ground.

Sheffield bound.......Salisbury City F.C. Manager, Nick Holmes and his family.
l/r: Lyndsey, (Matt's wife) Nick (Jr), Matt, Nick, Carolyn and Kim.

Left: This was a story of bags of effort, plenty of style, sackloads of chances, loads of pressure but only one goal and unfortunately Westbury scored as many, so it's all to be done again.

Forget the long punt and odd bounce, Kevin Sawyer, scores against his opposite number to make it 5-1 versus Lymington & New Milton in the 2003/04 season.

Kevin on his goal: It was the first time I'd taken a penalty in a game but I'd practised them in training.
Nick Holmes: I didn't think anyone else was up for it and Kev's got a terrific left foot.
Andy Cook: We practised them for the Westbury replay, just in case and Kevin was smashing them in.

The following six pages contain photos that I could not squeeze in elsewhere. Another magical season from the Whites – 2006/2007, fittingly is the 60th year of Salisbury City F.C. This one season sums up all that has gone before, top games, good crowds, exciting cup ties and plenty of fun. Long may it last !

Top 3 photos Southern Echo

Top 2 photos from VT F.C. v Salisbury 2nd Qualifying Round F.A. Cup. Holmes and Turk are in the thick of it all.

☆

left: Eastleigh v Salisbury 3rd Qual. Round F.A. Cup. Tommy letting them know he's about.

☆

☆

Five photos from 4th Qualifying Round F.A. Cup. Fisher Athletic v Salisbury City F.C. of happy fans and players ready for the off, during the match and team celebrating at the happy ending.

Happy players and fans from Salisbury City v Fleetwood Town
1st Round F.A. Cup.

Who will ever forget Salisbury City F.C. v Nottingham Forest
2nd Round F.A. Cup? – surely not anybody in the photos below,

☆

☆

FA CUP
2nd ROUND REPLAY

SALISBURY CITY FC
away to
NOTTINGHAM FOREST

COACH TICKET ONLY
Tuesday 12th December 2006

COACHES LEAVE FROM:
Coach Station, Millstream Approach, Central Car Park
Leaves at 2:00pm
AND THEN
Raymond McEnhill Stadium
Leaves at 2.30pm

ABSOLUTELY NO ALCOHOL & NO SMOKING ON THE COACH

COACH TICKET PRICE £13

☆

photo above pdw

These two facing pages feature the Raymac. Forest match and the replay at the City Ground Nottingham.

Above photo: with kind permission of Richard Hudd/Western Daily Press   Above photo Daily Echo

ADULT

E.ON F.A Cup Rnd 2 Replay

The City Ground is a smoke free venue
Forest v Salisbury City

Tue 12 Dec, 2006   Kick Off 7:45 pm

BRIDGFORD LOWER - BLOCK X

Block	Row	Seat Number	Price
X2	U	128	£10.00

Turnstile 49-56   Stair 10

Please quote client reference   95500   Away Supporters

Probably the best photo to finish with, the present home of S.C.F.C. seen from the air, The Ray McEnhill Stadium. By the time this book is printed it will have seen a few changes. Two 75-seater stands and full terracing will be in place opposite the main stand. Further terracing behind the 'City end' goal and on the fourth side to the far tea-bar, will have brought the Raymac. capacity up to over 5000...............Cheers again Ray, for that 'first big kick-off'. pdw

Busy, busy, busy to meet the looming deadline. This was a very, very, very cold day with a 60+ wind blowing straight down the pitch. Sometimes the camera tells fibs..........

as here it could be a lovely spring day and, like in the top photo of the Raymac................even the car park looks flat ! !   photos× 4 pdw

caricatures

These following drawings are not anybody's Top 10, 20, 30 or whatever; they just have that certain 'style'. Somewhere in their make-up is the key which the cartoonist latches on to; its all light-hearted, and brings the book nearly to its conclusion on a non-to serious note – maybe bringing a smile to your face ....if your not one of the drawings.

'the Whites' commander at the back Aaron Cook, whose No. 1 team after 'City' is the blues of Pompey.

Matty Tubbs, Matty, Matty Tubbs, scored many a goal for Salisbury

'Mooncat, Mooncat', frightens most no. 5s....without even touching the ball

'Saint's Alive', it's the boss ! !

'Big Kev', was probably the Whites best goal-keeper ever........... at taking penalties.

When Bashley embarrassed
Salisbury 6-1 at the
Raymac., Paul Sales easily
scored 4 of them.

Much travelled
`Danger Man',
Shaun Hale

Hope his initials means all for
the Whites ! ! !
Luke Prince

Salisbury managers = 3,
all seen by Scotty B.

All drawings
are by
Phil Smith
words
pdw

salisbury statistics

1947/48 F.A. Cup versus	res.	goalscorer	gate	1947/48 Amateur Cup versus	res.	goalscorer	gate
Winchester City(a)	1-0	Smith	1800	Chippenham United(h)	7-0	Fisher(3), Child, Rogers(3)	1800
Basingstoke Town(h)	5-1	Fisher(2), Colmer Rogers, Parker	1150	Swindon Victoria(h)	5-3	Miller(2), Rogers Fisher, Parker	n.a.
Newport I.O.W.(h)	0-0		2857	Purton(a)	1-1	Childs	n.a.
replay (a)	0-2		3000	*replay* (h)	4-0	Fisher(2), Miller, Noss	n.a.
				Pewsey (a)	2-3	Rogers, Fisher	n.a.

1947/48 Western League Division II versus	H	goalscorer	gate	A	goalscorer	gate
B.A.C. Res.	5-1	Child(3), Rogers, Smith	2700	4-2	Pearce(2), Child, Parker	n.a.
Cheltenham Rs	4-1	Fisher, Parker, Child, Rogers	1300	4-3	Child(2), Miller, Bayford	n.a.
Chippenham Town Rs	9-0	Rogers(5), Smith(2) Miller, Child	2000	1-0	Williams	n.a.
Cinderford Town	5-0	Fisher(3), Smith, Colmer	n.a.	0-1		n.a.
Dorchester Town	3-1	Fisher, Smith, Rogers	3000	5-1	Fisher(2), Parker, Williams, Child	n.a.
Douglas (Bristol)	7-0	Smith(2), Pearce, Abbott, Rogers, Parker, Child	2000	1-3	Scullard (pen)	n.a.
Frome Town	4-0	Miller(2), Fisher, Child	n.a.	5-0	Fisher(2), Child(2), Smith	n.a.
Hofmman Athletic	4-0	Bayford, Child, Williams, o.g.	n.a.	2-0	Bayford, Child	n.a.
Nt. Smelting Co.	9-2	Fisher(5), Rogers(3), Williams	n.a.	1-3	Child	n.a.
R.A.F. Colerne	11-1	Fisher(5), Howard(3), Parker Smith, Williams	n.a.	5-1	Rogers(2), Miller, Colmer, Fisher	n.a.
R.A.F. Locking	10-1	Cavenagh(4), Smith(2), Child(2), Abbott, Bayford	n.a.	3-0	Fisher(2), Parker	n.a.
R.A.F. Melksham	6-0	Pearce(2), Parker(2), Smith, Rogers	n.a.	8-2	Child(2), Parker(2), Rogers(2), Fisher, Smith	n.a.
Stonehouse	9-0	Fisher(2), Parker(2), Smith, Rogers, Abbott, Scullard, Child	3000	4-2	Fisher, Abbott, Parker	n.a.
Swindon Town Rs	3-1	Fisher(2), Scullard	2000	2-1	Abbott, Child	n.a.
Trowbridge Town Rs	3-0	Fisher(3)	1500	2-1	Scullard, Abbott	n.a.
Welton Rovers	2-1	Fisher, Scullard	n.a.	1-2	Colmer	n.a.
Weymouth	1-1	Parker	8902	2-1	Miller, Rogers	4200

Leading goalscorer for the 1947/48 season was Roy Fisher with 34 goals.

1947/48 Western League Division II

	P	W	D	L	F	A	Pts
Salisbury	34	29	1	4	145	33	59
Weymouth	34	26	4	4	148	37	56
Cheltenham Town Res	34	25	3	6	142	42	53
Welton Rovers	34	21	3	10	85	49	45
Frome Town	33	22	0	11	114	76	44
Hoffman Athletic	34	19	5	10	79	50	43
Trowbridge Town Res	33	17	5	11	92	59	39
Swindon Town Res.	34	17	4	13	95	76	38
Douglas	34	18	2	14	104	88	38
Dorchester Town	34	13	6	15	64	79	32
Cinderford Town	34	12	7	15	87	103	31
National Smelting Co.	34	13	5	16	80	102	31
Stonehouse	34	7	7	20	64	113	21
Chippenham Town Res.	34	8	4	22	63	117	20
R.A.F. Locking	33	9	1	23	52	126	19
R.A.F. Melksham	34	7	4	23	63	136	18
R.A.F. Colerne	33	6	4	23	64	146	16
B.A.C. Res.	34	2	1	31	48	154	5

Unplayed matches ignored in the final table.

1948/49 F.A. Cup versus	res.	goalscorer	gate
Purton (h)	1-0	Parker	3000
W.C.Mental Hos. (a)	3-0	Fisher, Parker(2)	n.a.
Peasdown MW (a)	3-2	Parker(2), Fisher	2500
Trowbridge Town (a)	1-4	Fisher	4546

1948/49 Amateur Cup versus	res.	goalscorer	gate
Shepton M (a)	8-2	Fisher(2), Rogers(2) Carter(2), Parker(2)	700
Welton Rovers (h)	3-2	Fisher(2). Rogers	n.a.
Frome Town(a)	1-4	Fisher	n.a.
replay(ineligible player)(h)	2-1	Carter, Rogers	2300
Purton(h)	3-1	Money, Parker(2)	2200
Barnstaple Town(a)	5-2	Fisher(2), Carter, Parker, Child	3111
Wimbledon(a)	1-2	Child	6500

1948/49 Western League Division I versus	H	goalscorer	gate	A	goalscorer	gate
Bath City Res	6-2	Rogers(4), Smith, Carter	n.a.	0-0		n.a.
Bristol City Colts	5-1	Smith(2), Abbott, Fisher, Parker	n.a.	3-1	Roger, Smith, Scullard	n.a.
Bristol Rovers Colts	1-1	Williams	n.a.	2-2	Child, Fisher	n.a.
Chippenham Town	3-1	Fisher, Scullard(2 penalties)	n.a.	3-4	Rogers(2), Parker	n.a.
Clandown	4-0	Fisher(3), Child	n.a.	1-2	Fisher	n.a.
Clevedon Town	4-0	Smith(2), Carter, Fisher	2300	3-4	Hall(2), Carter	n.a.
Glastonbury	4-1	Rogers(3), Smith	1700	2-4	Fisher(2)	n.a.
Paulton Rovers	0-1		n.a.	2-3	Fisher, Abbott	n.a.
Peasdown MW	3-0	Smith, Fisher, Parker	2100	0-3		n.a.
Poole Town	0-1		n.a.	4-0	Fisher(2), Smith, Child	n.a.
Portland United	1-0	Fisher	n.a.	1-1	Bligh	n.a.
Soundwell	3-1	Fisher, Carter, Parker	n.a.	0-1		n.a.
Street	2-1	Smith, Money	3000	3-4	Fisher(2), Parker	n.a.
Trowbridge Town	1-0	Fisher	6500	3-4	Carter, Parker, Fisher	4130
Wells City	3-0	Fisher, Carter, Smith	n.a.	3-2	Fisher, Roger, o.g.	n.a.
Weymouth Res	1-0	Child	5100	1-2	Rogers	5000
Yeovil Town Res	4-2	Scullard, Fisher, Child, o.g.	2000	2-2	Fisher, Smith	n.a.

Leading goalscorer for this season 1948/49 season was Roy Fisher with 24 goals.

Salisbury team for the opening fixture in Western League Division I versus Glastonbury was: Fountain, Duncan, Pickering, Abbott, Williams, Colmer, Rogers, Smith, Fisher, Parker and Child. Salisbury F.C. Supporters Club membership reached 1010 at beginning of February 1949. The Western League benefit match versus Weymouth at Victoria Park in August 1948 drew a crowd of 3400, Weymouth won 3-1.

1948/49 Western League Division I

	P	W	D	L	F	A	Pts
Glastonbury	34	24	6	4	93	50	54
Trowbridge Town	34	22	6	6	109	44	50
Weymouth	34	22	4	8	100	44	48
Chippenham Town	34	19	5	10	94	50	43
Street	34	18	4	12	90	58	40
Salisbury	**34**	**17**	**5**	**12**	**78**	**51**	**39**
Bristol Rovers Colts	34	12	12	10	65	63	36
Paulton Rovers	34	13	6	15	57	64	32
Wells City	34	14	4	16	51	67	32
Bath City Reserves	34	14	4	16	63	92	32
Poole Town	34	13	5	16	59	65	31
Soundwell	34	13	5	16	76	100	31
Peasdown M.W.	34	12	3	19	54	81	27
Clandown	34	12	3	19	55	102	27
Portland United	34	11	4	19	51	70	26
Yeovil Town Reserves	34	7	12	15	61	81	26
Clevedon	34	5	10	19	48	74	20
Bristol City Colts	34	7	4	23	57	105	18

1949/50 F.A. Cup versus	res.	goalscorer	gate	1949/50 Amateur Cup versus	res.	goalscorer	gate
Warminster Tn (h)	7-0	Carter(2), Fisher(2) Rogers(2), Parker	3200	Winchester City(a) *replay*(h)	1-1 6-5	Fisher Carter(2), Rogers, Parker, Fisher,	2319 3142
Bath City (a)	2-0	Child, Parker	5412			Norridge	
Clandown (a)	6-1	Fisher(2), Child(2) Carter, Parker	1600	Wealdstone (h)	4-1	Fisher(3) o.g.	5358
Trowbridge Town(a)	0-1		7719	Dulwich Hamlet (h)	0-2		7375

1949/50 Western League Division I							
versus	H	goalscorer	gate	A	goalscorer		gate
Bath City Res	4-0	Fisher, Parker,.Rogers, Carter	2000	3-1	Carter, Fisher, Heagren		n.a.
Bristol Rovers Colts	0-1		n.a.	1-1	Witt(penalty)		n.a.
Cheltenham Town Res	3-2	Rogers, Smith, Carter	n.a.	1-2	o.g.		n.a.
Chippenham Town	0-0		n.a.	2-7	Parker, Fisher		n.a.
Chippenham United	3-2	Parker(2), Child	2500	1-3	Perkins		1100
Clandown	3-4	Carter, Fisher, Witt	n.a.	0-2			n.a.
Glastonbury	1-2	Fisher	3000	0-2			n.a.
Paulton Rovers	6-0	Witt(3), Smith(2), Norridge	1700	1-5	Fisher		n.a.
Peasdown MW	3-2	Fisher(2), Howard	n.a.	0-3			n.a.
Poole Town	2-3	Fisher(2)	1900	1-4	Carter		n.a.
Portland United	2-0	Fisher, Abbott	n.a.	3-1	Fisher, Abbott, Heagren		n.a.
Soundwell	7-1	Fisher(2), Carter(2), Norridge Smith, Perkins	2300	2-0	Fisher(2)		n.a.
Street	1-2	Carter	2700	0-0			n.a.
Trowbridge Town	3-0	Norridge, Smith, Rogers	4100	3-5	Fisher, Carter, Scullard		3450
Wells City	0-4		n.a.	0-3			1100
Weymouth Res	2-1	Fisher(2)	2000	1-0	Fisher		4000
Yeovil Town Res	4-1	Rogers(2), Fisher, Smith	1200	1-2	Rogers		n.a.

Leading goalscorer for 1949/50 season was Roy Fisher with 22 goals.

Salisbury F.C. team versus Dulwich Hamlet on 28th January 1950 was: Amor, Duncan, Scullard, Reinman, Abbott, Money, Rogers, Carter, Fisher, Parker and Norridge. On the 24th April 1950 Salisbury played Clandown at home, at half-time the score was 0-4 but by full-time Salisbury had pulled back to 3-4 and were pressing at the final whistle. On 26th April 1950 Salisbury's Hants League team played host to Southampton A in a Hants League match. Appearing for the visitors were Wilkins, Dare, Judd and Sillett who were to make a considerable number of 1st-team appearances later. An ex-Salisbury old boy, Eric Fountain was in goal.

1949/50 Western League Division I	P	W	D	L	F	A	Pts
Wells City	34	22	7	5	87	43	51
Poole Town	34	22	7	5	88	45	51
Glastonbury	34	23	4	7	78	38	50
Trowbridge Town	34	22	5	7	104	40	49
Cheltenham Town Reserves	34	21	4	9	91	58	46
Chippenham United	34	16	8	10	57	49	40
Bristol Rover Colts	34	15	7	12	54	50	37
Chippenham Town	34	13	7	14	77	70	33
Street	34	12	9	13	71	75	33
Weymouth Reserves	34	13	5	16	67	49	31
Salisbury	**34**	**14**	**3**	**17**	**64**	**66**	**31**
Yeovil Town Reserves	34	13	5	16	55	102	31
Paulton Rovers	34	12	3	19	60	76	27
Peasedown M.W.	34	8	9	17	56	82	25
Portland United	34	8	6	20	44	74	22
Clandown	34	8	5	21	46	80	21
Soundwell	34	6	6	22	61	116	18
Bath City Reserves	34	5	6	23	45	103	16

1950/51 F.A. Cup versus	res.	goalscorer	gate	1950/51 Amateur Cup versus	res.	goalscorer	gate
Westbury United (h)	6-1	Fisher(3), Grayer Scullard, Smith	..n.a.	B'mouth Gas Wks(a)	3-0	Fisher, Carter, Grayer	1600
Chippenham United(h)	2-1	Fisher, Howard	3500	Walton & Hersham(a)	0-0		..n.a.
Clandown (h)	4-2	Fisher(2), Carter Grayer	3800	*replay*(h)	1-3	Fisher	5100
Trowbridge Town(h)	1-0	Howard	7000				
Gloucester City(a)	1-2	Smith	6500				

1950/51 Western League Division I

versus	H	goalscorer	gate	A	goalscorer	gate
Barnstaple Town	1-2	Howard	n.a.	2-2	Witt, Norridge	n.a.
Bristol Rovers Colts	2-3	Howard, Smith	n.a.	1-0	Grayer	n.a.
Cheltenham Tn Res	1-2	Fisher	n.a.	1-0	Smith	n.a.
Chippenham Town	1-0	Howard	n.a.	1-2	Fisher	n.a.
Chippenham United	2-1	Scullard, Grayer	n.a.	1-2	Heath	n.a.
Clandown	3-0	Fisher, Parker, Howard	n.a.	1-1	Howard	n.a.
Dorchester Town	1-1	Carter	n.a.	0-2		n.a.
Glastonbury	1-1	Fisher	n.a.	0-1		n.a.
Paulton Rovers	5-2	Fisher(3), Carter, Howard	n.a.	1-3	Fisher	n.a.
Peasdown MW	4-1	Smith(2), Witt(pen), Parker	n.a.	3-1	Grayer, Howard, Scullard	n.a.
Poole Town	0-2		n.a.	1-3	Fisher	n.a.
Portland United	8-2	Fisher(4), Parker(2), Carter, Grayer	n.a.	4-3	Fisher(4)	n.a.
Street	0-0		n.a.	1-5	Fisher	n.a.
Trowbridge Town	4-2	Heagren, Fisher, Carter, Grayer	n.a.	1-5	Grayer	n.a.
Wells City	3-3	Parker, Grayer, Norridge	n.a.	1-2	Fisher	n.a.
Weymouth Res	2-0	Fisher(2)	n.a.	2-2	Clemence(2)	n.a.
Yeovil Town Res	2-1	Smith, Howard	n.a.	4-1	Grayer(4)	n.a.

> Leading goalscorer for 1950/51 season was Roy Fisher with 22 goals.

25/11/50 Wiltshire played Sussex in Salisbury in the Southern Counties Amateur Championship. Team: Amor (Salisbury), Page (Swindon Town), Turner *(Calne & Harris), Davenport (Chippenham United), Haywood (Devizes Town), Haycock (Trowbridge Town), Howard (Salisbury), Hancock (Trowbridge Town),** Atyeo (Westbury United), Carter and Grayer (Salisbury). On 10th March 1951, Salisbury played host to London University in a friendly fixture. Salisbury: Amor, Duncan, Scullard, Heagren, Witt, Abbott, Howard, Carter, Fisher, Parker and Grayer. Somewhat surprisingly the visitors won 3-2. Grayer scored both Salisbury's goals.
*The present day Calne Town were originally Calne & Harris. Harris from the large sausage factory that dominated the area.
**John Atyeo went on to play for Portsmouth, Bristol City and he also represented England.

1950/51 Western League Division I

	P	W	D	L	F	A	Pts
Glastonbury	34	26	6	2	102	27	58
Wells City	34	22	9	3	83	39	53
Chippenham Town	34	18	8	8	86	48	44
Chippenham United	34	18	6	10	72	44	42
Trowbridge Town	34	17	7	10	83	49	41
Barnstaple Town	34	18	4	12	71	62	40
Poole Town	34	18	3	13	71	71	39
Salisbury	**34**	**14**	**7**	**13**	**65**	**58**	**35**
Dorchester Town	34	13	8	13	64	58	34
Street	34	13	8	13	74	69	34
Weymouth Res	34	13	6	15	54	56	32
Cheltenham Town Res	34	12	7	15	56	46	31
Bristol Rovers Colts	34	11	8	15	60	85	30
Clandown	34	10	9	15	49	58	29
Paulton Rovers	34	9	9	16	62	75	27
Portland United	34	6	7	21	56	112	19
Yeovil Town Res	34	8	3	23	38	79	19
Peasdown M.W.	34	1	3	30	25	123	5

1951/52 F.A. Cup				1951/52 Amateur Cup			
versus	**res.**	**goalscorer**	**gate**	**versus**	**res.**	**goalscorer**	**gate**
Calne Town (h)	2-0	Rolls(2)	2074	B'mouth Gas Wks(h)	6-1	Rolls(2), Heagren(2) Howard, Carter	1811
Frome Town(a)	3-2	Rolls(3)	n.a.				
Chippenham Town(h)	1-1	Smith	2662	Brentwood & Warley(a)1-2		Carter	1200
replay (a)	1-2	Dennis(penalty)	1400				

		1951/52 Western League Division I					
versus	**H**	**goalscorer**	**gate**	**A**	**goalscorer**		**gate**
Barnstaple Town	1-1	Dawson	2180	0-2			n.a.
Bath City Res	2-2	Fidler(2)	1250	1-2	Heagren (penalty)		1000
Bristol Rovers Colts	4-0	Howard(2), Rolls, Smith	1168	1-4	Duncan		...28
Cheltenham Tn Res	2-0	Howse, Fidler	1750	2-1	Fidler, Lister		1000
Chippenham Town	2-5	Norridge, Abbott	2069	0-6			800
Chippenham United	6-2	Trickett(3), Carter(2), Fisher	1350	1-1	Lidster		n.a.
Clandown	1-2	Rolls	n.a.	1-1	Trickett		300
Dorchester	4-0	Rolls(2), Smith(2)	1804	0-3			500
Glastonbury	3-3	Smith(2), Heagren	1721	1-3	Rolls		n.a.
Paulton Rovers	1-0	Howse	1250	3-4	Howse(2), Dennis (penalty)		700
Poole Town	2-3	Rolls, Smith	2063	3-0	Fidler (2 penalties), Fisher		n.a.
Portland United	3-3	Carter, Norridge, Rolls	1895	3-0	Trickett, Cutbush, Fisher		300
Stonehouse	0-2		1230	1-1	Howse		700
Street	3-3	Norridge, Rolls, Aitken	n.a.	0-3			500
Trowbridge Town	3-2	Heagren(2 penalties), Fisher	1790	1-4	Rolls		2140
Wells City	2-2	Fisher, Trickett	n.a.	0-2			650
Weymouth Res	5-0	Cutbush(3), Howse, Trickett	2500	0-1			2150

Leading goalscorer for 1951/52 season was **Fred Rolls** with 9 goals.

Salisbury team for the opening fixture versus Poole Town on 25th August 1951 was: Amor, Duncan, Sheppard, Young, Abbott, Bartlett, Howard, Smith, Rolls, Longlan and Norridge. Also in the same year on 24th of November Salisbury entertained Bournemouth Gasworks Athletic in the 4th Qualifying Round of the Amateur Cup winning 6-1. In the visitors line-up were No. 10 'Josh' Jenkins who two years earlier had assisted Salisbury in the Amateur Cup. At No. 7, was a young Derek Reeves aged 17, later to be a prolific scorer for Southampton.

Salisbury reached the semi-final of the Wiltshire Senior Cup. After beating Calne & Harris away 5-2 and Pinehurst Youth Centre at home 3-1, they lost to Westbury United 0-1 at Warminster in front of a gate of 2000.

1951/52 Western League Division I						
	P	**W**	**D**	**L**	**F**	**A**	**Pts**
Chippenham Town	34	23	4	7	103	41	50
Glastonbury	34	20	6	8	87	64	46
Barnstaple	34	18	6	10	87	62	42
Weymouth Res	34	18	5	11	84	54	41
Trowbridge Town	34	19	3	12	85	58	41
Stonehouse	34	15	7	12	82	61	37
Wells City	34	12	13	9	65	60	37
Bath City Res	34	14	8	12	53	51	36
Cheltenham Town Res	34	13	8	13	58	55	34
Street	34	14	6	14	65	71	34
Clandown	34	11	10	13	63	75	32
Salisbury	**34**	**10**	**9**	**15**	**62**	**68**	**29**
Dorchester Town	34	11	7	16	61	81	29
Chippenham United	34	10	8	16	59	70	28
Portland United	34	9	8	17	49	73	26
Paulton Rovers	34	10	5	19	64	96	25
Bristol Rovers Colts	34	6	11	17	46	75	23
Poole Town	34	8	6	20	50	106	22

1952/53 F.A. Cup				1952/53 Amateur Cup			
versus	res.	goalscorer	gate	versus	res.	goalscorer	gate
Welton Rovers(h)	7-1	Fisher(2), Cutbush(2) Martin(2), Fidler	2000	Clevedon Town (a)	1-2	Howse	800
Westbury United(h)	4-1	Fidler(2), Fisher Cutbush	2060				
Chippenham Town(h)	3-1	Sainsbury, Howse(2pen.)	2800				
Trowbridge Town(h)	0-2		4100				

1952/53 Western League Division I						
versus	H	goalscorer	gate	A	goalscorer	gate
Barnstaple Town	2-2	Cutbush, Witt	3640	2-4	Fisher, Cutbush	n.a.
Bath City Res	2-2	Howse, Rogers	n.a.	4-4	Honey(2), Sainsbury, Hibberd	2050
Bideford Town	0-5		2100	1-1	Abbott	1500
Bridgwater Town	5-1	Rogers(2), Heagren, Smith, Fisher	2060	3-3	Cutbush(2), Parker	1500
Chippenham Town	1-4	Fisher	1500	1-3	Sainsbury	1188
Chippenham United	0-2		2100	2-2	Smith, Fisher	700
Glastonbury	3-0	Smith(2), Heagren	n.a.	2-1	Honey, Glass	900
Clandown	4-1	Turner, Jenkins, Heagren(2)	1310	2-1	Fisher, Heagren	300
Dorchester Town	1-0	Hibberd	2300	3-2	Smith(2), Honey	700
Paulton Rovers	1-1	Fisher	1454	4-0	Honey, Glass, Fisher, Rogers	250
Portland United	2-1	Rogers, Honey	n.a.	1-1	Heagren	230
Stonehouse	2-1	Fisher, Heagren	1320	0-5		n.a.
Street	2-3	Cutbush, Heagren	n.a.	1-4	Honey	800
Trowbridge Town	2-4	Fisher, Rogers	2500	1-1	Cutbush	1600
Wells City	3-0	Smith, Glass, Fisher	1711	0-1		580
Weymouth Res	2-4	Smith, Jenkins	1503	1-1	Abbott	1490

Leading goalscorer for 1952/53 season was Roy Fisher with 10 goals.

On October 4th 1952 over 750 spectators visited Victoria Park to see the reserves play a friendly against the Royal Welsh Fusiliers. On November 15th, four coach-loads of Salisbury supporters travelled to Clevedon for the Amateur Cup match. Fulham visited Salisbury at Victoria Park on 25th April 1953 for a friendly, which the hosts won 2-0. The scorers were Jenkins and Fisher. The Fulham team consisted of Ronson, Gibson, Lowe, Smith, Ashen, Healey, Dwight, Cronin, Taylor, Newcombe and Chamberlain.

Salisbury were defeated 6-2 away at Pinehurst Youth Centre in the opening round of the Wiltshire Senior Cup. Pinehurst were a particularly strong side at this time.

1952/53 Western League Division I							
	P	W	D	L	F	A	Pts
Barnstaple Town	32	18	8	6	77	37	44
Street	32	19	6	7	89	43	44
Trowbridge Town	32	17	7	8	76	48	41
Bideford	32	13	13	6	79	52	39
Chippenham Town	32	17	3	12	84	58	37
Weymouth Res	32	16	5	11	75	58	37
Chippenham United	32	15	5	12	62	62	35
Salisbury	**32**	**11**	**10**	**11**	**60**	**65**	**32**
Glastonbury	32	15	1	16	61	49	31
Bath City Res	32	10	11	11	64	63	31
Stonehouse	32	11	8	13	57	58	30
Portland United	32	11	8	13	66	77	30
Bridgwater Town	32	12	4	16	58	73	28
Wells City	32	9	6	17	52	71	24
Clandown	32	7	9	16	40	74	23
Dorchester Town	32	8	5	19	46	74	21
Paulton Rovers	32	6	5	21	42	125	17

versus	res.	goalscorer	gate
1953/54 F.A. Cup			
Andover Town(h)	2-1	Long, Hall	3200
Chippenham Town(a)	2-4	Muckles(2)	1700

versus	res	goalscorer	gate
1953/54 Wilts Premier Shield			
Chippenham Town(h)	2-0	Long, Taylor	2096
Trowbridge Town(h)	2-0	Fleming, Booth	2689
Swindon Town(a)	1-2	Hall	3662

1953/54 Western League Division I

versus	H	goalscorer	gate	A	goalscorer	gate
Barnstaple Town	1-0	Smith	3480	1-3	Hall	1400
Bath City Res	3-0	Cutbush(2), Hall	2050	0-5		1200
Bideford Town	5-1	Glass, Hall, Long, Rogers, Booth	2150	2-2	Hall, Smith	1400
Bridgwater Town	1-0	Smith	2150	0-4		n.a.
Chippenham Town	4-2	Fleming, Hall(2), Hiscock	n.a.	1-2	Long	1200
Chippenham United	2-1	Hall, Hasty	2600	0-1		n.a.
Clandown	6-0	Long(2), Cutbush(2), Hall, Smith	2100	5-3	Muckles(2), Hall(2), Booth	200
Dorchester Town	2-2	Smith, Hall	n.a.	2-2	Cutbush, Hall	1527
Glastonbury	2-0	Rogers, Witt	n.a.	1-1	Smith	n.a.
Ilfracombe Town	2-1	Long, Cutbush	1420	0-0		800
Poole Town	0-3		2340	2-3	Long, Smith	1900
Portland United	4-1	Hall(2), Rickard, Long	n.a.	1-3	Hall	550
Stonehouse	5-1	Fidler(2), Hall(2), Smith	1100	2-5	Fleming, Taylor	900
Street	2-0	Long, Booth	1980	2-2	Hall(2)	850
Trowbridge Town	4-2	Heagren, Taylor, Fidler, Hall	2902	3-2	Hall(2), Long	2400
Wells City	4-0	Muckles(2), Fisher, Witt(penalty)	2100	1-2	Long	550
Weymouth Res	3-0	Booth, Smith, Hall	2054	1-6	Muckles	2300

Leading goalscorer for 1953/54 season was Bill Hall with 23 goals.

At Victoria Park on the 9th of January 1954 Wiltshire played Hampshire in the Southern Counties Amateur Championship. Salisbury's D. Cutbush, E. Fidler and R. Mutton played for Hampshire while R. Weeks played for Wiltshire. On the 1st of May of the same year, Salisbury's team for the final league fixture at home versus Chippenham Town was: Goodwin, Turner, Booth, Heagren, Witt, Fleming, Hiscock, Smith, Hall, Cutbush and Long.

1953/54 Western League Division I

	P	W	D	L	F	A	Pts
Weymouth Res	34	21	4	9	102	53	46
Poole Town	34	18	8	8	73	49	44
Trowbridge Town	34	19	5	10	78	62	43
Barnstaple Town	34	17	7	10	74	42	41
Chippenham Town	34	18	5	11	79	49	41
Salisbury	**34**	**17**	**6**	**11**	**74**	**60**	**40**
Portland United	34	18	3	13	71	63	39
Wells City	34	15	7	12	63	68	37
Bridgwater Town	34	15	6	13	72	76	36
Bideford Town	34	13	8	13	70	66	34
Dorchester Town	34	14	5	15	79	69	33
Chippenham United	34	13	6	15	60	63	32
Glastonbury	34	12	8	14	59	70	32
Street	34	12	8	14	55	69	32
Bath City Res	34	10	6	18	40	66	26
Ilfracombe Town	34	9	5	20	40	77	23
Stonehouse	34	7	6	21	51	80	20
Clandown	34	4	5	25	29	87	13

	1954/55 F.A. Cup		
versus	**res.**	**goalscorer**	**gate**
Frome Town(h)	2-3	Fleming(2 pen.)	3100

1954/55 Wilts Premier Shield

versus	res	goalscorer	gate
Trowbridge Tn(h)	3-3	Prentice, Fleming, Fisher	2000
Trowbridge Tn(a)	3-1	Heagren(2), Rogers	n.a.
Chippenham Utd(a)	3-0	Masters, Smith, C., Timms	1350
Swindon Town(a)	0-1		3350

1954/55 Western League Cup

versus	res	goalscorer	gate
Chippenham Utd(a)	1-1	Rogers	n.a.
Chippenham Utd(h)	3-3	Stiff, Prentice, Kew	n.a.
Ilfracombe Town(h)	4-2	Hasty(2), Fleming, Prentice	n.a.
Frome Town(h)	1-1	Smith, C.	n.a.
Frome Town(a)	0-1		n.a.

1954/55 Western League Division I

versus	H	goalscorer	gate	A	goalscorer	gate
Barnstaple Town	2-0	Prentice, Timms	2680	0-4		1700
Bath City Res	0-1		1740	1-1	Kew	1900
Bideford Town	2-2	Stiff, Masters	n.a.	2-2	Prentice(2)	n.a.
Bridgwater Town	4-1	Long, Booth, Hasty	2270	2-4	Prentice, Masters	450
Bristol City Colts	3-0	Rolls(3, 1 penalty)	2800	1-0	Pinchbeck	29
Bristol Rover Colts	2-1	Rolls, Cutbush	2060	0-2	(Played at Eastville Stadium)	5500
Chippenham Town	3-3	Fleming(2, 1 penalty), Taylor	1990	5-2	Prentice(3), Long, Taylor	800
Chippenham United	3-2	Stiff, Pinchbeck, Timms	n.a.	1-1	Rolls	800
Dorchester Town	0-2		2620	1-3	Rolls	1000
Glastonbury	5-1	Prentice(2), Taylor, Cutbush, Fleming	2750	2-1	Pinchbeck, Timms	250
Ilfracombe Town	2-1	Kew, Prentice	n.a.	4-2	Fisher(2), Prentice(2)	360
Poole Town	1-1	Taylor	2725	4-1	Prentice(2), Long, Fisher	900
Portland United	6-0	Fleming(2), Stiff(2), Hasty Prentice	1980	1-2	Haines	550
Street	4-2	Prentice(2), Kew, Timms	2550	2-1	Timms(2)	500
Trowbridge Town	0-0		1400	1-2	Smith	2480
Wells City	3-2	Hiscock(3, 1 penalty)	1880	1-1	Heagren	455
Weymouth Res	3-1	Pinchbeck(2), Prentice	1500	0-1		1200

> **Leading goalscorer for 1954/55 season was Andy Prentice with 18 goals.**

> The Salisbury team for the opening fixture at home to Street was: Goodwin, Targett, Lewis, Fleming, Witt, Cutbush, Stiff, Timms Kew, Prentice and Long. On the 26th of February 1955 Wiltshire played Hampshire at Victoria Park. Salisbury had two players, P. Hasty and R. Vaughan, in the Hampshire side and A. Anderson played for Wiltshire.

1954/55 Western League Division I

	P	W	D	L	F	A	Pts
Dorchester Town	34	23	5	6	103	46	51
Chippenham Town	34	21	7	6	83	39	49
Bath City Res	34	22	4	8	87	52	48
Salisbury	**34**	**17**	**8**	**9**	**71**	**50**	**42**
Portland United	34	18	6	10	89	70	42
Bideford	34	18	6	10	69	56	42
Bridgwater Town	34	18	5	11	91	69	41
Poole Town	34	13	12	9	80	62	38
Bristol Rover Colts	34	16	5	13	73	55	37
Barnstaple Town	34	13	8	13	69	66	34
Trowbridge Town	34	14	5	15	65	55	33
Bristol City Colts	34	11	4	19	53	62	26
Weymouth Res	34	10	6	18	49	67	26
Chippenham United	34	10	5	19	57	97	25
Glastonbury	34	8	9	17	51	89	25
Wells City	34	5	9	20	49	90	19
Street	34	7	4	23	51	100	18
Ilfracombe	34	5	6	23	35	100	16

1955/56 F.A. Cup

versus	res.	goalscorer	gate	versus	res.	goalscorer	gate
Devizes Town(a)	2-0	Abbott, Fleming	1360	Chippenham Utd(a)	6-2	Prentice(3), Abbott(2) Oakley	2700
Bulford United(h)	3-0	Booth, Abbott, Prentice	3700				
Frome Town(h)	3-0	Abbott(2), Knight	3800	Weymouth(a)	2-3	Oakley, Prentice	6900
				1st Round Proper			

1955/56 Wilts Premier Shield

versus	res	goalscorer	gate
Chippenham Utd(a)	3-1	Oakley, Abbott, Prentice	n.a.
Chippenham Tn(a)	3-0	Knight, Abbott, Clancy	n.a.
Swindon Town(a)	0-2		2946

1955/56 Western League Cup

versus	res	goalscorer	gate
Trowbridge Tn(h)	2-2	Abbott(2)	n.a.
Trowbridge Tn(a)	3-1	Abbott(2), Prentice	n.a.
Frome Town(a)	4-1	Oakley, Prentice(2), Abbott	n.a.
Torquay Res(h)	2-0	Hiscock, Gilfillan	n.a.
Portland United(h)	6-2	Abbott(5), Fleming	n.a.
Chippenham Tn(a)	0-0		n.a.
Chippenham Tn(h)	3-0	Prentice(2), Fleming	n.a.

1955/56 Western League Division I

versus	H	goalscorer	gate	A	goalscorer	gate
Barnstaple Town	0-0		2700	2-1	Prentice, Abbott	n.a.
Bideford Town	0-0		850	1-1	o.g.	n.a.
Bridgwater Town	7-0	Abbott(4), Knight, Hiscock, Prentice	n.a.	4-1	Oakley, Abbott, Knight, Booth	n.a.
Bristol City Colts	4-1	Prentice, Clancy	1540	1-2	Abbott	35
Bristol Rover Colts	2-0	Prentice, Fleming	2450	2-1	Prentice, Clancy	45
Chippenham Town	1-1	Fleming	3300	1-0	Mignot	n.a.
Chippenham United	2-0	Abbott, Prentice	n.a.	2-1	Prentice, Clancy	900
Dorchester Town	2-0	Abbott(2)	n.a.	0-1		n.a.
Frome Town	4-0	Abbott(2), o.g, Uren.	1450	2-1	Prentice(2)	1150
Glastonbury	1-1	Hiscock	1200	2-2	Knight, Abbott	200
Poole Town	1-1	Prentice	4004	0-2		3000
Portland United	1-2	Abbott	1500	1-0	Fleming	450
Trowbridge Town	0-2		n.a.	0-3		3146
Wells City	2-0	Uren, Abbott	1300	9-0	Abbott(6), Prentice, Clancy, Knight	950
Weymouth Res	3-4	Fleming, Abbott, Clancy	2400	1-2	Abbott	n.a.
Yeovil Town Res	5-1	Prentice(3), Fleming, Clancy	2380	1-0	Abbott	1750

Leading goalscorer for 1955/56 season was Stan Abbott with 24 goals.

Salisbury team for their 1st home fixture on 31st of August 1955 versus Trowbridge Town: Kingston, Stone, Booth, Timms, Tuck, Fleming, Oakley, Knight, Abbott, Smith and Clancy. Adversity struck twice in the 1956 season in away matches. On 14th January Salisbury played at Chippenham Town with 10 men when Harry Delew was taken to hospital after a motorcycle crash on the way to the game. Ray Mignot was rushed by car from Salisbury where he was due to play with the reserves, and arrived at half-time. He scored the only goal of the match 10 minutes later. On 3rd March a car accident on the way to Portland, deprived Salisbury of the services of Stan Abbott and Jackie Knight. Tommy Williams, acting trainer was pressed into service at centre-forward. Salisbury played throughout with 10 players. Eddie Fleming scored the only goal to record another 1-0 win

1955/56 Western League Division I

	P	W	D	L	F	A	Pts
Trowbridge Town	32	24	2	6	100	36	50
Poole Town	32	20	7	5	79	33	47
Dorchester Town	32	21	4	7	106	57	46
Chippenham Town	32	20	4	8	70	50	44
Salisbury	**32**	**17**	**7**	**8**	**64**	**31**	**41**
Bideford	32	14	10	8	58	50	38
Portland United	32	16	3	13	87	76	35
Barnstaple Town	32	15	4	13	61	66	34
Weymouth Res	32	10	12	10	63	70	32
Frome Town	32	10	7	15	69	64	27
Yeovil Town Res	32	11	5	16	57	86	27
Bristol Rover Colts	32	10	4	18	49	65	24
Bristol City Colts	32	8	7	17	43	63	23
Wells City	32	8	7	17	53	92	23
Bridgwater Town	32	7	5	20	59	98	19
Chippenham United	32	7	5	20	54	90	19
Glastonbury	32	3	9	20	47	92	15

1956/57 F.A. Cup

versus	res.	goalscorer	gate
Warminster Town(a)	6-1	Abbott(3), Prentice(2), Wheeler	1500
Chippenham Town(h)	1-2	Clancy	n.a.

1956/57 Wilts Premier Shield				1956/57 Western League Cup			
versus	res	goalscorer	gate	versus	res	goalscorer	gate
Chippenham Tn(h)	2-0	Prentice(2)	800	Poole Town(h)	2-6	Knight, Prentice	n.a.
Swindon Town(h)	1-0	Noyce	3000	Poole Town(a)	0-1		n.a.

1956/57 Western League Division I

versus	H	goalscorer	gate	A	goalscorer	gate
Barnstaple Town	6-0	Noyce(3), Clancy(2), Uren	n.a.	2-4	Abbott, Clancy	n.a.
Bideford Town	4-0	Clancy(2), Prentice, Abbott	n.a.	0-1		n.a.
Bridgwater Town	4-0	Prentice(2), Knight, Abbott	n.a.	2-1	Knight, Abbott	n.a.
Bristol City Colts	1-2	Prentice	n.a.	0-1		n.a.
Bristol Rover Colts	3-2	Fleming, Knight, Wheeler	1200	2-1	Noyce, Prentice	n.a.
Chippenham Town	6-2	Wheeler(2 pen), Abbott(2) Knight, Prentice	n.a.	1-1	Uren	n.a.
Chippenham United	5-2	Abbott(4), Clancy	n.a.	5-1	Abbott(2), Prentice(2), Fleming	n.a.
Dorchester Town0	3-2	Prentice(2), Abbott	n.a.	2-5	Fleming, Prentice	n.a.
Frome Town	5-1	Prentice(3), Noyce(2)	n.a.	2-0	McManus, Prentice	n.a.
Glastonbury	0-1		n.a.	1-3	Fleming	n.a.
Poole Town	1-0	Abbott	1800	0-3		n.a.
Portland United	4-0	Abbott(2), Knight, Prentice	n.a.	1-7	Prentice	n.a.
Taunton Town	2-0	Noyce(2)	n.a.	2-3	Prentice, Uren	n.a.
Torquay United Res	2-2	Abbott, McManus	n.a.	3-0	Knight, Noyce, Clancy	1345
Trowbridge Town	0-2		n.a.	2-2	Prentice, Wheeler	n.a.
Wells City	7-0	Prentice(4, 1 penalty), Noyce(2), Farrell	n.a.	4-2	Fleming(2), Wheeler, Prentice	n.a.
Weymouth Res	7-2	Prentice(3), Uren(2), Clancy Barfoot	n.a.	3-3	Prentice(3)	1900
Yeovil Town Res	2-2	McManus, Noyce	1270	4-2	Prentice(2), Abbott, Knight	n.a.

Leading goalscorer for 1956/57 season was Andy Prentice with 32 goals.

The Salisbury team for their 1st home fixture on 18th of August 1956 versus Bridgwater Town was: Kingston, King, Booth, Timms, Tuck, Fleming, Wheeler, Knight, Abbott, Prentice and Clancy.

1956/57 Western League Division I

	P	W	D	L	F	A	Pts
Poole Town	36	26	4	6	115	48	56
Trowbridge Town	36	21	5	10	83	55	47
Salisbury	**36**	**20**	**5**	**11**	**98**	**60**	**45**
Torquay United Res	36	18	8	10	91	55	44
Portland United	36	18	8	10	84	64	44
Bridgwater Town	36	17	7	12	58	54	41
Dorchester Town	36	16	7	13	83	70	39
Chippenham Town	36	16	7	13	77	67	39
Yeovil Town Res	36	18	2	16	79	73	38
Glastonbury	36	16	3	17	82	102	35
Bristol Rovers Colts	36	14	6	16	67	90	34
Weymouth Res	36	16	1	19	87	94	33
Barnstaple Town	36	14	4	18	76	70	32
Bideford	36	12	8	16	70	71	32
Taunton Town	36	11	9	16	59	71	31
Chippenham United	36	12	6	18	80	97	30
Bristol City Colts	36	13	4	19	58	74	30
Frome Town	36	10	2	24	46	91	22
Wells City	36	4	4	28	46	133	12

1957/58 F.A. Cup

versus	res.	goalscorer	gate
Westbury United(h)	4-2	Noyce(2), Prentice, Uren	n.a.
Trowbridge Town(h)	0-3		2700

1957/58 Wilts Premier Shield

versus	res	goalscorer	gate
Swindon Town(h)	0-2		n.a.

1957/58 Western League Cup

versus	res	goalscorer	gate
Dorchester Town(a)	3-2	Noyce(2), Delew	n.a.
Dorchester Town(h)	2-2	Noyce, Prentice	n.a.
Wells City(h)	2-1	McNulty, Kaile	n.a.
Glastonbury(a)	2-3	Allen, Prentice	n.a.

1957/58 Western League Division I

versus	H	goalscorer	gate	A	goalscorer	gate
Barnstaple Town	2-0	McNulty, Gale(penalty)	2800	0-0		n.a.
Bideford Town	0-0		n.a.	1-2	Noyce	n.a.
Bridgwater Town	1-3	Clancy	n.a.	1-2	Abbott	n.a.
Bristol City Colts	2-1	McNulty, Allen	n.a.	3-1	Abbott(2), Clancy	n.a.
Bristol Rover Colts	3-0	Abbott, Kaile, Farrell	n.a.	2-1	Allen, Uren	n.a.
Chippenham Town	1-1	o.g.	n.a.	0-0		n.a.
Chippenham United	1-0	Abbott	n.a.	0-0		n.a.
Cinderford Town	2-0	Abbott(2)	n.a.	1-0	McNulty	n.a.
Dorchester Town	0-2		n.a.	0-1		n.a.
Frome Town	2-1	Prentice, McNulty	n.a.	2-1	Prentice, Abbott	n.a.
Glastonbury	4-0	Prentice(2), Allen, Abbott	n.a.	1-1	Allen	n.a.
Minehead	4-2	Abbott(3), Kaile	n.a.	1-1	Kaile	n.a.
Portland United	4-1	Abbott, Clancy, Prentice, Gale	n.a.	4-2	Abbott, Gale, McNulty, o.g.	n.a.
Taunton Town	0-0		n.a.	1-1	Gale	n.a.
Torquay United Res	1-0	Jarvis	n.a.	2-0	McNulty, Allen	1372
Trowbridge Town	0-0		n.a.	1-2	McNulty	n.a.
Weymouth Res	1-0	Abbott	n.a.	2-2	Prentice, Clancy	n.a.
Yeovil Town Res	5-1	McNulty, Allen, Prentice McManus	n.a.	0-1		n.a.

Leading goalscorer for 1957/58 season was Stan Abbott with 15 goals.

For the first time Salisbury F.C. had three teams, Western League, Hampshire League and Bournemouth Senior League. On the 30th of April 1958 Salisbury beat Cinderford 2-0 and confirmed they would win the Championship. The team was: Kingston, Cole, Gibbons, Rushworth, Tuck, Farrell, Oakley, Allen, Abbott, McNulty and Clancy. Season tickets for both ground and stand with reserved seats until 10 minutes after kick-off cost £2-17s.6d (£2.87).

1957/58 Western League Division I

	P	W	D	L	F	A	Pts
Salisbury	36	18	11	7	55	30	47
Bridgwater Town	36	20	5	11	78	53	45
Dorchester Town	36	19	6	11	87	57	44
Barnstaple Town	36	17	7	12	83	48	41
Trowbridge Town	36	15	11	10	80	61	41
Bristol Rovers Colts	36	16	8	12	80	74	40
Torquay United Res	36	15	9	12	70	56	39
Bristol City Colts	36	16	7	13	70	59	39
Minehead	36	16	5	15	68	76	37
Frome Town	36	16	5	15	66	77	37
Ciderford Town	36	17	2	17	72	70	36
Taunton	36	11	13	12	48	55	35
Bideford Town	36	14	5	17	62	55	33
Weymouth Res	36	13	7	16	89	85	33
Chippenham Town	36	13	7	16	71	74	33
Glastonbury	36	12	7	17	50	79	31
Yeovil Town Res	36	13	4	19	66	92	30
Portland United	36	12	3	21	58	80	27
Chippenham United	36	5	6	25	51	123	16

1958/59 F.A. Cup

versus	res	goalscorer	gate	versus	res	goalscorer	gate
Bridport(a)	5-2	Alexander(2), Forester, Allen, Clancy	n.a.	Poole Town(a)	1-2	Allen	n.a.

1958/59 Wilts Premier Shield

1958/59 Western League Cup

versus	res	goalscorer	gate	versus	res	goalscorer	gate
Chippenham Tn(h)	3-1	Forrester, Gibbons, Purvis	n.a.	Chippenham Utd(h)	5-0	Forrester(2), Allen, Alexander, Purvis	n.a.
Swindon Town(a)	1-2	Stratton		Chippenham Tn(a)	2-0	Purvis(2)	n.a.
				Street(a)	5-1	Clancy(2), Alexander, Allen	n.a.
				Yeovil Res(a)	0-1		n.a.

1958/59 Western League Division I

versus	H	goalscorer	gate	A	goalscorer	gate
Barnstaple Town	2-0	Allen, McCowen	n.a.	3-1	Allen, Onslow, Purvis	n.a.
Bideford Town	3-1	Purvis(2), Allen	n.a.	0-3		n.a.
Bridgwater Town	2-5	McCowan, o.g.	n.a.	1-3	Allen	n.a.
Bristol City Colts	1-2	Alexander	n.a.	1-0	Onslow	n.a.
Bristol Rover Colts	2-0	Purvis, Allen	n.a.	2-1	Kaile, Purvis	n.a.
Chippenham Town	5-2	Purvis(2), Alexander, Clancy, McCowan	n.a.	2-1	Purvis(2)	n.a.
Cinderford Town	0-1		n.a.	3-0	Purvis(2), Alexander	n.a.
Dorchester Town0	3-1	Onslow(2), Alexander	n.a.	2-4	McCowan, Purvis	n.a.
Frome Town	6-2	Onslow(2), Purvis(3), o.g.	n.a.	2-1	Purvis(2)	n.a.
Glastonbury	6-0	Onslow(3), Clancy, Alexander McCowan	n.a.	1-0	Purvis	n.a.
Gloucester City	2-0	McCowan, Clancy	n.a.	2-0	Purvis, Allen	n.a.
Minehead	5-0	Purvis(4), Alexander	n.a.	3-1	Onslow, Allen, o.g.	n.a.
Poole Town	4-1	Allen(2), Purvis, Onslow	n.a.	3-3	Onslow(2), Allen	n.a.
Portland United	3-0	Allen, Clancy, Purvis	n.a.	2-2	Allen, Alexander	n.a.
Taunton Town	3-1	Forrester(2), Purvis	1710	2-1	Purvis, Onslow	n.a.
Torquay United Res	3-1	Rushworth,. Onslow(2)	n.a.	4-1	Allen, Alexander, Clancy, Kaile	n.a.
Weymouth Res	1-1	Clancy	n.a.	2-5	Forester, Alexander	n.a.
Yeovil Town Res	3-4	Purvis(2), o.g.	n.a.	2-4	Purvis, Kaile	n.a.

> Leading goalscorer for 1959/59 season was Derek Purvis with 30 goals.

> Eagerly awaiting the start of a new season a crowd of 800 turned up for a practice match on 16th of August 1958. The first team on the opening day fixture versus Taunton was: Kingston, Dooler, Gibbons, Rushworth, Compton, McGowan, Allen, Alexander, Purvis, Forester, Clancy.

1958/59 Western League Division I

	P	W	D	L	F	A	Pts
Yeovil Town Res	36	26	3	7	115	54	55
Salisbury	**36**	**24**	**3**	**9**	**91**	**53**	**51**
Dorchester Town	36	23	2	11	110	61	48
Bridgwater Town	36	21	6	9	81	57	48
Barnstaple Town	36	20	5	11	85	68	45
Chippenham Town	36	20	3	13	104	66	43
Bideford	36	15	11	10	83	60	41
Torquay United Res	36	18	3	15	70	70	39
Weymouth Res	36	18	2	16	84	63	38
Cinderford Town	36	15	4	17	60	63	34
Bristol Rovers Colts	36	14	6	16	73	77	34
Glastonbury	36	15	3	18	63	81	33
Taunton	36	15	2	19	53	68	32
Bristol City Colts	36	12	7	17	75	88	31
Portland United	36	13	5	18	68	82	31
Poole Town Res	36	10	7	19	63	91	27
Gloucester City Res	36	9	5	22	64	91	23
Minehead	36	6	7	23	50	111	19
Frome Town	36	4	4	28	52	140	12

1959/60 F.A. Cup

versus	res	goalscorer	gate	versus	res	goalscorer	gate
Portland United(a)	3-2	Watts(2), Clancy	n.a.	Barnet(h)	1-0	Onslow	4349
Warminster Town(a)	5-0	Watts(3), Onslow, Clancy	n.a.	*1st Round Proper*			
Poole Town(a)	1-0	Watts	n.a.	Newport County(h)	0-1		6368
Basingstoke Town(h)	2-2	Alexander(2)	3408	*2nd Round Proper*			
replay (a)	2-1-	Onslow, Allen	n.a.				

1959/60 Wilts Premier Shield

versus	res	goalscorer	gate
Chippenham Tn(h)	3-2	Onslow(2), Watts	n.a.
Chippenham Utd(h)	2-0	Watts(2)	n.a.
Swindon Town(a)	2-1	Harding, Watts	
Final			

1959/60 Western League Cup

versus	res	goalscorer	gate
Barnstaple Tn(h)	5-1	Alexander(2), Watts(2) Clancy	n.a.
Trowbridge Tn Res(a)	3-2	Watts(2), Kaile	n.a.
Bridgwater(h)	1-1	Watts	n.a.
replay (a)	0-1		

1959/60 Alan Young Cup

versus	res	goalscorer	gate
Yeovil Town Res(a)	2-0	Watts, Alexander	n.a.
Yeovil Town Res(h)	5-1	Watts, Clancy, Allen(2), Alexander	n.a.

1959/60 Western League Division I

versus	H	goalscorer	gate	A	goalscorer	gate
Barnstaple Town	1-1	Prosser	n.a.	4-2	Watts(3), Clancy	n.a.
Bath City Res	4-1	Watts(3), Onslow	n.a.	3-0	Allen, Kaile, McAlone	n.a.
Bideford Town	4-0	Watts(2), Allen, Clancy	n.a.	2-0	Watts(2)	n.a.
Bridgwater Town	3-1	Watts(2), Onslow	n.a.	0-5		n.a.
Bristol City Colts	1-0	Alexander	n.a.	4-0	Onslow(2), Watts, Clancy	n.a.
Bristol Rover Colts	1-1	Alexander	n.a.	1-1	McAlone	n.a.
Chippenham Town	2-2	Watts, McAlone	n.a.	2-1	Rushworth, Allen	n.a.
Dorchester Town	2-2	o.g., Watts	n.a.	0-1		n.a.
Glastonbury	4-0	Wicks(3), Alexander	n.a.	3-0	Watts(2), Clancy	n.a.
Gloucester City Res	2-1	Watts, Onslow	n.a.	2-1	Rushworth, Allen	n.a.
Minehead	7-2	Watts(3), Alexander(2), Gogan(2)	n.a.	0-3		n.a.
Poole Town Res	2-1	Harding, McAlone	n.a.	3-3	Allen, Watts, Kaile	n.a.
Portland United	0-1		n.a.	2-3	Watts, Onslow	n.a.
Taunton Town	5-0	Onslow(2), Kaile, Clancy, Watts	n.a.	1-1	Watts	n.a.
Torquay United Res	2-4	Onslow, Allen	n.a.	0-1		962
Trowbridge Town Res	1-0	Onslow	n.a.	9-1	Onslow(5), Watts(2), Allen, Cross	n.a.
Weymouth Res	3-0	Watts(2), Onslow	n.a.	0-1		n.a.
Yeovil Town Res	5-0	Onslow(2), Allen(2), Clancy	n.a.	0-2		n.a.

Leading goalscorer for 1959/60 season was Roy Watts with 29 goals.

1959/60 Western League Division I

	P	W	D	L	F	A	Pts
Torquay United Res	36	29	5	2	132	40	63
Salisbury	**36**	**20**	**7**	**9**	**85**	**43**	**47**
Chippenham Town	36	18	6	12	70	56	42
Bridgwater Town	36	18	5	13	79	62	41
Weymouth Res	36	18	4	14	72	58	40
Portland United	36	17	6	13	61	68	40
Bideford	36	15	8	13	61	62	38
Bath City Res	36	15	7	14	63	61	37
Yeovil Town Res	36	17	3	16	74	77	37
Poole Town Res	36	15	6	15	73	66	36
Dorchester Town	36	17	2	17	87	88	36
Minehead	36	12	11	13	68	72	35
Bristol Rovers Colts	36	13	8	15	79	80	34
Glastonbury	36	11	10	15	66	78	32
Barnstaple Town	36	13	5	18	50	65	31
Taunton Town	36	11	7	18	67	96	29
Bristol City Colts	36	12	4	20	65	82	28
Gloucester City Res	36	9	4	23	49	92	22
Trowbridge Town Res	36	5	6	25	36	91	16

1960/61 F.A. Cup

versus	res. goalscorer	gate		res	gate
Weymouth(a)	1-1 Watts	3338	*replay*(h)	0-2	2200

1960/61 Wilts Premier Shield

versus	res	goalscorer	gate
Swindon Town(a)	3-3		
Swindon Town(h)	3-0	Lloyd(2), Watts	1640
Trowbridge Tn(h)	3-1	Lloyd, Allen, Watts	2000

1960/61 Alan Young Cup

versus	res	goalscorer	gate
Torquay Reserves(h)	2-1	Hill, Allen	1309
Torquay Reserves(a)	4-1	Hill, Watts, Clancy, Lloyd	n.a.

1960/61 Western League Division I

versus	H	goalscorer	gate	A	goalscorer	gate
Barnstaple Town	8-1	Watts(4), McCartney(3), Harding	1088	2-1	Watts, Lloyd	n.a.
Bath City Res	3-1	Hill(2), Harding	542	3-1	Watts, McCartney, Lloyd	n.a.
Bideford Town	6-0	McCartney(3), Watts(2), Lloyd	1029	1-2	Lloyd	n.a.
Bridgwater Town	5-1	Hill(3), Harding, Watts	1036	1-1	Hill	n.a.
Bristol City Colts	4-1	Watts(2), Hill(2)	1266	6-2	Watts(2), Lloyd, Clancy, McAlone, McCartney	n.a.
Bristol Rover Colts	1-1	McCartney	1042	0-2		n.a.
Chippenham Town	3-1	Watts(2), McAlone	1742	1-0	Watts	n.a.
Dorchester Town	4-0	Watts(2), Lloyd, Prosser	1538	5-1	McCartney(2), Clancy, Lloyd McAlone	n.a.
Exeter City Res	5-4	Watts(3), Lloyd, Clancy	1305	0-1		n.a.
Glastonbury	3-1	McCartney(2), McAlone	n.a.	5-1	McCartney(4), Clancy	n.a.
Minehead	5-1	Watts(3), McCartney, Lloyd	568	1-1	McCartney	n.a.
Poole Town Res	3-1	Watts, Hill(2)	983	3-2	Watts, Allen, Harding	n.a.
Portland United	4-1	McCartney(2), Watts, Allen	1150	0-1		n.a.
Taunton Town	6-0	Watts(3), McCartney(2), Clancy	950	2-1	Hill(2)	n.a.
Torquay United Res	2-2	Watts(2)	1225	1-0	Clancy	1225
Trowbridge Town Res	9-1	Watts(4), Lloyd(2), McCartney(2) Clancy	797	7-0	Watts(4), Allen, Harding, McCartney	n.a.
Welton Rovers	6-1	Watts(2), Lloyd(2), Allen, McAlone	n.a.	4-1	Watts(3), Cross	n.a.
Weston-super-Mare	3-2	Watts(2), Lloyd	1208	3-0	Lloyd(2), McCartney	n.a.
Weymouth Res	3-1	Hill(2), Harding	1068	2-0	Watts(2)	n.a.
Yeovil Town Res	1-2	Hill	1309	4-1	Lloyd(2), Clancy, Harding	n.a.

Leading goalscorer for 1960/61 season was Roy Watts with 49 goals.

1960/61 Western League Division I

	P	W	D	L	F	A	Pts
Salisbury	40	31	4	5	135	42	66
Dorchester Town	40	26	6	8	115	63	58
Minehead	40	24	8	8	100	62	56
Torquay United Res	40	23	6	11	122	70	52
Bridgwater Town	40	18	12	10	88	71	48
Exeter City Res	40	21	5	14	99	68	47
Weymouth Res	40	19	9	12	91	79	47
Bristol City Colts	40	18	10	12	94	70	46
Welton Rovers	40	20	5	15	119	110	45
Portland United	40	16	10	14	93	87	42
Yeovil Town Res	40	18	5	17	73	73	41
Chippenham Town	40	18	5	17	79	81	41
Bristol Rovers Colts	40	12	12	16	80	74	36
Bath City Res	40	11	11	18	75	79	33
Weston-Super-Mare	40	13	7	20	76	98	33
Bideford	40	12	9	19	76	99	33
Glastonbury	40	13	4	23	66	114	30
Poole Town Res	40	8	9	23	57	87	25
Trowbridge Town Res	40	9	7	24	62	122	25
Barnstaple Town	40	8	4	28	55	111	20
Taunton Town	40	5	6	29	59	153	16

1961/62 F.A. Cup

versus	res	goalscorer	gate
Oxford United(a)	2-3	McCartney(2)	6300

1961/62 Wilts Premier Shield / Alan Young Cup

versus	res	goalscorer	gate	versus	res	goalscorer	gate
Chippenham Tn(h)	7-1	Stratton(4), Watts(2) Hill	n.a.	Dorchester Town(a)	1-4	Watts	n.a.
Chippenham Utd(h)	3-1	Watts, Stratton, Hill	n.a.	Dorchester Town(h)	4-2	Watts(2), McCartney, Clancy	n.a.

1961/62 Western League Division I

versus	H	goalscorer	gate	A	goalscorer	gate
Barnstaple Town	3-0	Watts, Stratton, Hill	n.a.	6-0	Watts(2), Hill(2), McCartney, Evans	n.a.
Bath City Res	5-0	Watts(2), Stratton(2), Clancy	n.a.	1-1	Hill	n.a.
Bideford Town	1-0	o.g.	n.a.	1-1	Watts	n.a.
Bridgwater Town	3-0	Stratton(2), Watts	n.a.	0-1		n.a.
Bridport	6-0	Hill(3), Watts(2), Clancy	2200	0-3		n.a.
Bristol City Colts	1-3	Watts		1-2	Hill	n.a.
Bristol Rover Colts	6-2	Watts(2), Hill(2), McCartney, Evans	n.a.	1-0	Hill	n.a.
Chippenham Town	3-1	Watts(3)	n.a.	1-2	Evans	n.a.
Dorchester Town	5-3	Watts(3), Allen, Stratton	n.a.	2-1	Watts, Stratton	n.a.
Glastonbury	5-1	Laverick, Watts, Allen, McAlone, o.g.	n.a.	2-0	Watts(2)	n.a.
Minehead	3-1	McCartney, Allen, Watts	n.a.	2-6	Stratton, Watts	n.a.
Poole Town Res	2-3	McCartney, McAlone	n.a.	3-1	Stratton(2), Watts	n.a.
Portland United	6-0	Hill(4), Stratton(2)	n.a.	1-0	Allen	n.a.
Taunton Town	9-0	Hill(4), Stratton(2), Clancy(2), McAlone	n.a.	3-1	Watts, Stratton, Cross	n.a.
Torquay United Res	1-0	Watts	n.a.	3-1	Watts(2), Hill	n.a.
Welton Rovers	2-3	Watts, McAlone	n.a.	2-0	McAlone, Hill	n.a.
Weston-super-Mare	1-2	Sevier	n.a.	2-1	Hill, o.g.	n.a.
Weymouth Res	1-0	Watts	n.a.	3-0	Clancy, Hill, Watts	n.a.
Yeovil Town Res	6-1	Watts(2), Stratton(2), Allen, Hill	n.a.	2-0	Stratton, Clancy	n.a.

> Leading goalscorer for 1961/62 season was Roy Watts with 34 goals. Dilwyn Hill's score of 24 was no mean total and with 18 from Dave Stratton Salisbury's strike force was something for opposing defences to fear.

1961/62 Western League Division I

	P	W	D	L	F	A	Pts
Bristol City Res	38	28	7	3	132	36	63
Salisbury	38	27	2	9	105	41	56
Bideford	38	21	11	6	84	49	53
Torquay United Res	38	20	5	13	95	78	45
Poole Town Res	38	19	5	14	115	85	43
Dorchester Town	38	19	5	14	102	85	43
Bridgwater Town	38	17	8	13	89	69	42
Minehead	38	17	8	13	80	68	42
Chippenham Town	38	17	6	15	79	71	40
Portland United	38	16	8	14	92	85	40
Weston-Super-Mare	38	14	11	13	63	68	39
Weymouth Res	38	16	6	16	85	71	38
Bath City Res	38	13	9	16	74	80	35
Bridport	38	11	8	19	72	93	30
Yeovil Town Res	38	13	3	22	74	99	29
Welton Rovers	38	11	7	20	61	104	29
Taunton Town	38	11	4	23	59	114	26
Bristol Rovers Colts	38	6	13	19	59	93	25
Barnstaple Town	38	8	7	23	52	120	23
Glastonbury	38	7	5	26	44	107	19

1962/63 F.A. Cup

versus	res.	goalscorer	gate
Chippenham Town(h)	2-2	Watts, Petherbridge	1323
replay(a)	1-3	Stratton	1100

1962/63 Alan Young Cup

versus	res	goalscorer	gate
Bristol City Reserves(h)	2-1	Stratton, Watts	750
Bristol City Reserves((a)	3-3	Pask(2), Allen	n.a.

1962/63 Western League Division I

versus	H	goalscorer	gate	A	goalscorer	gate
Andover	3-1	Watts(2), Allen	n.a.	0-2		n.a.
Barnstaple Town	2-0	Allen, Stratton	n.a.	4-3	Watts(2), Stratton, Petherbridge	n.a.
Bath City Res	5-2	Watts(3), Hill(2)	610	0-4		n.a.
Bideford Town	0-0		n.a.	0-0		n.a.
Bridgwater Town	0-2		n.a.	1-1	Watts	n.a.
Bridport	3-1	Miller, Pask, Watts	n.a.	3-2	Watts, Hill, Clancy	n.a.
Bristol City Res	2-2	Allen, Petherbridge	n.a.	1-2	McCall	700
Bristol Rover Colts	5-0	Stratton(3), Hill, Watts	800	5-0	Hill(2), Watts, Pask, (o.g.)	30
Chippenham Town	1-1	Allen	n.a.	1-0	Hill	n.a.
Dorchester Town	2-2	McManus, Watts	n.a.	2-2	Watts(2)	n.a.
Exeter City Res	2-0	McCall(2)	n.a.	1-1	Pugsley	n.a.
Glastonbury	1-1	Stratton	n.a.	2-3	Pask, Watts	n.a.
Minehead	1-0	o.g.	n.a.	3-2	Stratton(2), Watts	n.a.
Poole Town Res	4-0	Pask, Watts, McManus, o.g.	n.a.	0-4		n.a.
Portland United	4-0	Hill, Allen, McCall(2)	888	0-1		n.a.
Taunton Town	5-2	Watts(2), McCall, Allen Petherbridge	n.a.	4-0	Stratton(2), Hall, (o.g.)	n.a.
Torquay United Res	1-0	Hill	n.a.	1-0	Watts	n.a.
Welton Rovers	1-3	Hall	700	2-1	Watts, Hill	350
Weston-super-Mare	9-0	Watts, Allen, McCall(3), Hill(3), Petherbridge	n.a.	0-1		n.a.
Weymouth Res	4-3	Hill(3), Watts	350	1-2	Watts	n.a.
Yeovil Town Res	1-2	Watts	n.a.	2-3	Prosser, Watts	n.a.

> Leading goalscorer for 1962/63 season was Roy Watts with 27 goals.

1962/63 Western League Division I

	P	W	D	L	F	A	Pts
Bristol City Res	42	31	5	6	120	56	67
Bideford	42	29	7	6	115	51	65
Minehead	42	25	6	11	102	62	56
Andover	42	25	5	12	106	59	55
Bridgwater Town	42	23	8	11	77	48	54
Salisbury	**42**	**21**	**9**	**12**	**89**	**56**	**51**
Portland United	42	23	5	14	80	66	51
Weymouth Res	42	20	5	17	104	78	45
Yeovil Town Res	42	18	9	15	67	72	45
Barnstaple Town	42	19	6	17	81	75	44
Dorchester Town	42	17	9	16	92	81	43
Chippenham Town	42	15	12	15	92	60	42
Poole Town Res	42	17	7	18	82	77	41
Exeter City Res	42	15	10	17	55	74	40
Bath City Res	42	14	6	22	82	96	34
Weston-Super-Mare	42	11	9	22	72	108	31
Welton Rovers	42	11	8	23	71	107	30
Glastonbury	42	13	4	25	56	114	30
Torquay United Res	42	10	8	24	48	78	28
Bridport	42	9	8	25	66	111	26
Taunton Town	42	11	4	27	56	112	26
Bristol Rovers Colts	42	6	8	28	56	120	20

		1963/64 F.A. Cup	
versus	**res.**	**goalscorer**	**gate**
Warminster Town(a)	2-2	Palmer, Bevan	n.a.
replay(h)	4-0	Watts(2), Pask, Burt	690
Dorchester Town(a)	1-1	Henderson	832
replay(h)	1-3	Henderson	n.a.

		1963/64	Western League Division I			
versus	**H**	**goalscorer**	**gate**	**A**	**goalscorer**	**gate**
Andover Town	0-6		n.a.	1-3	Gilbert	n.a.
Barnstaple Town	2-0	Pierce, Cranmer, A.	n.a.	1-1	Stocks	n.a.
Bath City Reserves	1-1	Pierce	n.a.	3-2	Henderson(2), Collett	750
Bideford Town	1-2	Pierce	n.a.	1-2	Pierce	n.a.
Bridgwater Town	0-1		n.a.	0-2		n.a.
Bridport	0-0		n.a.	0-0		n.a.
Bristol City Reserves	3-1	Stocks, Pierce, Pask	1250	0-1		n.a.
Chippenham Town	1-0	Henderson	n.a.	3-2	Watts, Gilbert, Bevan	n.a.
Dorchester Town	2-0	Stocks, Pask	520	0-4		n.a.
Exeter City Reserves	3-1	Pierce, Watts, Palmer	n.a.	2-2	Henderson, Cranmer, A.	n.a.
Frome Town	4-2	Stocks(2), Pask, Cranmer, A.	n.a.	4-1	Henderson(2), Pierce, Ambrose	n.a.
Glastonbury	1-0	Watts	n.a.	3-1	Ambrose, Watts, Henderson	n.a.
Minehead	4-1	Henderson(2), Collett, Holmes	426	1-2	Watts	n.a.
Poole Town Reserves	5-1	Palmer(3), Watts, Pierce	n.a.	1-0	Henderson	n.a.
Portland United	5-4	Henderson(4), Ambrose	311	3-1	Stocks(2), Pask	n.a.
Taunton Town	3-0	Bevan, Ambrose, Henderson	n.a.	5-1	Pask(3), Pierce, Stocks	n.a.
Torquay United Res	0-0		597	1-2	Uren	597.
Welton Rovers	2-1	Pask, Watts	n.a.	0-2		n.a.
Weston-super-Mare	1-4	Henderson	n.a.	2-0	Henderson(2)	n.a.
Weymouth Reserves	1-3	o.g.	407	1-1	Ambrose	n.a.
Yeovil Town Reserves	8-2	Henderson(5), Watts, Collett, Holmes	517	1-1	Pierce	n.a.

> Leading goalscorer for 1963/64 season was Ian Henderson with 23 goals.

Ian Henderson, who arrived free from Andover at the start of the season with Malcolm Ambrose, departed for Welton Rovers at the end of it. He did, however, score 23 goals from 27 appearances. His principal strength was in the air and some said this led to Salisbury playing unattractive football. Salisbury beat Aldershot 3-0 in the Hants Senior Cup Final at the Dell, Stocks 2 and Watts being the scorers. There were no Premier Shield or Western Floodlight League matches played this year.

1963/64 Western League Division I

	P	W	D	L	F	A	Pts
Bideford	42	30	6	6	113	36	66
Bristol City Reserves	42	24	15	3	122	43	63
Bridgwater Town	42	25	10	7	82	32	60
Welton Rovers	42	24	6	12	84	54	54
Dorchester Town	42	19	14	9	94	56	52
Salisbury	**42**	**21**	**8**	**13**	**80**	**61**	**50**
Barnstaple Town	42	20	9	13	92	69	49
Minehead	42	20	8	14	96	85	48
Weymouth Reserves	42	16	12	14	94	74	44
Andover Town	42	17	10	15	89	78	44
Torquay United Reserves	42	18	7	17	81	73	43
Yeovil Town Reserves	42	17	9	16	73	99	43
Chippenham Town	42	15	8	19	75	62	38
Bath City Reserves	42	12	12	18	77	92	36
Frome Town	42	11	11	20	69	97	33
Weston-super-Mare	42	11	11	20	58	86	33
Glastonbury	42	11	9	22	70	91	31
Exeter City Reserves	42	8	15	19	73	100	31
Poole Town Reserves	42	11	6	25	56	98	28
Bridport	42	7	14	21	40	100	28
Portland United	42	10	5	27	63	127	25
Taunton Town	42	8	9	25	37	105	25

1964/65 F.A. Cup

versus	res.	goalscorer	gate	
Dorchester Town(h)	3-3	Stocks(2), Ambrose	n.a.	
replay(a)	3-1	Ambrose, Stocks, Palmer	n.a.	
Poole Town(h)	1-1	Stocks	1453	
replay(a)	1-0	Ambrose	n.a.	
Portland United(h)	5-1	Penk, Bevan, Ambrose, Pask(2)	1125	
Yeovil Town(h)	2-1	Stocks(2)	3391	
P'borough United(a)	1-5	Stocks	10,095	*1st Round Proper*

1964/65 Western League Division I

versus	H	goalscorer	gate	A	goalscorer	gate
Andover	1-1	Pierce	n.a.	0-4		n.a.
Barnstaple Town	3-0	Pierce(3)	257	2-0	Cranmer, Stocks	n.a.
Bath City Res	4-0	Pask, Eckersall(2), Cranmer	n.a.	7-1	Stocks, Ambrose, Penk(3), Pask, o.g.	n.a.
Bideford Town	0-4		n.a.	0-2		n.a.
Bridgwater Town	2-1	Pierce(2)	n.a.	0-4		n.a.
Bridport	2-0	Cranmer, Pask	n.a.	1-1	Palmer	n.a.
Bristol City Res	1-4	Penk	n.a.	1-3	Gilbert	n.a.
Chippenham Town	1-0	Ambrose	800	2-2	Hale, Bailey	n.a.
Dorchester Town	5-2	Gilbert, Pierce(2), Cranmer, Stocks	n.a.	2-1	Pask, Ambrose	n.a.
Exeter City Res	5-1	Penk, Stocks(2), Hasty, Ambrose	n.a.	0-1		n.a.
Frome Town	2-2	o.g. Pierce	n.a.	0-2		n.a.
Glastonbury	5-0	Stocks(2), Pask(2), Pierce	n.a.	3-5	Gilbert(2), Tyrell	n.a.
Minehead	5-0	Stocks(2), Hasty(2), Pierce	408	1-2	Pask	n.a.
Poole Town Res	4-1	Pierce(2), Hasty, Penk	n.a.	2-1	Darnton, Ambrose	n.a.
Portland United	1-1	Pierce	n.a.	5-2	Fitch, Stocks, Ambrose(2), Pask	n.a.
Taunton Town	0-0		n.a.	1-2	Pierce	n.a.
Torquay United Res	0-0		n.a.	2-3	Pierce, Pask	n.a.
Welton Rovers	0-2		950	1-5	Stocks	n.a.
Weston-super-Mare	1-2	Penk	n.a.	2-2	Penk(2)	n.a.
Weymouth Res	0-2		n.a.	1-0	Hasty	n.a.
Yeovil Town Res	4-0	Bevan, Stocks, Hasty, Gilbert	n.a.	1-1	Stocks	n.a.

Leading goalscorer for 1964/65 season was Barry Pierce with 16 goals.

The basic squad for the Western League team comprised Stevens, Palmer, Fitch, Rutter (from February 1965), Henry (ex-Aldershot), Gilbert, Pask (ex-Basingstoke), Ambrose, Penk (ex-Saints), Pierce (ex-Exeter), Alfie Cranmer, Stocks and Hasty.

1964/65 Western League Division I

	P	W	D	L	F	A	Pts
Welton Rovers	42	35	3	4	148	36	73
Bideford	42	32	6	4	120	29	70
Minehead	42	27	7	8	88	42	61
Dorchester Town	42	26	4	12	89	53	56
Weston-Super-Mare	42	22	9	11	89	58	53
Weymouth Res	42	24	4	14	96	46	52
Bridgwater Town	42	20	9	13	74	59	49
Torquay United Res	42	21	5	16	74	59	47
Bristol City Res	42	21	4	17	96	82	46
Salisbury	**42**	**17**	**9**	**16**	**80**	**67**	**43**
Frome Town	42	17	8	17	66	71	42
Exeter City Res	42	18	5	19	92	84	41
Chippenham Town	42	16	8	18	75	82	40
Glastonbury	42	15	6	21	69	109	36
Yeovil Town Res	42	15	5	22	65	99	35
Andover	42	13	8	21	74	66	34
Bath City Res	42	12	6	24	54	98	30
Bridport	42	11	7	24	60	99	29
Taunton Town	42	10	8	24	54	104	28
Barnstaple Town	42	11	5	26	51	89	27
Portland United	42	6	8	28	40	122	20
Poole Town Res.	42	5	2	35	49	149	12

1965/66 F.A. Cup

versus	res	goalscorer	gate
Newbury Town(h)	4-0	Harley,(3), Pask	833
Andover(a)	3-0	Harley, Davidson, Knight	n.a.
Portland United(h)	0-3		1277

1965/66 Western League Cup

versus	res	goalscorer	gate	versus	res	goalscorer	gate
Glastonbury(a)	2-1	Knight, Gilbert	n.a.	Weston-super-Mare(h)	4-0	Naysmith(2), Gilbert,	n.a.
Frome Town(h)	1-1	Gilbert	n.a			Knight	
Glastonbury(h)	0-0		n.a.	Weston-super-Mare(a)	2-4	Pearce, Pask	n.a.
				Frome Town(a)	0-0		n.a.

1965/66 Western League Division I

versus	H	goalscorer	gate	A	goalscorer	gate
Andover	3-2	Knight(2), Pearce	564	1-3	Harley	n.a.
Barnstaple Town	3-0	Pearce, Knight, Gilbert	648	0-1		n.a.
Bideford Town	2-0	Tout, Naysmith	300	3-1	Knight, Harley, Tout	n.a.
Bridgwater Town	1-1	Tout	548	1-3	Gilbert	n.a.
Bridport	1-2	Davidson	419	1-1	Pearce	n.a.
Bristol City Colts	2-0	Pearce, o.g.	276	5-0	Tout(2), Harley, Knight, o.g.	n.a.
Dorchester Town	3-0	Harley, Knight, Davidson	375	2-2	Knight, Gilbert	n.a.
Exeter City Res	4-0	Rutter(p), Knight, Harley, Pask	750	1-6	Rutter	n.a.
Frome Town	1-1	Gilbert	597.	0-2		n.a.
Glastonbury	2-1	Harley(2)	277	0-3		n.a.
Minehead	0-0		377	1-1	Pask	n.a.
Portland United	2-3	Knight(2)	702	1-2	Gilbert	n.a.
Taunton Town	2-0	Pask, Harley	717	2-4	Knight, Harley	n.a.
Torquay United Res	2-2	Harley, Knight	980	1-1	Harley	n.a.
Welton Rovers	2-3	Harley, Knight	702	1-4	Donnelly	n.a.
Weston-super-Mare	0-1		591	5-2	Knight(2). Rutter, Harley, o.g.	n.a.
Weymouth Res	3-4	Knight(2), Pearce	755	4-1	Pearce(2), Knight, Gilbert	n.a.

> Leading goalscorer for 1965/66 season was John Knight with 18 goals.

> Barry Fitch and Phil Gilbert only missed two league games in the season.

> The surnames of Salisbury's first two goalscorers in the F.A. Cup match versus Andover Town which went 3-0 in Salisbury's favour had a famous American motorcycle name about them, Harley Davidson.

1965/66 Western League Division I

	P	W	D	L	F	A	Pts
Welton Rovers	34	25	9	0	105	28	59
Portland United	34	23	2	9	75	50	48
Bideford	34	19	8	7	90	49	46
Andover	34	16	8	10	74	57	40
Minehead	34	13	12	9	46	44	38
Frome Town	34	14	9	11	53	53	37
Glastonbury	34	12	11	11	61	46	35
Taunton Town	34	15	5	14	73	69	35
Bridgwater Town	34	12	10	12	63	62	34
Salisbury	**34**	**12**	**8**	**14**	**62**	**57**	**32**
Torquay United Res	34	11	10	13	56	56	32
Exeter City Res	34	13	4	17	63	70	30
Weymouth Res	34	11	8	15	65	76	30
Weston-Super-Mare	34	12	5	17	48	61	29
Bridport	34	12	5	17	57	90	29
Dorchester Town	34	9	5	20	41	79	23
Barnstaple Town	34	7	8	19	35	59	22
Bristol City Colts	34	4	5	25	33	94	13

		1966/67 F.A. Cup					
versus	**res**	**goalscorer**	**gate**	**versus**	**res**	**goalscorer**	**gate**
Cowes Sports(h)	4-1	Harley(2), Hodgkins, Allen	600	Fareham Town(a)	2-2	Reid, Gilbert	1473
Waterlooville(a)	2-0	Hodgkins, Allen	n.a.	*replay*(h)	1-2	Fitch	n.a.
				first competitive match under floodlights at Victoria Park			

		1966/67 Wilts Premier Shield					
versus	**res**	**goalscorer**	**res**	**versus**	**res**	**goalscorer**	**gate**
Chippenham Tn(h)	5-1	Hodgkins(4), Fitch	n.a.	Trowbridge(a)	6-0	Tyler(3), Pearce, Ambrose Pask	1003

		1966/67 Western League Division I				
versus	**H**	**goalscorer**	**gate**	**A**	**goalscorer**	**gate**
Andover	1-1	Pask	450	4-2	Hodgkins(2), Fitch, o.g.	n.a.
Barnstaple Town	5-1	Hodgkins(2), Harley, Tout, Gilbert	384	0-0		n.a.
Bideford Town	2-1	Hodgkins(2)	578	0-3		n.a.
Bridgwater Town	1-1	Hodgkins	996	1-6	Gilbert	n.a.
Bridport	3-0	Fitch(2), Pearce	700	2-0	Tyler, Ambrose	n.a.
Bristol City Colts	2-0	Hodgkins, Gilbert	495	2-0	Allen, Middleton	n.a.
Dorchester Town	2-3	Stratton, Phillips	550	1-1	Pearce	n.a.
Exeter City Res	1-0	o.g.	671	1-2	Harley	n.a.
Frome Town	3-0	Harley, Reid(2)	740	4-2	Hodgkins(2), Tyler(2)	n.a.
Glastonbury	2-1	Hodgkins, Stratton	450	3-2	Gilbert(2), o.g.	n.a.
Minehead	0-1		674	2-0	Pask, Hodgkins	n.a.
Portland United	1-0	Gilbert	470	3-0	Pask, Hodgkins, Harley	150
Plymouth Argyle Colts	3-5	Hodgkins(2), Tout	482	1-1	Hodgkins	737
St Luke's College	2-1	Ambrose(2)	447	1-1	Hodgkins	n.a.
Taunton Town	2-1	Harley(2)	576	5-3	Tyler(2), Pearce(2), McCarthy	n.a.
Torquay United Res	1-2	Fitch	551	0-0		n.a.
Welton Rovers	1-4	Hodgkins	700	2-0	Hodgkins(2)	n.a.
Weston-super-Mare	2-1	Allen, Ambrose	n.a.	2-2	Tyler(2)	n.a.
Weymouth Res	4-0	Pask(2), Swain(2)	n.a.	4-1	Hodgkins(3), Ambrose	n.a.
Yeovil Town Res	2-3	Hodgkins, Pask	498	5-0	Hodgkins(2), Ambrose, Allen,Pearce	n.a.

> Leading goalscorer for 1966/67 season was Geoff Hodgkins with 26 goals.

1966/67 Western League Division I							
	P	W	D	L	F	A	Pts
Welton Rovers	40	29	7	4	102	37	65
Minehead	40	25	10	5	98	42	60
Bridgwater Town	40	25	7	8	93	47	57
Salisbury	**40**	**22**	**9**	**9**	**83**	**54**	**53**
Dorchester Town	40	22	8	10	89	48	52
Bideford	40	23	6	11	76	47	52
Glastonbury	40	20	9	11	71	54	49
Exeter City Res	40	17	7	16	54	63	41
Torquay United Res	40	15	9	16	66	56	39
Andover	40	13	13	14	69	60	39
Portland United	40	15	7	18	61	76	37
Frome Town	40	17	1	22	60	82	35
Bristol City Colts	40	13	8	19	63	64	34
Weston-Super-Mare	40	12	9	19	52	69	33
Taunton Town	40	11	10	19	67	77	32
Plymouth Argyle Colts	40	12	8	20	66	97	32
Bridport	40	11	8	21	50	80	30
Weymouth Res	40	12	4	24	39	75	28
St Lukes College	40	10	7	23	61	90	27
Barnstaple Town	40	8	8	24	50	92	24
Yeovil Town Res	40	8	5	27	52	111	21

1967/68 F.A. Cup

versus	res	goalscorer	gate	versus	res	goalscorer	gate
Fareham Town(a)	2-2	Hodgkins, Tyler	728	Newport I.O.W.(h)	3-0	Pearce, Hodgkins, Ashe	767
replay(h)	5-1	Gilbert, Hodgkins,	1771	Dorchester Town(a)	2-1	Donohoe, Phillips	1105
		Pearce(2), Tyler		Swindon Town(a)	0-4	12,193	
Cowes Sports(a)	1-1	Phillips	n.a.	*1st Round Proper*			
replay(h)	5-1	Phillips, Ashe,	1555				
		Hodgkins(2), Donohoe					

1967/68 Wilts Premier Shield

versus	res	versus	gate
Chippenham Tn(h)	9-0	Gilbert(2), Donohue(2)	608
		Hall(2), Tyler(2), Saunders	
Trowbridge Tn(a)	1-0	Ashe	n.a.
Trowbridge Tn(h)	1-1	Hall	911

1967/68 Western League Division I

versus	H	goalscorer	gate	A	goalscorer	gate
Andover	4-1	Hodgkins(3), Donohoe	1105	3-2	Hodgkins, Collins, Saunders	n.a.
Barnstaple Town	7-0	Gilbert(3), Tyler, Bichard,	604	3-2	Ashe, Pearce, Hodgkins	n.a.
		(o.g.) (2)				
Bath City Res	0-2		919	2-1	Ashe, Hodgkins	n.a.
Bideford Town	2-0	Hodgkins(2)	760	0-2		n.a.
Bridgwater Town	2-1	Ashe, Donohoe	1192	0-4		787
Bridport	2-0	Gilbert(2)	679	0-1		n.a.
Bristol City Colts	0-0		444	2-0	Hodgkins(2)	n.a.
Devizes Town	7-0	Hodgkins(3), Saunders	752	6-3	Hodgkins(2), Gilbert, Saunders	n.a.
		Gilbert, Pierce(2)			Pearce(2)	
Dorchester Town	1-0	Ashe	715	4-2	Donohoe(3), Hall	500
Frome Town	3-0	Tyler(2), Pearce	591	2-0	Hodgkins, Phillips	n.a.
Glastonbury	2-1	Hall, Hodgkins	487	1-2	Gilbert	350
Minehead	7-1	Saunders, Pearce, Tyler(3)	685	0-2		n.a.
		Hodgkins, Fitch				
Plymouth Argyle Colts	0-2		640	0-1		n.a.
Portland United	4-0	Donohoe(2), Hall(2)	563	1-1	Hodgkins	n.a.
St Luke's College	7-1	Gilbert, Hodgkins,	658	5-1	Pearce, Hodgkins(2) Fitch	150
		Donohoe(3), Ashe, Fitch			Phillips	
Taunton Town	5-1	Tyler, Phillips, Donohoe(3)	425	3-0	Hodgkins, Donohoe, Phillips	n.a.
Torquay United Res	4-0	Hodgkins(2), Hall, (o.g.)	1253	0-1		n.a.
Welton Rovers	2-0	Hall, Hodgkins	727	1-0	Hodgkins	n.a.
Weston-super-Mare	9-0	Hodgkins(2), Ashe(2),	680	0-0		300
		Donohoe(2), Gilbert(2), Hall				
Yeovil Town Res	2-0	Tyler, Donohoe	285	2-0	Hodgkins, Ambrose	n.a.

> Leading goalscorer for 1967/68 season was Geoff Hodgkins with 30 goals.

1967/68 Western League Division I

	P	W	D	L	F	A	Pts
Bridgwater Town	40	27	8	5	92	41	62
Salisbury	40	28	3	9	105	35	59
Glastonbury	40	24	7	9	103	64	55
Bath City Res	40	21	9	10	81	63	51
Frome Town	40	22	6	12	98	72	50
Minehead	40	18	13	9	72	49	49
Dorchester Town	40	17	14	9	81	50	48
Welton Rovers	40	20	6	14	74	55	46
Plymouth Argyle Colts	40	18	7	15	76	72	43
Bridport	40	18	5	17	68	58	41
Torquay United Res	40	17	7	16	58	55	41
Andover	40	17	5	18	61	66	39
Taunton Town	40	11	15	14	76	68	37
Bideford	40	13	9	18	52	63	35
St Luke's College	40	12	9	19	60	78	33
Portland United	40	10	12	18	39	80	32
Bristol City Colts	40	9	10	21	33	59	28
Weston-Super-Mare	40	9	10	21	40	79	28
Barnstaple Town	40	8	6	26	48	91	22
Devizes Town	40	7	7	26	56	113	21
Yeovil Town Res	40	5	10	25	36	98	20

1968/69 F.A. Cup

versus	res.	goalscorer	gate
Ryde Sports(a)	7-1	Hodgkins(4), Tyler(3)	335
Thorneycroft Ath(h)	4-0	Tyler(3), Ashe	853
Waterlooville (a)	2-4	Tyler, Gilbert	458

1968/69 Beazer Homes Southern League Cup

versus	res	goalscorer	gate
Weymouth(a)	0-1		2225
Weymouth(h)	0-3		2076

1968/69 Beazer Homes Southern Division

versus	H	goalscorer	gate	A	goalscorer	gate
Ashford	6-1	Tyler(6, 2 pens)	656	1-3	Hodgkins	605
Banbury United	3-0	Tyler (pen.) Hodgkins(2)	795	0-2		550
Barry Town	2-1	Ashe, Hodgkins	613	1-1	Foley	200
Bath City	1-3	Hodgkins	2424	0-2		3083
Bexley United	4-0	Muxworthy(3), Tyler	834	3-0	Tyler, Donohoe, Hodgkins	700
Brentwood Town	2-1	Moxham, Tyler	1123	1-2	Donohoe	1225
Cambridge City	0-2		1174	0-1		2001
Canterbury	1-0	Tyler	690	2-1	Bichard, Fitch	347
Corby Town	3-0	Hodgkins(2), Tyler	786	0-1		493
Crawley Town	2-2	Ashe, Gilbert	669	0-2		925
Dartford	1-3	Tyler	619	2-2	Muxworthy, Tyler	1198
Dunstable Town	0-0		1267	0-2		514
Folkestone Town	0-2		646	0-1		655
Gloucester City	0-1		1284	2-1	Foley, Hodgkins	2051
Gravesend & N'fleet	2-0	Foley, Hodgkins	1147	3-2	Foley, Hodgkins, Donohoe	824
Hastings United	1-0	Muxworthy	707	1-3	Hodgkins	1320
Merthyr Tydfil	3-0	Tyler(2), o.g.	584	3-3	Muxworthy, Hodgkins(2)	300
Ramsgate Athletic	2-0	Hodgkins(2)	780	3-2	Hodgkins, Tyler Foley	744
Tonbridge	7-1	Tyler(4, 1 pen), Hodgkins Gilbert, Muxworthy	823	3-0	Hodgkins, Donohoe, o.g	276
Trowbridge	2-1	Ashe, Hodgkins	1302	0-0		1825
Wisbech Town	1-0	Tyler	557	1-3	Tyler	593

Leading goalscorer for 1968/69 season was Alan Tyler with 23 goals.

1968/69 Beazer Homes Southern Division

	P	W	D	L	F	A	Pts
Brentwood Town	42	26	12	4	94	37	64
Bath City	42	26	10	6	96	40	62
Gloucester City	42	25	9	8	100	53	59
Crawley Town	42	21	13	8	65	32	55
Corby Town	42	22	6	14	81	65	50
Dartford	42	20	8	14	79	51	48
Ramsgate Athletic	42	19	9	14	72	57	47
Salisbury	**42**	**20**	**6**	**16**	**69**	**52**	**46**
Cambridge City	42	18	10	14	73	63	46
Banbury United	42	16	12	14	67	72	44
Trowbridge Town	42	15	14	13	70	60	44
Folkestone Town	42	19	5	18	53	59	43
Canterbury City	42	17	7	18	67	63	41
Ashford	42	16	8	18	72	73	40
Bexley United	42	15	9	18	62	75	39
Hastings United	42	15	9	18	58	69	39
Wisbech Town	42	11	13	18	57	70	35
Dunstable Town	42	14	6	22	73	99	34
Merthyr Tydfil	42	10	7	25	49	101	27
Barry Town	42	8	10	24	39	78	26
Gravesend & Northfleet	42	8	9	25	51	79	25
Tonbridge	42	2	6	34	36	137	10

1969/70 F.A. Cup				1969/70 F.A. Trophy			
versus	**res**	**goalscorer**	**gate**	**versus**	**res**	**goalscorer**	**gate**
Ryde Sports(a)	1-1	Tyler	346	L. Gornal Athletic(h)	4-2	Hodgkins(2), Tyler(2)	741
replay(h)	3-2	Ashe, Hodgkins, Gilbert	880				
Thorneytcroft A.(a)	4-3	Tyler(2), Smith(2)	200	Lockheed Leamington (a)	4-0	Hodgkins, Smith	704
Fareham Town(h)	1-0	Moxham	845			Moxham(2)	
Andover Town(a)	0-0		1586	Poole Town(h)	1-1	Hodgkins	885
replay(h)	3-0	Tyler, Moxham, Harding	2144	*replay*(a)	0-1		400
Weymouth(h)	0-1		2456				

1969/70 Wilts Premier Shield				1969/70 Beazer Homes Southern League Cup			
versus	**res**	**goalscorer**	**gate**	**versus**	**res**	**goalscorer**	**gate**
Chippenham Tn(h)	2-0	Paddy Smith, Tyler	669	Weymouth(h)	0-3		1443
Trowbridge Tn(h)	1-1	Marwood	n.a.	Weymouth(a)	0-4		2164
Trowbridge Tn(a)	0-2		550				

1969/70 Beazer Homes Southern Division						
versus	**H**	**goalscorer**	**gate**	**A**	**goalscorer**	**gate**
Ashford	0-0		548	0-0		848
Banbury United	0-2		506	1-3	Crook	438
Barry Town	1-0	Tyler	996	2-1	Tyler(2)	352
Bedford Town	1-1	Marwood	598	1-3	Marwood	261
Bexley United	2-1	Tyler, Moxham	522	2-3	Hodgkins, Fitch	545
Cambridge City	0-0		634	0-5		1893
Canterbury City	1-1	Bichard	966	0-0		216
Cheltenham Town	2-0	Harding, Tyler	838	0-3		643
Corby Town	0-0		540	0-1		540
Dartford	3-1	Tyler(2), Marwood	732	1-3	Tyler	841
Dunstable Town	2-1	Hodgkins, Smith	695	0-2		126
Folkestone Town	5-1	Marwood(2), Tyler(2), Foley.	525	1-1	Hodgkins	359
Gravesend & N'fleet	1-1	Tyler	918	1-1	Hodgkins	821
Guildford City	0-0		607	2-4	Marwood, Tyler	1163
Hastings United	1-0	Gilbert	444	0-2		793
Merthyr Tydfil	0-0		1162	1-1	Smith	796
Ramsgate Athletic	0-1		583	1-1	Muxworthy	795
Rugby Town	6-0	Marwood(3), Holder, Moxham(2)	666	0-3		481
Tonbridge	0-1		678	0-1		245
Trowbridge	2-1	Tyler(2)	1665	0-1		1069
Wisbech Town	2-0	Tyler(2)	597	5-2	Marwood(2), Husbands, Smith, Foley	246

1969/70 Beazer Homes Southern Division							
	P	**W**	**D**	**L**	**F**	**A**	**Pts**
Bedford Town	42	26	9	7	92	37	61
Cambridge City	42	26	8	8	104	43	60
Dartford	42	24	11	7	88	46	59
Ashford	42	19	15	8	71	42	53
Rugby Town	42	20	10	12	81	65	50
Trowbridge Town	42	20	8	14	72	65	48
Hastings United	42	18	11	13	67	51	47
Guildford City	42	19	9	14	68	58	47
Banbury United	42	19	8	15	86	72	46
Cheltenham Town	42	20	5	17	78	81	45
Canterbury City	42	15	13	14	61	57	43
Corby Town	42	14	15	13	57	53	43
Folkestone Town	42	19	5	18	56	54	43
Ramsgate Athletic	42	14	13	15	53	57	41
Salisbury	**42**	**13**	**13**	**16**	**47**	**53**	**39**
Gravesend & Northfleet	42	13	11	18	62	71	37
Bexley United	42	10	11	21	58	76	31
Dunstable Town	42	11	9	22	52	82	31
Merthyr Tydfil	42	9	11	22	40	80	29
Barry Town	42	11	6	25	39	76	28
Wisbech Town	42	11	3	28	58	116	25
Tonbridge	42	4	10	28	46	101	18

1970/71 F.A. Cup				1970/71 F.A. Trophy			
versus	res	goalscorer	gate	versus	res	goalscorer	gate
Portland United(h)	3-0	Marwood, Norton, Stevens	n.a.	Frome Town(h)	3-1	Stevens(2), Norton	740
Poole Town(h)	0-1		952	Bodmin Town(h)	5-1	Tyler, Dixon, Marwood, Husbands(2)	497
				Bilston Town(h)	0-1		769

1970/71 Wilts Premier Shield				1970/71 Beazer Homes Southern League Cup			
versus	res	goalscorer	gate	versus	res	goalscorer	gate
Trowbridge Tn(h)	1-1	Gilbert	819	Hastings Unitedd(a)	0-0		757
Trowbridge(a)	5-2	Moxham(2), Tyler(2), Dixon	1270	Hastings United(h)	1-3	Husbands	1250
Chippenham Tn(a)	2-0	Stevens(2)	267				
Chippenham Tn(h)	2-2	Walker(2)	315				

1970/71 Beazer Homes Southern Division						
versus	H	goalscorer	gate	A	goalscorer	gate
Banbury United	1-1	Dixon	660	1-2	Marwood	551
Barry Town	5-1	Stevens(3), Moxham, o.g.	490	1-2	Soutar	n.a
Bexley United	2-3	Soutar, o.g.	458	0-1		n.a
Burton Albion	0-2		435	0-2		1039
Canterbury	4-0	Husbands, Dixon, Soutar Stevens	469	2-0	Tyler, Crook	130
Cheltenham Town	4-2	Stevens(3), Soutar	618	2-2	Stevens, Moxham	375
Corby Town	2-1	Stevens, Dixon	640	2-2	Stevens, Dixon	321
Crawley Town	0-0		582	2-3	Marwood, Tyler	744
Dunstable Town	4-0	Walker, Stevens, Soutar, Moxham	592	1-0	Tyler	158
Folkestone Town	3-4	Tyler(2), Husbands	964	0-4		1297
Gravesend & N'fleet	1-2	Stevens	564	1-5	Marwood	536
Guildford City	1-1	Stevens	1228	0-3		2215
Hastings United	2-1	Dixon, Tyler	590	0-3		516
Merthyr Tydfil	2-1	Husbands, Stevens	966	0-1		1458
Ramsgate Athletic	4-3	Stevens, Crook(2), Moxham	477	1-1	Tyler	652
Rugby Town	0-0		711	0-1		556
Stevenage Athletic	3-0	Husbands, Dixon, Moxham	542	1-0	Moxham	723
Tonbridge	0-1		381	3-0	Stevens, Dixon, Soutar	559
Trowbridge	0-2		568	1-3	Dixon	562

> Leading goalscorer for the previous 1969/70 season was Alan Tyler with 16 goals.
> Leading goalscorer for this season 1970/71 season was John Stevens with 16 goals.

1970/71 Beazer Homes Southern Division

	P	W	D	L	F	A	Pts
Guildford City	38	22	10	6	76	36	54
Merthyr Tydfil	38	19	12	7	52	33	50
Gravesend & Northfleet	38	19	10	9	74	42	48
Folkestone Town	38	20	8	10	83	53	48
Burton Albion	38	19	10	9	56	37	48
Rugby Town	38	17	14	7	58	40	48
Ramsgate Athletic	38	20	5	13	83	54	45
Trowbridge Town	38	19	7	12	78	55	45
Bexley United	38	17	11	10	57	45	45
Crawley Town	38	15	11	12	84	68	41
Hastings United	38	13	12	13	51	50	38
Banbury United	38	13	11	14	58	53	37
Corby Town	38	14	8	16	57	60	36
Salisbury	**38**	**13**	**7**	**18**	**56**	**60**	**33**
Cheltenham Town	38	8	15	15	44	58	31
Stevenage Athletic	38	12	7	19	55	79	31
Tonbridge	38	8	8	22	48	83	24
Barry Town	38	9	6	23	35	82	24
Dunstable Town	38	8	4	26	32	81	20
Canterbury City	38	5	4	29	37	105	14

1971/72 F.A. Cup versus	res	goalscorer	gate
Westbury Utd(h)	4-0	Bennett, Fitch, Parker, Moxham	465
Bath City(h)	2-1	Moxham, Bennett	985
Basingstoke Town	2-4	Moxham, Bennett	1213

1971/72 F.A. Trophy versus	res	goalscorer	gate
Andover Town(a)	0-0		n.a.
replay(h)	4-3	Bennett, Parker, Soutar(2)	725
Welton Rovers(h)	3-1	Stevens(2), Moxham	536
Dorchester Town(a)	1-1	Stevens	n.a.
replay(h)	0-2		606

1971/72 Wilts Premier Shield versus	res	goalscorer	gate
Chippenham Tn(h)	4-2	Bennett(2), Stevens, o.g.	249
Swindon Town(a)	1-4	Bennett	1472
Swindon Town(h)	1-3	Bennett	608

1971-72 Beazer Homes Southern League Cup versus	res	goalscorer	gate
Waterlooville(h)	0-3		500
Trowbridge Tn(a)	4-1	Husbands(2), Stevens(2)	n.a.
Basingstoke Tn(a)	0-2		891
Winchester City(a)	1-3	Moxham)	n.a.
Andover Town(h)	2-0	Stevens, Wrintmore	706
Crawley Town(h)	4-0	Bennett(2), Moxham(2)	460
Metropolitan Police(a)	0-3		250

1971/72 Beazer Homes Southern Division						
versus	H	goalscorer	gate	A	goalscorer	gate
Andover	1-2	Stevens	527	0-2		573
Ashford Town	1-0	Bennett	296	1-1	Bennett	573
Basingstoke Town	2-2	Parker, Bennett	342	4-0	Parker(2), Bennett, Norman	n.a.
Bexley United	4-1	Fitch, Bennett, Moxham(2)	385	3-2	Fitch, Bennett, Moxham	n.a.
Canterbury City	2-2	Bennett, Parker	498	1-2	Parker	n.a.
Crawley Town	3-0	Soutar(2), Bennett	749	1-4	Husbands	n.a.
Hastings United	0-1		248	4-1	Bennett(2), Parker, Husbands	176
Maidstone United	1-0	Husbands	504	1-3	Wrintmore	n.a.
Metropolitan Police	1-2	Husbands	495	0-1		479
Ramsgate Athletic	2-2	Husbands, Bennett	238	0-0		624
Tonbridge	0-1		458	2-2	Bennett, Husbands	n.a.
Trowbridge Town	3-2	Bennett, Moxham, o.g.	364	2-3	Bennett, Soutar	n.a.
Waterlooville	1-1	Husbands	331	1-2	Bennett	800
Winchester City	1-0	Norman	359	1-2	Stevens	n.a.
Woodford Town	1-0	Fitch	483	1-3	Parker	n.a.

Leading goalscorer for 1971/72 season was Dave Bennett with 15 goals.

1971/72 Beazer Homes Southern Division	P	W	D	L	F	A	Pts
Waterlooville	30	15	9	6	40	22	39
Ramsgate Athletic	30	14	11	5	42	27	39
Maidstone United	30	14	10	6	48	28	38
Crawley Town	30	15	5	10	67	55	35
Metropolitan Police	30	15	3	12	48	41	33
Tonbridge	30	12	9	9	37	34	33
Bexley United	30	14	4	12	52	46	32
Basingstoke Town	30	14	4	12	37	36	32
Andover	30	11	9	10	32	34	31
Ashford Town	30	12	4	14	43	48	28
Salisbury	**30**	**10**	**7**	**13**	**45**	**44**	**27**
Winchester City	30	10	7	13	40	47	27
Hastings United	30	10	7	13	28	42	27
Trowbridge Town	30	8	7	15	41	49	23
Canterbury City	30	7	8	15	39	56	22
Woodford Town	30	4	6	20	22	52	14

1972/73 F.A. Cup

versus	res	goalscorer	gate
Westbury United(h)	9-1	Moxham(2), Taylor(2), Wookey, Bennet(2), Elliot, Duncan	446
Andover(a)	1-0	Moxham	735
Frome Town(a)	0-0		n.a.
replay(h)	0-1		860

1972/73 F.A. Trophy

versus	res	goalscorer	gate
Guildford City(h)	1-0	Viney	830
Bletchley(a)	1-1	Bennett	n.a.
replay(h)	0-2		554

1972/73 Wilts Premier Shield

versus	res	goalscorer	gate
Swindon Town(h)	3-1	Elliott, Husbands, Gorman	686
Trowbridge Tn(h)	0-1		429
Trowbridge Tn(a)	0-2		

1972/73 Beazer Homes Southern League Cup

versus	res	goalscorer	gate
Minehead(h)	2-0	Wookey, Taylor	643
Minehead(a)	0-1		n.a.
Andover Town(a)	4-1	Wookey(2), Bennett, Glover	558
Cheltenham Tn(a)	3-1	Elliott, Duncan, Wookey	n.a.
Weymouth(h)	2-2	Husbands(2)	553
Weymouth(a)	1-2	Wookey	n.a.

1972/73 Beazer Homes Southern Division

versus	H	goalscorer	gate	A	goalscorer	gate
Andover	0-0		967	1-3	Norman	357
Ashford	2-0	Bennett, Wookey	633	0-3		545
Basingstoke Town	0-1		647	0-4		n.a.
Bath City	0-1		465	1-2	Norman	1527
Bexley United	0-0		544	0-0		644
Bideford	0-2		291	2-2	Wookey, Bennett	n.a.
Bletchley	0-1		353	2-1	Husbands, Bennett	n.a.
Bognor Regis Town	2-1	Bennett, Wookey	622	3-0	Fitch, Bennett, Wookey	n.a.
Canterbury	2-1	Husbands, Elliott	229	0-0		n.a.
Crawley Town	3-1	Bennett, Elliot, Wookey	297	2-0	Taylor, Norman	n.a.
Dorchester Town	1-1	Moxham	350	1-1	Duncan	168
Dunstable Town	5-0	Duncan, Norman, Moxham, Husbands, o.g.	372	3-1	Bennett, Wookey, Duncan	n.a.
Gravesend & N'fleet	1-3	Norman	572	1-4	Wookey	720
Hastings United	0-1		388	3-1	Bennett, Taylor, Wookey	352
Maidstone	2-0	Norman, Powell	444	0-1		1208
Metropolitan Police	0-0		299	1-5	Moxham	n.a.
Minehead	2-1	Bennett, Elliott	447	0-2		500
Tonbridge	0-2		489	1-0	Bennett	549
Trowbridge	2-3	Gorman, Husbands	521	1-0	Bennett	424
Wealdsone	0-0		349	0-4		n.a.
Winchester City	1-0	Bennett	226	3-3	Bennett(3)	n.a.

Leading goalscorer for 1972/73 season was Dave Bennett with 15 goals.

1972/73 Beazer Homes Southern Division

	P	W	D	L	F	A	Pts
Maidstone United	42	25	12	5	90	38	62
Tonbridge	42	26	7	9	70	44	59
Ashford Town	42	24	7	11	90	40	55
Bideford	42	19	14	9	70	43	52
Minehead	42	20	12	10	65	47	52
Gravesend & Northfleet	42	22	7	13	81	55	51
Bath City	42	18	11	13	56	54	47
Wealdstone	42	16	12	14	81	61	44
Bletchley Town	42	14	13	15	54	51	41
Hastings United	42	14	13	15	53	53	41
Andover	42	15	11	16	62	70	41
Canterbury City	42	14	12	16	51	59	40
Basingstoke Town	42	14	12	16	48	57	40
Crawley Town	42	14	11	17	59	76	39
Metropolitan Police	42	15	8	19	82	75	38
Trowbridge Town	42	15	8	19	65	77	38
Bexley United	42	12	14	16	54	64	38
Salisbury	**42**	**14**	**10**	**18**	**49**	**60**	**38**
Bognor Regis Town	42	12	9	21	41	66	35
Dorchester Town	42	10	12	20	47	73	32
Winchester City	42	7	11	24	41	79	25
Dunstable Town	42	4	10	28	38	105	18

1973/74 F.A. Cup				1973/74 F.A. Trophy			
versus	res	goalscorer	gate	versus	res	goalscorer	gate
Westbury United(a)	2-0	Duncan, White	n.a.	Basingstoke Town(a)	1-1	Smith(A)	n.a.
Bridport(a)	1-0	Smith	n.a.	replay(h)	3-0	Cook, Norman, White	463
Weymouth(a)	0-2		n.a.	Chatham Town(a)	0-2		n.a.

1973/74 Wilts Premier Shield				1973/74 Beazer Homes Southern League Cup			
versus	res	goalscorer	gate	versus	res	goalscorer	gate
Chippenham Tn(h)	6-1	Williams, Smith, A.(2) Presley(2), Weller	n.a.	Dorchester Town(h)	1-4	Weller	517
Swindon Town(h)	0-1		442	Dorchester Town(a)	1-5	Smith, A.	407
Swindon Town(a)	0-4						

1973/74 Beazer Homes Southern Division						
versus	H	goalscorer	gate	A	goalscorer	gate
Andover	1-4	Cook	411	1-2	Smith	307
Ashford	2-1	Smith(2)	n.a.	1-1	Smith	n.a.
Basingstoke Town	4-1	Williams(2), Smith, Weller	624	1-0	Williams	307
Bath City	0-0		n.a.	0-1		n.a.
Bexley United	0-1		n.a.	0-2		n.a.
Bideford	0-1		n.a.	1-2	Norman	n.a.
Bognor Regis Town	1-1	Smith	510	0-1		n.a.
Canterbury	1-3	Williams	166	2-2	Williams(2)	n.a.
Crawley Town	5-2	Smith(2), Weller, Lake, Presley	n.a.	2-2	Weller(2), 1 penalty	n.a.
Dorchester Town	1-0	Smith	n.a.	2-2	Smith, Presley	n.a.
Gravesend & N'fleet	2-4	Cook, Williams	210	1-6	Hunt	544
Hastings United	1-0	Kelly	293	0-4		n.a.
Metropolitan Police	0-0		150	0-0		n.a.
Minehead	0-3		n.a.	2-2	Slade, Weller	270
Poole Town	1-0	Burden	435	0-1		n.a.
Ramsgate Athletic	2-1	Williams, Presley	n.a.	0-2		269
Trowbridge	0-1		n.a.	2-1	Smith(2)	820
Waterlooville	2-1	Norman, Smith	n.a.	0-1		n.a.
Wealdstone	1-2	Weller	536	1-2	Taylor	1420

Leading goalscorer for 1973/74 season was Alan Smith with 10 goals.

1973/74 Beazer Homes Southern Division

	P	W	D	L	F	A	Pts
Wealdstone	38	26	7	5	75	35	59
Bath City	38	20	8	10	55	34	48
Waterlooville	38	16	15	7	55	38	47
Minehead	38	16	15	7	69	52	47
Bideford	38	17	12	9	61	51	46
Poole Town	38	18	9	11	67	47	45
Bexley United	38	18	7	13	50	42	43
Hastings United	38	16	9	13	45	36	41
Basingstoke Town	38	14	11	13	55	44	39
Gravesend & Northfleet	38	13	13	12	58	52	39
Bognor Regis Town	38	13	12	13	48	54	38
Ashford Town	38	14	8	16	41	42	36
Ramsgate Athletic	38	13	9	16	46	44	35
Dorchester Town	38	10	13	15	40	48	33
Canterbury City	38	9	12	17	37	46	30
Trowbridge Town	38	8	14	16	44	61	30
Salisbury	**38**	**10**	**9**	**19**	**40**	**60**	**29**
Metropolitan Police	38	9	11	18	37	61	29
Andover	38	11	3	24	38	70	25
Crawley Town	38	6	9	23	35	79	21

1974/75 F.A. Cup

versus	res	goalscorer	gate
Cowes(h)	3-0	Guy, Green, Hibberd	269
Basingstoke Town(a)	1-1	Christopher	n.a.
replay(h)	3-1	Green(2), Christopher	n.a.
Alton Town(a)	3-1	Guy(2), Green	309
Cheltenham Town(a)	1-4	Christopher(p)	1374

1974/75 F.A. Trophy

versus	res	goalscorer	gate
Andover Town(h)	0-0		334
replay(a)	2-2	Hibberd, Guy	n.a.
2nd replay(a)	2-0	Green, Christopher	n.a.
Chippenham Town(a)	1-2	Christopher	n.a.

1974/75 Wilts Premier Shield

versus	res	goalscorer	gate
Chippenham Tn(h)	0-2		n.a.

1974/75 Beazer Homes Southern League Cup

versus	res	goalscorer	gate
Basingstoke Tn(h)	1-1	Green	n.a.
Basingstoke Tn(a)	2-2	Green(2)	n.a.
Basingstoke Tn(a)	5-0	Green(2), Guy(2), Christopher	n.a.
Crawley Town(a)	2-0	Guy, Hibberd	n.a.
Bedford Town(a)	0-1		n.a.

1974/75 Beazer Homes Southern Division)

versus	H	goalscorer	gate	A	goalscorer	gate
Andover	2-2	Green, Hunt	n.a.	1-1	Guy	227
Ashford	1-3	Christopher	n.a.	0-1		n.a.
Basingstoke Town	1-2	Christopher	n.a.	1-2	Iles	310
Bexley United	3-0	Iles(2), Guy	n.a.	2-2	Guy, Christopher	n.a.
Bideford	0-1		n.a.	1-1	Fitch	n.a.
Bognor Regis Town	2-2	Eyden, Christopher	227	0-2		n.a.
Canterbury	1-0	Christopher	166	1-2	Christopher	201
Crawley Town	3-2	Green, Guy, Weller	n.a.	0-1		n.a.
Dorchester Town	0-1		n.a.	1-0	Syrett	n.a.
Folkestone & Shepway	2-1	Green, Christopher	n.a.	2-1	Green, Guy	n.a.
Gravesend & N'fleet	1-1	Fairclough	n.a.	0-2		n.a.
Hastings United	1-0	Christopher	n.a.	2-2	Thomas, Christopher	n.a.
Hillingdon Borough	0-4		265	1-3	Christopher	519
Metropolitan Police	2-0	Christopher(2)	n.a.	1-2	Green	n.a.
Minehead	0-7		n.a.	0-2		n.a.
Poole Town	4-2	Green, Iles(2), Thomas	n.a.	3-3	Christopher(2), Guy	n.a.
Ramsgate Athletic	1-1	Green	n.a.	0-1		n.a.
Trowbridge Town	1-1	Green	425	1-4	Lock	n.a.
Waterlooville	1-1	Christopher(p)	349	2-3	Christopher, Guy	n.a.

> Leading goalscorer for 1974/75 season was Paul Christopher with 16 goals.

1974/75 Beazer Homes Southern Division

	P	W	D	L	F	A	Pts
Gravesend & Northfleet	38	24	12	2	70	30	60
Hillingdon Borough	38	22	8	8	87	45	52
Minehead	38	21	9	8	74	33	51
Ramsgate	38	19	11	8	70	37	49
Bexley United	38	19	7	12	61	44	45
Waterlooville	38	17	11	10	67	49	45
Ashford Town	38	16	12	10	64	55	44
Basingstoke Town	38	16	11	11	64	50	43
Canterbury City	38	16	9	13	54	43	41
Hastings United	38	13	14	11	54	45	40
Poole Town	38	11	13	14	50	60	35
Metropolitan Police	38	11	13	14	54	66	35
Folkestone & Shepway	38	10-	14	14	53	57	34
Andover	38	12	8	18	52	71	32
Bognor Regis Town	38	10	11	17	49	64	31
Salisbury	**38**	**9**	**11**	**18**	**45**	**66**	**29**
Trowbridge Town	38	10	9	19	48	76	29
Bideford	38	10	8	20	40	71	28
Dorchester Town	38	8	10	20	40	63	26
Crawley Town	38	3	5	30	31	102	11

1975/76 F.A. Cup				1975/76 F.A. Trophy			
versus	res	goalscorer	gate	versus	res	goalscorer	gate
Trowbridge Town(h)	3-1	Green(2), Christopher	n.a.	Workingham Town(a)	2-0	Green, Fitch	n.a.
Swaythling Athletic(a)	1-0	Guy	n.a.	Fareham Town(h)	1-1	Green	n.a.
Frome Town(h)	1-0	Hibberd	n.a.	*replay*(a)	0-1		n.a.
Weymouth(h)	4-5	Green(2), Hibberd, Guy	1050				

1975/76 Wilts Premier Shield				1975/76 Beazer Homes Southern League Cup			
versus	res	goalscorer	gate	versus	res	goalscorer	gate
Swindon Town(a)	1-1	o.g.	n.a.	Poole Town(a)	1-1	Christopher	n.a.
Swindon Town(h)	0-1		953	Poole Town(h)	1-0	Guy	n.a.
				Dorchester Town(h)	1-3	Green	n.a.

1975/76 Beazer Homes Southern Division

versus	H	goalscorer	gate	A	goalscorer	gate
Andover	2-0	Green, Guy	585	2-0	Green, Syrett	351
Ashford	6-1	Green(2), Guy(3), Selby	n.a.	1-3	Green	n.a.
Basingstoke Town	3-3	Hughes, Hibberd, o.g.	n.a.	3-4	Christopher(2), Guy	n.a.
Bexley United	0-1		n.a.	2-0	Green, Guy	n.a.
Bognor Regis Town	3-3	Guy(2), Andrews	n.a.	2-0	Andrews(2)	n.a.
Canterbury	3-1	Andrews, Guy, Christopher	n.a.	5-1	Green(2), Guy, Christopher, Andrews	n.a.
Crawley Town	1-0	Christopher	n.a.	1-1	Green	n.a.
Dartford	1-3	Guy	278	1-0	Green	n.a.
Dorchester Town	3-2	Selby, Andrews(2)	453	3-1	Guy, Green, Hibberd	n.a.
Folkestone & Shepway	2-1	Green, Guy	n.a.	0-0		n.a.
Guildford & Dorking	0-0		n.a.	2-1	Green, Hibberd	n.a.
Hastings United	3-3	Green(2), Guy	172	1-2	Selby	n.a.
Metropolitan Police	0-0		n.a.	2-2	Green, Guy	n.a.
Minehead	1-5	Andrews	n.a.	2-2	Christopher, o.g.	n.a.
Poole Town	0-1		n.a.	1-2	Andrews	n.a.
Ramsgate Athletic	3-1	Guy, Selby, o.g.	n.a.	3-1	Andrews, Guy(2)	n.a.
Romford	1-1	Fitch	n.a.	1-2	Guy	n.a.
Trowbridge	4-2	Green(2), Selby, Christopher	n.a.	1-1	Guy	n.a.
Waterlooville	3-0	Green, Christopher, Andrews	335	1-2	Green	n.a.

Leading goalscorer for 1975/76 season was Colin Guy with 20 goals.

1975/76 Beazer Homes Southern Division

	P	W	D	L	F	A	Pts
Minehead	38	27	8	3	102	35	62
Dartford	38	26	4	8	84	46	56
Romford	38	21	9	8	66	37	51
Salisbury	**38**	**17**	**11**	**10**	**73**	**53**	**45**
Hastings United	38	15	15	8	67	51	45
Poole Town	38	20	2	16	57	57	42
Bexley United	38	14	13	11	62	53	41
Waterlooville	38	13	13	12	62	54	39
Basingstoke Town	38	13	12	13	69	71	38
Ashford Town	38	14	8	16	67	73	36
Canterbury City	38	11	13	14	53	60	35
Folkestone & Shepway	38	10-	14	14	36	51	34
Metropolitan Police	38	9	14	15	46	58	32
Trowbridge Town	38	11	10	17	48	75	32
Guildford & Dorking United	38	9	13	16	43	50	31
Bognor Regis Town	38	6	17	15	44	72	29
Ramsgate	38	9	10	19	57	76	28
Crawley Town	38	9	10	19	46	66	28
Andover	38	9	10	19	42	62	28
Dorchester Town	38	11	6	21	45	69	28

1976/77 F.A. Cup

versus	res	goalscorer	gate
Farnborough Town(a)	0-4		n.a.

1976/77 F.A. Trophy

versus	res	goalscorer	gate
Frome Town(h)	1-1	Green	n.a.
replay(a)	4-0	Andrews, Green, Verity, Selby	n.a.
Bideford(a)	1-2	Myers	n.a.

1976/77 Wilts Premier Shield

versus	res	goalscorer	gate
Chippenham Town(a)	2-0	Guy, Christopher	n.a.
Swindon Town(a)	0-4		n.a.
Swindon Town(h)	3-0	Christopher(2), Verity	n.a.

1976/77 Beazer Homes Southern League Cup

versus	res	goalscorer	gate
Andover Town(a)	4-1	Myers, Andrews, Christopher, Verity	n.a.
Andover Town(h)	1-0	Guy	n.a.
Poole Town(h)	5-1	Guy(2), Christopher, Myrers, Green	n.a.
Worcester City	1-2	Guy	n.a.

1976/77 Beazer Homes Southern Division

versus	H	goalscorer	gate	A	goalscorer	gate
Andover	1-0	Green	n.a.	4-2	Guy(2), Green, Christopher	346
Ashford Town	2-3	Verity, Christopher	n.a.	2-1	Myers, Guy	n.a.
Aylesbury United	3-0	Guy(2), Green	n.a.	4-0	Green(2), Guy(2)	402
Barnet	1-0	Andrews	450	0-1		1196
Basingstoke Town	1-1	Christopher	745	6-3	Guy(2), Green(2), Christopher, Myers	550
Bognor Regis Town	2-2	Harrison, Lock	531	3-1	Green(3)	n.a.
Canterbury	3-0	Green(2), Christopher	514	2-1	Christopher, Guy	n.a.
Crawley Town	1-0	Guy	n.a.	5-0	Green(2), Verity, Andrews Christopher	n.a.
Dorchester Town	1-1	Verity	1368	0-0		619
Folkestone & Shepway	2-2	Guy(2)	527	1-1	o.g.	n.a.
Hastings United	1-1	Andrews	699	0-5		n.a.
Metropolitan Police	2-2	Green, Guy	n.a.	4-0	Andrews, Green(2), Hughes	n.a.
Poole Town	0-0		n.a.	0-2		n.a.
Romford	1-1	Guy	617	0-2		1508
Tonbridge	2-0	Selby, Guy	n.a.	1-1	Green	n.a.
Trowbridge	1-3	Verity	873	0-2		n.a.
Waterlooville	1-0	Christopher	n.a.	0-1		n.a.

Leading goalscorer for 1976/77 season was Alan Green with 18 goals.

1976/77 Beazer Homes Southern Division

	P	W	D	L	F	A	Pts
Barnet	34	23	8	3	65	25	54
Hastings United	34	18	11	5	47	18	47
Waterlooville	34	19	6	9	50	25	44
Dorchester	34	16	11	7	48	30	43
Salisbury	**34**	**15**	**11**	**8**	**57**	**39**	**41**
Romford	34	18	5	11	47	32	41
Poole Town	34	17	7	10	40	35	41
Trowbridge Town	34	15	8	11	47	39	38
Crawley Town	34	14	9	11	53	42	37
Folkestone & Shepway	34	12-	11	11	39	42	35
Basingstoke Town	34	12	10	12	51	43	34
Canterbury City	34	6	16	12	36	46	28
Bognor Regis Town	34	9	9	16	33	50	27
Tonbridge AFC	34	9	9	16	33	50	27
Metropolitan Police	34	5	12	17	37	61	22
Andover	34	4	11	19	17	49	19
Ashford Town	34	5	8	21	32	65	18
Aylesbury United	34	5	6	23	27	68	16

1977/78 F.A. Cup

versus	res	goalscorer	gate
Cowes(h)	5-1	Verity(2), Green(2) Christopher	n.a.
Hungerford Town(a)	1-0	Christopher	n.a.
Frome Town(a)	2-2	Green, Andrews	n.a.
replay(h)	1-0	Verity	1072
Minehead(h)	1-1	Andrews	1240
replay(a)	1-2	Green	n.a.

1977/78 F.A. Trophy

versus	res	goalscorer	gate
Wokingham Town(a)	2-1	Cotton, Christopher	n.a.
Boreham Wood(a)	0-0		n.a.
replay(h)	1-0	Andrews	n.a.
Cheltenham Town(h)	1-2	Husbands	520

1977/78 Wilts Premier Shield

versus	res	goalscorer	gate
Chippenham Tn(h)	3-0	Cotton(2), Andrews	n.a.
Swindon Town(a)	2-1	Christopher, Andrews	n.a.
Swindon Town(h)	0-0		

1977/78 Beazer Homes Southern League Cup

versus	res	goalscorer	gate
Barry Town(h)	2-2	Husbands, Cotton	n.a.
Barry Town(a)	1-3	Green	

1977/78 Beazer Homes Southern Division

versus	H	goalscorer	gate	A	goalscorer	gate
Addlestone	5-1	Christopher(2), Cotton, Husbands, Marsh	625	3-1	Green(2), Christopher	987
Andover	3-0	Andrews(2), Husbands	n.a.	2-0	Christopher, Marsh	n.a.
Ashford	3-0	Green, Husbands, Marsh	466	0-2		n.a.
Aylesbury United	0-2		993	1-0	Marsh	987
Basingstoke Town	2-0	Green, Christopher	610	3-2	Verity, Christopher, Chalklin	n.a.
Bognor Regis Town	2-0	Verity, Christopher	444	0-0		n.a.
Canterbury City	4-1	Verity(2), Christopher, Marsh	384	4-0	Green(2), Cotton, Andrews	n.a.
Chelmsford City	3-1	Christopher(2), Green	n.a.	1-1	Marsh	n.a.
Crawley Town	2-0	Green, Andrews	n.a.	1-0	Cotton	n.a.
Dorchester Town	2-2	Green, Husbands	n.a.	1-2	Christopher	n.a.
Folkestone & Shepway	2-3	Verity, Christopher	603	1-2	Andrews	n.a.
Hounslow Town	0-1		411	3-1	Green(2), Christopher	n.a.
Margate	0-0		1286	1-1	Marsh	800
Poole Town	1-0	Green	n.a.	1-0	Selby	n.a.
Romford	0-0		440	0-0		n.a.
Taunton Town	2-0	Marsh(2)	528	0-2		n.a.
Tonbridge	2-0	Husbands, Marsh	n.a.	1-0	Cotton	n.a.
Trowbridge	1-1	Green	759	0-0		n.a.
Waterlooville	2-0	Cotton, Husbands	n.a.	1-1	Marsh	600

> Leading goalscorers for 1977/78 season were Paul Christopher and Alan Green with 13 goals each.

1977/78 Beazer Homes Southern Division

	P	W	D	L	F	A	Pts
Margate	38	24	10	4	92	32	58
Dorchester Town	38	23	10	5	67	31	56
Salisbury	**38**	**21**	**10**	**7**	**60**	**27**	**52**
Waterlooville	38	19	13	6	66	36	51
Romford	38	17	15	6	58	37	49
Aylesbury United	38	20	7	11	56	42	47
Trowbridge Town	38	16	11	11	65	59	43
Chelmsford City	38	15	11	12	58	46	41
Folkestone & Shepway	38	16-	9	13	64	56	41
Taunton Town	38	15	10	13	57	54	40
Addlestone	38	14	10	14	57	60	38
Crawley Town	38	14	9	15	61	60	37
Basingstoke Town	38	11	11	16	44	50	33
Tonbridge AFC	38	13	5	20	64	77	31
Ashford Town	38	9	13	16	39	60	31
Hounslow	38	10	10	18	43	62	30
Bognor Regis Town	38	9	8	21	52	69	26
Poole Town	38	8	10	20	43	68	26
Andover	38	4	12	22	30	68	20
Canterbury City	38	2	6	30	31	113	10

1978/79 F.A. Cup

versus	res	goalscorer	gate
Welton Rovers(h)	4-0	McCarthy, Hallam Andrews, o.g..	n.a.
Bath City(h)	0-2		n.a.

1978/79 F.A. Trophy

versus	res	goalscorer	gate
Paulton Rovers(a)	2-1	Andrews, McCarthy	n.a.
Tiverton Town(h)	1-1	McCarthy	n.a.
replay(h)	4-0	Ransome(2), McCarthy, Andrews	n.a.
Bridgwater Town(a)	1-1	Andrews	n.a.
replay(h)	2-1	Andrews, Christopher	n.a.
Taunton Town(h)	0-2		

1978/79 Wilts Premier Shield

versus	res	goalscorer	gate
Chippenham Tn(a)	2-0	Christopher, Ransome	n.a.
Swindon Town(h)	0-0		n.a.
Swindon Town(a)	3-0	Christopher, Ashton Bobby Andrews	n.a.

1978/79 Beazer Homes Southern League Cup

versus	res	goalscorer	gate
Dorchester Town(a)	0-5		n.a.
Dorchester Town(h)	1-2	Booth	289

1978/79 Beazer Homes Southern Division

versus	H	goalscorer	gate	A	goalscorer	gate
Addlestone	1-0	Andrews	n.a.	0-0		n.a.
Andover	1-2	Christopher	n.a.	1-2	Ashton	n.a.
Ashford	3-0	Ashton(2), Christopher	n.a.	1-1	Ashton	n.a.
Aylesbury United	4-1	Ashton(2), McCarthy, Fry	149	1-2	Ashton	302
Basingstoke Town	0-0		n.a.	1-1	McCarthy	n.a.
Bognor Regis Town	1-0	Ashton	243	2-1	Marsh(2)	n.a.
Canterbury City	1-0	Hallam	243	3-0	Ashton(2), Christopher	n.a.
Chelmsford City	1-1	Fry	n.a.	3-0	Andrews(2), Ashton	n.a.
Crawley Town	2-0	Christopher, Andrews	n.a.	3-4	Verity, Fry, Andrews	n.a.
Dover	0-2		n.a.	0-4		n.a.
Dunstable Town	3-1	Andrews, Fry, Verity	n.a.	3-1	o.g. Ashton, Andrews	n.a.
Folkestone & Shepway	0-4		n.a.	1-2	Fry	n.a.
Gosport Borough	0-3		304	0-1		750
Hounslow Town	1-1	o.g.	n.a.	0-2		n.a.
Minehead	1-0	Andrews	370	2-0	Bletsoe	n.a.
Poole Town	0-1		n.a.	1-1	o.g.	n.a.
Taunton Town	2-4	Fry(2)	n.a.	0-0		1000
Tonbridge	0-1		290	2-4	Christopher, Fry	328
Trowbridge	1-1	Ashton	769	1-2	Booth	410
Waterlooville	0-0		n.a.	0-1		n.a.

Leading goalscorer for 1978/79 season was Brian Ashton with 13 goals.

1978/79 Beazer Homes Southern Division

	P	W	D	L	F	A	Pts
Dover	40	28	9	3	88	20	65
Folkestone & Shepway	40	22	6	12	84	50	50
Gosport Borough	40	19	11	10	62	47	49
Chelmsford City	40	20	7	13	65	61	47
Minehead	40	16	13	11	58	39	45
Poole Town	40	15	15	10	48	44	45
Hounslow	40	16	12	12	56	45	44
Waterlooville	40	17	10	13	52	43	44
Trowbridge Town	40	15	12	13	65	61	42
Aylesbury United	40	16	9	15	54	52	41
Taunton Town	40	16	9	15	53	51	41
Bognor Regis Town	40	17	7	16	58	58	41
Dunstable	40	18	4	18	57	55	40
Tonbridge AFC	40	15	10	15	43	47	40
Salisbury	**40**	**13**	**10**	**17**	**47**	**51**	**36**
Basingstoke Town	40	12	11	17	49	62	35
Addlestone	40	12	9	19	56	64	33
Andover	40	12	6	22	47	69	30
Ashford Town	40	10	10	20	28	53	30
Crawley Town	40	9	9	22	44	75	27
Canterbury City	40	6	3	31	31	98	15

1979/80 F.A. Cup

versus	res	goalscorer	gate
Newport I.O.W.(h)	4-3	Christopher(2)Andrews Fry	
Horsham YMCA(h)	3-1	Fry, Cox, Ashton	455
Poole Town(h)	3-0	Christopher(2), Ashton	617
Worcester City(h)	2-1	Christopher(2)	1512
Millwall(h)	1-2	Hibbs	8805

1979/80 F.A. Trophy

versus	res	goalscorer	gate
Croydon(h)	1-0	Verity	319
Oxford City(a)	0-1		

match was played at 'the Dell' Southampton

1979/80 Wilts Premier Shield

versus	res	goalscorer	gate
Chippenham Tn(a)	0-0		n.a.
Chippenham Tn(h)	1-2	Bobby Andrews	n.a.

1979/80 Beazer Homes Southern League Cup

versus	res	goalscorer	gate
Taunton Town(h)	2-0	Andrews, Christopher	n.a.
Taunton Town(a)	0-1		n.a.
Ashford Town(h)	0-1		n.a.

1979/80 Beazer Homes Southern Division

versus	H	goalscorer	gate	A	goalscorer	gate
Addlestone	2-2	Ashton, (o.g.)	406	0-1		n.a.
Andover	1-3	Christopher	308	1-1	Lennard	n.a.
Ashford	0-1		233	1-2	Green	n.a.
Aylesbury United	0-1		215	1-2	Ashton	340
Basingstoke Town	1-2	Andrews	338	1-1	Hibbs	n.a.
Bognor Regis Town	0-0		478	0-1		n.a.
Canterbury City	1-1	Ashton	328	1-2	Christopher	n.a.
Chelmsford City	3-1	Ashton(2), Verity	405	2-3	Green(2)	n.a.
Crawley Town	0-0		240	1-0	Cox	n.a.
Dartford	0-0		336	0-0		n.a.
Dorchester Town	1-2	Ashton		1-2	Andrews(p)	n.a.
Dover	2-1	Durbridge, Green	222	1-2	Andrews	n.a.
Dunstable Town	0-4		n.a.	1-4	Christopher	n.a.
Fareham Town	1-1	Dowthwaite	422	1-0	Andrews	n.a.
Folkestone & Shepway	2-2	Ashton, Hibbs	210	1-1	Andrews	n.a.
Gosport Borough	0-2		379	1-0	Verity	222
Hastings United	3-0	Cook, Hallam, Ashton	318	0-1		n.a.
Hillingdon Borough	0-1		280	1-2	Christopher	n.a.
Hounslow Town	2-0	Green, Andrews	290	0-1		n.a.
Margate	2-1	Tindall, Green		0-2		n.a.
Poole Town	0-1			0-1		n.a.
Tonbridge	6-1	Green(3), Tindal(2), Guy	296	4-0	Green(3), Guy	n.a.
Waterlooville	0-0		168	1-2	Andrews	n.a.

Leading goalscorer for 1979/80 season was Alan Green with 12 goals.

1979/80 Beazer Homes Southern Division

	P	W	D	L	F	A	Pts
Dorchester	46	25	12	9	81	53	62
Aylesbury United	46	25	11	10	73	40	61
Dover	46	22	13	11	78	48	57
Gosport Borough	46	21	15	10	70	50	57
Dartford	46	21	14	11	66	45	56
Bognor Regis Town	46	20	15	11	66	38	55
Hillingdon Borough	46	19	16	11	64	41	54
Dunstable	46	17	19	10	93	64	53
Addlestone	46	20	13	13	72	57	53
Hastings United	46	19	15	12	74	65	53
Fareham Town	46	16	16	14	61	53	48
Waterlooville	46	17	12	17	67	64	46
Andover	46	16	13	17	65	65	45
Poole Town	46	16	13	17	49	64	45
Canterbury City	46	15	14	17	56	60	44
Hounslow	46	14	15	17	44	57	43
Margate	46	17	8	21	51	62	42
Folkestone & Shepway	46	14	11	21	54	63	39
Ashford Town	46	12	14	20	54	71	38
Crawley Town	46	13	11	22	55	72	37
Chelmsford City	46	9	18	19	47	69	36
Basingstoke Town	46	9	15	22	48	79	33
Salisbury	**46**	**10**	**12**	**24**	**47**	**58**	**32**
Tonbridge AFC	46	3	9	34	31	128	15

1980/81 F.A. Cup

versus	res	goalscorer	gate
Trowbridge Town(h)	1-1	Green	600
replay(a)	1-2	Haysom	n.a.

1980/81 F.A. Trophy

versus	res	goalscorer	gate
Hampton(a)	2-2	Oakley, Christopher(p)	n.a.
replay(h)	2-1	Tindal, Oakley	322
Llanelli(a)	2-1	Green, Legg	n.a.
Dawlish(h)	2-1	Legg, Verity	278
Bridgend(a)	0-2		135

1980/81 Beazer Homes Southern League Cup

versus	res	goalscorer	gate
Andover Town(h)	6-1	Green(3), Christopher, Lennard, Tindal	402
Andover Town(a)	1-1	Hibbs	n.a.
Bognor Regis Tn(h)	0-2		305

1980/81 Beazer Homes Southern Division

versus	H	goalscorer	gate	A	goalscorer	gate
Addlestone	2-1	Haysom, Green	219	0-2		n.a.
Andover	3-1	Legg(2), Guy	435	0-0		n.a
Ashford	2-0	Green, Tindal	245	4-0	Green(3), Oakley	n.a
Aylesbury	1-3	Guy	221	1-3	Green	410
Basingstoke Town	2-0	Green, Christopher(p)	550	0-1		n.a.
Bognor Regis Town	1-3	Green	n.a.	0-2		n.a.
Canterbury City	0-2		188	2-1	Green, Legg	n.a.
Chelmsford City	3-1	Green, Oakley, Tindal	n.a.	2-0	Haysom, Hibbs	n.a
Crawley Town	0-3		173	2-1	Legg, Guy	n.a.
Dartford	0-1		336	1-5	Oakley	n.a
Dorchester Town	1-2	Guy	n.a.	1-2	Green	300
Dover	4-2	Christopher(2), Green, Shurben	315	1-3	Christopher	n.a.
Dunstable	1-2	o.g.	356	1-4	Guy	n.a
Fareham Town	2-2	Legg(2)	n.a.	1-1	Legg	n.a.
Folkestone & Shepway	0-0		207	0-0		n.a
Gosport	0-2		375	0-3		356
Hastings United	0-2		201	0-6		n.a.
Hillingdon Borough	2-0	Tindal, Christopher	222	0-1		n.a.
Hounslow Town	0-1		235	1-5	Tindal	n.a.
Margate	7-1	Green(3), Christopher, Tindall Legg, Summers	295	0-0		n.a.
Poole Town	1-2	Oakley	406	0-2		n.a.
Tonbridge	3-0	Guy(3)	221	3-1	Hibbs(2), Green	n.a.
Waterlooville	0-0		363	2-2	Green(2)	n.a.

Leading goalscorer for 1980/81 season was Alan Green with 18 goals.

1980/81 Beazer Homes Southern Division

	P	W	D	L	F	A	Pts
Dartford	46	26	14	6	76	39	66
Bognor Regis Town	46	25	13	8	95	43	63
Hastings United	46	24	14	8	87	43	62
Gosport Borough	46	24	12	10	84	52	60
Waterlooville	46	19	21	6	67	50	59
Dorchester Town	46	21	13	12	84	56	55
Dover	46	22	10	14	70	50	54
Poole Town	46	19	14	13	70	56	52
Addlestone	46	21	9	16	66	57	51
Dunstable	46	19	13	14	73	68	51
Aylesbury United	46	20	10	16	66	60	50
Hounslow	46	17	13	16	65	55	47
Hillingdon Borough	46	16	15	15	50	49	47
Basingstoke Town	46	16	14	16	69	58	46
Crawley Town	46	18	4	24	64	78	40
Ashford Town	46	12	15	19	55	76	39
Tonbridge AFC	46	12	15	19	44	68	39
Chelmsford City	46	13	12	21	54	78	38
Canterbury City	46	12	13	21	40	59	37
Salisbury	**46**	**14**	**8**	**24**	**57**	**76**	**36**
Folkestone	46	11	11	24	47	65	33
Margate	46	11	7	28	65	117	29
Fareham Town	46	5	18	23	31	73	28
Andover Town	46	6	10	30	41	94	22

1981/82 F.A. Cup				1981/82 F.A. Trophy			
versus	res	goalscorer	gate	versus	res	goalscorer	gate
Wealdstone(a)	0-4		569	Gloucester(a)	1-2	Andrews	324

1981/82 Beazer Homes Southern League Cup			
versus	res	goalscorer	gate
Basingstoke Tn(a)	2-1	Coak, Tindal	n.a.
Basingstoke Tn(h)	2-2	McDougall, Verity	761
Minehead(a)	3-2	Thompson, Haysom, Green	n.a.
Gloucester City(a)	0-2		n.a.

1981/82 Beazer Homes Southern Division						
versus	H	goalscorer	gate	A	goalscorer	gate
Addlestone	2-6	Verity, Haysom	181	1-2	Thompson	n.a.
Andover	0-2		215	2-1	Tindal, Cranmer	n.a.
Ashford	2-0	Hibbs, Thompson	162	1-2	Harvey	n.a.
Aylesbury	1-1	Oakley	416	1-2	Verity	157
Basingstoke Town	1-3	Tavener	236	1-0	Hibbs	761
Canterbury City	3-1	MacDougall(3)	356	1-1	Thompson	n.a.
Chelmsford City	0-0		163	2-1	Thompson, Tindal	n.a.
Crawley Town	3-0	Leigh, Hibbs(2)	164	3-1	Andrews, Oakley, Thompson	n.a.
Dorchester Town	0-0		263	1-2	Chisholm	n.a.
Dover	3-0	Leigh, Hibbs, Thompson	212	1-3	Harvey	n.a.
Dunstable	4-2	Andrews, Thompson(3)	168	0-2		n.a.
Fareham Town	1-1	Thompson	327	0-0		n.a.
Folkestone & Shepway	3-0	Thompson, Hibbs, Christopher	207	3-1	Coak, Hibbs, Green	n.a.
Gosport	1-0	Oakley	224	1-1	Hibbs	n.a.
Hastings United	0-5		218	0-2		n.a.
Hillingdon Borough	4-3	Hibbs, Leigh, Tavener, Christopher	238	2-1	Thompson(2)	n.a.
Hounslow Town	2-4	Thompson, Haysom	150	0-0		n.a.
Poole Town	0-4		221	0-2		n.a.
Thanet United	2-0	Hibbs, Thompson	150	1-2	Thompson	n.a.
Tonbridge	1-1	Hibbs	240	3-5	Thompson(2), Tavener	n.a.
Waterlooville	2-1	Hibbs, Andrew(p)	380	0-3		n.a.
Wealdstone	2-4	Marsh(2)	252	1-4	Thompson	n.a.
Welling United	1-1	Green	214	1-4	Tindal	n.a.

Leading goalscorer for 1981/82 season was Ian Thompson with 19 goals.

1981/82 Beazer Homes Southern Division							
	P	W	D	L	F	A	Pts
Wealdstone	46	32	8	6	100	32	72
Hastings United	46	31	9	6	79	34	71
Dorchester Town	46	21	18	7	76	41	60
Gosport Borough	46	26	8	12	76	45	60
Fareham Town	46	20	14	12	58	48	54
Poole Town	46	19	15	12	92	63	53
Waterlooville	46	22	9	15	75	53	53
Welling United	46	19	13	14	70	48	51
Addlestone	46	17	17	12	71	53	51
Chelmsford City	46	20	11	15	64	53	51
Aylesbury United	46	19	12	15	79	61	50
Basingstoke Town	46	18	12	16	74	61	48
Dover	46	19	8	19	61	63	46
Ashford Town	46	16	14	16	52	56	46
Tonbridge AFC	46	19	7	20	62	70	45
Dunstable	46	18	8	20	63	68	44
Salisbury	**46**	**16**	**10**	**20**	**64**	**81**	**42**
Hounslow	46	15	11	20	59	83	41
Hillingdon Borough	46	14	10	22	46	58	38
Canterbury City	46	10	16	20	49	78	36
Crawley Town	46	9	12	25	46	81	30
Folkestone	46	10	6	30	49	101	26
Andover	46	4	11	31	39	100	19
Thanet United	46	5	7	34	37	110	17

1982/83 F.A. Cup				1982/83 F.A. Trophy			
versus	res	goalscorer	gate	versus	res	goalscorer	gate
Calne Town(h)	3-2	Howarth, Thompson(2)	179	Barnstaple Town(h)	1-1	Thompson(p)	176
Slough Town(a)	0-2		539	*replay*(a)	0-2		164

1982/83 Beazer Homes Southern League Cup			
versus	res	goalscorer	gate
Andover Town(a)	2-1	Newark, Hibbs	240
Andover Town(h)	2-1	Thompson, Hibbs	216
Waterlooville(a)	2-4	Christopher, o.g.	n.a

1982/83 Beazer Homes Southern Division						
versus	H	goalscorer	gate	A	goalscorer	gate
Andover	2-0	Haysom, Thompson	294	0-0		n.a.
Ashford Town	5-1	Thompson(2), Brooks, Hibbs, Frost	159	3-1	Thompson, Leigh, Battams	n.a.
Basingstoke Town	1-2	Howarth	195	2-0	Thompson, Christopher	n.a.
Cambridge City	2-0	Hibbs, Thompson	166	3-2	Thompson(p), Howarth, Christopher	n.a.
Canterbury City	3-1	Thompson(2), Leigh	205	0-4		n.a.
Crawley Town	2-2	Hibbs, Thompson	190	2-1	Thompson(2)	n.a.
Dover	1-1	Brooks	180	2-2	Thompson(2)	n.a.
Dunstable Town	0-0		208	2-2	Christopher(2)	n.a.
Erith & Belvedere	2-1	Brooks, Leigh	203	0-0		n.a.
Fisher Athletic	3-1	Thompson(2), Christopher	235	2-3	Thompson, Frost	n.a.
Folkestone	3-3	Thompson, Hayson, Hibbs	240	1-3	Brooks	n.a.
Hillingdon Borough	3-2	Hibbs, Thompson(p), o.g.	209	0-1		n.a.
Hounslow Town	0-1		161	1-1	Thompson	n.a.
Road Sea S'hampton	1-4	Brooks	302	2-3	Thompson(2)	n.a.
Thanet United	6-1	Howarth(3), Ames, Haysom, Thompson	177	1-0	Haysom	n.a.
Tonbridge AFC	3-2	Christopher, Leigh, Thompson(p)	153	0-2		n.a.
Woodford Town	0-2		203	0-0		n.a.

> Leading goalscorer for 1982/83 season was Ian Thompson with 24 goals.

Ten new clubs joined the Southern League as it reverted to a three-division format – this was after the S.L. had offered the Isthmian League one of their Alliance promotion places. Minehead quit the Southern League set-up, but new-comers who did well included, Fisher Athletic who won the division and RS Southampton who made the big step-up from the Hampshire League. Salisbury's top scorer Ian Thompson nearly went to Man. City for £16,000 but a last minute hitch saw him arrive at Bournemouth, where in the following season he scored the winning goal that knocked Manchester United out of the F.A. Cup.

1982/83 Beazer Homes Southern Division

	P	W	D	L	F	A	Pts
Fisher Athletic	34	23	5	6	79	34	74
Folkestone	34	22	6	6	79	41	72
Road Sea Southampton	34	21	7	6	66	30	70
Dunstable	34	19	5	10	57	39	62
Hillingdon Borough	34	14	11	9	41	30	53
Salisbury	**34**	**14**	**10**	**10**	**58**	**49**	**52**
Crawley Town	34	14	9	11	51	43	51
Ashford Town	34	13	10	11	51	41	49
Tonbridge AFC	34	14	5	15	57	57	47
Hounslow	34	11	12	11	46	47	45
Canterbury City	34	12	9	13	52	63	45
Cambridge City	34	12	5	17	56	63	41
Dover	34	11	7	16	35	52	40
Thanet United	34	10	5	19	30	61	35
Basingstoke Town	34	8	10	16	37	56	34
Woodford Town	34	6	9	19	29	57	27
Andover Town	34	6	8	20	28	53	26
Erith & Belvedere	34	5	9	20	26	62	24

1983/84 F.A. Cup				1983/84 F.A. Trophy			
versus	**res**	**goalscorer**	**gate**	**versus**	**res**	**goalscorer**	**gate**
Flackwell Heath(h)	1-0	Frost(p)	180	Maesteg Park(a)	1-1	Haysom	80
				replay(h)	3-0	Beal(2), Paterson	225
Sholing Sports(a)	1-2	Smith	242	Weston-super-Mare(h)	4-2	Diaper, Battams	284
						Cramner, Smith	
				Gloucester City(h)	2-2	Butler, Paterson	335
				1st replay(a)	3-3	Frost, Slade,	400
						Paterson	
				2nd replay(a)	0-2		530

1983/84 Beazer Homes Southern League Cup			
versus	**res**	**goalscorer**	**gate**
Gosport Borough(h)	1-2	Beal	231
Gosport Borough(a)	2-2	Smith, B., o.g.	220

1983/84 Beazer Homes Southern Division						
versus	**H**	**goalscorer**	**gate**	**A**	**goalscorer**	**gate**
Addlestone	2-0	Paterson, Slade	167	0-2		143
Andover	0-0		203	2-0	Paterson, Slade	299
Ashford Town	4-2	Smith(2), Diaper, Frost	194	1-2	Paterson	115
Basingstoke Town	0-1		354	1-2	Smith	303
Cambridge City	3-1	Paterson(2, 1 penalty), Battams	209	0-0		116
Canterbury City	2-1	Cranmer, Slade	227	2-3	Paterson(2)	52
Chatham Town	1-1	Frost(p)	195	0-3		150
Crawley Town	2-2	Goddard, Beal	146	0-2		254
Dover Athletic	3-2	Dawtry(p), Slade, Hibbs	198	3-0	Paterson(2), Smith	150
Dunstable Town	3-2	Smith(2), Cranmer	193	4-2	Paterson(2) Hibbs, Smith	113
Erith & Belvedere	4-1	Paterson(3), Haysom	195	1-1	Slade	98
Hillingdon Borough	3-1	Ames(2), Smith	240	1-1	Beal	96
Hounslow Town	2-0	Paterson, Slade	148	1-1	o.g.	98
Poole Town	0-1		233	1-2	Dawtry	316
R.S. Southampton	1-0	Slade	371	0-1		252
Thanet United	1-0	Hibbs	172	0-1		130
Tonbridge AFC	4-1	Beal, Slade, Smith, Ames	217	1-3	Dawtry	328
Waterlooville	3-4	Slade(2), Frost(p)	293	2-1	Slade(2)	220
Woodford Town	0-0		169	3-1	Frost(p), Beal, Paterson	47

Leading goalscorer for 1983/84 season was Tommy Paterson with 16 goals.

1983/84 Beazer Homes Southern Division							
	P	**W**	**D**	**L**	**F**	**A**	**Pts**
Road Sea Southampton	38	26	6	6	83	35	84
Crawley Town	38	22	9	7	68	28	75
Basingstoke Town	38	20	9	9	54	36	69
Tonbridge AFC	38	20	9	9	61	44	69
Addestone & Weybridge	38	19	11	8	58	34	68
Poole Town	38	20	7	11	68	42	67
Hillingdon Borough	38	18	11	9	43	20	65
Ashford Town	38	19	5	14	65	47	62
Salisbury	**38**	**17**	**8**	**13**	**61**	**48**	**59**
Cambridge City	38	13	9	16	43	53	48
Canterbury City	38	12	9	17	44	52	45
Waterlooville	38	12	9	17	56	69	45
Dover Athletic	38	12	9	17	51	74	45
Chatham Town	38	11	10	17	46	56	43
Andover Town	38	12	6	20	35	54	42
Erith & Belvedere	38	11	9	18	43	68	42
Dunstable	38	10	8	20	38	65	38
Thanet United	38	9	8	21	40	65	35
Woodford Town	38	7	8	23	30	69	29
Hounslow	38	4	12	22	30	58	24

1984/85 F.A. Cup				1984/85 F.A. Trophy			
versus	res	goalscorer	gate	versus	res	goalscorer	gate
Marlow Town(h)	3-1	Slade, Tutton, White	185	Weston-super-Mare(a)	1-1	Cranmer	197
Newport I.O.W.(h)	4-1	Dawtry, Paterson, Tutton, o.g.	210	*replay*(h)	3-0	Paterson, Slade o.g	162
				Taunton Town(h)	7-0	Paterson(2),	232
Hungerford(h)	0-0		316			Slade(2) Dawtry,	
replay(a)	0-3		457			Beal, Newark	
				Frome Town(a)	1-7	Slade	239

1984/85 Beazer Homes Southern League Cup			
versus	res	goalscorer	gate
RS Southampton(a)	1-4	Haysom	218
Dorchester Town(h)	0-1		172
Poole Town(a)	0-2		248
RS Southampton(h)	2-1	Dowtry, Beal	194
Dorchester Town(a)	3-2	Rushton, Patterson, Slade	110
Poole Town(h)	0-1		180

1984/85 Beazer Homes Southern Division)						
versus	H	goalscorer	gate	A	goalscorer	gate
Addlestone	2-1	Slade, Newark	166	1-0	Paterson	60
Andover	1-2	Haysom(p)	289	0-2		272
Ashford	2-1	Dawtry, Orchard	173	2-1	Haysom, Orchard	73
Basingstoke Town	0-3		251	0-3		447
Cambridge City	2-2	Paterson, Slade	382	1-0	Newark	190
Canterbury City	2-0	Paterson, Slade	255	1-2	Dawtry	78
Chatham Town	3-0	Newark, Cranmer, Orchard	187	5-3	Dawtry(2), Tutton, Paterson, Slade	99
Dorchester Town	3-0	Paterson, Slade, Dawtry(p)	218	1-2	Dawtry(p)	92
Dover Athletic	2-0	Cranmer, Tutton	198	3-1	Paterson, Slade, Dawtry(p)	151
Dunstable	2-0	Haysom, McMenemy(p)	201	1-1	Paterson	111
Erith & Belvedere	2-2	Slade, Orchard	178	1-0	Cox	98
Gosport	2-1	Beal, Smith	186	0-5		1200
Hillingdon Borough	1-0	Dawtry(p)	190	0-2		105
Poole Town	0-0		261	1-3	o.g.	189
Sheppey United	2-4	Tutton, Dawtry(p)	203	0-1		140
Thanet United	3-1	Paterson(2), o.g.	203	1-1	Dawtry	150
Tonbridge	0-3		248	0-1		195
Waterlooville	2-1	Cranmer, Tutton	205	2-0	Slade, o.g.	120
Woodford Town	1-3	Orchard	111	3-2	Newark(2), Cranmer	20

Leading goalscorer for 1984/85 season was Kevin Dawtry with 10 goals.

1984/85 Beazer Homes Southern Division							
	P	W	D	L	F	A	Pts
Basingstoke Town	38	24	9	5	61	22	81
Gosport Borough	38	22	6	10	78	41	72
Poole Town	38	20	12	6	69	38	72
Hillingdon Borough	38	19	10	9	51	23	67
Thanet United	38	19	9	10	63	47	66
Salisbury	**38**	**19**	**5**	**14**	**55**	**54**	**62**
Sheppey United	38	18	6	14	49	45	60
Addlestone & Weybridge	38	16	9	13	68	54	57
Waterlooville	38	15	10	13	71	63	55
Canterbury City	38	15	7	16	61	64	52
Woodford Town	38	13	13	12	46	53	52
Tonbridge AFC	38	16	3	19	59	62	51
Andover Town	38	15	5	18	42	54	50
Dorchester Town	38	13	7	18	45	60	46
Cambridge City	38	11	11	16	59	71	44
Chatham Town	38	12	8	18	44	66	44
Ashford Town	38	10	9	19	54	69	39
Dunstable	38	8	10	20	35	56	34
Dover Athletic	38	7	7	24	39	78	28
Erith & Belvedere	38	6	8	24	36	65	26

1985/86 F.A. Cup				1985/86 F.A. Trophy			
versus	res	goalscorer	gate	versus	res	goalscorer	gate
Fareham Town(a)	2-2	Paterson, Orchard	172	Maesteg Park(h)	4-1	Courtney(2), Dawtry, Johnson	210
replay(h)	0-5		291	Bideford(h)	2-0	o.g., Dawtry	266
				Merthyr Tydfil(a)	1-1	Cranmer, B.	301
				replay(h)	2-1	Dawtry, Paterson	372
				Worthing(a)	0-1		387

1985/86 Beazer Homes Southern League Cup			
versus	res	goalscorer	gate
Poole Town(a)	3-1	Paterson, Orchard, Dawtry	n.a.
Andover Town(h)	1-0	Diaper	251
Basingstoke Town(a)	3-1	Cranmer, Barry(2), Dawtry	220
Andover Town(a)	1-0	Paterson	211
Poole Town(h)	1-0	Courtney	206
Basingstoke Town(h)	3-0	Cranmer, Calvin(2), Dawtry	180
Trowbridge Town(a)	0-0		267
Trowbridge Town(h)	1-4	Paterson	297

1985/86 Beazer Homes Southern Division						
versus	H	goalscorer	gate	A	v	gate
Andover	1-1	Dawtry	395	2-1	Cranmer, B., Dawtry	172
Ashford	2-0	Paterson, Cranmer, B.	202	3-2	Courtney(2), Dawtry(p)	
Burnham & Hillingdon	2-0	Courtney, Cranmer, B.	189	0-2		
Cambridge City	0-2		229	0-0		268
Canterbury City	3-1	Dawtry(2), Courtney	202	2-2	Johnson, Paterson	50
Chatham Town	2-1	Dawtry, Courney	165	3-1	Chambers, White, Dawtry	50
Corinthian	4-2	Paterson(2), Courtney(2)		1-2	Dawtry	
Dorchester Town	3-0	Courtney(2), Paterson	207	2-0	Paterson(2)	118
Dover Athletic	3-2	Dawtry(2), Paterson	212	3-2	Courtney(2), Paterson	234
Dunstable	3-1	Dawtry(p), Paterson, White	230	1-3	Courtney	100
Erith & Belvedere	1-1	Paterson	163	0-0		
Hastings Town	3-3	Dawtry, Courtney, Paterson	189	3-5	Johnson(3)	340
Poole Town	2-0	Cranmer, B., Paterson	347	1-2		350
Ruislip	5-1	Barber(2), Dawtry, Orchard Cranmer, B.	205	2-1	Paterson, Dawtry	48
Sheppey United	4-0	Paterson, Chambers, Russell, Courtney	139	0-2		116
Thanet United	4-0	Paterson(2), Dawtry, Cranmer	220	2-1	Orchard(2)	54
Tonbridge	4-1	Courtney(2), Dawtry, Paterson	141	1-4	Dawtry	
Trowbridge	2-2	Dawtry, Paterson	297	1-1	Dawtry	320
Waterlooville	2-0	Cranmer, B., Paterson	433	1-0	Orchard	120
Woodford Town	3-0	Courtney, Dawtry(p), Haysom	314	3-2	Cranmer, B., Paterson, Dawtry(p)	130

Leading goalscorer for 1985/86 season was Kevin Dawtry with 21 goals.

1985/86 Beazer Homes Southern Division							
	P	W	D	L	F	A	Pts
Cambridge City	40	23	11	6	87	41	80
Salisbury	40	24	8	8	84	51	80
Hastings Town	40	23	9	8	83	51	78
Dover Athletic	40	23	6	11	89	53	75
Corinthian	40	20	9	11	78	45	69
Tonbridge AFC	40	17	13	10	65	51	64
Dunstable	40	17	11	12	70	61	62
Ruislip	40	17	6	17	67	66	57
Erith & Belvedere	40	14	12	14	35	40	54
Waterlooville	40	16	6	18	52	58	54
Burnham & Hillingdon	40	16	6	18	44	59	54
Canterbury City	40	13	13	14	58	58	52
Trowbridge Town	40	13	13	14	57	63	52
Sheppey United	40	14	10	16	43	53	52
Thanet United	40	13	7	20	58	63	46
Woodford Town	40	12	10	18	49	62	46
Poole Town	40	12	7	21	55	63	43
Ashford Town	40	10	12	18	45	65	42
Chatham Town	40	8	15	17	53	70	39
Andover Town	40	10	8	22	52	92	38
Dorchester Town	40	5	8	27	35	94	23

460   *Salisbury City F.C. – The first 60 years*

1986/87 F.A. Cup

versus	res	goalscorer	gate
Bridgend Town(h)	2-1	McGregor, Carmichael	164
Trowbridge Town((a)	0-2		540

1986/87 F.A. Trophy

versus	res	goalscorer	gate
Weston-super-Mare(h)	1-3	Carmichael	153

1986/87 Beazer Homes Southern League Cup

versus	res	goalscorer	gate
Trowbridge Town(h)	2-3	McGreggor(2)	180
Poole Town(a)	2-2	Carmichael, Paterson	150
Dorchester Town(a)	0-0		200
Dorchester Town(h)	1-0	Barry Andrews	141
Poole Town((h)	1-1	Denny Mundee	197
Trowbridge Town(a)	2-3	Barry Andrews, Denny Mundee	320

1986/87 Beazer Homes Premier Division

versus	H	goalscorer	gate	A	goalscorer	gate
Alvechurch	0-0		205	0-3		256
Aylesbury United	1-2	Mundee, D.	311	0-3		670
Basingstoke Town	2-1	McGregor(2).	443	0-3		340
Bedworth United	2-1	Cranmer, B., Bolson	220	1-0	Thompson	186
Bromsgrove Rovers	0-0		314	0-5		462
Cambridge City	1-4	Carmichael	270	1-2	Mundee, D.	400
Chelmsford City	0-0		248	0-0		630
Corby Town	2-2	Courtney, Dawtry	213	1-2	McGregor	271
Crawley Town	2-0	Mundee, D., Eddie	228	2-3	Wilson, Carmichael	255
Dartford	1-2	D. Mundee	232	1-2	Bolson	631
Dudley Town	1-2	McGregor	232	2-1	Eddie, Carmichael	150
Fareham Town	3-1	Mundee, B.(2), Andrews	252	1-2	Eddie	197
Fisher Athletic	1-5	McGregor	257	2-2	Thompson(2)	288
Folkestone	3-0	Thompson, Mundee D., Eddie	316	3-1	C. Cramner, Eddie, Carmichael	170
Gosport Borough	1-2	Mundee, B.	231	4-0	Mundee, B., Andrews, Thompson, McGregor	251
King's Lynn	5-2	Andrews(2), Carmichael(2), Courtney	205	2-1	Mundee, D.(2)	284
Redditch United	1-5	Newark	266	0-2		169
Shepshed Charterhouse	2-4	Carmichael, Mundee, D.	234	0-5		253
Willenhall Town	2-0	McGregor, Carmichael	156	0-3		115
Witney Town	0-0		142	0-2		145
Worcester City	1-3	Courtney	181	1-4	Andrews(p)	645

> Leading goalscorers for 1986/87 season were Matt Carmichael and Denny Mundee with 8 goals each.

1986/87 Beazer Homes Premier Division

	P	W	D	L	F	A	Pts
Fisher Athletic	42	25	11	6	72	29	86
Bromsgrove Rovers	42	24	11	7	82	41	83
Aylesbury United	42	24	11	7	72	40	83
Dartford	42	19	12	11	76	43	69
Chelmsford City	42	17	13	12	48	45	64
Cambridge City	42	14	20	8	68	52	62
Redditch United	42	16	14	12	59	54	62
Alverchurch	42	18	8	16	66	62	62
Corby Town	42	14	17	11	65	51	59
Worcester City	42	16	11	15	62	55	59
Shepshed Charterhouse	42	16	10	16	59	59	58
Bedworth United	42	15	12	15	55	51	57
Crawley Town	42	14	11	17	59	60	53
Fareham Town	42	11	17	14	58	49	50
Willenhall Town	42	13	11	18	48	57	50
Basingstoke Town	42	12	12	18	53	78	48
Witney Town	42	12	12	18	29	56	48
Gosport Borough	42	11	13	18	42	57	46
Salisbury	42	12	7	23	52	82	43
King's Lynn	42	9	13	20	48	72	40
Dudley Town	42	9	9	24	39	76	36
Folkestone	42	8	11	23	36	79	35

1987/88 F.A. Cup				1987/88 F.A. Trophy			
versus	res	goalscorer	gate	versus	res	goalscorer	gate
Barry Town(h)	0-1		261	Dorchester Town(h)	1-0	Cranmer, C.	225
				Witney Town(h)	1-2	Thompson	255

1987/88 Wilts Premier Shield				1987/88 Beazer Homes Southern League Cup			
versus	res	goalscorer	gate	versus	res	goalscorer	gate
Swindon Town(h)	1-5	Thompson	328	Waterlooville(a)	2-6	Carmichael, Denny Mundee	200
				Fareham Town(h)	0-0		276
				Hounslow F.C.(a)	1-2	Denny Mundee	125
				Waterlooville(h)	1-1	Denny Mundee	225
				Fareham Town(a)	0-2		126
				Hounslow F.C.(h)	0-1		136

1987/88 Beazer Homes Premier Division						
versus	H	goalscorer	gate	A	goalscorer	gate
Andover	2-2	Mundee, D., Cranmer, B.	297	0-0		650
Baldock Town	1-0	Cranmer, C.	252	1-1	Platt	150
Burnham	1-0	Sanders	267	1-0	Thompson	75
Bury Town	1-1	Mundee, D.	222	0-0		285
Canterbury City	2-0	Thompson, Mundee, D.	289	1-0	Sanders	48
Chatam Town	3-0	Sanders, Mundee, D., Green	208	5-1	Mundee, D.(3), Shaw(2)	26
Corinthian	2-0	Sanders, Cranmer, B.	226	1-0	Cranmer, C.	531
Dover Athletic	2-4	Diaper, Green	614	3-2	Mundee, D.(2), Tate	114
Dunstable	1-1	Mundee, D.	248	1-2	Cranmer, B.	106
Erith & Belvedere	1-3	Johnson	215	3-2	Carmichael, Thompson, D., Mundee	234
Folkestone	3-0	Platt, C. Cranmer, D. Mundee	189	1-1	Thompson	250
Gravesend & N'fleet	1-0	Cranmer, B.	299	0-0		214
Hastings Town	2-0	Thompson, Cranmer, C.	221	1-1	Sanders	106
Hounslow	2-0	Johnson, Cranmer, C.	213	6-2	Mundee, D.(3), Cranmer, C.(2), Brooks	432
Poole Town	2-1	Platt(2)	380	2-1	Sanders(2)	30
Ruislip	6-0	Carmichael(2), Thompson(2), Mundee, D., McGregor	205	0-0		111
Sheppey United	1-0	Carmichael	243	3-2	Platt(2), Cranmer, C.	179
Thanet United	1-1	Mundee, D.	286	2-0	Platt, Cranmer, B.	232
Tonbridge	3-0	D. Mundee, C. Cranmer,.	222	1-0	D. Mundee	

Leading goalscorer for 1987/88 season was Denny Mundee with 20 goals.

This was the year when the Southern League took on a major sponsorship in the form of Beazer Homes for an agreed three-year period (extended later); this applied to Premier and feeder regional divisions.

1987/88 Beazer Homes Southern Division

	P	W	D	L	F	A	Pts
Dover Athletic	40	28	10	2	81	28	94
Waterlooville	40	27	10	3	88	33	91
Salisbury	**40**	**24**	**11**	**5**	**71**	**33**	**83**
Gravesend & Northfleet	40	20	12	8	60	32	72
Thanet United	40	17	13	10	60	38	64
Andover Town	40	17	13	10	64	58	64
Dunstable	40	17	12	11	78	56	63
Burnham	40	17	10	13	61	45	61
Bury Town	40	17	7	16	80	67	58
Erith & Belvedere	40	16	9	15	52	56	57
Sheppey United	40	14	10	16	58	52	52
Hastings Town	40	14	10	16	62	70	52
Tonbridge AFC	40	14	8	18	51	56	50
Poole Town	40	13	10	17	69	70	49
Baldock Town	40	12	12	16	44	53	48
Hounslow	40	11	8	21	41	76	41
Folkestone	40	9	11	20	47	76	38
Corinthian	40	9	10	21	49	67	37
Ruislip	40	5	13	22	33	80	28
Canterbury City	40	7	6	27	33	87	27
Chatham Town	40	7	5	28	39	88	26

1988/89 F.A. Cup

versus	res	goalscorer	gate
Newbury Town(h)	4-2	Cranmer, C., Kilgour, Chalk, Green	202
Pagham(h)	2-3	Kilgour, Dawtry	175

1988/89 F.A. Trophy

versus	res	goalscorer	gate
Bridgend(a)	6-1	Green(2), Chalk, Platt, Thompson, Dawtry	68
Andover Town(a)	5-2	Platt(3), Dawtry, o.g.	296
Merthyr Tydfil(h)	0-5		863

1988/89 Wilts Premier Shield

versus	res	goalscorer	gate
Trowbridge Town(h)	1-2	Chalk	133

1988/89 Beazer Homes Southern League Cup

versus	res	goalscorer	gate
Waterlooville(h)	1-2	Wright	154
Waterlooville(a)	3-1	Platt(2), Dawtry	257
Fareham Town(h)	3-2	Platt, Dawtry, Thompson	174
Fareham Town(a)	3-0	Dawtry, Sanders, Chalk	204
Gloucester City(h)	0-2		220
Gloucester City(a)	2-3	Sanders, Butler	470

1988/89 Beazer Homes Southern Division

versus	H	goalscorer	gate	A	goalscorer	gate
Andover	1-1	Wright	307	2-2	Dawtry, o.g.	259
Baldock Town	1-3	Platt	231	1-2	Sanders	241
Buckingham Town	0-1		198	0-0		97
Burnham	2-3	Cranmer C., o.g.	136	1-4	Shaw	120
Bury Town	3-1	Platt(2), Chalk	126	0-1		380
Canterbury City	3-2	Chalk, Thompson, Platt	168	1-0	Green	
Chelmsford City	1-2	Sanders	253	1-4	Platt	1122
Corinthian	1-1	Green		0-1		50
Dunstable	4-0	Dawtry(2), Chalk, Cranmer, B.	190	5-0	Platt(3), Chalk, Green	122
Erith & Belvedere	2-1	Chalk(2)	156	2-1	Sanders, Dawtry	104
Folkestone	0-2		240	0-1		141
Gravesend & N'fleet	5-0	Chalk(2), Cranmer, B., Cranmer, C, Diaper	230	0-2		505
Hastings Town	0-2		156	2-5	Platt, Kilgour	343
Hounslow	0-1		212	2-1	Shaw, Dawtry	104
Poole Town	2-0	Chalk, Kilgour	242	0-3		474
Ruislip	4-1	Platt(2), Sanders, Dawtry	167	5-1	Sanders(2), Platt(2), Chalk	64
Sheppey United	5-0	Dawtry(3), Cranmer, B., Shaw	175	0-1		
Thanet United	5-2	Chalk(3), Sanders(2)	217	3-1	Platt(2), Wright	204
Tonbridge	3-2	B. Cranmer, Dawtry, Kilgour	228	3-1	Chalk(2), Sanders	168
Trowbridge Town	2-0	Rayfield, Platt	344	1-1	Green	
Witney Town	4-0	Green(2), Chalk, Dawtry	137	2-1	Platt, Cranmer, C.	158

Leading goalscorer for 1988/89 season was Ian Chalk with 16 goals.

1988/89 Beazer Homes Southern Division

	P	W	D	L	F	A	Pts
Chelmsford City	42	30	5	7	106	38	95
Gravesend & Northfleet	42	27	6	9	70	40	87
Poole Town	42	24	11	7	98	48	83
Bury Town	42	25	7	10	75	34	82
Burnham	42	22	13	7	78	47	79
Baldock Town	42	23	5	14	69	40	74
Hastings Town	42	21	11	10	75	48	74
Hounslow	42	21	6	15	75	60	69
Salisbury	**42**	**20**	**5**	**17**	**79**	**58**	**65**
Trowbridge	42	19	7	16	59	52	64
Folkestone	42	17	8	17	62	65	59
Corinthian	42	13	13	16	59	69	52
Canterbury City	42	14	8	20	52	60	50
Witney Town	42	13	11	18	61	71	50
Dunstable	42	11	14	17	42	57	47
Buckingham Town	42	12	10	20	56	79	46
Erith & Belvedere	42	11	10	21	48	63	43
Andover Town	42	11	9	22	56	90	42
Sheppey United	42	10	8	24	50	90	38
Thanet United	42	7	15	20	47	95	36
Tonbridge AFC	42	7	6	29	50	98	27
Ruislip	42	6	8	28	47	112	26

1989/90 F.A. Cup

versus	res	goalscorer	gate
Sholing Sports(h)	6--0	Chalk(2), Shaw, Green Sanders, Cranmer, C.	174
Poole Town(h)	1-1	Chalk	305
replay(a)	1-3	Dawtry	524

1989/90 F.A. Trophy

versus	res	goalscorer	gate
Lewes(h)	4-4	Green(3), Dawtry	186
replay(a)	1-1	Williams(p)	215
2nd *replay*(h)	4-2	Shaw, Dawtry, Chalk, Sanders	289
Staines(a)	2-3	Cranmer, C., Dawtry	589

1989/90 Wilts Premier Shield

versus	res	goalscorer	gate
Calne Town(a)	4-2	Chalk(2), Sanders, o.g.	134
Swindon Town(n)	0-3		250
(*played at Downton*)			

1989/90 Beazer Homes Southern League Cup

versus	res	goalscorer	gate
Dorchester Town(a)	3-5	Chalk, o.g., Williams	199
Dorchester Town(h)	1-0	Chalk	208

1989/90 Beazer Homes Southern Division

versus	H	goalscorer	gate	A	goalscorer	gate
Andover	3-0	Cranmer, B., Sanders, Chalk	257	2-0	Chalk, Williams	229
Baldock Town	2-2	Sanders, Williams	190	2-1	Chalk, Cranmer, C.	182
Bashley	0-1		343	1-2	Baylis	408
Buckingham Town	1-3	Dawtry	189	1-1	Chalk	194
Burnham	1-5	Cranmer, B.	302	0-0		75
Bury Town	1-1	Shaw	369	1-1	Chalk	704
Canterbury City	2-1	Sanders, Hurdwell	289	1-0	Chalk	113
Corinthian	2-0	Dawtry, Williams(p)	141	0-2		130
Dunstable	1-1	Shaw	207	2-1	Chalk, Sanders	155
Erith & Belvedere	0-1		223	4-0	Cranmer, B., Sanders, Chalk, Dawtry	163
Fareham	1-1	o.g.	267	6-1	Sanders(2), Cranmer, C., Shaw, Chalk, Green	203
Folkestone	3-4	Sanders, Green, Williams(p)	285	0-3		291
Hastings Town	2-0	Cranmer, B., Chalk	224	2-0	Chalk, Green	
Hounslow	0-1		222	4-0	Cranmer, B., Williams, Sanders Chalk	105
Hythe Town	2-0	Sanders, Syrett, D.	381	1-5	Thompson	308
Margate	1-2	Chalk	180	2-1	Cranmer, C., Williams(p)	240
Poole Town	2-0	Cranmer, B., Chalk	605	2-2	Bayliss, o.g.	472
Sheppey United	2-0	Chalk, Syrett, D.	195	4-2	Chalk(2), Cranmer, C.(2)	174
Trowbridge Town	3-0	Syrett, Cranmer B., Williams(p)	675	1-1	Chalk	454
Witney Town	3-0	Cranmer, B., Chalk, Shaw	263	0-2		144
Yate Town	2-1	Cranmer, B., Chalk	220	2-1	Chalk, Hurdwell	227

> Leading goalscorer for 1989/90 season was Ian Chalk with 21 goals.

1989/90 Beazer Homes Southern Division

	P	W	D	L	F	A	Pts
Bashley	42	25	7	10	80	47	82
Poole Town	42	23	8	11	85	60	77
Buckingham Town	42	22	10	10	67	46	76
Dunstable	42	20	14	8	56	38	74
Salisbury	**42**	**21**	**9**	**12**	**72**	**50**	**72**
Hythe Town	42	20	12	10	69	48	72
Trowbridge Town	42	20	9	13	79	64	69
Hastings Town	42	20	9	13	64	54	69
Bury Town	42	18	12	12	76	62	66
Baldock Town	42	18	11	13	69	52	65
Burnham	42	17	11	14	77	52	62
Fareham Town	42	14	14	14	49	53	56
Yate Town	42	16	6	20	53	52	54
Witney Town	42	16	6	20	54	56	54
Canterbury City	42	14	10	18	52	52	52
Margate	42	12	15	15	46	45	51
Folkestone	42	14	9	19	61	83	51
Andover Town	42	13	11	18	54	70	50
Hounslow	42	11	5	26	39	82	38
Erith & Belvedere	42	8	11	23	34	73	35
Corinthian	42	6	10	26	44	93	28
Sheppey United	42	6	7	29	35	83	25

1990/91 F.A. Cup

versus	res	goalscorer	gate
Uxbridge(h)	1-1	Smith	199
replay(h)	2-1	Smith(p), Chalk	134
Hungerford Town(h)	2-0	Smith(2)	265
Bournemouth(h)	4-0	Smith(2, 1 penalty), Airey, Sanders	501
Farnborough(h)	0-3		937

1990/91 F.A. Trophy

versus	res	goalscorer	gate
Andover(a)	2-1	Chalk, Smith	593
Barry(h)	0-0		337
replay(a)	1-0	o.g.	342
VS Rugby(h)	1-4	Smith	542

1990/91 Wilts Premier Shield

versus	res	goalscorer	gate
Chippenham Town(h)	4-1	Green, Airey, Smith, J., Sanders	n.a.
Calne(n)	0-2		n.a.
(played at Westbury)			

1990/91 Beazer Homes Southern League Cup

versus	res	goalscorer	gate
Andover Town(a)	3-2	Smith, J.(2), Chalk	537
Andover Town(h)	2-0	Smith, J.(2)	485
Bashley(h)	2-1	Smith, J.(2)	329
Bashley(a)	2-0	Smith, Airey	344
Dorchester Town(h)	1-1	Airey	292
Dorchester Town(a)	0-0		476

1990/91 Beazer Homes Southern Division

versus	H	goalscorer	gate	A	goalscorer	gate
Andover	3-1	O'Donnell(2), Smith	231	1-0	Cranmer, B.	464
Ashford	1-0	Thomson	273	2-2	Smith(p), Airey	330
Baldock Town	2-0	Smith(2)	201	0-0		372
Buckingham Town	2-0	Dowding(2)	386	1-0	Green	264
Burnham	1-0	Smith(p)	297	1-1	O'Driscoll	135
Bury Town	1-1	Smith(p)	256	0-2		337
Canterbury City	6-2	Smith, Sanders, Airey, Green Cranmer, B., Wright	198	1-3	Smith(p)	97
Corinthian	0-1		205	2-0	Smith(2)	35
Dunstable Town	3-1	Smith(2), Cranmer, B.	220	3-2	Smith, Chalk, Cranmer, B.	
Erith & Belvedere	2-0	Green, O'Donnell	245	1-0	Smith	180
Fareham Town	1-1	Shaw	289	1-1	Smith	224
Gosport Borough	1-1	Smith(p)	335	1-1	Smith	136
Hastings Town	4-1	Smith(3), Airey	262	1-2	Chalk	309
Hythe Town	3-1	Cranmer, B., Airey, Smith	302	1-0	Smith	358
Margate	2-2	Smith (2, 1 penalty)	288	0-1		243
Newport I.O.W.	2-1	Chalk, Smith(p)	350	2-1	Smith, Sanders	366
Sudbury Town	1-1	Thomson	461	0-3		585
Trowbridge Town	1-0	Cranmer, B.	469	2-2	Sanders, Dowding	841
Witney Town	2-0	Sanders, Airey	221	4-1	Smith, Cranmer, B., Green, O'Donnell	162
Yate Town	1-0	Smith	325	0-3		281

> Leading goalscorer for 1990/91 season was Jimmy Smith with 28 goals.

1990/91 Beazer Homes Southern Division

	P	W	D	L	F	A	Pts
Buckingham Town	40	25	8	7	73	38	83
Trowbridge Town	40	22	12	6	67	31	78
Salisbury	**40**	**22**	**11**	**7**	**63**	**39**	**77**
Baldock Town	40	21	9	10	66	52	72
Ashford Town	40	22	5	13	82	52	71
Yate Town	40	21	8	11	76	48	71
Hastings Town	40	18	11	11	66	46	65
Hythe Town	40	17	9	14	55	44	60
Andover Town	40	16	6	18	69	76	54
Margate	40	14	11	15	52	55	53
Burnham	40	12	16	12	57	49	52
Bury Town	40	15	5	20	58	74	50
Sudbury Town	40	13	10	17	60	68	49
Newport I.O.W.	40	13	9	18	56	62	48
Gosport Borough	40	12	11	17	47	58	47
Witney Town	40	12	11	17	57	75	47
Dunstable	40	9	15	16	48	63	42
Canterbury City	40	12	6	22	60	83	42
Erith & Belvedere	40	10	6	24	46	73	36
Fareham Town	40	9	9	22	46	74	36
Corinthian	40	5	12	23	34	78	27

1991/92 F.A. Cup				1991/92 F.A. Trophy			
versus	res	goalscorer	gate	versus	res	goalscorer	gate
Thatcham(a)	1-1	Green	321	Cwmbran Town(h)	1-0	Smith(p)	206
replay(h)	3-0	Cranmer, B, Phillips, Gomersall	221	Taunton Town(h)	4-1	Green(2), Chalk Smith	212
Poole Town(h)	2-0	Chalk, Smith(p)	220	Wokingham Town(a)	0-0		357
Thame Utd(a)	4-0	Smith(2), Gomersall, O'Donnel	420	*replay*(h)	1-0	Green	274
				Wycombe Wanderers(a)	0-2		2917
Farnborough Town(h)	1-7	Gomersall	808				

1991/92 Wilts Premier Shield				1991/92 Beazer Homes Southern League Cup			
versus	res	goalscorer	gate	versus	res	goalscorer	gate
Chippenham Town(h)	3-1	Loveridge, Gomershall, Pearson	117	Andover Town(h)	1-0	Chalk	220
Trowbridge Town(h)	1-2	Chalk	n.a.	Andover Town(a)	1-0	Pearson	263
				Waterlooville(a)	2-0	Smith, J.(2)	64
				Waterlooville(h)	3-1	Chalk, Smith, J.(2)	107
				Gloucester City(h)	1-2	Smith, J.	216
				Gloucester City(a)	2-0	Pearson, Smith, J.	382
			Quarter Finals	Dorchester(h)	0-1		244
			Quarter Finals	Dorchester(a)	0-2		450

1991/92 Beazer Homes Southern Division						
versus	H	goalscorer	gate	A	goalscorer	gate
Andover	0-0		374	1-1	Hobson	363
Ashford	1-3	Gomersall	167	2-2	Fletcher(2)	393
Baldock Town	2-3	Smith, Gomersall	208	1-1	Loveridge	269
Braintree Town	2-2	Gomersall, Chalk	214	0-2		198
Buckingham Town	0-0		137	0-0		106
Burnham	0-0		173	2-3	Smith (2, 1 penalty)	122
Bury Town	5-0	Gomersall(2), Pearson(p), Maskell, Morrison	97	3-0	Gomersall, Woods, o.g.	64
Canterbury City	3-1	Smith(2), Sanders	175	3-1	Chalk(2), Gomersall	71
Dunstable Town	1-2	Chalk	163	1-1	Fletcher	107
Erith & Belvedere	4-2	Smith(3, 1 penalty), Gomersall	184	1-0	Green	141
Fareham Town	0-1		244	4-0	Fletcher, Pearson(p), Sanders, Maskell	185
Gosport Borough	3-2	Darby, Chalk, Maskell	155	3-0	Green, Fletcher, Smith	112
Hastings Town	1-1	Smith	210	1-2	Pope	730
Havant Town	0-0		187	1-3	Loveridge	199
Hythe Town	0-1		96	1-3	Gomersall	257
Margate	5-1	Pearson(2), Chalk(2), Mulkern	179	0-1		286
Newport I.O.W.	2-2	Chalk, Green	204	1-1	Payne	225
Sittingbourne	0-2		166	2-2	Loveridge, Smith(p)	303
Sudbury Town	0-0		239	3-1	Gomersall, Chalk, Sanders	219
Weymouth	2-2	Chalk, Sanders	422	0-1		1334
Witney Town	3-1	Smith(2), Chalk	176	3-0	Sanders, Hobson, Green	125

Leading goalscorer for 1991/92 season was Jimmy Smith with 13 goals.

1991/92 Beazer Homes Southern Division

	P	W	D	L	F	A	Pts
Hastings Town	42	28	7	7	80	37	91
Weymouth	42	22	12	8	64	35	78
Havant Town	42	21	12	9	67	46	75
Braintree	42	21	8	13	77	58	71
Buckingham Town (3pts deducted)	42	19	15	8	57	26	69
Andover Town	42	18	10	14	73	68	64
Ashford Town	42	17	12	13	66	57	63
Sudbury Town	42	18	9	15	70	66	63
Sittingbourne (6pts deducted)	42	19	10	13	63	41	61
Burnham	42	15	14	13	57	55	59
Baldock Town	42	16	10	16	62	67	58
Salisbury	**42**	**13**	**16**	**13**	**67**	**51**	**55**
Hythe Town	42	15	10	17	61	62	55
Margate	42	13	16	13	49	56	55
Newport I.O.W.	42	13	10	19	58	63	49
Dunstable	42	12	12	18	55	67	48
Bury Town	42	14	4	24	52	94	46
Witney Town	42	11	12	19	55	76	45
Fareham Town	42	12	8	22	45	71	44
Erith & Belvedere	42	11	10	21	44	67	43
Canterbury City	42	8	14	20	43	69	38
Gosport Borough	42	6	9	27	32	65	27

1992/93 F.A. Cup				1992/93 F.A. Trophy			
versus	res	goalscorer	gate	versus	res	goalscorer	gate
Trowbridge Town(h)	6-2	Gomersall(3), Payne, Sanders, Maskell	425	Worcester City(a)	1-2	Sanders	649
Thatcham Town(h)	4-0	Gomersall, Fletcher Maskell, Hobson	292				
Brockenhurst(a)	3-1	Sanders(2), Bale	451				
Witney Town(a)	2-1	Loveridge, Bale	544				
Marlow(a)	3-3	Loveridge, Sanders, Fletcher	940				
replay(h)	2-2	Chalk, Sanders	1854	*Salisbury City lost on penalties* 3-4			

1992/93 Wilts Premier Shield				1992/93 Beazer Homes Southern League Cup			
versus	res	goalscorer	gate	versus	res	goalscorer	gate
Calne Town(h)	1-3	Gomershall	n.a.	Havant(h)	3-1	Sanders, Emms, Bale	157
				Havant(a)	2-0	Maskell, Hobson	121
				Fareham(h)	1-0	Fletcher	131
				Witney(h)	1-2	Hung Dang	157

1992/93 Beazer Homes Southern Division						
versus	H	goalscorer	gate	A	goalscorer	gate
Andover	3-3	Hung Dang, Hobson, Maskell	395	5-0	Chalk(2), Loveridge, Emms, Pearson	381
Ashford	2-0	Emms,. Chalk	377	1-0	Sanders	350
Baldock Town	1-0	Maskell(p)	179	0-0		435
Braintree Town	1-2	Fletcher	224	1-5	Bale	215
Buckingham Town	1-4	Wilston	173	4-2	Emms, Odey, Sanders, Bale	55
Burnham	4-0	Sanders(2), Chalk, Green	171	0-0		127
Bury Town	5-3	Odey(2), Chalk(2), Sanders	283	3-0	Dang(2), Phillips	110
Canterbury City	4-0	Dang, Payne, Bale, Chalk	201	2-1	Browne, Fletcher	114
Dunstable	1-0	Odey	283	0-1		127
Erith & Belvedere	4-1	Chalk, Sanders,.Maskell(p), Bale	263	3-2	Chalk, Odey, Payne(p)	127
Fareham Town	2-0	Loveridge, Payne	411	2-1	Dang, o.g.	120
Fisher Athletic	4-1	Odey(3). Bale	294	2-2	Odey, Browne	104
Gravesend & N'fleet	3-0	Sanders, Odey, Maskell	469	0-2		502
Havant Town	2-1	Sanders(2)	179	2-0	Emms, Sanders	274
Margate	2-0	Odey, Sanders	251	5-3	Loveridge, Sanders, Fletcher Chalk, Odey	275
Newport I.O.W.	2-1	Emms, Fletcher	238	2-0	Sanders, Maskell	237
Poole Town	2-1	Odey, Bale	414	0-4		228
Sittingbourne	1-2	Odey	573	1-0	Dang	1167
Sudbury Town	3-1	Sanders(2), Hobson	284	1-1	Maskell(p)	421
Wealdstone	1-0	Payne(p)	271	3-4	Hobson, Chalk, Loveridge	210
Witney Town	1-1	Loveridge	168	1-1	Maskell	178

> Leading goalscorer for 1992/93 season was Sean Sanders with 15 goals.

1992/93 Beazer Homes Southern Division							
	P	W	D	L	F	A	Pts
Sittingbourne	42	26	12	4	102	43	90
Salisbury City	42	27	7	8	87	50	88
Witney Town	42	25	9	8	77	37	84
Gravesend & Northfleet	42	25	4	13	99	63	79
Havant Town	42	23	6	13	78	55	75
Sudbury Town	42	20	11	11	89	54	71
Erith & Belvedere	42	22	5	15	73	66	71
Ashford Town	42	20	8	14	91	66	68
Braintree Town	42	20	6	16	95	65	66
Margate	42	19	7	16	65	58	64
Wealdstone	42	18	7	17	75	69	61
Buckingham Town	42	16	11	15	61	58	59
Baldock Town	42	15	9	18	59	63	54
Poole Town	42	15	7	20	61	69	52
Fareham Town	42	14	8	20	67	65	50
Burnham	42	14	8	20	53	77	50
Canterbury City	42	12	10	20	54	76	46
Newport I.O.W.	42	9	16	17	44	56	43
Fisher Athletic	42	8	9	25	38	98	33
Andover Town	42	7	9	26	42	99	30
Dunstable	42	5	14	23	42	92	29
Bury Town	42	8	5	29	46	119	29

1993/94 F.A. Cup				1993/94 F.A. Trophy			
versus	res	goalscorer	gate	versus	res	goalscorer	gate
Waterlooville(a)	0-1		295	Poole Town(h)	1-3	Odey	256

1993/94 Wilts Premier Shield				1993/94 Beazer Homes Southern League Cup			
versus	res	goalscorer	gate	versus	res	goalscorer	gate
Melksham Town(h)	5-0	Chalk(2), Sanders(2), Shaw	129	Poole Town(a)	5-1	Browne, Jantschew, Chalk(2), Odey	130
				Poole Town(h)	0-1		218
Poole Town(h)	0-1		218	Weymouth(h)	2-2	Sanders(2)	204
Trowbridge Town(a)	0-2		282	Weymouth(a)	3-1	Sanders, Shaw, Hobson	354
				Trowbridge Tn(h)	1-0	Odey	271
				Dorchester Tn(h)	4-0	Sanders(2), Hobson(2)	322
				Sudbury Town(a)	2-2	Sanders, Hobson	265
				Sudbury Town(h)	1-4	Browne	482

1993/94 Beazer Homes Southern Division						
versus	H	goalscorer	gate	A	goalscorer	gate
Ashford	1-2	Cranmer	250	1-1	Browne	219
Baldock Town	2-0	Odey, Sanders	385	0-2		301
Braintree Town	5-1	Sanders(2), Cranmer, Hobson, Odey	324	1-0	Milsom	156
Buckingham Town	2-1	Odey, Baird	271	1-0	Emms	112
Burnham	5-2	Odey(4), Sanders	189	2-1	Sanders, Hobson	135
Bury Town	6-1	Odey(3), Payne, Wickens, Sanders	192	5-1	Odey, Sanders, Chalk, Browne, Emms	160
Canterbury City	1-1	Browne	252	2-0	Chalk, o.g.	55
Dunstable Town	2-0	Odey, Chalk	265	1-1	Baird(p)	88
Erith & Belvedere	1-0	Odey	243	2-0	Odey, Sanders	95
Fareham Town	3-2	Odey(2), Chalk	193	1-1	Sanders	213
Fisher 93	6-0	Sanders(3), Odey(2), Emms	255	2-0	Payne, Sanders	103
Gravesend & N'fleet	1-4	Browne(p)	492	0-0		611
Havant Town	1-0	Morgan	334	0-1		411
Margate	2-2	Odey(2)	332	4-1	Browne, Sanders, Shaw, Cranmer	312
Newport I.O.W.	1-1	Milsom	282	3-3	Odey, Sanders, Chalk	302
Poole Town	3-2	Odey(2), Chalk	222	0-1		235
Sudbury Town	1-0	Cranmer	345	3-1	Odey(2), Chalk	321
Tonbridge Angels	2-0	Baird, Odey	182	5-0	Odey(2), Sanders, Bale, Wright	551
Wealdstone	4-0	Chalk(2), Sanders, Hobson	329	3-2	Odey(2), Emms	261
Weymouth	3-1	Odey, Hobson(2)	471	1-1	Blackler	680
Witney Town	1-1	Baird	361	0-1		221

Leading goalscorer for 1993/94 season was Paul Odey with 31 goals.

1993/94 Beazer Homes Southern Division						
	P	W	D	L	F	A	Pts
Gravesend & Northfleet	42	27	11	4	87	24	92
Sudbury Town	42	27	8	7	98	47	89
Witney Town	42	27	8	7	69	36	89
Salisbury City	**42**	**26**	**10**	**6**	**90**	**39**	**88**
Havant Town	42	27	4	11	101	41	85
Ashford Town	42	24	13	5	93	46	85
Baldock Town	42	26	7	9	76	40	85
Newport I.O.W.	42	22	8	12	74	51	74
Margate	42	20	8	14	76	58	68
Weymouth	42	18	9	15	71	65	63
Tonbridge Angels	42	19	5	18	59	62	62
Buckingham Town	42	14	14	14	43	42	56
Braintree Town	42	16	7	19	72	84	55
Fareham Town	42	12	12	18	54	75	48
Poole Town	42	13	6	23	54	86	45
Burnham	42	10	9	23	53	92	39
Fisher '93	42	9	10	23	52	81	37
Dunstable	42	9	7	26	50	91	34
Erith & Belvedere	42	9	5	28	40	72	32
Canterbury City	42	8	7	27	35	80	31`
Wealdstone	42	6	7	29	45	95	25
Bury Town	42	3	5	34	36	121	14

1994/95 F.A. Cup

versus	res	goalscorer	gate
Totton(h)	5-0	Emms(2), Burns Coleman, Chalk	249
Worcester City(h)	2-0	Chalk, Coleman	433
Poole Town(h)	3-2	Batty, Clements, Sanders	487
Waterlooville(h)	3-3	Batty(2), Chalk	539
replay(a)	1-0	Batty	519
Ashford(h)	2-3	Chalk, Lovell	760

1994/95 F.A. Trophy

versus	res	goalscorer	gate
Newport I.O.W (a)	4-2	Chalk(2), Browne, Batty	230
Bognor Regis Town(h)	0-0		438
replay(a)	2-4	Coleman, Chalk	140

1994/95 Wilts Premier Shield

versus	res	goalscorer	gate
Warminster Town(h)	1-2	Lovell	130

1994/95 Beazer Homes Southern League Cup

versus	res	goalscorer	gate
Bashley(h)	2-2	Coleman(2)	236
Bashley(a)	0-2		207

1994/95 Beazer Homes Southern Division

versus	H	goalscorer	gate	A	goalscorer	gate
Ashford	3-1	Lovell(2), Carroll	295	3-2	Manson(2), Clements	424
Baldock Town	1-0	Chalk	257	7-0	Lovell(3), Carroll, Emms, Batty, Browne	205
Bashley	5-0	Chalk(2), Lovell, Burns, Browne(p)	244	2-1	Chalk, Batty	357
Braintree Town	2-1	Emms, Sanders	207	0-3		152
Burnham	1-0	Chalk	343	2-1	Manson(2)	141
Bury Town	1-0	Chalk	282	3-0	Morrell(2), Payne	100
Clevedon Town	3-0	Lovell, Chalk, Mulkern	322	1-1	Lovell	371
Erith & Belvedere	5-1	Emms(2), Lovell(2), Browne(p)	379	6-0	Lovell(2), Clements, Carroll, Chalk, Guy	120
Fareham Town	2-1	Carroll, Emms	447	2-0	Chalk, Emms	279
Fisher 93	1-0	Lovell	257	2-2	Lovell, o.g.	120
Havant Town	1-0	Browne	1054	1-0	Clements	423
Margate	5-2	Carroll(2), Clements, Lovell, Chalk	228	2-0	Emms, Lovell	307
Newport I.O.W.	0-3		462	2-0	Lovell, Chalk	293
Poole Town	2-1	Manson, Sanders	487	1-0	Lovell	211
Tonbridge Angles	3-3	Sanders, Chalk, Manson	360	1-2	Lovell	476
Waterlooville	0-2		539	2-0	Lovell, Chalk	377
Wealdstone	3-1	Chalk(2), Browne(p)	627	2-1	Lovell(2)	224
Weston-super-Mare	0-0		401	1-1	Chalk	360
Weymouth	1-1	Carroll	585	0-3		991
Witney Town	3-0	Clements, Lovell, Batty	309	1-1	Browne	235
Yate Town	4-2`	Lovell(3), Chalk	211	1-0	Chalk	203

Leading goalscorer for 1994/95 season was Jason Lovell with 26 goals.

1994/95 Beazer Homes Southern Division

	P	W	D	L	F	A	Pts
Salisbury City	42	30	7	5	88	37	97
Baldock Town	42	28	10	4	92	44	94
Havant Town	42	25	10	7	81	34	85
Waterlooville	42	24	8	10	77	36	80
Ashford Town	42	21	12	9	106	72	75
Weston-super-Mare	42	18	13	11	82	54	67
Bashley	42	18	11	13	62	49	65
Weymouth	42	16	13	13	60	55	61
Newport I.O.W.	42	17	10	15	67	67	61
Witney Town	42	14	14	14	57	57	56
Clevedon Town	42	14	13	15	73	64	55
Tonbridge Angles	42	14	12	16	74	87	54
Margate	42	15	7	20	60	72	52
Braintree Town	42	12	13	17	64	71	49
Wealdstone	42	13	8	21	76	94	47
Yate Town	42	11	13	18	57	75	46
Fisher 93c	42	9	16	17	54	70	43
Bury Town	42	11	8	23	59	86	41
Erith & Belvedere	42	10	9	23	49	94	39
Poole Town	42	10	8	24	53	79	38
Fareham Town	42	10	8	24	46	91	38
Burnham	42	7	7	28	40	89	28

1995/96 F.A. Cup				1995/96 F.A. Trophy			
versus	res	goalscorer	gate	versus	res	goalscorer	gate
Hungerford Town(h)	5-2	Browne, Harbut, Chalk Manson, Guy	373	Fisher '93(h)	2-0	Chalk, Emms	319
				Sudbury Town(h)	2-2	Carroll, Paskins	332
Newport I.O.W.(h)	1-3	Browne(p)	412	*replay*(a)	2-2	Noble(p), Chalk	251
				replay(a)	2-3	Noble, o.g.	213

1995/96 Wilts Premier Shield				1995/96 Dr Martins Southern League Cup			
versus	res	goalscorer	gate	versus	res	goalscorer	gate
Westbury Utd(h)	3-2	Browne, De Gordon, Manson	84	Poole Town(h)	5-0	Blackler, Emms, Paskins, Hewitt , Clements	239
Trowbridge Tn(h)	2-1	De Gordon(2)	168	Poole Town(a)	6-0	Chalk(3), Emms, Browne, Clements	117
Chippenham Tn(n)	2-0	Harbut(2)	207	Dorchester Tn(h)	2-1	Sandrey, Chalk	145
(at Westbury)				Trowbridge Tn(a)	1-1	o.g.	303
				Trowbridge Tn(h)	2-1	Carroll(2)	238
				Newport A.F.C.(a)	2-1	Sandrey, Manson	571
				Baldock Town(a)	0-0		104
				Baldock Town(h)	1-1	o.g.	355

1995/96 Dr Martins Premier Division						
versus	H	goalscorer	gate	A	goalscorer	gate
Atherstone	2-0	Manson, Clements	333	1-3	Chalk	244
Baldock Town	1-2	Hobson	351	2-4	Manson, Guy	280
Burton Albion	2-0	Emms, Chalk	376	1-0	Manson	466
Cambridge City	1-0	Carroll	272	3-1	Lovell, Browne(p), Manson	257
Chelmsford City	0-0		355	0-0		556
Cheltenham Town	3-3	Noble, Browne, Clements	547	3-3	Emms,. Carroll, Spencer	548
Crawley Town	2-1	Browne(p), Lovell	272	0-2		722
Dorchester Town	1-0	Carroll	422	2-0	Sandrey, Masters	1032
Gloucester City	3-3	Manson(3)	483	0-2		1576
Gravesend & N'fleet	2-0	Manson(2)	425	1-1	Lovell	429
Gresley Rovers	1-4	Carroll	337	2-2	Webb, o.g.	582
Halesowen	2-3	Manson, Hobson	391	0-2		652
Hastings Town	3-4	Manson, Emms, Chalk	334	2-6	Blackler, Manson	444
Ilkeston Town	0-2		381	1-2	Carroll	340
Merthyr Tydfil	0-0		402	0-1		321
Newport AFC	1-3	Chalk	340	1-1	Manson	648
Rushden & Diamonds	0-2		569	0-3		1532
Stafford Rangers	2-1	Chalk, Manson	379	1-2	Browne	433
Sudbury Town	3-0	Paskins(2), Harbut	345	3-3	Sanders, Carroll, Chalk	325
VS Rugby	1-0	Masters	302	1-0	Sandrey	250
Worcester City	3-1	Browne, Spencer, Webb	316	0-2		435

Leading goalscorer for 1995/96 season was Gary Manson with 14 goals.

1995/96 Dr Martins Premier Division

	P	W	D	L	F	A	Pts
Rushden & Diamonds	42	29	7	6	99	41	94
Halesowen Town	42	27	11	4	70	36	92
Cheltenham Town	42	21	11	10	76	57	74
Gloucester City	42	21	8	13	65	47	71
Gresley Rovers	42	20	10	12	70	58	70
Worcester City	42	19	12	11	61	43	69
Merthyr Tydfil	42	19	6	17	67	59	63
Hastings Town	42	16	13	13	68	56	61
Crawley Town	42	15	13	14	57	56	58
Sudbury Town	42	15	10	17	69	71	55
Gravesend & Northfleet	42	15	10	17	60	62	55
Chelmsford City	42	13	16	13	46	53	55
Dorchester Town	42	15	8	19	62	57	53
Newport A.F.C.	42	13	13	16	53	59	52
Salisbury City	42	**14**	**10**	**18**	**57**	**69**	**52**
Burton Albion	42	13	12	17	55	56	51
Atherstone United	42	12	12	18	58	75	48
Baldock Town	42	11	14	17	51	56	47
Cambridge City	42	12	10	20	56	68	46
Ilkeston Town	42	11	10	21	53	87	43
Stafford Rangers	42	11	4	27	58	90	37
V.S. Rugby	42	5	10	27	37	92	25

1996/97 F.A. Cup

versus	res	goalscorer	gate
Godalming & G'ford(h)	0-0		318
replay(a)	2-0	Browne(p), Webb	342
Cheltenham Town(a)	3-4	Emms, Webb, Harbut	714

1996/97 F.A. Trophy

versus	res	goalscorer	gate
Witney Town(h)	1-0	Lovell	381
Harrow Borough(a)	2-2	Boyce(p), o.g.	174
replay(h)	2-1	Emms(2)	175
Hastings(a)	3-1	Emms, Webb, Chalk	389
1st Round proper			
Dorchester(h) 2nd Round	1-1	Browne	727
replay(a)	2-3	Cranmer, Chalk	713

1996/97 Wilts Premier Shield

versus	res	goalscorer	gate
Warminster Town(h)	4-1	Emms(2), Chalk, Baird	366
Westbury United(h)	3-0	Chalk(3)	113
Swindon Supermarine(a)	0-2		n.a.

1996/97 Dr Martens Southern League Cup

versus	res	goalscorer	gate
Bashley(a)	3-2	Webb(2), Emms	122
Bashley(h)	3-0	Webb(2) Boyce	235
Newport I.O.W.(h)	3-1	Boyce(2), Browne	189
Weymouth(h)	1-3	Boyce	180

1996/97 Dr Martens Premier Division

versus	H	goalscorer	gate	A	goalscorer	gate
Ashford Town	0-1		421	1-0	Emms	456
Atherstone United	3-2	Emms, Lovell, Chalk	284	0-4		213
Baldock Town	2-3	Webb, Harbut	212	1-1	Chalk	323
Burton Albion	1-1	Preston	339	1-1	Webb	724
Cambridge City	2-2	Browne(p), Chalk	257	1-1	Harbut	213
Chelmsford City	1-1	Webb	247	2-1	Harbut, Boyce	961
Cheltenham Town	1-2	Harbut	310	2-0	Lovell, Harbut	1017
Crawley Town	1-0	Sandrey	340	2-2	Chalk, Webb	482
Dorchester Town	0-0		1024	2-4	Chalk(2)	868
Gloucester City	0-4		489	3-1	Webb(2), Harbut	1863
Gravesend & N'fleet	4-1	Harbut(3), Boyce(p)	324	2-3	Browne, Spencer	601
Gresley Rovers	1-1	Harbut	285	0-5		720
Halesowen Town	1-2	Preston	285	2-1	Lovell, Boyce(p)	833
Hastings Town	2-1	Chalk Boyce	281	3-2	Chalk(2), Webb	387
Kings Lynn	2-0	Harbut, Webb	362	1-1	Boyce	888
Merthyr Tydfil	1-3	Browne	167	3-2	Boyce, Emms(2)	610
Newport A.F.C.	0-0		472	1-3	Chalk	563
Nuneaton Borough	1-1	Boyce	460	0-4		830
Sittingbourne	0-1		254	1-2	Webb	584
Sudbury Town	2-1	Sanders, Harbut	170	1-0	Cranmer	490
Worcester City	1-1	Chalk	452	2-0	Webb, Harbut	746

> Leading goalscorer for 1996/97 season was Robbie Harbut with 13 goals.

1996/97 Dr Martens Premier Division

	P	W	D	L	F	A	Pts
Gresley Rovers	42	25	10	7	75	40	85
Cheltenham Town	42	21	11	10	76	44	74
Gloucester City	42	21	10	11	81	56	73
Halesowen Town	42	21	10	11	77	54	73
King's Lynn	42	20	8	14	65	61	68
Burton Albion	42	18	12	12	70	53	66
Nuneaton Borough	42	19	9	14	61	52	66
Sittingbourne	42	19	7	16	76	65	64
Merthyr Tydfil	42	17	9	16	69	61	60
Worcester City	42	15	14	13	52	50	59
Atherstone United	42	15	13	14	46	47	58
Salisbury City	**42**	**15**	**13**	**14**	**57**	**66**	**58**
Sudbury Town	42	16	7	19	72	72	55
Gravesend & Northfleet	42	16	7	19	63	73	55
Dorchester Town	42	14	9	19	62	66	51
Hastings Town	42	12	15	15	49	60	51
Crawley Town	42	13	8	21	49	67	47
Cambridge City	42	11	13	18	57	65	46
Ashford Town	42	9	18	15	53	79	45
Baldock Town	42	11	8	23	52	90	41
Newport A.F.C.	42	9	13	20	40	60	40
Chelmsford City	42	6	14	22	49	70	32

1997/98 F.A. Cup				1997/98 F.A. Trophy			
versus	res	goalscorer	gate	versus	res	goalscorer	gate
Chard Town(h)	3-0	Browne, Puckett, Webb	274	Berkhamstead Town(a)	1-2	Chalk	112
Weston-super-Mare(h)	2-2	Harbut(2)	305				
replay(a)	2-2	Fletcher, Browne(p)	210	*Salisbury won 4-3 on penalties*			
Taunton Town(h)	3-0	Preston, Puckett, Chalk	403				
Kings Lynn(a)	0-5		1946				

1997/98 Wilts Premier Shield				1997/98 Dr Martins Southern League Cup			
versus	res	goalscorer	gate	versus	res	goalscorer	gate
Warminster Town(h)	6-0	Chalk(2), Sotoudeh(2) Puckett, Holmes	97	Trowbridge Town(h)	2-3	Browne, Winter	273
				Trowbridge Town(h)	4-3	Puckett(2), Harbut, o.g.	141
Trowbridge Town(h)	2-1	Bush, Browne	117	Bashley(h)	1-6	Harbut	137
Melksham	0-0	*(played at Swindon Melksham won on penalties)*					

1997/98 Dr Martens Premier Division						
versus	H	goalscorer	gate	A	goalscorer	gate
Ashford Town	0-0		315	1-1	Chalk	339
Atherstone United	2-1	Bright, Chalk	294	3-0	Webb(2), Preston	221
Bath	1-0	Harbut	403	0-5		513
Bromsgrove Rovers	2-0	Bright, Chalk	343	2-2	Puckett, Housley	369
Burton Albion	0-2		301	2-1	Thompson, Bright	751
Cambridge City	1-1	Whale	246	1-3	Harbut	322
Crawley Town	2-6	Chalk, Browne(p)	685	0-1		1314
Dorchester Town	0-3		472	0-1		1088
Forest Green Rovers	0-2		506	2-3	Thompson, Bright	862
Gloucester City	2-3	Browne, Hobson	434	1-1	Bartlett	328
Gresley Rovers	1-0	Chalk	574	1-1	Bright	418
Halesowen Town	1-0	Chalk	306	1-4	Chalk	447
Hastings Town	2-0	Whale, Finlayson	375	0-2		446
Kings Lynn	2-3	Holmes, Braybrook	408	0-3		738
Merthyr Tydfil	2-5	Chalk, Finlayson	324	0-0		619
Nuneaton Borough	2-2	Bright, Braybrook	371	1-2	Housley	1174
Rothwell Town	0-0		450	2-2	Bright, Holmes	202
Sittingbourne	4-0	Browne(2), Emms, Preston	221	3-0	Sandrey, Puckett, Chalk	417
St Leonards Stamcroft	2-0	Whale, Puckett	413	2-6	Bright, Chalk	436
Tamworth	3-2	Braybrook, Whale, Finlayson	347	1-1	Bright	453
Worcester City	1-1	Holmes	280	0-2		713

Leading goalscorer for 1997/98 season was Ian Chalk with 10 goals.

1997/98 Dr Martens Premier Division							
	P	W	D	L	F	A	Pts
Forest Green Rovers	42	27	8	7	93	55	89
Merthyr Tydfil	42	24	12	6	80	42	84
Burton Albion	42	21	8	13	64	43	71
Dorchester Town	42	19	13	10	63	38	70
Halesowen Town	42	18	15	9	70	38	69
Bath City	42	19	12	11	72	51	69
Worcester City	42	19	12	11	54	44	69
King's Lynn	42	18	11	13	64	65	65
Atherstone United	42	17	12	13	55	49	63
Crawley Town	42	17	8	17	63	60	59
Gloucester City	42	16	11	15	57	57	59
Nuneaton Borough	42	17	6	19	68	61	57
Cambridge City	42	16	8	18	62	70	56
Hastings Town	42	14	12	16	67	70	54
Tamworth	42	14	11	17	68	65	53
Rothwell Town	42	11	16	15	55	73	49
Gresley Rovers	42	14	6	22	59	77	48
Salisbury City	**42**	**12**	**12**	**18**	**53**	**72**	**48**
Bromsgrove Rovers	43	13	6	23	67	85	45
Sittingbourne	42	12	8	22	47	66	44
Ashford Town	42	8	5	29	34	85	29
St Leonards Stamcroft	42	5	10	27	48	97	25

| 1998/99 F.A. Cup | | | | | 1998/99 F.A. Trophy | | | |
versus	res	goalscorer		gate	versus	res	goalscorer	gate
Dorchester(a)	3-0	Emms, Randall, Ferrett		616	Carshalton Athletic(h)	2-1	Ferrett, Sales	335
Hungerford Town(a)	1-1	Rofe		386	Woking(a)	1-2	Bright	1614
replay(h)	3-2	Sales(2), Harbut		421				
Carshalton Athletic(a)	6-0	Housley(3), Sales,		278				
		Harbut, Randall						
Hull City(h)	0-2	*1st Round Proper*		2573				

| 1998/99 Wilts Premier Shield | | | | | 1998/99 Dr Martins Southern League Cup | | | |
versus	res	goalscorer		gate	versus	res	goalscorer	gate
Warminster Town(h)	9-0	Sales(4), Bowers,		108	Bashley(a)	1-1	Sales	215
		Chalk(2), Hayter(2)			Bashley(h)	2-2	Randall, Sales	253
Highworth Town(a)	2-1	Emms, Bowers		107				
Swindon Supermarine(h)	2-1	Curtis, Fearon		320				

1998/99 Dr Martens Premier Division						
versus	H	goalscorer	gate	A	goalscorer	gate
Atherstone United	0-2		360	0-2		211
Bath	3-2	Chalk(2), Fearon	682	5-3	Sales, Harbut, Bowers(2), Randall	716
Boston	0-0		521	1-3	Randall	782
Bromsgrove Rovers	1-0	Hayter	494	2-0	Sales, Rofe	348
Burton Albion	0-2		560	2-1	Sales, Bright	690
Cambridge City	4-1	Randall(2), Ferrett, Holmes	308	3-1	Randall(p), Emms, Sales	275
Crawley Town	0-2		279	1-1	Randall(p)	835
Dorchester Town	3-3	Randall, Sales, Harbut	367	0-4		571
Gloucester City	1-1	Sales	667	2-1	Bowers, Randall(p)	448
Grantham Town	1-0	Randall	419	1-2	Randall	730
Gresley Rovers	2-2	Harbut, Fearon	352	1-4	Randall(p)	571
Halesowen Town	1-2	Sales	771	3-3	Bright, Sales, Hayter	537
Hastings Town	1-0	Randall	462	2-3	Chalk, Braybrook	376
Ilkeston Town	0-0		337	0-3		483
Kings Lynn	2-2	Sales, Harbut	449	3-3	Winter, Sales, Chalk	652
Merthyr Tydfil	1-0	Harbut	763	1-0	Hayter	431
Nuneaton Borough	1-1	Housley	1050	1-0	Hayter	1404
Rothwell Town	0-2		363	0-1		175
Tamworth	2-1	Sales, Housley	421	1-2	Housley	519
Weymouth	1-0	Randall	932	1-1	Randall	951
Worcester City	2-0	Bowers, Bright	317	0-0		703

Leading goalscorer for 1998/99 season was Adrian Randall with 13 goals.

1998/99 Dr Martens Premier Division

	P	W	D	L	F	A	Pts
Nuneaton Borough	42	27	9	6	91	33	90
Boston United	42	17	16	9	69	51	67
Ilkeston Town	42	18	13	11	72	59	67
Bath City	42	18	11	13	70	44	65
Hastings Town	42	18	11	13	57	49	65
Gloucester City	42	18	11	13	57	52	65
Worcester City	42	18	9	15	58	54	63
Halesowen Town	42	17	11	14	72	60	62
Tamworth	42	19	5	18	62	67	62
King's Lynn	42	17	10	15	53	46	61
Crawley Town	42	17	10	15	57	58	61
Salisbury City	**42**	**16**	**12**	**14**	**56**	**61**	**60**
Burton Albion	42	17	7	18	58	52	58
Weymouth	42	14	14	14	56	55	56
Merthy Tydfil	42	15	8	19	52	62	53
Atherstone United	42	12	14	16	47	52	50
Grantham Town	42	14	8	20	51	58	50
Dorchester Town	42	11	15	16	49	63	48
Rothwell Town	42	13	9	20	47	67	48
Cambridge City	42	11	12	19	47	68	45
Gresley Rovers	42	12	8	22	49	73	44
Bromsgrove Rovers	42	8	7	27	38	84	31

1999/2000 F.A. Cup				1999/2000 F.A. Trophy			
versus	res	goalscorer	gate	versus	res	goalscorer	gate
Welton Rovers(a)	3-1	Shepherd(3)	254	Tonbridge Angels(h)	2-0	Housley, Sales	471
Maidenhead United(a)	1-0	Sales	354	Sutton United(h)	2-5	Shepherd, Sales	644
Oxford City(a)	1-2	Shepherd	461				

1999/2000 Wilts Premier Shield				1999/2000 Dr Martins Southern League Cup		
versus	res	goalscorer	gate	versus	res goalscorer	gate
Devizes Town(a)	1-2	Sales	148	Newport I.O.W.(h)	1-4 Sales	258

1999/2000 Dr Martens Premier Division						
versus	H	goalscorer	gate	A	goalscorer	gate
Atherstone	1-0	Housley	374	3-0	Smith(2 penalties), Shepherd	165
Bath City	1-3	Sales	721	4-4	Chalk, Bowers, Emms, Sales	1175
Boston United	1-2	Sales	593	0-6		1228
Burton Albion	0-3		515	1-4	Sales	842
Cambridge City	4-0	Sales(2), Shepherd, Andersen	371	3-1	Sales(2), Chalk	449
Clevedon Town	1-2	Bowers	370	2-1	Sales, Bowers	348
Crawley Town	4-1	Miles, Harbut(2), Sales	460	1-4	Bowers	557
Dorchester Town	1-1	Sales	557	4-4	Shepherd(2), McMenemy, Savage(p)	626
Gloucester City	2-0	Shepherd, Chalk	535	3-3	Sales(2), Shepherd	408
Grantham Town	5-0	Sales(3), Shepherd, Bowers	379	1-5	Shepherd	250
Halesowen Town	2-0	Sales, Shepherd	391	1-3	Smith(p)	353
Havant & W'ville	1-2	Bowers	394	1-0	Sheherd	417
Ilkeston Town	1-2	Emms	352	0-6		539
King's Lynn	2-3	Sales, Miles	463	0-2		552
Margate	2-0	Sales, Rofe	509	0-2		356
Merthyr Tydfil	2-3	Powell, Harbut	405	1-1	Sales	652
Newport AFC	1-2	Miles	618	0-0		640
Rothwell Town	4-2	Sales(3), Chalk	404	2-3	Shepherd, Sales	227
Tamworth	1-1	Sales	527	2-1	Shepherd, Powell	574
Weymouth	1-1	Smith	627	0-1		872
Worcester City	1-3	Sales	381	3-2	Emms, Chalk, Bartley	720

> Leading goalscorer for 1999/2000 season was Paul Sales with 26 goals.

1999/2000 Dr Martens Premier Division							
	P	W	D	L	F	A	Pts
Boston United	42	27	11	4	102	39	92
Burton Albion	42	23	9	10	73	43	78
Margate	42	23	8	11	64	43	77
Bath City	42	19	15	8	70	49	72
Kings Lynn	42	19	14	9	59	43	71
Tamworth	42	20	10	12	80	51	70
Newport AFC	42	16	18	8	67	50	66
Clevedon Town	42	18	9	15	52	52	63
Ilkeston Town	42	16	12	14	77	69	60
Weymouth	42	14	16	12	60	51	58
Halesowen Town	42	14	14	14	52	54	56
Crawley Town	42	15	8	19	68	82	53
Havant & Waterlooville	42	13	13	16	63	68	52
Cambridge City	42	14	10	18	52	66	52
Worcester City	42	13	11	18	60	66	50
Salisbury City	**42**	**14**	**8**	**20**	**70**	**84**	**50**
Merthy Tydfil	42	13	9	20	51	63	48
Dorchester Town	42	10	17	15	56	65	47
Grantham Town	42	14	5	23	63	76	47
Gloucester City	42	8	14	20	40	82	38
Rothwell Town	42	5	14	23	48	85	29
Atherstone United	42	5	13	24	30	76	28

2000/01 F.A. Cup				2000/01 F.A. Trophy			
versus	res	goalscorer	gate	versus	res	goalscorer	gate
Clevedon Town(a)	4-2	Emms, Bowers, Smith(2)(1 penalty)	302	Bashley(a)	0-1		257
Dorchester Town(a)	3-4	Sales(2), Smith	817				

2000/01 Wilts Premier Shield				2000/01 Dr Martins Southern League Cup		
versus	res	goalscorer	gate	versus	res goalscorer	gate
Chippenham Tn(h)	1-0	o.g.	128	Havant & Waterlooville(a)	2-2 Sanders, Smith	192
Westbury United(a)	4-0	Corcoran(2), Chalk, Sales	n.a.		*(lost 3-2 on penalties)*	
Melksham Town(h)	2-1	Emms, Shepherd	244			
Bemerton H.H.	1-0	Richardson	738			

2000/01 Dr Martens Premier Division						
versus	H	goalscorer	gate	A	goalscorer	gate
Bath	4-4	Turk(2), Sales, Lloyd, o.g.	575	1-0	Gibbon	710
Burton Albion	1-0	o.g.	559	0-5		1085
Cambridge City	2-1	Turk, Bowers	432	2-1	Sales, Shepherd	510
Clevedon Town	4-1	Sales(2), Shepherd(2)	375	1-3	Sales	272
Crawley Town	1-1	Sales	422	1-5	Sales	1053
Dorchester Town	0-2		556	1-2	Sales	544
Fisher Athletic '93	3-0	Sales, Smith, Emms	370	2-1	Smith(p), Shepherd	143
Folkestone Invicta	0-0		428	1-2	Smith	424
Halesowen Town	2-1	Sales, Braybrook	490	0-3		405
Havant & W'ville	0-0		298	1-3	Shepherd	477
Ilkeston Town	2-0	Shepherd, Bartlett	424	1-1	Shepherd	362
King's Lynn	1-4	Smith	320	1-2	Smith	507
Margate	0-1		623	1-1	Shepherd	925
Merthyr Tydfil	2-2	Turk, Smith	475	0-1		456
Moor Green	3-1	Sales(3)	331	2-0	Sales, Smith	312
Newport AFC	4-0	Shepherd, Emms(2), Smith	571	3-1	Bowers(2), Marwood	563
Stafford Rangers	4-1	Shepherd, Wakefield(2), Sales	510	2-4	Bowers, Smith	658
Tamworth	1-3	Smith	513	1-4	Wakefield	535
Welling United	1-1	Harbut	421	1-2	Corcoran	432
Weymouth	3-2	Bowers, Sales, Corcoran	617	1-3	Shepherd	770
Worcester City	2-0	Sales, Bowers	255	1-0	Sales	1005

> Leading goalscorer for 2000/01 season was Paul Sales with 18 goals.

2000/01 Dr Martens Premier Division

	P	W	D	L	F	A	Pts
Margate	42	28	7	7	75	27	91
Burton Albion	42	25	13	4	76	36	88
King's Lynn	42	18	11	13	67	58	65
Welling United	42	17	13	12	59	55	64
Weymouth	42	17	12	13	69	51	63
Havant & Waterlooville	42	18	9	15	66	54	63
Stafford Rangers	42	18	9	15	70	59	63
Worcester City	42	18	8	16	52	53	62
Moor Green	42	18	8	16	50	53	62
Newport A.F.C.	42	17	10	15	70	61	61
Crawley Town	42	17	10	15	61	54	61
Tamworth	42	17	8	17	58	55	59
Salisbury City	**42**	**17**	**8**	**17**	**64**	**69**	**59**
Ilkeston Town	42	16	11	15	51	61	59
*Bath City	42	15	13	14	67	68	55
Cambridge City	42	13	11	18	56	59	50
Folkestone Invicta	42	14	6	22	49	74	48
Merthyr Tydfil	42	11	13	18	49	62	46
Clevedon Town	42	11	7	24	61	74	40
*Fisher Athletic '93	42	12	6	24	51	85	39
Dorchester Town	42	10	8	24	40	71	38
Halesowen Town	42	8	13	21	47	69	37

*3 points deducted for fielding ineligible player

2001/02 F.A. Cup				2001/02 F.A. Trophy			
versus	**res**	**goalscorer**	**gate**	**versus**	**res**	**goalscorer**	**gate**
Tiverton Town(h)	3-3	Shepherd, Bowers, Emms	586	Tooting & Mitcham(a)	0-3		261
replay(a)	1-3	Mathie	779				

2001/02 Wilts Premier Shield				2001/02 Dr Martins Southern League Cup			
versus	**res**	**goalscorer**	**gate**	**versus**	**res**	**goalscorer**	**gate**
Swindon Supermarine(a)	1-2	Underhay	156	Weymouth(a)	0-4		399

2001/02 Dr Martens League Premier Division						
versus	**H**	**goalscorer**	**gate**	**A**	**goalscorer**	**gate**
Bath City	0-1		455	0-1		697
Cambridge City	1-1	King	393	3-1	King, Richardson, Crook	273
Chelmsford City	1-2	King	379	2-3	Davies, Cook	451
Crawley Town	0-4		637	0-4		637
Folkestone Invicta	2-0	King, Turk	366	0-2		366
Havant & W'ville	2-0	Turk, King	340	0-2		505
Hednesford Town	1-0	Underhay(p)	300	0-6		650
Hinckley Athletic	1-1	Cooper	375	1-2	King	308
Ilkeston Town	1-1	Sales	397	1-0	King	547
Kettering Town	1-2	King	539	0-4		1295
King's Lynn	0-3		324	1-2	King(p)	683
Merthyr Tydfil	1-2	Turk	439	2-3	King(2)	501
Moor Green	5-0	Bowers, King(2, 1 penalty), Wallace, Griffin	330	1-1	Speakman	277
Newport County	0-2		460	0-0		810
Newport I.O.W.	1-1	Sales	481	0-0		557
Stafford Rangers	1-4	King	382	0-3		698
Tamworth	1-2	King(p)	444	1-5	Turk	2240
Tiverton Town	0-3		417	0-1		528
Welling United	0-1		199	1-5	Davies	516
Weymouth	2-3	Blackham, Speakman	545	1-2	Crook	701
Worcester	1-1	Davies	315	0-6		886

> **Leading goalscorer for 2001/02 season was Ryan King with 15 goals.**

Salisbury City's home match versus Tiverton Town was played on that momentous day of Tuesday 11th September 2001. After watching those horrendous hours unfold in America on all T.V. screens most persons thought that the game would be postponed. Salisbury certainly seemed to be in a daze and in a game with their minds seemingly elsewhere, losing 3-0. Tamworth were pipped by Kettering Town for promotion in their final game needing to win but only managing a draw.

2001/02 Dr Martens League Premier Division							
	P	**W**	**D**	**L**	**F**	**A**	**Pts**
Kettering Town	42	27	6	9	80	41	87
Tamworth	42	24	13	5	81	41	85
Havant & Waterlooville	42	22	9	11	74	50	75
Crawley Town	42	21	10	11	67	48	73
Newport County	42	19	9	14	61	48	66
Tiverton Town	42	17	10	15	70	63	61
Moor Green	42	18	7	17	64	62	61
Worcester City	42	16	12	14	65	54	60
Stafford Rangers	42	17	9	16	70	62	60
Ilkeston Town	42	14	16	12	58	61	58
Weymouth	42	15	11	16	59	67	56
Hinckley United	42	14	13	15	64	62	55
Folkestone Invicta	42	14	12	16	51	61	54
Cambridge City	42	12	16	14	60	70	52
Welling United	42	13	12	17	69	66	51
Hednesford Town	42	15	6	21	59	70	51
Bath City	42	13	11	18	56	65	50
Chelmsford City	42	13	11	18	63	75	50
Newport I.O.W.	42	12	12	18	38	61	48
King's Lynn	42	11	13	18	44	57	46
Merthyr Tydfil	42	12	8	22	53	71	44
Salisbury City	**42**	**6**	**8**	**28**	**36**	**87**	**26**

2002/03 F.A. Cup				2002/03 F.A. Trophy			
versus	res	goalscorer	gate	versus	res	goalscorer	gate
Bideford(h)	1-2	King	482	Dartford(h)	2-0	Funnell, King	410
				Erith & Belvedere(h)	2-2	Thomas, Brown	431
				replay(a)	0-2		93

2002/03 Wilts Premier Shield				2002/03 Dr Martins Southern League Cup			
versus	res	goalscorer	gate	versus	res	goalscorer	gate
Chippenham Town(h)	3-3	Crook, Sotoudeh, o.g.	368	Dorchester Town(h)	3-2	Wallace(2), Turk	441
Chippenham Town(a)	2-0	Wallace, Sotoudeh	381	Newport I.O.W.(a)	2-3	Wallace, Turk	n.a.
Swindon Supermarine(h)	3-1	Wallace, Strong, Purches	639				

2002/03 Dr Martens League Eastern Division

versus	H	goalscorer	gate	A	goalscorer	gate
Ashford	3-1	Wallace, Strong, Funnell	555	1-0	Phillips	106
Banbury United	0-0		663	1-0	Brown	1042
Bashley	2-2	Bowers, Funnell	823	1-3	Emms	520
Burnham	5-2	Brown, Wallace, Thomas, Emms, Bowers	470	1-1	Turk	158
Chatham Town	2-0	Brown, Turk	539	2-0	Davies, Turk	209
Corby Town	3-1	Davies, Wallace(2)	446	4-0	Wallace, Brown, Davies, Turk	70
Dartford	3-0	King, Emms, Bowers	433	4-1	Brown, Bowers(2), Bartlett	182
Dorchester Town	0-0		554	1-5	Wallace	469
Erith & Belvedere	2-1	Funnell, Brown	374	2-3	King, Bowers	153
Eastbourne Borough	1-2	Burt	561	0-0		357
Fisher Athletic	3-1	Wallace (3, 1 penalty)	462	1-0	Wallace	103
Fleet Town	2-1	Bowers, McGlashan	435	2-0	Strong, Bartlett	287
Histon	3-2	Thomas, Burt, Bowers	488	1-1	Bowers	241
King's Lynn	2-1	Turk, Brown	475	1-3	Brown	691
Newport I.O.W.	3-2	Cook, Burt, Bowers	613	4-0	Crook, King, Funnell, Wallace	258
Rothwell Town	0-0		393	1-0	Funnell	261
Sittingbourne	3-0	Turk, Wallace(2)	363	2-3	Bartlett, Wallace	210
Spalding United	1-0	Thomas	507	4-1	Turk(2), Wallace, Funnel	106
Stamford	2-1	Brown, Strong	468	0-0		302
St Leonards	3-2	Funnell, McGlashan, Wallace(p)	359	2-0	Crook, Purches	81
Tonbridge Angles	2-0	Funnell, Brown	469	1-2	Strong	639

Leading goalscorer for 2002/03 season was Adam Wallace with 16 goals.

2002/03 Dr Martens League Eastern Division

	P	W	L	D	F	A	Pts
Dorchester	42	28	9	5	114	40	93
Eastbourne Borough	42	29	6	7	92	33	93
Stamford	42	27	6	9	80	39	87
Salisbury City (3pts deducted)	**42**	**27**	**8**	**7**	**81**	**42**	**86**
Bashley	42	23	12	7	90	44	81
King's Lynn	42	24	7	11	98	62	79
Rothwell Town	42	22	10	10	77	52	76
Banbury	42	21	11	10	75	50	74
Tonbridge Angles	42	20	11	11	71	55	71
Histon	42	20	7	15	99	62	67
Ashford Town	42	18	9	15	63	57	63
Sittingbourne	42	15	8	19	57	69	53
Burnham	42	15	7	20	62	79	52
Fisher Athletic	42	15	5	22	57	80	50
Chatham Town	42	14	5	23	54	84	47
Newport I.O.W.	42	12	6	24	53	87	42
Dartford	42	11	8	23	48	78	41
Erith & Belvedere	42	11	6	25	65	96	39
Corby Town	42	9	11	22	49	84	38
Fleet Town	42	8	8	26	34	80	32
Spalding United	42	4	6	32	40	108	18
St. Leonards	42	4	4	34	38	116	16

2003/04 F.A. Cup

versus	res	goalscorer	gate
Odd Down(h)	4-0	Cooper, Turk, Strong(2)	418
Taunton Town(h)	4-1	Cook,(2), Strong, Crook	551
Westbury United(h)	1-1	Cooper	570
replay(a)	2-1	Turk, Phillips	478
Havant & W'ville(a)	4-3	Turk(2), Thomas, Crook	494
Lymington & N.Milton(h)	5-1	Wallace(2), Thomas, Crook, Sawyer(goal-keeper)(p)	1190
Sheffield Wednesday(a)	0-4		11,419

2003/04 F.A. Trophy

versus	res	goalscorer	gate
Clevedon Town(h)	0-1		376

1st round proper

2003/04 Wilts Premier Shield

versus	res	goalscorer	gate
Swindon Town(h)	0-0		313
Swindon Town(a)	2-3	Phillips(2)	110

2003/04 Dr Martins Southern League Cup

versus	res	goalscorer	gate
Newport I.O.W.(a)	2-3	Turner(2)	123

2003/04 Dr Martens League Eastern Division

versus	H	goalscorer	gate	A	goalscorer	gate
Ashford	2-1	Davis, Strong	591	2-0	Davis, o.g.	242
Banbury United	1-1	Tubbs	601	1-0	Phillips	256
Bashley	5-1	Strong(3), Funnell, Phillips	582	4-2	Wallace(2), Turk, o.g.	344
Burgess Hill Town	0-1		557	0-1		217
Burnham	1-1	Turner	357	1-2	Wallace	153
Chatham	1-1	Tubbs	701	3-2	Wallace(2), Tubbs	187
Corby Town	2-0	Tubbs(2)	561	1-2	Phillips	107
Dartford	3-1	Davis, Tubbs, Strong	505	3-0	Turner, Tubbs, Crook	244
Eastleigh	0-4		554	2-1	Wallace, Thomas	528
Erith & Belv	3-0	Davis, Strong, Phillips	380	3-0	Howes, Tubbs(2)	101
Fisher Athletic	2-1	Phillips, Tubbs	559	1-2	Davis	116
Fleet Town	1-0	Wallace	519	5-1	Wallace(3), Tubbs, Crook	207
Folkestone Inv.	1-1	Strong	463	2-2	Tubbs(2)	401
Hastings United	3-2	Phillips Tubbs(2)	537	4-1	Tubbs(2) Turk, Wallace	202
Histon	0-0		473	1-2	Davis	269
King's Lynn	0-3		903	2-0	Turk, Tubbs	936
Newport I.O.W.	2-0	Bartlett, Davis	701	1-1	Strong	300
Rothwell Town	1-1	Phillips	542	2-0	Thomas, Phillips	126
Sittingbourne	3-0	Tubbs, Wallace, Thomas	609	0-1		279
Stamford	1-1	Wallace	406	0-2		228
Tonbridge Angels	1-1	Phillips	924	2-2	Strong, Funnell	496

Leading goalscorer for 2003/04 season was Matt Tubbs with 19 goals.

2003/04 Dr Martens League Eastern Division

	P	W	D	L	F	A	Pts
King's Lynn	42	28	7	7	90	35	91
Histon	42	26	10	6	96	41	88
Tonbridge Angels	42	27	7	8	82	46	88
Eastleigh (3pts deducted)	42	27	4	11	88	40	82
Folkestone Invicta.	42	20	15	7	91	45	75
Salisbury City	**42**	**21**	**11**	**10**	**73**	**45**	**74**
Stamford	42	20	11	11	63	45	71
Banbury United	42	19	10	13	65	57	67
Burgess Hill Town	42	19	7	16	67	54	64
Sittingbourne	42	18	8	16	61	55	62
Bashley	42	18	7	17	66	58	61
Ashford Town	42	15	9	18	51	53	54
Chatham Town	42	13	10	19	49	67	49
Fisher Athletic	42	13	10	19	61	81	49
Corby Town	42	12	9	21	44	75	45
Dartford	42	13	6	23	48	81	45
Burnham (3pts deducted)	42	12	11	19	52	76	44
Hastings United	42	12	7	23	60	91	43
Newport I.O.W.	42	11	7	24	42	69	40
Rothwell Town	42	9	11	22	30	47	38
Erith & Belvedere	42	7	10	25	45	84	31
Fleet Town	42	5	7	30	35	114	22

2004/05 F.A. Cup

versus	res	goalscorer	gate
Exmouth United(a)	2-1	Phillips, Tubbs	253
Frome Town(h)	1-1	Davis, C.	
replay(a)	3-0	Phillips, Tubbs, Turk	665
Weston-super-Mare(a)	3-1	Davis, C(2), Matthews	543
Slough Town(a)	2-3	Matthews, Wallace(p)	1194

2004/05 F.A. Trophy

versus	res	goalscorer	gate
Thurrock(h)	0-4		471

2004/05 Wilts Premier Shield

versus	res	goalscorer	gate
Chippenham Town(a)	4-3	Wallace(3), Phillips	234
Chippenham Town(h)	0-2		237

2004/05 Bryco Rymans League Cup

versus	res	goalscorer	gate
Leyton(h)	2-0	Wallace, Matthews	234
Slough Town(a)	0-3		193

2004/05 Ryman Isthmian Premier

versus	H	goalscorer	gate	A	goalscorer	gate
Billericay Town	1-0	Davis, C.	450	0-0		482
Braintree Town	0-0		553	2-2	Wallace, Phillips	311
Chelmsford City	0-2		556	3-1	Phillips, Tubbs, Howes	394
Cheshunt	1-0	Phillips	523	2-2	Bond, Hale	121
Dover Athletic	0-0		417	1-2	Davis, C.(p)	659
Eastleigh	0-0		1151	0-3		702
Folkestone Invicta	1-0	Wallace (penalty)	530	1-3	Wallace	361
Hampton & Richmond	2-1	Bond, Davis, C.(penalty)	523	2-3	Andy Cook, Phillips	181
Harrow Burough	1-2	Matthews	532	2-3	Phillips, Cook, S	141
Hendon	2-1	Wallace(2)	498	2-1	Turk, Jones	377
Heybridge Swifts	1-1	Turk	444	2-1	Tubbs, Sawyer(goal-keeper)(p)	293
Kingstonian	1-0	Tubbs	502	4-0	Aaron Cook, Hale, Davis, C., Tubbs	251
Leyton	0-2		509	2-3	Davis, C, Turk	144
Northwood	1-4	Matthews	347	3-0	o.g., Turk, Tubbs	172
Slough Town	0-0		655	0-1		431
Staines Town	1-3		511	2-2	Tubbs, Wallace(p)	348
Tonbridge Angels	1-0	Davis, C.	477	3-2	Wallace(2), Davis, C.	274
Wealdstone	3-1	Phillips,.Tubbs, Davis, C.	704	2-4	Davis, C., Wallace	322
Windsor & Eton	5-1	Wallace(2), Davis, C., Tubbs Matthews	487	1-2	Turk	189
Worthing	1-2	Phillips	487	1-5	Cook, S.	331
Yeading	1-3	Davis C.	431	2-1	Davis, C., Matthews	261

Leading goalscorer for 2004/05 season was Adam Wallace with 12 goals.

2004/05 Ryman Isthmian Premier

	P	W	D	L	F	A	Pts
Yeading(C)	42	25	11	6	74	48	86
Billericay Town (play-offs)	42	23	11	8	78	40	80
Eastleigh (play-offs) (promoted)	42	22	13	7	84	49	79
Braintree Town (play-offs)	42	19	17	6	67	33	74
Leyton (play-offs)	42	21	8	13	71	57	71
Hampton & Richmond	42	21	8	13	64	53	71
Heybridge Swifts	42	18	9	15	76	65	63
Chelmsford City	42	17	11	14	63	58	62
Staines Town	42	17	9	16	59	53	60
Worthing	42	16	11	15	50	45	59
Hendon	42	17	7	18	48	60	58
Salisbury City	**42**	**16**	**9**	**17**	**60**	**64**	**57**
Slough Town	42	15	10	17	61	66	55
Folkestone Invicta.	42	14	10	18	51	53	52
Windsor & Eton	42	12	14	16	48	62	50
Harrow Borough	42	13	10	19	41	54	49
Northwood	42	14	7	21	49	66	49
Wealdstone	42	13	8	21	60	73	47
Cheshunt(R)	42	12	11	19	58	71	47
Tonbridge Angels(R)	42	11	10	21	47	73	43
Dover Athletic(R)	42	10	9	23	50	66	39
Kingstonian(R)	42	7	5	30	43	93	26

2005/06 F.A. Cup

versus	res	goalscorer	gate
Clevedon Town(a)	1-1	Tubbs	264
replay (h)	4-2	Tubbs(2), Turk, o.g. Matthews	506
Yate Town(a)	2-0	Widdrington, Tubbs	371
Merthyr Tydfil(a)	1-2	Tubbs	615

2005/06 F.A. Trophy

versus	res	goalscorer	gate
Paulton Rovers(a)	1-1	Sales	150
replay(h)	3-1	Haddow, Heath(2)	336
Clevedon(h)	2-1	Davis, Tubbs	552
Newport County(h)	3-0	Haddow, Sales, Widdrington	806
Trophy 1st Round Proper			
2nd Round Proper			
Harlow(h)	1-0	Tubbs(p)	731
3rd Round Proper			
Canvey Island(a)	1-0	Haddow	534
Stalybridge Celtic(h)	0-0		1533
replay			
Stalybridge Celtic(a)	1-0	Tubbs	704
Quarter Final			
Exeter City(a)	1-3	Matthews	3653

2005/06 Wilts Premier Shield

versus	res	goalscorer	gate
Swindon(a)	0-1		200
Swindon(h)	4-1	Wilde(3), Matthews	194
Chippenham Town(h)	0-1		803

2005/06 Errea Southern League Cup

versus	res	goalscorer	gate
Aylesbury United(h)	3-0	Matthews(2), Heath	226
Cirencester(h)	3-2	Cook Andy, Wilde, Heath	280
(abandoned)			
Cirencester(h)	3-4	Tubbs(3)	205

2005/06 Southern Premier

versus	H	goalscorer	gate	A	goalscorer	gate
Aylesbury United	3-0	Matthews(2), Heath	763	3-1	Sales(2), Turk	214
Banbury United	1-3	Turk	495	2-1	Prince, Matthews	588
Bath City	0-0		1478	2-0	Widdrington, Tubbs	787
Bedford Town	1-0	Tubbs	571	0-1		479
Chesham United	6-0	Sales(3), Haddow, Tubbs(2)	557	4-1	Tubbs, Davis(p), Sales, Haddow	252
Cheshunt	5-0	Turk(2), Bond, Aaron Cook, Tubbs	1400	1-0	Andy Cook	136
Chippenham Town	2-1	Tubbs(p), Sales	1907	1-2	Turk	851
Cirencester Town	3-0	Sales(2), Tubbs	506	5-2	Ferrett, Haddow, Sales(2), Wilde	188
Evesham United	1-0	Regis	774	2-2	Sales, Tubbs	238
Gloucester City	2-0	Sales, Haddow	1609	2-1	Davies, Turk	551
Granham Town	3-0	Sales(2), Tubbs	875	0-1		282
Halesowen Town	0-1		767	1-0	Sales	401
Hitchin Town	3-0	Prince, Turk, Matthews	976	3-0	Matthews(3)	388
King's Lynn	1-0	Tubbs(p)	922	3-1	Turk(2), Holgate	1821
Mangotsfield United	2-2	Turk, Haddow	826	0-0		395
Merthyr Tydfil	2-0	Davis(p), Matthews	761	1-0	Tubbs	333
Northwood	3-0	Tubbs(2), Davies	759	2-2	Turk, Widdrington	234
Rugby Town	3-0	Sales(2), Tubbs	587	3-1	Prince, Sales(2)	262
Team Bath	0-1		690	2-1	Sales, Tubbs	337
Tiverton Town	1-0	Sales	980	1-0	Tubbs	629
Yate Town	3-1	Browne, Davis(p), Tubbs	800	0-1		320

Leading goalscorer for 2005/06 season was Paul Sales 22 goals.
Tubbs and Paul Sales together were the Southern Premier Leagues top scorers with 49 goals in all competitions.

2005/06 Southern Premier

	P	W	D	L	F	A	Pts
Salisbury City (C)	42	30	5	7	83	27	95
Bath City (play-offs)	42	25	8	9	66	33	83
King's Lynn (play-offs)	42	25	7	10	73	41	82
Chippenham Town (play-offs)	42	22	11	9	69	45	77
Bedford Town (play-offs) (promoted)	42	22	10	10	69	53	76
Yate Town	42	21	5	16	78	74	68
Banbury United	42	17	11	14	66	61	62
Halesowen Town	42	15	15	12	54	45	60
Merthyr Tydfil	42	17	9	16	62	58	60
Magnotsfield United	42	15	13	14	67	67	58
Grantham Town	42	15	11	16	49	49	56
Tiverton Town	42	14	10	18	69	65	52
Gloucester City	42	14	10	18	57	60	52
Hitchin Town	42	13	12	17	59	76	51
Rugby Town	42	13	11	18	58	66	50
Cheshunt	42	13	9	20	57	70	48
Team Bath	42	14	6	22	55	68	48
Cirencester Town	42	14	4	24	49	68	46
Northwood	42	12	6	24	53	88	42
Evesham United (R)	42	9	14	19	46	58	41
Aylesbury Town (R)	42	9	12	21	43	69	39
Chesham United (R)	42	9	9	24	43	84	36

2006/07 F.A. Cup

versus	res	goalscorer	gate
VTFC(a)	3-0	Sales, Bond, McGregor	370
Eastleigh(a)	1-0	Sales	1402
Fisher Athletic(a)	1-0	Aaron Cook	432
Fleetwood United(h)	3-0	Tubbs, Holmes, Bartlett	2648
1st *Round Proper*			
Nottingham Forest(h)	1-1	Tubbs	3100
replay(a)	0-2	2nd *Round Proper*	6177

2006/07 F.A. Trophy

versus	res	goalscorer	gate
Enfield(h)	2-1	Matthews(2, 1p)	1452
Woking(h)	3-1	Tubbs(2, 1p)Turk	967
1st *Round Proper*			
Southport(h)	2-1	Turk(2)	1183
2nd *Round Proper*			
Kettering(a)	2-0	Tubbs(2)	1795
3rd *Round Proper*			
Stevenage(a)	0-3		2148
4th *Round Proper*			

2006/07 Conference South Play-offs (2 legs home/away)

versus	H	goalscorer	gate	A	goalscorer	gate
Bishop's Stortford	3-1(a.e.t)	Tubbs, Matthews, Fowler	1920	1-1	Matthews	1049

2006/07 Conference South Play-off Final – Broadhall Way Stadium, Stevenage, 13th May

	gate
SALISBURY CITY F.C. 1 v BRAINTREE TOWN 0	
Tubbs	3167

2006/07 Conference South

versus	H	goalscorer	gate	A	goalscorer	gate
Basingstoke Town	0-0		1431	1-1	Prince	1131
Bedford Town	3-1	Clay, Tubbs, Haddow	1146	2-1	Tubbs(2, 1 penalty)	576
Bishop's Stortford	3-1	Tubbs, Browne, Bond	1142	1-1	Aaron Cook	651
Bognor Regis Town	2-1	Aaron Cook, Matthews	1221	1-1	Matthews	508
Braintree Town	0-1		1072	0-0		889
Cambridge City	2-0	Turk, Matthews	791	3-1	Prince, Brown M, McGregor	304
Dorchester Town	1-1	Sales	1378	3-0	Prince, Sales, Aaron Cook	657
Eastbourne Borough	1-2	Marvin Brown	1297	0-1		745
Eastleigh	1-0	Bond	1688	1-0	Sales	1426
Farnborough Town	0-1		1117	1-0	Prince	545
Fisher Athletic	3-0	Sales, Tubbs, o.g.	754	4-1	Turk(2), Matthews, Tubbs(p)	247
Havant & Waterl'ville	1-1	Tubbs	1062	1-3	Tubbs	607
Hayes	0-0		804	4-0	Turk, Tubbs(2), Sales	343
Histon	0-3		1784	2-4	Tubbs(2)	707
Lewes	1-1	Tubbs(p)	849	0-1		724
Newport County	2-1	Matthews, Turk	1101	3-4	Matthews, Tubbs(2)	1014
Sutton United	1-0	Prince	965	1-0	Tubbs	584
Thurrock	0-0		1112	5-1	Turk, Tubbs(p), Sales, Matthews(2)	238
Welling United	1-0	Tubbs	1197	2-1	Prince, Matthews	364
Weston-super-Mare	0-0		966	1-1	Sales	421
Yeading	4-0	Sales, Matthews(2), Bartlett	621	3-1	Tubbs(2)(p), Beswetherick	193

Leading goalscorer for 2006/07 was Matt Tubbs with 20 goals

2006/07 Conference South

	P	W	D	L	F	A	Pts
Histon (C)	42	30	4	8	85	44	94
Salisbury City (play-offs) (promoted)	**42**	**21**	**12**	**9**	**65**	**37**	**75**
Braintree Town (play-offs)	42	21	11	10	51	38	74
Havant & Waterlooville (play-offs)	42	20	13	9	75	46	73
Bishop's Stortford (play-offs)	42	21	10	11	72	61	73
Newport County	42	21	7	14	83	57	70
Eastbourne Borough	42	18	15	9	58	42	69
Welling United	42	21	6	15	65	51	69
Lewes	42	15	17	10	67	52	62
Fisher Athletic	42	15	11	16	77	77	56
Farnborough Town (deducted 10pts)	42	19	8	15	59	52	55
Bognor Regis Town	42	13	13	16	56	62	52
Cambridge City	42	15	7	20	44	52	52
Sutton United	42	14	9	19	58	63	51
Eastleigh	42	11	15	16	48	53	48
Yeading	42	12	9	21	56	78	45
Dorchester Town	42	11	12	19	49	77	45
Thurrock	42	11	11	20	58	79	44
Basingstoke Town	42	9	16	17	46	58	43
Hayes (R)	42	11	10	21	47	73	43
Weston-super-Mare(R)	42	8	11	23	49	77	35
Bedford Town(R)	42	8	7	27	43	82	31

Leading goalscorers for the whites

	Player	Debut	League	Cup	Total
1	Roy Watts	59/60	147	33	180
2	Ian Chalk	88/89	125	51	176
3	Roy Fisher	47/48	119	44	163
4	Alan Green	73/74	91	45	136
5	Jeff Hodgkins	66/67	80	36	116
6	Paul Sales	98/99	88	22	110
7	Paul Christopher	73/74	68	40	108
8	Sean Sanders	87/88	73	24	97
9	Andy Prentice	54/55	72	21	93
10	Alan Tyler	66/67	60	30	90
11	Matt Tubbs	03/04	67	21	88
12	Jimmy Smith	90/91	55	31	86
13	Stan Abbott	55/56	58	21	79
14	Colin Guy	74/75	51	23	74
15	Cyril Smith	47/48	59	13	72
16	Ian Thompson	81/82	56	14	70
17	Kevin Dawtry	83/84	49	20	69
18	Dilwyn Hill	60/61	56	4	60
18a	Tommy Paterson	83/84	44	16	60
18b	Dennis Rogers	47/48	44	16	60
19	Bill Clancy	55/56	46	12	58
20	Barry Cranmer	81/82	46	10	56
21	Bobby Andrews	75/76	36	18	54
22	Roger Emms	92/93	34	18	52
22a	Wayne Turk	2000/01	41	11	52
23	Ian Allen	58/59	41	10	51
24	Paul Odey	92/93	45	4	49
25	Phil Gilbert	63/64	31	16	47
25a	Jack Parker	47/48	30	17	47
26	Adam Wallace	01/02	42	3	45
27	Dave Bennett	71/72	25	19	44
28	Simon Browne	92/93	25	15	40
28a	Bernie Pask	62/63	31	09	40
29	Vic Carter	48/49	22	17	39
30	Roy Onslow	58/59	32	5	37
30a	Dave Stratton	61/62	29	8	37
31	Robbie Harbut	95/96	25	10	35
31a	Mike Hibbs	79/80	25	10	35
32	Dave Husbands	70/71	22	12	34
32a	Robbie Matthews	01/02	12	22	34
32b	Joe McCartney	60/61	31	3	34
33	Peter Childs	47/48	27	6	33
33a	Graham Moxham	68/69	15	18	33
33b	Derek Purvis	58/59	30	3	33
33c	John Stevens	70/71	20	13	33

Six goals by Stan Abbott 1955/56 (Wells (a) and Alan Tyler 1968/69 (Ashford (h) are still Salisbury City F.C. records, likewise three consecutive hat-tricks by Alan Green 1980/81 still holds.

Brief history of the Western and Southern Leagues

The Western League was formed in 1892 with just nine clubs. A second division was formed in 1894. Many Southern League clubs, which included London clubs took part in this competition but in 1909 it was disbanded. After WWI the league was again formed with two divisions intact but in 1922, 1925 and 1960 this second division collapsed.

In 1890, an attempt was made to form a league in southern England. This failed, through the 'old boys club' which was dominant in public schools in this area. Two years later Woolwich Arsenal, who had been expelled from the London F.A. and all cup competitions for adopting professionalism at their A.G.M., sent out a circular to what they considered suitable clubs for the formation of a Southern League. It was attended by 26 clubs, a motion was put, carried and seconded with clubs names entered but in the end this also failed. On the 12th January 1894, officials of Millwall Athletic arranged a meeting, also with the purpose of forming a Southern League. Many clubs attended including: Chatham, Clapton, Ilford, Luton Town, Reading and the 2nd Scots Guards. In a further meeting other clubs were invited but only Royal Ordnance Factories and Swindon Town accepted. A late redrawal by the 2nd Scots Guard saw Southampton St Mary's being accepted.

Moving on to the end of WWII, season 1946/7, the Southern League then had a membership of 17 clubs. Two of these had noteworthy success in the F.A. Cup against Football League clubs. Yeovil Town beat Sunderland in 1948/9 and Bedford held Arsenal 2-2 in 1955/6 and then beat Newcastle United at St James's Park in 1963/4. In 1958/9 two divisions were formed both regional, when 13 new clubs were elected. New clubs were welcomed and admitted in 1963/4 making both divisions up to 22. It was decided in 1971 to regionalize Division I. Not all the extra clubs adapted well, with Woodford Town and Winchester City soon returning to lower level football.

In 1979 the Southern League provided 13 founder members to the newly formed Alliance Premier (now Vauxhall Conference); they were: AP Leamington, Barnet, Bath City, Gravesend & Northfleet, Kettering Town, Maidstone United, Nuneaton Borough, Reddich United, Telford United, Wealdstone, Weymouth, Worcester City and Yeovil Town.

Then in 1982 the Southern League reverted back to a Premier Division composed of the top clubs from the two regional divisions and the relegated Alliance clubs supplemented by two regional divisions. This format existed up until the 2003/4 season when a Conference North and South were created from the top 13 clubs from the regional North, South and Isthmian leagues. These leagues fed into the Conference National.

That very briefly is the history of the Southern League. As all clubs within its fold hanker for promotion, some probably with Football League ambitions the light at the end of the tunnel seemingly never to arrive, one can take heart looking at the many clubs that have risen from Southern League Football. Clubs like Tottenham Hotspur who went on to win the League Championship and became the first team to do 'the double' (also winning in Europe). Also Southampton, QPR, Bristol City and Rovers, Portsmouth, Crystal Palace, Norwich, Swindon Town, West Ham and Fulham. Other famous clubs that featured in this league with their reserve teams include Arsenal.

In 1910/11 at the bottom of Southern League Division II were the old now disbanded Salisbury City; they had been members since 1906. The league had contained, among others, Stoke, Cardiff City, Walsall, Reading, Tom Pentre and Merthy Town.

☆
Salisbury
City
1905
☆

*photo
supplied by
Colin Clark*

So is it not possible, with more support and a bit more sponsorship that the present day Salisbury City F.C. could once again rise to those dizzy heights of success, and make 'our forefathers' of Salisbury City smile once again.............. *Peter D. Wood*

index

This index is for all names that appear in text matter only, not Football Extra or Statistics.

<u>underlined</u> = photograph